UE

The Foreign Office
and Foreign Policy, 1898–1914

The celebration of the Queen's Birthday at the Foreign Office
on 1 June 1891

# The Foreign Office
# and Foreign Policy, 1898-1914

ZARA S. STEINER

*Fellow of New Hall*
*University of Cambridge*

CAMBRIDGE
AT THE UNIVERSITY PRESS
1969

Published by the Syndics of the Cambridge University Press
Bentley House, 200 Euston Road, London N.W.1
American Branch: 32 East 57th Street, New York, N.Y. 10022

© Cambridge University Press 1969

Library of Congress Catalogue Card Number: 70-85739
Standard Book Number: 521 07654 4

Printed in Great Britain
by Alden & Mowbray Ltd at the Alden Press, Oxford

# Contents

# List of Plates

Acknowledgements for permission to reproduce these plates are due to Mr Nigel Nicolson (5*c*), Miss Sybil Crowe (5*a*, 7), the Radio Times Hulton Picture Library (5*d*), the R.I.B.A. Sir Banister Fletcher Library (2*a*, *b*), the *Illustrated London News* (1*b*, 6, 8), H.M. Treasury and Cabinet Office Library (1*a*) and the publishers John Murray (5*b*).

vii

# Preface

This is a study of the Foreign Office in one of the most crucial periods of its development. I have sought to show how and why the Foreign Office, in the years before 1914, assumed an integral part in the process of formulating foreign policy. What follows is the history of an emergent department of state. In these pages I hope to recount the story of the civil servants who staffed this department. I attempt to trace and detail the influence they had on diplomacy during the decisive pre-war period.

There have been many studies of diplomacy, that metier of head-waiters who, as one modern dramatist puts it, are sometimes invited to sit down at the table. More recently, there have been studies of the administration and enactment of foreign relations. These have focussed on both the constitutional and institutional aspects of the making of policy. I have tried to do something different though no doubt complementary. I have tried to analyse the actual work and underlying stance of those men who began as clerks, exercising influence within a narrow, often traditional bureaucratic radius, and who, by the time world war began, had won a permanent place in the conception of British foreign affairs.

A study of this kind involves special problems of scope. It is not too difficult to present a purely administrative history of the Foreign Office over such a restricted time-span. Further documents will come to light allowing us to fill in this or that gap. What I have set out to do is to deal with the personalities and political interplay of the individuals involved. This is the portrait of an institution seen from the perspective of the personalities and casts of mind of the people that constituted its everyday life. Obviously, there are dangers in this approach. I have had invaluable help both from surviving relatives and contemporaries of the fascinating group of men with whom I deal. Inevitably, a gap remains between the blurred immediacies of personal encounter and the deceptive clarity of a written record. I must take the blame for any inaccuracies of perspective; but the recently dead are the most difficult subjects to portray accurately.

Much of this book depends upon letters, minutes and memoranda written by officials in haste and without thought of publicity. They often reflect first impressions, emotional responses, or temporary hypotheses and are rarely the result of prolonged reflection or historical analysis. Civil servants did not have the time to give form to their brief jottings and were not encouraged to make official pronouncements. Differences of personality and style can easily lead the historian to mistaken impressions. There is a natural tendency to regard the more prolific or more intelligent writers as the most influential and more important figures of their day. Though the historian is always at the mercy of his documentation, the papers used in this study raise special (though fascinating) issues of judgement.

But there is a more significant dilemma of methodology. My study deals with the anatomy of decision. How are decisions made, what complex chain of intuition and reason, of ignorance and awareness, relates the initial dim intent to the final formulation? Any complete answer involves areas beyond the historian's normal terms of reference. These include psychology, sociology and, one occasionally feels, the craft of the astrologer. Even when abundantly available, documents are only stones in a complex mosaic. Moreover, I have limited my study to the internal dynamics of the making of foreign policy. While fully cognizant of their importance, I touch only briefly on such aspects of the context of foreign policy as the role of the sovereign, the interventions of the Cabinet and Committee of Imperial Defence, the influence of Parliament, of the City, and of the press. But this special focus is not an arbitrary one. In the period under scrutiny, the servants of the Foreign Office had little doubt that diplomacy—'the art of the possible'—ought to be conducted by a professional elite in an arena well removed from the vagaries of political amateurism and public debate. It was not Eyre Crowe alone who 'rather looked down on Secretaries of State than up to them and regarded Foreign Office clerks as the really important people'. The public should be led, not responded to or even taught. Had these remarkable *clercs* not taken so exalted a view of their mysteries, had they not gone so far in insulating themselves from the community at large, the arts of diplomacy would not have been so drastically discredited when the lights went out in Europe. Much of the resentment against 'striped pants in Whitehall' points back to a period when the outsider, however informed or intelligently concerned, did not get past the door.

My own study is neither a defence of nor an attack on the 'old diplomacy'. It is a description of that diplomacy at work from the central professional focus of Whitehall. Though explicitly and designedly a chapter in the larger history of the Civil Service and an assessment of the permanent official in modern affairs, this book should also throw additional light on the vexed problem of the dissolution of classical power-relations in Europe and the coming of catastrophe.

This study was first begun under the direction of the late Professor David Owen of Harvard University who not only read sections of this book but repeatedly argued that this monograph was worth doing. Mr F. H. Hinsley of St John's College, Cambridge, has encouraged me to publish some of this material in article form and has read the final manuscript with his usual care, patience and understanding. I am also indebted to Professor John Grenville of Leeds University whose critical comments were most useful and illuminating.

Mr C. H. Fone, formerly of the Foreign Office Library, and Mr C. L. Robertson of the Printed Books Library (Foreign Office) not only found many of the documents and photographs used in this book but took the time to discuss key questions with me. The late Sir Harold Nicolson lent me his father's unpublished manuscripts and gave me a good deal of information about the period. Miss Sybil Crowe of St Hilda's College, Oxford, has given me permission to reproduce pages from her father's *Lesebuch* and told me many facts about her father that I could not have found in the archives. I must also record my special debt to the Dowager Lady Hardinge of Penshurst and Lord Ponsonby of Shulbrede whose hospitality made my researches agreeable as well as profitable. I am grateful to the Duke of Devonshire, the Marquess of Salisbury and Earl St Aldwyn for permission to quote from papers in their private possession. Like all students of this period, most of my work was done in the Public Record Office and in the Foreign Office Library and these records have been used by permission of the Controller of H.M. Stationery Office. Mrs J. Ashman of the Churchill College Library typed the manuscript and gave me considerable assistance in preparing the book for the press.

My debt to my husband lies not in traditional expressions of loyal support but in his disbelief that the job would ever get done.

Z. S. S.

# List of Abbreviations

| | |
|---|---|
| BD | British Documents on the Origins of the War, 1898–1914 |
| Cmd. 7748, 7749 | The Fifth Report of the Royal Commission on the Civil Service, Command Paper 7748, 7749 |
| DDF | Documents Diplomatiques Français, 1871–1914 |
| DGP | Die Grosse Politik der Europäischen Kabinette, 1871–1914 |
| PP | Parliamentary Papers |

# CHAPTER 1

# The old Foreign Office

*The background of history*

The history of the Foreign Office as a separate administrative department is a short one though its origins can be traced to the medieval period. In 1253 John Maunsell was actually designated 'secretarius noster' and was put in charge of the royal seal used for personal correspondence. The present secretary of state for foreign affairs is his administrative descendant. In 1430 the office was divided and during the Stuart period this became permanent practice. Under Charles II this duality led to a division in function. One secretary, the southern secretary, controlled the correspondence with Spain, Flanders, Italy and Ireland. The northern secretary supervised Holland, the Baltic countries, Germany, France and Turkey. The division was formalized in 1640 and subsequent changes, like the original separation, were due to religious and dynastic developments on the continent. The dual secretariat lasted until 1782 when Burke's economical reforms changed the system of administration by separating domestic from foreign business. The Northern Department became the Foreign Office and Charles James Fox the first secretary of state for foreign affairs. The Southern Department became the Home Office and retained control over Irish and Colonial affairs.[1]

After 1782 the history of British foreign policy became the history of successive foreign secretaries. For the first twenty-five years of its independent existence, the Foreign Office was overshadowed by the figure of the younger Pitt. Then a series of great ministers, Castlereagh, Canning and Palmerston, raised the foreign secretaryship to a position of commanding importance. Lord Salisbury once said that there were but two offices in the British Empire too difficult to be adequately filled by men of good average ability—the premiership and the foreign secretaryship.[2]

[1] For the history of the secretaries of state, see Florence Evans, *The Principal Secretary of State, 1558–1680* (Manchester, 1923); Mark Thompson, *The Later Secretaries of State, 1681–1782* (Oxford, 1932). Material also in D. B. Horn, *The British Diplomatic Service, 1689–1789* (Oxford, 1961).
[2] Algernon Cecil, *British Foreign Secretaries, 1807–1916* (London, 1927), p. 5.

I

In the nineteenth century, high birth and personal fortune were the self-evident prerequisites for ministerial office. There were seventeen foreign secretaries between 1815 and 1914 and all, with two exceptions (Canning and Grey) were peers or the sons of peers. The great families of England dominated the roster: Derby, Granville, Clarendon, Rosebery, Salisbury and Grey. Between Palmerston and Grey almost all the foreign secretaries sat in the House of Lords, a practice which gave these ministers the time and privacy necessary to conduct their affairs according to the conventions of the 'old diplomacy'.[1] In the Upper House, such men became national figures while their departments remained secretarial adjuncts, self-contained and immune from outside criticism.

Most foreign secretaries came to office with several years of political experience behind them. Many had sat in the Commons before inheriting their titles; most had served in one of the major departments of state, frequently as parliamentary under-secretary. For the majority, this office represented the summit of ambition. Palmerston, Rosebery and especially Salisbury preferred the Foreign Office to their premierships. Salisbury's preference was so strong that, after a brief and unsuccessful experiment at separation, he combined both offices rather than relinquish his immediate control over foreign affairs. In reverse, only the Foreign Office was considered important enough to interest a former prime minister, as Lord John Russell showed in Palmerston's Cabinet of 1859.

Once appointed, the same men returned to the Foreign Office in subsequent ministries. Changes were rarely made during the life of a Cabinet and length of service was remarkable, even by Victorian standards. Palmerston, who dominated English diplomacy for most of his active life, sat in the foreign secretary's chair for seventeen years. Between 1854 and 1914 there were only eleven foreign secretaries, fewer political chiefs than in any other department.[2] It was not uncommon for one man to serve for three or four terms in different ministries. Such experienced politicians naturally enjoyed a special position within their Cabinets and enjoyed a greater degree of independence than most of their colleagues. In fact, the Cabinet proved a poor check on the work of the Foreign Office and most ministers stood somewhat in awe of their foreign secretary. Few Cabinet members had the time for a detailed study of foreign affairs. They intervened sporadically, save in moments of crisis, and in the day-to-day business of diplomacy, the

[1] Derby and Russell were the two exceptions and they transferred to the Lords before the end of their terms. Palmerston was a peer of Ireland and thus could sit in the Commons.

[2] Six ministers held office once, three (Granville, Derby and Rosebery) twice, Clarendon three times and Salisbury four.

foreign secretary had a free hand. Only the prime minister kept a close watch and the relationship of the premier with his foreign secretary remained one of the most important factors in the changing patterns of British diplomacy.[1]

Within his own department, the foreign secretary did what he wished. The burden of work on the Victorians was heavy and in some cases overpowering. Even Palmerston, who enjoyed his responsibilities, complained: 'The life I lead is like that of a man who on getting out of bed every morning should be caught up by the ends of one of the arms of a windmill and whirled round and round until he was again deposited at night to rest.'[2] Nevertheless, he continued to conduct his affairs with a small department to which he delegated little responsibility. This is as much a commentary on the character of mid-nineteenth-century diplomacy as it is on the energy and devotion of successive ministers.

Castlereagh completely ignored his staff. Canning did all his own drafting but took an active interest in the efficiency of the office. Palmerston drove his clerks relentlessly.[3] They were besieged with demands for factual information and corrected drafts. They were subjected to a constant stream of complaint about slackness, slovenly penmanship and poor grammar. Despite frayed tempers and hurt feelings, Palmerston's passion for order had its effect. A rather disorganized scrivener's office was turned into a more-than-adequate secretarial department. The political divisions (Turkish, French, German and Spanish) were made as important as the administrative (Chief Clerk's, Treaty, Consular and Slave Trade) and the work throughout the office was supervised by one of the two under-secretaries. These under-secretaries, though constantly badgered and sadly taxed, were 'no more than clerks and did not interfere in matters of policy'.[4] Palmerston wrote all important despatches himself and left only minor administrative details to his clerks.[5] He wanted abstracts made, despatches copied, queries answered and papers properly circulated but he did not wish for or seek advice.

The number of despatches handled by the Foreign Office increased steadily (6,000 in 1829; 30,000 in 1849; 51,000 in 1869; 102,000 in 1898;

[1] F. Gosses, *The Management of British Foreign Policy before the First World War* (Leiden, 1948), p. 144.
[2] Sir Charles Webster, *The Foreign Policy of Palmerston, 1830–41* (London, 1951), vol. 1, p. 58.
[3] Sir Charles Webster, *The Art and Practice of Diplomacy* (London, 1961), pp. 181–96.
[4] *Ibid.* p. 189.
[5] 'Lord Palmerston, you know, never consults our Under-Secretary. He merely sends out questions to be answered or papers to be copied when he is here in the evenings, and our only business is to obtain from the clerks the information that is wanted.' Sir John Tilley and Stephen Gaselee, *The Foreign Office* (London, 1933), p. 3.

111,000 in 1905) but the Foreign Office grew at a much slower pace.[1] Canning's department already included most of the personnel used by subsequent foreign secretaries. It consisted of two under-secretaries, a chief clerk, three senior clerks, thirteen junior clerks, a librarian and sub-librarian, a private secretary, a précis writer, a translator, a Turkish interpreter and a collector and transcriber of papers.[2] At mid-century, the office had about forty people and subsequent increases were due primarily to the introduction of supplementary and staff clerks, grammar-school men hired at lower salaries to do the non-confidential work of the administrative departments. Even on the eve of the First World War, after a major internal reform, the Foreign Office staff numbered 176 persons including some forty door-keepers, cleaners and others. The cost of the establishment both at home and abroad came to less than a million pounds annually.[3]

One of the key administrative changes within the nineteenth-century Foreign Office was the emergence of the permanent under-secretary as the

[1] In 1796 the Foreign Office consisted of:

|  | SALARY |
|---|---|
| 2 under-secretaries | £1,500 each |
| 1 chief clerk | £1,000 |
| 1 senior clerk | £650 |
| 1 senior clerk | £480 |
| 9 junior clerks | £80–£300 |

In 1861:

| 2 under-secretaries—1 permanent | — |
|---|---|
| 1 assistant under-secretary | — |
| 1 chief clerk | £1,250 + £200 special allowance |
| 2 senior clerks | £700–£850 |
| 8 assistant clerks | £570–£610 |
| 23 junior clerks—third to first class | £100–£395 |

In 1914:

| 2 under-secretaries—1 permanent | £2,500 including personal allowance of £500 |
|---|---|
| 3 assistant under-secretaries | £1,000–£1,500 |
| 1 controller of commercial and consular affairs | £1,200 |
| 1 chief clerk | £1,000–£1,260 |
| 7 senior clerks | £900–£1,000 |
| 10 assistant clerks | £700–£800 |
| 28 junior clerks | £200–£500 |

Cmd. 7748, pp. 8, 12. For 1861 figures see Reports from Committees, (2) Diplomatic Service, vol. 6, 1861, pp. 486–7.

[2] Tilley and Gaselee, The Foreign Office, p. 48. The chief clerk's department had a clerk.
[3] Lord Strang, The Foreign Office (London, 1955), p. 30. The expenditure on the Foreign Office was always moderate. In 1869–70 the cost was £63,079. A. Ward and G. P. Gooch, Cambridge History of British Foreign Policy (Cambridge, 1923), vol. III, p. 627.

top official in the departmental hierarchy.[1] In Castlereagh's day there was little difference between the permanent under-secretary and the 'governmental' under-secretary.[2] The man closest to the foreign secretary held the superior position regardless of title but the work of the department was shared between the under-secretaries. There was little distinction in either status or duty. Though the foreign secretary tended to retain the services of the senior under-secretary this was not a hard and fast rule and the minister could select the man he wanted for the position. Attempts were made to establish a salary differential between the two under-secretaries but this did not become an established practice until 1831 when a Select Committee on Reduction of Salaries confirmed the distinction on the grounds that under-secretaries 'who habitually remain in office during different changes in administration and thus made a profession of official life should be distinguished from those who merely appear for short periods'. Palmerston protested against this decision but it was during his administration that the permanent under-secretary began to establish the special place of his post in the Foreign Office hierarchy. Palmerston tended to rely on Backhouse (his permanent under-secretary) for the efficient administration of the office and the majority of the intra-office minutes are in Backhouse's hand.[3] After a sharp quarrel with the chief clerk, the superior administrative position of the permanent under-secretary was firmly established.[4] But the latter was also emerging as the chief figure on the political side, a trend reinforced by the growing importance of the political divisions which expanded in power and

*1900–1901:*

| Foreign Office | £79,000 |
| Diplomatic and Consular Services | £467,000 |
| Secret Service | £53,000 |
| | [at disposal of foreign secretary] |

*1913–1914:*

| Foreign Office | £67,500 |
| Diplomatic and Consular Services | £699,000 |
| Secret Service | £50,000 |

Figures from *Expenditure, Civil Government Charges, Accounts and Papers, 1901*, vol. XXXVII; *1913–1914*, vol. I.

[1] E. Parry-Jones, 'Under-Secretaries of State for Foreign Affairs, 1782–1855', *The English Historical Review* XLIX (1934), 308–20. Most of the following information comes from the important thesis of Dr Mary Anderson, 'Edmund Hammond, Permanent Under-Secretary of State for Foreign Affairs, 1854–1873', University of London, 1955.

[2] The term 'under-secretary' was first applied to the secretary of state's chief assistant in the latter part of the seventeenth century.

[3] C. Webster, *The Art and Practice of Diplomacy*, p. 190.

[4] V. Cromwell, 'An Incident in the Development of the Permanent Under-Secretaryship at the Foreign Office', *Bulletin of the Institute of Historical Relations* (May 1960), 99–113.

prestige.[1] It became the general practice for the permanent under-secretary to control the most vital of these departments. Correspondence handled by one under-secretary was still seen by the other and most parliamentary business (i.e. the preparation of Blue Books) was still jointly done. During Palmerston's tenure, moreover, the purely party character of the parliamentary under-secretary was not yet defined. From 1831 until 1841 (1835–6 excepted) he did not sit in either House of Parliment and from 1841 to 1851, though usually a member of the Commons, he rarely took his seat.

The situation evolved further under Palmerston's less forceful successors. Foreign secretaries like Granville and Clarendon were more inclined to ask for their under-secretaries' opinions and judgements. It was Edmund Hammond (1854–73), Clarendon's choice as permanent under-secretary, who gave a new and lasting importance to the position.[2] Hammond had already served for thirty years in the department. Though highly conservative, Hammond felt he 'was bound to advise and to recommend to the secretary of state what he thought should be done'.[3] Hammond offered his advice freely on a wide range of political questions and his minutes became the basis of many outgoing despatches. On minor matters his views were often decisive and in general he exercised a restraining influence on British diplomacy. Hammond also played a key role in the appointment of ministers (with whom he corresponded regularly) and had almost exclusive control over the selection of consuls, particularly in the Far East, an area in which he took a special interest.[4]

During his years as permanent under-secretary, Hammond successfully ousted his parliamentary colleague from the political business of the Foreign Office. By 1865 Hammond supervised four of the five political departments. While the parliamentary under-secretary continued to see all despatches and drafts before they went to the foreign secretary, he became almost exclusively concerned with parliamentary business and spent a good deal of his time at Whitehall. In 1865, despite Hammond's protest, a Commercial Department was created which came under the parliamentary under-secretary's control and this 'black hole' remained one of the

---

[1] Until 1841 the four administrative departments (Chief Clerk, Consular, Treaty and Slave Trade) were of more importance than their three political counterparts and were run by senior clerks rather than clerk assistants. As the pressure of diplomatic business increased, Palmerston was forced to raise the status of the political departments and their heads so that by 1841 the latter were second only in rank and pay to the under-secretaries and chief clerk.

[2] Clarendon first looked outside the Foreign Office for a new permanent under-secretary to replace Addington. But when his first choice refused the office, he selected Hammond. See Anderson, 'Edmund Hammond, Permanent Under-Secretary of State for Foreign Affairs, 1854–1873', p. 52.

[3] *Ibid.* p. 100.          [4] *Ibid.* pp. 218, 242.

latter's few links with the internal organization of the Foreign Office.[1]

Hammond's influence depended upon relations with his chiefs. He was close to Clarendon and Granville but Russell did not confide in him and often disregarded his advice. Moreover, Hammond still performed much of the traditional work of his predecessors—writing first drafts, preparing abstracts of incoming despatches and even copying and ciphering in moments of crisis. There was little delegation of responsibility; even senior clerks were expected only to arrange the papers for the under-secretaries and foreign secretary. Despite the recommendations of successive Treasury officials, the Foreign Office resisted efforts to introduce 'copying checks' into the department. Yet Hammond argued that his office had to be staffed by clerks and not diplomats, whom he tended to mistrust. Hammond wanted 'gentlemen by birth and habits and feelings'. To copy despatches the office needed pleasant, industrious, trustworthy scribes, not brilliant scholars.[2]

Hammond's successors, Charles Tenterden, Julian Pauncefote and Philip Currie, did not radically extend the powers of their office. Tenterden, who was Hammond's choice for the position, was equally conservative in his views and in his management of the Foreign Office. He thwarted all efforts to modernize the office; the term 'Tenterdenism' was used to characterize the old-fashioned bureaucratic shuffle of the office.[3] Yet it seems that Tenterden was 'quite first-rate as an official, intellectually keen, clever as a man . . .'[4] Tenterden's papers show that he wrote a number of key memoranda, some for ambassadors leaving for their posts, one on the Treaty of San Stefano which Disraeli found invaluable at the Congress of Berlin, another on Egypt for Lord Salisbury, of acknowledged utility.[5] The permanent head dealt directly with the prime minister and other Cabinet ministers. In a memorandum on the Eastern question in 1876, he not only proposed what the Government should do but personally urged the Cabinet to strongly support Lord Salisbury.[6] In 1880 he recommended a meeting with Gladstone to decide government policy in Greece. 'There is no time to be lost' he warned his chief, 'or you will find yourself in a crisis in another

[1] S. Gwynn and G. Tuckwell, *The Life of the Rt. Hon. Sir Charles Dilke*, (London, 1917), vol. I, p. 349; Anderson, 'Edmund Hammond, Permanent Under-Secretary of State for Foreign Affairs, 1854–1873', pp. 204–5.

[2] *Ibid.* p. 190.     [3] Tilley and Gaselee, *The Foreign Office*, p. 110.

[4] T. H. Escott, *The Story of British Diplomacy. Its Makers and Movements* (London, 1908), p. 364.

[5] The Tenterden papers (FO 363) are in 4 volumes; volume II is missing. FO 363, vol. I, pt 2, Dufferin to Tenterden, 5 May 1879; vol. I, pt 3, Disraeli to Tenterden, 2 July 1878; vol. IV Salisbury to Tenterden, 27 April 1879.

[6] *Ibid.* vol. V, memorandum by Tenterden, 19 October 1876.

fortnight.'[1] Tenterden had his own views on a variety of subjects—Egypt, Greece, the composition of Blue Books, the right of Cabinet ministers to the retention of the confidential print. Though he may have insisted that every paper be sent to the secretary of state for decision, he did not hesitate to give advice.

Like Hammond, Tenterden was the channel of communication between the Foreign Office and diplomats abroad. Some wrote to him once or twice a month and even the powerful Lord Dufferin was anxious to receive his semi-official communications. Responsible for the discipline of his department and for the work of the missions abroad, Tenterden was extremely doubtful about the benefits of the newly-instituted system of open competition. Commenting about the failure to recruit adequate student dragomans for Constantinople, Tenterden wrote to Dufferin '[open competition] affords no means of proper selection. The Crammers can teach most things but they cannot teach manners.'[2] Tenterden presided over the Foreign Office during the Marvin scandal. He tracked down the temporary clerk from the Treaty Department who revealed the terms of the Disraeli–Shubaloff agreement to the *Globe* but suffered both physically and emotionally from the experience.

Tenterden was succeeded by Julian Pauncefote, a rather unexpected appointment by Lord Granville. Pauncefote had been brought into the Foreign Office from the Colonial Office to serve as the first legal assistant secretary.[3] Though he was a first-rate administrator, he was considered an outsider and was never fully at home in his new position. It was under his leadership, however, that the reorganization begun under Tenterden was completed. In 1881 eight departments were created: Eastern (Europe), Western (Europe), American and Asiatic Consular (African), Commercial, Library, Treaty and Chief Clerk's Department. The work of supervising them was divided between the permanent under-secretary and the assistant under-secretaries. In the same year lower division clerks were introduced into the Commercial and Consular Departments and a year later into the Chief Clerk's Department. Pauncefote took the lead in enlarging and rationalizing those departments which were too dispersed to handle the increased work load of the Foreign Office. He had also hoped to reform

1 FO 363, vol. v, memorandum by Tenterden, 8 June 1880.
2 *Ibid.* vol. i, pt 2, Tenterden to Dufferin, 28 October 1881.
3 Even after his promotion, Pauncefote continued to do the legal work of the Foreign Office. A second assistant under-secretary was added to help him with the diplomatic business. Although a legal assistant (later called 'legal adviser') was later appointed, the second assistant under-secretary remained, a third one appointed in 1898, and a fourth in 1914. The first assistant under-secretary had been added to the staff in 1858.

the Consular and Commercial Departments but bureaucratic inertia, Treasury parsimony and mixed views about the overseas commercial functions of the Foreign Office prevented any major changes.

Sir Philip Currie (1889–94) was an old and intimate friend of Lord Salisbury's and had already served him twice as private secretary. He had been for many years an assistant under-secretary and was thoroughly familiar with the procedures of the office. Currie was a complete contrast to Pauncefote. He was, according to T. H. Escott, a 'brilliant, if rather flighty, worker and thoroughly trained man-of-the-world' who shone in society and moved easily in journalistic circles. Though Lord Salisbury did not believe it was the duty of his officials to make decisions or offer unsolicited advice, he did discuss diplomatic questions with Currie and invited comment. The two men worked well together and Currie was rewarded with the embassy at Constantinople.

Lord Hammond's original extension of the powers of the permanent under-secretary had no further consequences. The combination of strong chiefs and conservative civil servants prevented any further modernization of Whitehall. In this respect the Foreign Office began to lag behind the other major departments of state—a lag the more paradoxical in view of the growing complexity and urgency of foreign policy. The appointment of Thomas Sanderson to replace Lord Currie in 1894 assured the continuance of the status quo.

Over these years some modernization of the physical structure of the Foreign Office did take place. The old Northern Department had been located in the Lottery Office, Whitehall.[1] In 1761 Bute moved his premises to Cleveland Row, St James's, where the Foreign Office began its independent life. In 1786 the department was moved to a house owned by the Duke of Dorset which was part of one of the old Tennis Courts at Whitehall. At the end of 1793 the Foreign Office was transferred to Lord Sheffield's private house in Downing Street. Other houses, both to the left and right, were gradually acquired. These seem to have been 'in such a state of dilapidation as to render it inexpedient to expend any large sum on their substantial repair'.[2] Sir Horace Rumbold's description of these quarters is eloquent '. . . dingy and shabby to a degree, made up of dark offices and labyrinthine passages—four houses at least tumbled into one, with floors at uneven

---

[1] All of this information about the early history of the Foreign Office has been collected by Colin L. Robertson of the Foreign Office Library who has very generously allowed me to look at his notes, plans and pictures in the Printed Books Library at Cornwall House. His information corrects earlier accounts which tend to be unreliable for the eighteenth century.

[2] House of Commons 466, Select Committee on Public Offices (Downing Street), 29 July 1839.

levels and wearying corkscrew stairs that men cursed as they climbed—a thorough picture of disorder, penury and meanness'.[1] In these grim premises rose the many Foreign Office legends—the heavy printing machines in the attic imperilling the lives of the clerks below, the cat entombed behind the giant volumes of *The Times* whose malodorous scent created an office scandal, peashooters and water spouters leaning out of the Foreign Office windows, young clerks enjoying themselves in 'the Nursery' with their foils, sticks and boxing gloves. Though the walls of the houses had to be propped with beams and the inhabitants claimed 'they were almost in constant terror for their lives' nothing was done until the ceiling of Lord Malmesbury's office collapsed on his table. Even that arch-conservative Edmund Hammond agreed that the building had given out.

There then began the famous 'battle of the styles'. The original winning design for the Foreign Office was discarded and Sir Gilbert Scott was commissioned to plan the new building for Downing Street. His first design (1858) for a giant Gothic structure (which was to become the Midland Hotel) was rejected by Palmerston who wanted a cheaper, lighter and 'more cheerful' structure in the Italian style. Scott then produced a Byzantine building— a 'regular mongrel affair' according to Palmerston. The Commons divided (as did the journals of the day) between the advocates of the Gothic and the defenders of the Italian or Paladian. Palmerston prevailed; the final design by Scott owed a great deal to the suggestions of the Premier and was broadly Italian with 'an occasional infusion of Gothic'. While the old buildings were knocked down and the new office built, the Foreign Office moved to Pembroke House and Malmesbury House in Whitehall Gardens (1861–8). Palmerston did not live to see his Venetian palace, which is still used today. Disraeli opened the building with its great double staircase and enormous reception rooms in 1868. To contemporaries, the Foreign Office had, architecturally at least, come of age.

### Bureaucracy and recruitment

The transfer of the Foreign Office to its new quarters did not signify a radical break with the old ways. The forces of inertia and the sensibilities of its members continued to exercise great influence. From the angle of vision of Whitehall, Salisbury was in every sense Palmerston's successor. Thus it is during Lord Salisbury's last administration that we can best observe the Foreign Office in its vintage years before the onset of the new regime I shall be describing in this study.

[1] Sir Horace Rumbold, *Recollections of a Diplomatist* (London, 1901), vol. I, p. 109.

The old Foreign Office was 'just easy enough to be agreeable, just ceremonious enough to possess distinction, and just industrious enough to do its work'.[1] In 1895 it consisted of four political (Western, Eastern, American and Asiatic, African and Protectorates—divisions made in a somewhat arbitrary fashion) and five administrative (Chief Clerk's Office, Commercial and Sanitary, Consular, Library, Treaty) departments.[2] In 1899, due to the pressure of business, American and Asiatic affairs were at last divided.[3] And in the following year the African protectorates were placed in a single department apart from the rest of African business.[4] All the political work as well as some of the important administrative business was handled by the first-division clerks, some fifty men, called, collectively, the diplomatic establishment. The second-division staff, which was separately recruited and graded, was employed only in the non-political departments.[5] The division between the two staffs was rigid and there was little transfer from one to the other.

Each department had at least one senior or principal clerk and four to six assistant and junior clerks. The typical political department occupied three rooms; the senior clerk and assistant's room, the junior clerks' or second room, and a third room in which other junior clerks did their copying. Departments tended to acquire their own flavour. When Sanderson was chief of the Eastern Department, it was reputedly the most aristocratic in the office and a proper dress consisting of bowler, stiff collar and morning suit was *de rigueur*. Although a duke had been passed up 'as potentially difficult to handle', most of the honorary clerks came here. Francis Bertie,

[1] Ward and Gooch, *Cambridge History of British Foreign Policy*, vol. III, p. 599.
[2] The old designations, Northern and Southern, were still sometimes used and within departments the affairs of certain countries were handled separately. There are, for instances, references to the German Department though no such separate department really existed. See Appendix 1 for the list of departments and countries included.
[3] Satow Papers, Campbell to Satow, 1 June 1899. 'The department has become impossible owing to the stress of the China work. However, this was a blessing in disguise as America . . . has been taken away now and constituted a separate department. We got another senior clerk and two juniors out of the Treasury. We now deal with China, Japan and Siam only, which is quite enough.'
[4] The protectorates were gradually handed over to the Colonial Office. In 1904 British Central Africa and in 1905 British East Africa (after a fight between Lord Lansdowne and the Commissioner of East Africa, Sir Charles Eliot), Somaliland and Uganda were transferred. Zanzibar was administered by an assistant under-secretary who knew little if anything about its affairs. Fortunately, a senior clerk of the African Department took an active interest in the island and later became its agent and consul-general.
[5] In accordance with the civil service regulations of 1870, the staff of the Foreign Office was divided into an upper and lower division; renamed, after 1890, the first and second divisions. Second-division clerks were recruited from school and had little in common with the diplomatic establishment. They were not used in the political departments on the grounds that they should not handle secret documents.

its subsequent head, would not, moreover, tolerate a straw hat and was a thorough perfectionist.[1] The African Department, on the other hand, became the home of the rough country gentlemen with pipes. The European departments tended to be more important than their non-European counterparts partly because of the amount of commercial and consular work associated with Africa, Latin America and the Far East. For most of the staff, the pace was leisurely and the atmosphere informal. The department, John Tilley relates, was like a family with no 'Misters or Sirs' permitted and duties and hours thoroughly respectable.[2] Clerks were expected to attend the office from late morning until early evening—like the 'fountains in Trafalgar Square—they played from ten to four, with an interval for lunch'. Official hours were from twelve to six.

The foreign secretary remained the dominating figure who totally controlled the proceedings of his department. But beneath Lord Salisbury the chain of command was clearly defined. As in earlier times, the permanent under-secretary was the ranking member of the diplomatic establishment. Sir Thomas Sanderson supervised the work of the two key political departments (Eastern and Western) and a variety of administrative ones. A large number of the despatches and telegrams passed through his hands before they reached the foreign secretary. He sometimes commented briefly on them and subsequently checked that the foreign secretary's instructions were properly carried out. When Lord Salisbury was absent or occupied, he dealt with foreign representatives and domestic matters. He was held responsible for the smooth operation of his establishment and served as a link between the office and its embassies.

Immediately below the permanent under-secretary, three assistant under-secretaries supervised the political and administrative divisions of the Foreign Office. It was not uncommon for each to direct a political department and one or more administrative ones. For example, Francis Bertie, between 1898 and 1902, supervised the African, Far Eastern and Consular Departments. If an assistant under-secretary had acquired special knowledge of a difficult problem or country, he generally managed that area in addition to his normal

---

1 Tilley and Gaselee, *The Foreign Office*, pp. 130–45 for details. 'Bertie . . . contributed to our enjoyment by showing us how high he could kick or how to cut candles in two with a sword; although he had by then abandoned and even came to discourage, stump cricket' (pp. 130–1). Bruce Lockhart claims that in his day football was played in the Foreign Office corridors. Sir Robert H. Bruce Lockhart, *Memoirs of a British Agent* (London, 1932), pp. 44–5. It is reported by Owen O'Malley that Sanderson demanded that Eyre Crowe wear a top hat and not a bowler during the season. 'You say I am not to wear a bowler', Crowe had replied. 'Very well, your instructions shall be carried out', and for the rest of the summer he came to the office in a straw hat. Sir Owen O'Malley, *Phantom Caravan* (London, 1954), p. 47.
2 Tilley and Gaselee, *The Foreign Office*, p. 131.

load. Thus, Francis Villiers supervised a section of the Western Department in addition to the American, Consular and Treaty Departments between 1900 and 1906. One department might, under such a flexible system, be controlled by two or three under-secretaries. The senior assistant under-secretary was generally given one of the more important political areas while the newest appointment was left with the unwelcome job of helping the parliamentary under-secretary in the Commercial Department. The major function of these three men was to assemble all the necessary information and past papers needed by the foreign secretary. Incoming despatches were read and passed on to Lord Salisbury, sometimes with a brief query or suggestion. According to the latter's instructions, the assistant might prepare a draft for the minister's approval and then prepare the final despatch.

Even under Lord Salisbury, the senior clerks were men of some importance. Each senior clerk was the head of only one department and frequently stayed there for eight to twelve years. All the business of the department passed through their hands and they gradually built up funds of detailed knowledge about their areas. In the African, American and Asiatic Departments, they were the office experts. Nevertheless, with the exception of the head of the African Department, most of the work done by the senior clerks was of a clerical nature.[1] They supervised the keeping of the registers in which all despatches were recorded, they checked the final drafts of all letters to be despatched, prepared the confidential print and saw that the communications for the Queen, prime minister and Cabinet were properly circulated. They were also responsible for handling parliamentary questions and Blue Books, a most time-consuming operation.[2]

The junior clerks worked in the second room of each department. It was typical of the old Foreign Office that a man of fifteen years' experience was the 'print boy' who registered in volumes all papers sent to the printer and distributed the printed copies among the pigeon-holes assigned to the various posts abroad. If the senior clerk was absent, one of his assistants

[1] See note on Percy Anderson and Clement Hill, pp. 44–5.

[2] In 1901 Lord Cranborne, the parliamentary under-secretary, suggested that an assistant in each department be made responsible for this kind of work. See Appendix 5. Two years later a Parliamentary and Blue Book (known as the latter) Department was created with two assistant clerks. They were to have the print filed and edited in such a way as to produce Blue Books at short notice. Both William Tyrrell and John Tilley were employed here. Little time was saved and each of these men in turn combined their Blue Book work with acting as secretary to the Committee of Imperial Defence. In 1911 the Parliamentary Department (as it was called by everyone) was enlarged to include a head, an assistant and four clerks. Despite its name, its main function was that of ciphering and deciphering telegrams. See *Foreign Office Lists* and Tilley and Gaselee, *The Foreign Office*, pp. 155–6.

13

might prepare a brief memorandum, paraphrases of telegrams or routine despatches. The registers and volumes of printed papers were kept by the assistants.

As occupants of the third room, the junior clerks spent leisurely afternoons; their main raison d'être was the handling of the secret despatches and telegrams they copied.

The duties of the third room were multifarious but simple. We docketed the newly arrived letters ... we ciphered and deciphered telegrams; ... we 'put by' in their proper files the papers which had been acted on; we made up, that is, packed and fastened up, the bags for our missions abroad. The only original work which I can remember to have done was a small contribution to the annual departmental memorandum.[1]

Arthur Ponsonby testified before the McDonnell Commission in 1914, 'I had been nearly nine years in the service, and my work was still to copy out despatches, to put numbers on papers, to sort confidential prints, and, more especially to do up despatch bags with sealing wax and red tape'.[2] Almost all the junior clerks did similar work and spent their days copying, ciphering and deciphering, 'blueing', and indexing.[3] It is not surprising that one participant and critical observer wrote '... members of the Foreign Office lived a pleasant routine existence which stultified their education, dulled their wits and deprived them of every kind of initiative'.[4] Clerks were scribes performing the same kind of work as their Palmerstonian predecessors. This in a world tremendously altered amid other departments turning to very different styles.

A typical day at the Foreign Office began when the diplomatic bags arrived before noon and one of the four resident clerks registered their contents. Telegrams were deciphered and sent directly to the foreign secretary or, if he were absent, to the permanent under-secretary. Incoming despatches were folded in four, marked with a number, the date of receipt and a brief sketch of the contents (the docket) and then sent to the under-secretaries or senior clerks who arrived about one o'clock. If the diplomatic bags came after twelve, despatches were registered in the second room, telegrams ciphered and docketed and prepared for the scrutiny of the super-

---

[1] Tilley and Gaselee, *The Foreign Office*, pp. 127–8.          [2] Cmd. 7749, Q. 39,397.

[3] 'Blueing' was the name given to the process of copying telegrams for distribution. The Queen got the first copy. Until the end of her reign she demanded that all papers sent for her inspection should be written by hand except those already in print. Ward and Gooch, *Cambridge History of British Foreign Policy*, vol. III, p. 607.

[4] John D. Gregory, *On the Edge of Diplomacy, Rambles and Reflections, 1902–28* (London, 1929), p. 18. For a similar complaint that life at the Foreign Office was unbearably dull see Ponsonby MSS. Copy of letter by Ponsonby 8 May 1902 in Appendix 4.

vising under-secretary. The latter read the despatch, minuted it and added the proper direction for having the papers printed and circulated. He might append a brief observation or reminder of related matters before sending the despatch to the foreign secretary. If he felt he should see a foreign representative or member of another department, he requested permission before acting. It had been customary for each despatch box on its way to the foreign secretary to pass through the hands of the under-secretary not directly concerned but this practice seems to have ceased by the time of Lord Salisbury's last administration.[1] Informal morning conversations appear to have replaced the earlier procedure.

Many of the documents sent to Lord Salisbury were simply initialled and returned to the department for filing. The archives suggest that he glanced through a large proportion of these despatches even when they were of the most trivial nature. Where the question required personal attention, Salisbury conferred with the relevant ambassador at his office during the afternoon. Brief records were kept of these conversations and sent back to the appropriate departments. In most cases, Salisbury appended a laconic comment in his red ink to indicate how the problem should be settled.

Where departmental action was required or information requested, the material was returned to the under-secretary or senior clerk who subsequently drafted the despatch. The senior clerk sent the draft to the 'third room' where the juniors prepared the final copies for Salisbury's signature. After 1878, a ministerial confidential print (a list of incoming telegrams and despatches) was circulated each morning in pouches prepared in the third room of the Eastern Department.[2]

If they [Cabinet members] did not return their pouches quickly they had to go without news; the more high-handed juniors not allowing them to have more than two at a time ... It was commonly believed that Ministers did not read much of what was sent to them, and not infrequently put it in their waste-paper baskets, at the risk of the contents being sold to the enemy.[3]

These prints, and certain despatches, were sent to the Queen and Cabinet members at the discretion of the foreign secretary.

[1] Ward and Gooch, *Cambridge History of British Foreign Policy*, vol. III, p. 587.
[2] The ministerial confidential print should be distinguished from the departmental confidential print. The material for the former was selected by the foreign secretary and was sent only to the Queen and Cabinet. The departmental confidential print was far more complete than the ministerial but still did not contain all the despatches and telegrams received at the Foreign Office. See BD IX (2), pp. xi, xii.
[3] Tilley and Gaselee, *The Foreign Office*, p. 137. FO 800/176. Bertie to Salisbury, 2 October 1890. 'Waste paper baskets and not the fire are frequently the receptacles for discarded Cabinet Papers.' Salisbury's ironic minute 'The weather is fortunately getting colder'.

When the printed material was ready and sorted, the junior clerks prepared the diplomatic bags and delivered them to the Queen's messengers at Charing Cross Station at about eight in the evening. Bags for more remote places were prepared once a month. Expertness in sealing, like clear writing, was the mark of a first-rate junior and the eight o'clock rush was a typical feature of the old Foreign Office. The next day, between the hours of eleven and one, the new telegrams were deciphered and blued, letters were docketed and sent up with past papers to the senior clerk. There was time for friends and visitors, the atmosphere was urbane and the work far from taxing.

If the Foreign Office was a small, self-contained establishment, its tone and ethos were created by the caste from which it recruited its staff. All the clichés about the Foreign Office staff were true; it was indeed the stronghold of the aristocracy and everything was done to preserve its class character and clannish structure. The Foreign Office had responded slowly to public pressure for a more open form of recruitment. In 1850, despite a storm of protest from the permanent officials, a Treasury committee under Charles Trevelyan attacked this 'citadel of privilege' and in subsequent years questions were raised in Parliament about recruitment into the Diplomatic Service. It was, however, the preparation and publication of the Northcote–Trevelyan report in 1853 which stirred the Foreign Office into action. Lord Clarendon bowed to the storm and between 1856 and 1857 qualifying examinations (on subjects suggested by the Foreign Secretary and approved by the Civil Service commissioners) were instituted for candidates who had already secured the foreign secretary's official nomination. A candidate was tested in handwriting, French translation and dictation and the ability to make an abstract or précis. As Clarendon subsequently nominated three candidates for each vacant place, an element of competition was introduced. When candidates received the same marks, a German translation and reading test was used to distinguish between them. The standard was not high. Charles Spring-Rice told a Select Committee in 1861 that the 'test is not much more than an ordinary boy of fourteen, with a poor education, ought to be able to answer'.[1] A 'qualifying examination' for diplomatic attachés about the same time was far more exacting and seems to have discouraged recruitment.

There was further pressure from the Treasury and Civil Service commissioners and in 1871 the Foreign Office adopted a more stringent examination which made entrance into the office more difficult than into the Diplomatic Service. This new examination consisted of eight compulsory papers—spell-

[1] Cmd. 7748, p. 75.

ing, arithmetic, précis-writing, English composition, French translation, dictation and conversation, Latin, German translation and a general intelligence test. Optional subjects included a further test in German, Ancient Greek, Italian, Spanish, Books I to IV of Euclid, a combined test of European geography and history (1783 to 1847) and a paper in the constitutional history of England. Additional changes were made in the subjects tested and the marks allotted to each paper but this combined system of nomination and competitive examination remained basically unaltered until Lord Lansdowne's time. In 1880 Lord Granville established a scheme of 'limited' competition for the Diplomatic Service and in 1892, after the publication of a highly critical report by the Ridley Commission (1886–90), the same examinations were given to both sets of candidates though each was separately graded and appointed. On the whole, the Commission reported 'The Foreign Office commands the ablest men'.[1] To enter either competition the candidate had to secure the nomination of the foreign secretary and 'it was the weight carried by the position and interest of parents and sponsors, rather than the qualities of the candidates themselves, which decided the chance of a nomination'.[2] Though nominations could be secured at an early age, the young men had to be between eighteen and twenty-four to sit the examination and the Foreign Office fixed the number of men allowed to compete annually (often at a ratio of six men to every open place). Recruits for the Diplomatic Service were understood to have private incomes; there was no similar limitation on Foreign Office clerks, who began to earn as soon as they were appointed.[3]

Men from families totally unknown to Lord Salisbury or his private secretary did not apply. The examinations reflected the education offered to young men of the upper class. In 1895 a nominated candidate took papers in Latin, German, French, English Composition, General Intelligence, Geography, History of Modern Europe and Arithmetic. He was also tested in handwriting and précis; Italian, Spanish, Portuguese, Russian and shorthand were optional papers. As the age for examination was low and special preparation required in languages, candidates proceeded from school to a year or two of residence abroad and then to a cramming establishment (usually Scoones on Garrick Street) where the aspirants would

[1] *Ibid.* p. 6.   [2] *Ibid.* p. 7.
[3] Compare the salaries of clerks with those of diplomats (pp. 4 and 175). For his first two years abroad the attaché was not paid at all. Only at the top of the ladder, ambassadorial salaries far exceeded that of the permanent under-secretary. This created great difficulties when, for instance, Hardinge and then Nicolson, both ambassadors, came to the Foreign Office as permanent under-secretaries.

prepare the required books and learn the necessary secretarial skills. Training abroad was a necessity since the obligatory papers in French and German were particularly difficult. Even university men could not succeed without additional drill.[1] This period of prolonged training obviously restricted the class of men able to apply.

In 1904, in order to increase the number of university graduates and broaden the educational backgrounds of candidates, Lord Lansdowne raised the age of entrance to twenty-two and suggested that applicants 'take the ordinary civil service examination provided that a high standard in French and German could be maintained'.[2] To encourage the necessary specialization in languages, candidates took fewer papers (totalling fewer points) than required for Class I of the Home Civil Service. This meant, of course, that unsuccessful candidates were not eligible for domestic appointments. Nevertheless, apart from the French and German papers, the candidate could choose any of the subjects offered by the Civil Service Commission. The competition was intense, particularly after 1907 when men who had secured nominations could choose the year in which they wished to sit the examination and the earlier limitations on the number of examinees was abolished. In 1908 eight men competed for one place. Two were appointed. If the Foreign Office remained 'the last choice reserve of administration practised as a sport' the gentlemen selected were not without ability.

In the same year (1907), nominations for both the Foreign Office and Diplomatic Service were transferred from the foreign secretary to a Board of Selection. This Board was composed of the permanent under-secretary of state, who presided, the foreign secretary's principal private secretary, one or more members of the Diplomatic Service and one of the heads of the political departments of the Foreign Office. The assistant private secretary was also a member. The Board met twice a year to interview candidates who had received permission to apply and then made its recommendations to the foreign secretary.[3] Its creation was intended to put entrance into the

---

[1] John Tilley went through this typical training. He started at a good preparatory school, took a scholarship at Eton, went to King's College and read for the Classics Tripos. During his last year at King's, his name was entered on Lord Salisbury's list of candidates and he went abroad to perfect his French and to learn German. After three months with a *curé de campagne* near Tours and a year with a German family at Dresden, he returned to London and went to Scoones, where he read the required history texts and gained the necessary secretarial skills. At the age of twenty-four, he successfully stood for his examination. Sir John Tilley, *London to Tokyo* (London, 1943), pp. 9–20. See also Sir Harold Nicolson, *Some People* (London, 1926).

[2] Cmd. 7749, Q. 38,693.

[3] Candidates still had to get the foreign secretary's permission to appear before the Board. This was freely given and the Board itself rejected only 2 per cent of the prospective candidates. Cmd. 7748, p. 10.

Foreign Office on a more genuine competitive basis. In fact it admitted precisely the same kind of individual whom the foreign secretary and private secretary would have chosen by their own unaided aristocratic lights.

> I think your Board of Selection will generally take what we may call perhaps one type of man, because he is the type of man who is fit for this international career called diplomacy. All . . . speaking metaphorically, speak the same language; they have the same habits of thought, and more or less the same points of view, and if anybody with a different language came in, I think he would be treated by the whole diplomatic service more or less with suspicion.[1]

The Selection Board, though it did not ask inquisitorial questions about the candidate's background, had little difficulty in discovering his 'upbringing, the schools he had attended, what particular things he cared for in life and all that sort of thing'.[2] Few men who did not conform to the generally accepted pattern applied and fewer still slipped through the net.

The character of the Foreign Office did not change until the very last years of peace. In the period between 1898 and 1907, when the Board of Selection was established, over half the successful candidates came from aristocratic or gentry backgrounds.[3] The remainder were recruited from the professional middle class (barristers, army and navy officers, consular service, teachers). Only one candidate came from a merchant family and Scotsmen and non-conformists were conspicuously absent. There were no Jews. Even in 1911, when Owen O'Malley joined the Western Department as a junior, four of its six members were the scions of noble families.[4] Yet the lists of 1912 and 1913 suggest that the catchment area was slowly widening.[5] There was a noticeable increase in the number of successful recruits from professional families. A further change was to occur in 1919 with the grim end of 'la belle époque'.

The educational homogeneity of the men in the Foreign Office is even more striking and did much to create that mandarin tone which still merits public comment today. In 1898 ten of the top fourteen senior officials had been educated at one of the five leading public schools, Eton, Harrow, Winchester, Rugby and Charterhouse. Eton dominated the list; between 1908 and 1913 nine out of sixteen candidates were Etonians. John Tilley describes the Foreign Office in 1919: '. . . half were Etonians, that is 22 out

---

[1] *Ibid.* Q.42,519.    [2] *Ibid.* Q.40,788.
[3] R. Nightingale, *The Personnel of the British Foreign Office, 1851–1929*, Fabian Tract 232 (London, 1929). *Foreign Office Lists*; *Dictionary of National Biography*; Cmd. 7749, Appendix LXXXIV.
[4] O'Malley, *The Phantom Caravan*, p. 34.
[5] Donald C. Watt, *Personalities and Poilicies* (South Bend, Indiana, 1965), p. 41. Duff Cooper, the son of a surgeon, and Maurice Peterson, whose father was Principal of McGill University, both entered in 1913.

of 44, and that was not because any special favour was shown to Eton, but because the sort of people who wanted nominations mostly came from Eton'.[1]

In one sense at least the Lansdowne proposals did succeed. Between 1898 and 1907 only a little over half the Foreign Office clerks were university men; all of these had gone either to Oxford or Cambridge. Between 1908 and the outbreak of war, all but one of the successful candidates had gone to a university, ten to Oxford, four to Cambridge.[2]

Q. Have you had any candidates applying to come before your board from other universities such as provincial universities?
A. You mean besides Oxford and Cambridge; I remember one or two cases—people at Durham and elsewhere and one or two from Trinity College, Dublin and I think even a colonial one.[3]

The aristocratic bias in the Diplomatic Service was even more marked and the social circle narrowed rather than expanded in the pre-war period. The great families of England were well represented. Among the twenty-three secretaries appointed between 1908 and 1913, eight were the sons of lords and two were baronets. There was the same predominance of Etonians which one found at the Foreign Office; between 1908 and 1914 the number increased rather than diminished.[4] The Civil Service commissioners pressed William Tyrrell, Grey's private secretary, on this point. 'I should doubt whether that applies to the recruits we have had in the last five years; I would not be certain. I should certainly say that, speaking generally, they come from the public schools.'[5]

Foreign Office clerks soon joined a London club: St James's, Brooks', White's or Travellers'. In view of their requisite political neutrality, it is surprising how many were also members of the Carlton. This inner circle had easy links with diplomats and members of Parliament. But it tended to exclude members of the Consular Service and all too many of the increasingly important world of business and industry. Within the Foreign Office the newly-appointed clerk was placed in any department which had a vacancy and was generally transferred after two years.[6] Clerks were encouraged to

---

[1] Tilley and Gaselee, *The Foreign Office*, p. 88.    [2] See Appendix 3.
[3] Cmd. 7749, Q .26,873. Men read a variety of Honours subjects though there was a decided trend away from Classics or 'Greats'. There were some Firsts among the successful candidates.
[4] In the years 1908–13 inclusive no fewer than 25 out of 37 came from Eton. Among unsuccessful candidates the proportion was 44 out of 86. Cmd. 7749, p. 15, Appendix LXXXIV.
[5] *Ibid.* Q .40,791; 40, 792.
[6] The case of John Tilley is not atypical. Tilley started as a junior clerk in the Eastern Department in 1893; transferred to the Asiatic Department in 1894 and was sent to serve on the Venezuelan arbitration commission during Lord Salisbury's last administration. He returned to England and served for three years in the Consular Department. He then decided (perhaps to get out of the Consular Department) that he would like to serve abroad and arranged an exchange with one of

spend time in one of the many non-European departments though these assignments were never popular; the Commercial Department was considered particularly dull.[1] For most, promotion was inevitable and seniority the general rule until the grade of senior clerk. Men went 'Hackney coach-like from Bottom to Top, by dint of mere living'.[2] The top prize, the permanent under-secretaryship, usually went to one of the assistant under-secretaries; consequently the appointment of Charles Hardinge in 1906 and Arthur Nicolson in 1910, from the Diplomatic Service, aroused considerable comment, some adverse.[3]

Foreign Office officials rarely took diplomatic posts because they could not afford the more expensive life of an envoy. No positive inducement in either pay or promotion was offered to facilitate such exchanges, despite the repeated recommendations of various select committees. Thus Thomas Sanderson, with the exception of two short missions abroad, spent his entire forty-seven years of service in London. In Lord Salisbury's day, first-hand knowledge came from private travel: 'I have heard in former days surprise expressed that there was actually in, say the China Department, no one who knew China at first hand . . . their absence did not much matter because the Secretary of State was in direct touch with the man on the spot.'[4] If a clerk wished to go abroad, he had to get in touch with a man of his own rank, arrange an exchange and then seek out the private secretary for a final confirmation. Newly-appointed attachés spent about six months in one of the Foreign Office departments but not more than three or four diplomatists were attached to Salisbury's office at any one time.

Only at the very highest levels had a tradition of transfer from the Foreign Office to the Diplomatic Service developed. Both Julian Pauncefote and

the first secretaries at the embassy in Constantinople. On returning home (1909) he was promoted to the rank of senior clerk and was put in charge of the African Department. In 1913, he became chief clerk, a key appointment. After the war, he was promoted to the rank of assistant under-secretary. In 1921 he was made ambassador to Brazil and in 1926 ambassador to Japan. Sir John Tilley, *London to Tokyo* (London, 1943), passim.

1 The Commercial Department from 1903 was run by a fierce disciplinarian, Algernon Law, who became controller of commercial and consular affairs in 1912. Nevertheless, the Commercial and Consular Departments were 'the most inefficient in the Foreign Office. The senior clerks who ran them, were men who had lost all ambition and who had abandoned hope of future promotion.' The department did the widest variety of commercial work from representing British commercial interests abroad to collecting data for other departments on a range of subjects extending from finance and manufacture to the protection abroad of wild birds and their plumage. See Bruce Lockhart *Memoirs of a British Agent*, p. 46. Ward and Gooch, *Cambridge History of British Foreign Policy*, vol. III, pp. 624–5.

2 Russell Papers, Palmerston to Russell, 20 October 1839, quoted in Anderson, 'Edmund Hammond, Permanent Under-Secretary of State for Foreign Affairs, 1854–73', p. 42.

3 Hardinge was the first ambassador appointed permanent under-secretary since Addington.

4 Tilley and Gaselee, *The Foreign Office*, p. 164.

Philip Currie left Whitehall for missions or embassies as did Francis Bertie and Francis Villiers under Lord Lansdowne and Louis Mallet under Sir Edward Grey. It is also true that after 1906 the permanent under-secretary, Charles Hardinge, did encourage more exchanges at lower levels.[1] By 1914, one of the three assistant under-secretaries and six of the seven senior clerks had spent some time abroad or had served in a diplomatic post. Yet the initiative still came from the clerk or diplomatist and only a restricted number of exchanges were allowed in any one year. The Foreign Office, moreover, did not always make use of overseas experience; a clerk returning from a year at Vienna might well be assigned to the China Department.

Throughout the period and, in fact, until 1919, there was considerable feeling against amalgamation. Eyre Crowe argued, before the Royal Commission of 1914, that exchanges should only take place among junior clerks. 'It is difficult because you must have men more or less of the same standing, and you cannot allow the office to be over-run by too many senior men coming from outside, because it depletes the departments of experienced clerks.'[2] Like Hammond and Sanderson, Crowe believed that only clerks trained in the office could handle the work properly. The clerks were inclined to regard diplomatists as 'amateurs' and 'social butterflies', unaccustomed to work or to regular hours. Arthur Ponsonby commented: 'It would not be too much to say that there is at present a certain antagonism between the two services. Diplomats feel that they are entirely at the mercy of the officials at home. The Foreign Office clerk, accustomed to regular routine work, regards the diplomatist in the light of an amateur.'[3]

This was the kind of Foreign Office which served Lord Salisbury. One must judge its competence in the context of its own time. Its aristocratic bias was shared by all the foreign offices and diplomatic services of Europe. Foreign secretaries were 'grand seigneurs'. Even when, as was true in some European capitals, the middle class came to staff the domestic departments, the foreign ministries remained the strongholds of the aristocracy. Diplomatic life abroad was socially exclusive and expensive. Diplomatists shared certain common traditions and assumptions which were only partially obscured by national differences. At Whitehall a few men dealt with a vast and varied correspondence. A tradition of loyalty and intimacy as well as life-long service was a distinguishing and very positive asset of the 'old Foreign Office'. Salisbury was seconded by a devoted, hard-working staff with great

[1] For a table of annual exchanges between 1906 and 1914 see Doreen Collins, *Aspects of British Politics, 1904–1919* (London, 1965), p. 66.
[2] Cmd. 7749, Q.36,954.   [3] *Ibid.* pp. 318–19.

reserves of knowledge and experience. Charges of aristocratic exclusiveness or lack of specialization had only limited meaning in a Victorian setting. A common background and education, similar habits of behaviour and thought, and a powerful 'esprit de corps' combined to create a strong department.

Yet if one looks more closely at the operations of the Foreign Office during Lord Salisbury's administration, one can notice certain changes in the work of this bureaucracy which were to have far-reaching results in subsequent years. For while neither the social composition of the department nor its exclusive atmosphere was to alter, the functions which its members performed were to expand, bringing new power and problems to the office. Responsibilities had to be shared with other departments, strategic considerations became more important. Within the office, there were certain anachronisms of attitude and organization—the gap between ability and responsibility, the unequal distribution of work, the disorder in keeping records—which were noticed by observant clerks. Various suggestions were made to make the Foreign Office more efficient and practices were adopted which brought the department into line with its domestic counterparts.

## Lord Salisbury's last administration

Socially and in most of its personal and indeed mechanical aspects, the Foreign Office remained as I have described. Two main factors were, however, to militate against these often archaic and leisurely proceedings. After 1898 Lord Salisbury's failing strength brought on important changes in the actual structure of decision-making. This was true both at Cabinet level and at Whitehall. Simultaneously, the pressure and complication of international affairs mounted. These two factors, in conjunction, were to bring about changes within the framework of the Foreign Office. The most significant of these, at first scarcely perceptible, was the devolution of new powers and responsibilities into the hands of the senior permanent officials.

In 1895 Lord Salisbury was at the peak of his career and considered the most influential diplomatist in Europe. As always, he preferred his work at the office to his duties as prime minister. He had never overcome his innate political shyness and reserve and loathed the social functions which formed an essential part of a party chief's duties. He remained suspicious of the new democratic currents and had little zest for political manœuvre or electoral battle. Much of his time was spent at Hatfield working on the despatch boxes which arrived daily or tinkering with one of the many practical gadgets with which his home was filled.

Already in his lifetime, this 'strange, powerful, inscrutable, brilliant' man was a legend among politicians and diplomats. Winston Churchill, still a very young man, wrote of him as 'the venerable, august Lord Salisbury, Prime Minister since God knew when'. London was a choice post and ambassadors eagerly sought interviews with the Premier. Though inaccessible to all but a few close intimates, Salisbury was a man of great charm and wit. He often spoke with unusual frankness not only on questions of immediate interest but on broader problems of more long-range importance. At times, his subtlety and humour led to misunderstandings and his willingness to enter into academic discussions tended to rouse suspicions, particularly at the Wilhelmstrasse.

As could be predicted, for most of his working life Salisbury had little trouble with his Cabinet. The Prime Minister allowed his colleagues a free hand and rarely intervened in their departmental concerns. The coalition of 1895, however, was a weak one and though the Unionists were a minority they held certain key ministries. Disputes were not uncommon and Salisbury was called upon to keep the peace at the Cabinet table. Chamberlain was particularly restive and imperial affairs dominated many Cabinet discussions. Hicks Beach, a true Gladstonian Chancellor of the Exchequer, had little sympathy with the demands of the service departments for increased funds and constantly vetoed requests for government guarantees for British firms abroad.[1] During the Boer War, the clashes over arms expenditure reached crisis proportions. Moreover, Lord Lansdowne, the secretary of state for war, was particularly sensitive about the criticisms hurled at his office and Lord Salisbury stepped in more than once to prevent him from resigning.[2]

Despite these differences, Salisbury scrupulously consulted the Cabinet on all important foreign decisions and deferred to their wishes in the few instances when they ran counter to his own. He took special pains to keep his ministers fully informed and proposed that all important despatches be printed at once so that his colleagues could read them within a day or two of reception.[3] In addition to the ministerial confidential print, despatches sent to the Prime Minister were also circulated to a select inner circle particularly concerned with foreign affairs.[4] Whether they always read the con-

[1] Lady Victoria Hicks Beach, *Life of Sir Michael Hicks Beach* (London, 1932), vol. II, p. 153.
[2] FO 277, Salisbury to Lansdowne, 2 February 1896. Lord Newton, *Lord Lansdowne: a Biography* (London, 1929), pp. 149–51.
[3] Sanderson MSS, Salisbury to Sanderson, 14 November 1898.
[4] This group usually included the Duke of Devonshire, president of the Council and head of the Defence Committee, Arthur Balfour, first lord of the Treasury, Joseph Chamberlain, colonial

fidential print or the despatches is doubtful but Salisbury was completely open in his dealings with his colleagues.[1]

Within the Cabinet it was often left to the Prime Minister to decide what the consensus of his colleagues was. Until 1898 Salisbury had little difficulty in maintaining his ascendancy though he failed to convince the Cabinet to take positive action to counter the Russian challenge at Constantinople in December 1895.[2] An irate Conservative commented in *The Times* in 1898: 'It is a well known fact that Lord Salisbury and Lord Salisbury alone, is responsible for everything that is done and left undone in the region of foreign affairs. Neither the Cabinet nor the Party exercise the slightest influence or control in that *mare clausum*.'[3]

By this date, however, the situation had changed. One critic wrote: 'Lord Salisbury's strength, mental and physical, perceptibly waned. In the later days of his foreign secretaryship he had apparently lost hold of all details in the conduct of his affairs, and his colleagues became alarmed lest some untoward event should occur.'[4] Faced with numerous crises all over the world, the Cabinet disintegrated. Important issues were insufficiently discussed and too much time was wasted on trivialities and irrelevant questions.[5] Cabinet decisions were not always clear, and during the Boer War confusion at Downing Street added to the difficulties in the field. Arguing against Lord Salisbury's refusal to publish the Spion Kop despatches, Lord Lansdowne complained to Balfour 'I was quite unaware of any such decision but our decisions are very often impalpable and perhaps I ought to have been able to construct one from materials afforded by Devonshire's yawns, and casual interjections around the table'.[6] Some of the weaknesses in British policy at the turn of the century were due to Salisbury's ill-health and loss of control over his cabinet.

Though only sixty-nine, a youthful age by Gladstonian standards, the Prime Minister was obviously ageing. His eyes bothered him, his girth increased at an alarming rate and his bronchitis recurred as periodically as the London fogs. The once famous sharpness and pungent humour began

secretary, Lord George Hamilton, secretary of state for India and, of course, the Queen. Goschen, Lansdowne and Hicks Beach were also kept informed of matters touching their departments.
[1] Sanderson complained that despatches failed to distract Balfour from the pursuit of the golf ball or the Duke of Devonshire from his pheasants. The Duke kept Derby days and Ascot as sacred holidays. As he was deaf and subject to attacks of fatigue, he did not always take an active role in Cabinet discussions. Sanderson MSS, Sanderson to Salisbury, 15 November 1898.
[2] John Grenville, *Lord Salisbury and Foreign Policy* (London, 1964), pp. 50–3.
[3] *The Times*, 5 May 1898.
[4] Lord Askwith, *Life of Lord James of Hereford* (London, 1930), p. 256.
[5] Grenville, *Lord Salisbury and Foreign Policy*, p. 308.
[6] Balfour MSS, Lansdowne to Balfour, 24 April 1900.

to fade. His store of patience, never very large, decreased and his trips to Whitehall either for Cabinet meetings or official visits became even less frequent than usual. He had in the past often interrupted official visits by wagging his foot at the offending diplomat or cutting his visitor short. Now the Premier became an excellent subject for the cartoonist—a corpulent, tricycle-riding aristocrat who failed to recognize his own staff. In fact, he retained great influence and often proved more able to conduct business to Britain's advantage than his more vigorous colleagues. But as his hold over the Cabinet diminished, it was argued that he was physically unable to transact the business required of him. Even after his recovery from illness in the spring and summer of 1898, he took frequent trips to Beaulieu on the Riviera or to the Vosges to rest and restore his energies. In his last days at the Foreign Office, he 'sat in a crumpled heap like Grandpa Smallweed—evidently wearied out'.[1]

The Cabinet grew increasingly restive and a crisis with Russia in the Far East in addition to the difficulties in South Africa stirred its leading members. During Salisbury's absences abroad, the Foreign Office was left in the hands of Arthur Balfour, the Premier's nephew and heir apparent. Though lazy about paper work, Balfour had an excellent analytical mind and was a good negotiator. But he lacked Salisbury's standing and principles and was sometimes ineffectual as the leader of the Cabinet. His responsibilities at the Foreign Office were not clearly defined; he seems to have received all important despatches. Balfour worked closely with the permanent officials but disregarded their advice when it ran counter to his own opinions. 'I am refusing to do anything with regard to papers about either Crete or West Africa', he wrote to Sanderson. 'It is right that I should be kept informed but I do not think two people can, with advantage, give directions at the same time.'[2] There was, however, a duality of leadership which created an atmosphere of confusion.[3]

The important point was that Arthur Balfour sympathized with those who found Salisbury's policy inadequate for the needs of the moment.

[1] Viscount Esher, *Journals and Letters of Reginald, Viscount Esher*, ed. M. V. Brett and Oliver, Viscount Esher (London, 1934), vol. I, p. 44.

[2] FO 277, Balfour to Sanderson, 16 April 1898.

[3] FO 800/176, Bertie to Grey, 12 January 1912. Francis Bertie was assistant under-secretary at the time, and was later to recall 'Lord Salisbury had no affection for the agreement [Anglo-German Portuguese agreement of 1898] but that was, I think, partly because he had hoped to stave off the German Government and thought that his nephew had been too ready to conclude the negotiation. Besides this, in the later days of Lord Salisbury's time as Secretary of State for Foreign Affairs, he and Arthur Balfour were not always at one and the uncle was rather jealous of the nephew in his management of the Foreign Office during the uncle's absence.'

Though he characteristically 'sat on the fence', he did not check Joseph Chamberlain's attempts to work out an agreement with the Germans. For it was Joseph Chamberlain, more than any other minister, who attempted to reshape British diplomacy and who gave British policy its contradictory complexion. Chamberlain started from very different principles than Lord Salisbury and pursued his goals by very different means. He was alarmed by Britain's weakness everywhere in the world and the Far Eastern crisis intensified his fear that Russia and France would join against her. As the Boer crisis became more imminent, his pessimism deepened. Salisbury proceeded from an assumption of strength; the imperial rivalries did not affect England's position. Chamberlain believed in public statements and in dynamic gestures; Salisbury in quiet diplomacy and private words. Many of Chamberlain's interventions in foreign affairs were perfectly justified as imperial matters and foreign relations were inextricably connected. But in the West African settlement, in the Delagoa Bay negotiations and the Alaskan Boundary dispute with the United States, the Colonial Secretary pushed Salisbury to take a more determined line. More than once Salisbury gave way to Chamberlain against his own better judgement.

In his search for allies, whether the United States, Japan or Germany, Chamberlain initiated discussions with which Salisbury had little sympathy. These endeavours repeatedly failed; the talks with Berlin came to little, and complicated rather than simplified relations between the two powers.[1] Salisbury had good reasons for deploring Chamberlain's public diplomacy; the latter's speeches often provoked the opposite effect to the one intended. Yet the Prime Minister neither publicly nor privately rebuked Chamberlain. His ill-health and desire to preserve the unity of the Cabinet during the difficult days of the Boer crisis explain his acquiescence.[2] He tried to repair the damage through his own public speeches (the 'dying nations' speech of 2 May 1898), or privately in conversations with foreign ambassadors, but after 1898 he never effectively checked the impression that there were two heads of the Foreign Office proposing different lines of policy.

Two years later Salisbury totally lost the support of his colleagues. George Goschen, Lansdowne, Selborne, Devonshire and even Arthur Balfour did not share Salisbury's basic optimism. Each feared a Russian offensive at English expense and were as alarmed as Chamberlain at Britain's weakness. Matters came to a head in the autumn of 1900 when a majority

---

[1] For the best discussion of the Salisbury–Chamberlain dispute, see Grenville, *Lord Salisbury and Foreign Policy*, chapter 7.

[2] See for instance, FO 277, Salisbury to Lansdowne, 1 September 1900.

of the Cabinet forced Salisbury to conclude an agreement with Germany in China which he rightly felt to be worthless and unnecessary.[1] But the feeling of the Cabinet was against him and he bowed to the majority will. His colleagues attributed his 'masterly inactivity' to a general physical and mental decline and were anxious for him to retire. Only the Chancellor of the Exchequer shared Salisbury's apparently outdated views and 'Black Michael' was an increasingly isolated figure who belonged to a vanishing world of free trade, open competition and private investment abroad. In the long run, Salisbury's judgements proved to be sound and his predictions justified. But his days were numbered. Under great pressure, he reorganized his Cabinet in the autumn of 1900 and, to the relief of all, retired from the Foreign Office. The way was now clear for a new course.

Lord Salisbury's loss of authority occurred at a time when the British position was under attack in many different parts of the world. Both the French and the Germans considered (and dismissed) invasion plans during the Boer War. There were not only the inherited problems of the past to consider (i.e. the Straits and Turkey) but new challenges in the Far East, in the Middle East and in Africa. Great Britain was clearly feeling the effects of the emergence of other great nations in the non-European world. Other ministers intervened in the making of policy and there were numerous Cabinet discussions of alternative lines of diplomacy. Within the Foreign Office, senior officials took a more active share in the daily decision-making process. Even if Lord Salisbury had retained his full powers, some further delegation of responsibility to the senior officials would have become necessary. Under the circumstances, it was natural that the permanent under-secretary, at least, should attempt to ease the foreign secretary's lot.

At first these changes at Whitehall were barely perceptible. While Salisbury stayed at the Foreign Office the relations between the Foreign Secretary and his staff did not alter. The Palmerstonian tradition was maintained. Salisbury's relations with his staff were formal though he was personally close to his permanent under-secretary. The Prime Minister had always been contemptuous of bureaucracies in general and retained a low opinion of the so-called expert, whether in his own office or elsewhere, particularly in the service departments.[2] But he was a tireless worker and

[1] Grenville, *Lord Salisbury and Foreign Policy*, pp. 310–17.
[2] Lady Gwendolen Cecil, *Life of Robert, Marquis of Salisbury* (London, 1931–2), vol. III, p. 218. Devonshire Papers, Goschen to the Duke of Devonshire, 6 September 1895. 'I would not be too impressed by what soldiers tell you about the strategic importance of these places. If they were allowed full scope they would insist on the importance of garrisoning the moon in order to protect us from Mars.'

expected his subordinates to perform their functions efficiently.[1] Salisbury fully trusted his clerks and did not attempt to conceal his transactions.[2] It is simply that he believed there was a fundamental distinction between his power and their duties and he maintained this separation long after his officials began to assume more salient responsibilities. It was not only that Salisbury wanted clerks and not advisers or experts. He had a particular view of the way in which parliamentary government should function. The foreign secretary was responsible to the Cabinet, the Government to Parliament and the people. Permanent officials, however, were responsible to no one outside their departments and could not be held publicly accountable. As a result, Salisbury believed that they should not make decisions. By the turn of the century, this restricted view of the civil servant's role had been successfully challenged in other government departments. At the Colonial Office, for instance, civil servants were taking a not inconsiderable role in the determination of policy. But Salisbury remained loyal to an older and, perhaps, a more democratic view of the parliamentary system. It was Lord Lansdowne who first realized that the Foreign Office could not remain isolated from a general trend which was the direct result of the growing specialization of government business. During Salisbury's tenure of office there was no doubt where responsibility rested. There was no talk of 'grey eminences' or a foreign secretary misled by his advisers.

The changing role of the civil service was also obscured by the continuity of tone and attitude within the department. The office was run by Eric Barrington, Salisbury's private secretary for twelve years, and Henry Foley, the Foreign Secretary's précis writer, 'the perfect incarnation of the Foreign Office private secretary, handsome, slim, immaculately frock-coated with elegant manners'.[3] These men dealt with all the administrative problems of the day and the private secretary's office, which had already acquired the reputation of being an *imperium in imperio*, continued to play its key role in the staffing and discipline of the diplomatic services. It was Eric Barrington, acting in Salisbury's name, who recommended candidates for examinations

---

[1] Grenville, *Lord Salisbury and Foreign Policy*, p. 16. Grenville, relying on St John Brodrick's memoirs claims that 'his staff could calculate almost to the minute when a despatch they had sent would be returned to them for action'.

[2] I have found that contrary to what Lord Salisbury's daughter has written about his earlier administrations, the Foreign Secretary kept his officials fully informed of his proceedings in his last years. Though he continued his copious correspondence with diplomats abroad, there is little in these letters which cannot be found in the official archives. They are only an additional source of information for understanding Salisbury's diplomacy. Grenville has come to the same conclusion, *Lord Salisbury and Foreign Policy*, pp. 12–13. For the contrary view see G. Cecil, *Life of Lord Salisbury*, vol. IV, p. 21; BD III, Appendix A (p. 409), memorandum by Eyre Crowe, 1907.

[3] Sir Francis Oppenheimer, *Stranger Within* (London, 1960), p. 147.

and who arranged appointments for the consular services. Within the Foreign Office he was responsible for the promotions, transfers and movements of the junior clerks. He decided who was to be promoted and transferred, who was to move up by seniority and who by merit. Similarly, at the lower levels, Barrington played a significant part in determining diplomatic assignments. Petitions, complaints, requests for leave, funds and transfers, came to him first before formal applications were made to the Chief Clerk's Department. The private secretary's room was the obvious repository for office gossip and diplomatists always dropped in during visits home. The position was one of honour and distinction and was generally held by a senior clerk marked for future advancement.

Even by the standards of his day, Barrington was considered a snob, anxious to maintain the high social tone of his office. Junior clerks took great pains with their dress before entering his presence.[1] In all respects, however, Barrington's role was secretarial and administrative rather than political. In almost constant attendance, Barrington probably knew more about Salisbury's diplomacy than any other man in the office. He arranged appointments, kept records of Salisbury's conversations with visitors and saw most of Salisbury's correspondence.[2] In the Prime Minister's absence, he sometimes received foreign diplomats and shared with the permanent under-secretary the task of liaison with the press and diplomatic staff. But Barrington took no share in the shaping of policy. Salisbury was delighted to leave all administrative problems to his secretary but it seems highly doubtful whether he ever discussed general questions of diplomacy with Barrington or whether the latter would have ever offered advice on a political issue. This pattern changed only after Barrington left the private secretary's office and Sir Edward Grey replaced Lord Lansdowne.

Continuity was not restricted to the private secretary's office and powers. The position of the parliamentary under-secretary too had changed little since the decisive division of responsibility under Lord Hammond. This

---

[1] Tilley and Gaselee, *The Foreign Office*, p. 207.
[2] Barrington served Lord Lansdowne as well as Lord Salisbury as did Henry Foley until his death. The Private Secretary was assisted by a précis writer and two assistant private secretaries chosen from the regular Foreign Office staff. In 1889 a 'lady typewriter' was introduced into this inner sanctum; by 1914 the well-known Mrs Fulcher had a department of 11 (Ward and Gooch, *Cambridge History of British Foreign Policy*, vol. III, p. 606). The foreign secretary also had a parliamentary private secretary who did not belong to the Foreign Office staff at all. He was usually a young member of Parliament who relieved his chief of a part of his social obligations. The post, though unsalaried and social, provided an excellent introduction into ministerial circles and the young man often went from this position to that of a parliamentary under-secretary (Gosses, *The Management of British Foreign Policy*, p. 46).

under-secretary was not an important Foreign Office figure though a man of some political consequence. In this period he was always a politician rather than a civil servant and was picked by the foreign secretary from the ranks of the most promising party men.[1] Under Lord Salisbury he was responsible for defending the Government's policy in the Commons, a duty which required the reading of all despatches of any importance. He had to see the foreign secretary as often as possible to learn of the latest Cabinet decisions. During domestic debates, he sat in a small room in the basement of Westminster Hall reading through the contents of the red despatch boxes. Grey commented on his own industry: 'In fact, whenever foreign affairs were to come up in the House, I went there much better equipped than I had ever been at school or university.'[2] The parliamentary under-secretary not only had to attend Westminster on supply days and at question time when foreign affairs were discussed but he had to be present at all divisions, an additional burden which was finally dropped in 1898.[3]

Despite the time-consuming nature of the job, the parliamentary under-secretary's independence was severely limited. His replies to written questions were prepared for him by the heads of the departments and were often checked by the permanent under-secretary or by Lord Salisbury. His speeches in important debates were generally discussed in advance. His initiative was restricted to supplementary questions and details of wording. Rash remarks were rare and statements carefully guarded.[4] Consequently, although the parliamentary under-secretary knew an enormous amount about the contents of British policy, he had little influence on the course of events.

Grey had accepted this secondary role under Lord Rosebery but Lord Curzon found it nerve-racking and degrading.[5] He was constantly petitioning Salisbury for more information or details about policy decisions. 'I can't tell you', he complained, 'how anxious and even how miserable I am. And next week I have got to be defending all this without the slightest idea what the Cabinet really thinks or by what steps they arrive at their mysterious conclusions.'[6] Curzon sent the Foreign Secretary numerous memoranda

---

[1] Gosses, *Management of British Foreign Policy*, pp. 150–1.

[2] Grey of Fallodon, Viscount, *Twenty-Five Years* (London, 1933), vol. I, p. 30. Grey was parliamentary under-secretary to Kimberley and Rosebery.

[3] Balfour Papers, Salisbury to Brodrick, 4 October 1898. Lord Salisbury admitted that this practice would have driven him insane.

[4] Grey, *Twenty-Five Years*, vol. I, p. 18. See also Gosses, *Management of British Foreign Policy*, p. 151.

[5] Grey, *Twenty-Five Years*, vol. I, p. 32.

[6] Earl of Ronaldshay, *The Life of Lord Curzon* (London, 1928), vol. I, p. 253.

on Far Eastern and Middle Eastern (particularly Persian) matters and even tried to make something of the one Foreign Office department over which he had any control—the Commercial and Sanitary.[1] In March 1898 he was invited to the Cabinet to express his views on the Far Eastern situation and shared the responsibility for the decision to ask China for the lease of Wei-hai-Wei.[2] Nevertheless, Curzon's successful interventions were few and he left the office with relief.

His successor, St John Brodrick, was obviously reluctant to assume the position and wrote to Salisbury:

These doubts were in part based on the great increase in 'supplementary questions' in recent years which besides being very embarrassing from the public standpoint affect me personally, as being rather deaf, I feel somewhat uncertain of doing justice to them . . . I ought to add that I have been somewhat perturbed by the accounts given me by my two predecessors in the office of the pressure under which they have done their work. George Curzon had admittedly been broken down by it; E. Grey told me he had felt the strain acutely and that the House of Commons interruptions made it, even in quiet times, barely possible for him to keep pace with his work.[3]

To assist Brodrick, the Commercial Department was given to an assistant under-secretary to manage and his parliamentary duties were considerably lightened.[4] Supplementary questions were limited in number and arrangements made with the Whips regarding attendance in the Commons. These departmental responsibilities were not restored.

Like Lord Curzon, Brodrick was a political figure who also attempted to intervene in policy decisions. In June 1900 he proposed to Salisbury that Britain join Russia and Japan in an effort to rescue the Legations during the Boxer rebellion. More important, he gave his support to the

---

[1] D. C. M. Platt, *Finance, Trade and Politics, British Foreign Policy, 1815–1914* (Oxford, 1968), p. 231.

[2] Ian Nish, *The Anglo-Japanese Alliance* (London, 1966), p. 55.

[3] Salisbury MSS. Unbound Brodrick Correspondence, Brodrick to Salisbury, 2 October 1898.

[4] Since 1874 the parliamentary under-secretary had directed the Commercial Department of the Foreign Office. From 1880–91 and from 1895 until 1899, he was also made responsible for the supervision of all foreign commercial questions. As a result of strong protests from Curzon and Brodrick, this aspect of the secretary's work was dropped. The daily work was done by an assistant under-secretary under Brodrick's general supervision. In 1904 the name of the parliamentary under-secretary was eliminated and only the assistant under-secretary listed. In 1911 and 1912 the parliamentary under-secretary is again named supervisor but in April 1912 Algernon Law was made controller of commercial and consular affairs and the two departments (Commercial and Sanitary and Consular) were put under his control. FO 366/391, Brodrick to Salisbury, 17 February 1899. For additional information on the background of this department and Brodrick's suggestions for improving the status and usefulness of the commercial attachés and commercial agents, see Platt, *Finance, Trade and Politics, British Foreign Policy, 1815–1914*, p. 393 and his Appendix I.

Cabinet revolt against Salisbury's China policy in the autumn of 1900.[1] Both Curzon's and Brodrick's intervention were signs of Salisbury's weakening control over diplomacy. The formal position of the parliamentary under-secretary had not changed; in practice, however, Cabinet discussions of alternative policies allowed the successive holders of this office an opportunity to voice their own opinions. Curzon and Brodrick only reflected the general restlessness in the party. For the most part, parliamentary under-secretaries had to be content with Cabinet contacts, a public platform and the promise of an illustrious future. Grey became foreign secretary, Curzon was made viceroy of India and Brodrick became secretary of state for war.

Though the outward pattern of Thomas Sanderson's activities followed the same line of continuity, he was in fact to take over some of the responsibilities of his minister. The Permanent Under-Secretary thought of himself as the chief of a department whose job it was to carry out the instructions of the Secretary of State.[2] He was really concerned with the machinery of his office, the handwriting of his clerks, the accuracy of their copies, the correctness of their forms. 'It [handwriting] is not a small matter. Handwriting when thoroughly formed or deformed is not easily altered later in life; and it is almost impossible for the reader to give full attention to a paper when half his mental power is occupied in deciphering it.'[3] Complaints about late bags, missing despatches and poorly kept registers always came to his desk. This last great 'super-clerk' did not consider it his primary duty to give advice or make suggestions to Lord Salisbury except on the rare occasions when the latter solicited his views. Sanderson judged his administrative responsibilities to be as important as his diplomatic duties; he was probably the last permanent under-secretary to do so.[4]

'Lamps' had come to Whitehall at the age of eighteen after leaving Eton because of his father's business failure.[5] He had made his way up the

---

[1] In the case of Brodrick, see J. Amery, *Life of Joseph Chamberlain* (London, 1951), IV, 139. Grenville, *Lord Salisbury and Foreign Policy*, p. 308. George W. Monger, *The End of Isolation* (London, 1963), p. 19. Brodrick also supported Curzon's Persian proposals in 1900.

[2] He supervised the Western and Eastern Departments, the Chief Clerk's and Treaty Departments and the Library.

[3] T. Sanderson, *Observations on the Use and Abuse of Red Tape for the Juniors in the Eastern and Western Departments*, London 1891.

[4] Eyre Crowe during his permanent under-secretaryship (1920–25) was also to become preoccupied with the administrative details of his office but he undoubtedly would have put his advisory functions at the top of his list of responsibilities.

[5] Lord Vansittart, *The Mist Procession* (London, 1956), p. 45. 'He had thick glasses and thin legs, was a great listener to the great, a well-stored official of noted and unoriginal ability, who became suddenly formidable when he fused into a Department.'

Foreign Office ladder through a series of private secretaryships. Although he was personally closest to Lord Derby, about whom he wrote an interesting memoir, he and Lord Salisbury worked well together and his final promotions were due to Salisbury's appreciation of his talents.[1] Sanderson was noted for his industry, his prodigious memory and his ability as a draftsman. 'Your powers of drafting are quite unequalled. I wish it were possible to carry out the ideas which Lord Ampthill used to be so fond of, committing all the important drafting to one hand—as I believe is done at the French Foreign Office.'[2] The final wording of almost every major agreement during these years shows evidence of Sanderson's pen. He and Francis Bertie prepared the form of the Anglo-German agreement in August 1898, the final drafts of the two Anglo-French agreements on Africa, and the October 1900 agreement with Germany.

Though Sanderson was stiff in manner and regarded by some as a fussy chief, he had a sharp sense of humour sometimes bordering on the macabre which must have delighted Salisbury.[3] The Permanent Under-Secretary was not a man without artistic accomplishments; he wrote a series of delightful morality stories for children, played the flute with skill and was an active member of the Royal Society of Arts.[4] He was always looking for scientific books which might divert his chief, and towards the end of Salisbury's life a note of personal warmth is to be found in their correspondence.

Despite what he professed, Sanderson was taking an active part in the formulation of policy. Although he did not prepare memoranda on crucial issues, he did enable Lord Salisbury to get through an every-increasing volume of business. As the Foreign Secretary did most of his work at Hatfield, Sanderson was often the link between the Foreign Office and its political chief. As head of both the Western and Eastern Departments, Sanderson was kept in daily touch with all the more important political proceedings of the period.

As he possessed a well ordered and methodical mind and a marvellously retentive memory not only for general principles, but also for details of all dimensions, he early acquired the reputation of being a walking encyclopaedia of Foreign Office lore,

[1] Salisbury MSS. Sanderson unbound correspondence. Sanderson to Salisbury, 28 December 1893.

[2] *Ibid.* Salisbury to Sanderson, 20 August 1892.

[3] In later years Sanderson suffered from a number of physical disabilities which increased his irritability. His letters are quite witty and far more striking than those of his chief critic, Francis Bertie (Salisbury MSS, Sanderson to Salisbury, 1 April 1898: 'I am now a sort of standing dish at Arthur Balfour's breakfast... when his attention is divided, as it was this morning, between me and a fresh herring, there are alternatively moments of distraction while he is concentrating on the herring, and moments of danger when he is concentrating on foreign affairs').

[4] He also belonged to St James's, Travellers' and the Athenaeum.

and his colleagues often said of him, not altogether in jest, that he carried with him in his head all the archives of that venerable institution.[1]

He knew, as he instructed his clerks to learn, 'the sizes of the various islands of the Samoan archipelago and whether the various inhabitants do or do not wear trousers'.[2] By handling a large correspondence and by retaining the details of many previous negotiations, Sanderson could supply Lord Salisbury with the history and papers of almost any diplomatic problem of the moment. On one occasion, during Lord Salisbury's discussions with Count Hatzfeldt in 1900, Sanderson's close scrutiny of the proposed treaty saved Salisbury from a geographic error which would have further weakened the already feeble Anglo-German Chinese agreement.[3]

In practice, Sanderson had an important share in the daily making of policy. The harmony between Salisbury and Sanderson was so complete that the Prime Minister rarely rejected one of Sanderson's suggestions. During the Cretan crisis of 1898, the Foreign Secretary repeatedly initialled drafts which were composed by Sanderson in the first instance.[4] During the Persian negotiations of 1898 and 1899, Sanderson suggested the procedure to be followed and prepared the drafts used for discussions with the Chancellor of the Exchequer, the Imperial Bank of Persia and the Persian Government.[5] He forwarded the British minister's despatches from Teheran with critical comments of his own and offered alternative suggestions for propping the Persians up financially. A recent study of the Persian question in this period concludes on this point:

Sanderson, often after consultation with Lee Warner or Godley [officials at the India Office] prepared the papers which were to be decided in Hatfield, or himself went there to receive instructions from his chief. Through that mere fact there was left to him the formulation of the great mass of correspondence, a mass in which Salisbury intervened only seldom to make a correction or addition.[6]

Again, after Lord Salisbury had made it clear that he did not want a dispute with France over Newfoundland, Sanderson found the formula used in the many unsuccessful attempts to settle the repeated squabbles between the Foreign and Colonial Offices on the vexed question of the Newfoundland

[1] Obituary in *The Times*, 21 March 1923.
[2] Sanderson, *Observations on Use and Abuse of Red Tape*.
[3] FO 64/1507, minute by Sanderson, Salisbury to Hatzfeldt, 4 October 1900; BD II, no. 38.
[4] See FO 65/1551, no. 56b, 26 February 1898; FO 65/1552, no. 185, 18 June 1898. 'Do you wish to modify or supplement this answer?' 'No, I think it is quite right.'
[5] FO 60/601, minute by Sanderson, 16 May 1898; FO 60/630, Durand to Salisbury, 19 March 1899; telegram no. 8, Salisbury to Durand, 21 March 1899; Hamilton to Sanderson, 7 July 1899.
[6] J. V. Plass, *England zwischen Russland und Deutschland, 1899–1907* (Hamburg, 1966), pp. 45–6. My translation of the German.

fishing rights.[1] Obviously, on every major issue, Fashoda, the decision to negotiate with Germany, the talks with the United States—Salisbury made his own decisions and Sanderson merely implemented his orders. But in a large number of minor questions which made up the bulk of daily business, Salisbury accepted Sanderson's suggestions and the latter's drafts became the final form of a despatch.

In addition to the work connected with the actual running of the Western and Eastern Departments, Sanderson often saw foreign diplomats in Salisbury's absence. He more than once soothed the feathers of a ruffled German ambassador, listened to the woes of the angry King of Siam and dealt with many a minor diplomat with a burning grievance. There were times when he and Lord Salisbury discussed general questions of diplomacy, most often at Hatfield, where Sanderson was a constant visitor. During the autumn of 1900 the Prime Minister seems to have expressed his strong doubts about the feasibility of an agreement with Germany in the Far East.

Lord Salisbury asked me what the object of the Germans could be in asking for the agreement. I told him I thought they would like to show that their Chinese policy was a moderate one which had our support, and also that they probably considered that they had done a good stroke of business in obtaining from us a pledge not to swallow up the Yangtsze whole.[2]

These conversations allowed Sanderson both to deal with foreign emissaries and to supplement Salisbury's personal correspondence with short but informative notes which went to British envoys overseas in almost every bag.

Sanderson handled relations with the press, received editors and on occasions intervened with *The Times* to moderate its anti-Russian or anti-German tone.[3] The Under-Secretary saw the Reuters' agent regularly and not only gave him items of news but answered any questions he thought useful. He could count on this information appearing in publications both in India and throughout the Far East.[4] As there was no press secretary or press bureau, all of these conversations were highly informal and Sander-

---

[1] FO 27/3443, Sanderson to Salisbury, 22 June 1899, Sanderson backed the judgement of Villiers, the assistant under-secretary in charge of Newfoundland, against Joseph Chamberlain; *ibid.* minute by Sanderson, 12 December 1899; FO 27/3521, memorandum by Sanderson, 25 August 1900; Law Officers to Foreign Office, 31 October 1900.

[2] Lascelles MSS (FO 627), vol. III, pt 1, Sanderson to Lascelles, 17 October 1900; BD II, no. 98. BD II, pp. 84–8.

[3] See pp. 186–7 for a fuller discussion.

[4] Salisbury MSS. A/95, minute by Eric Barrington, 10 August 1897. Bertie complained that the Reuters' agent put a series of fishing questions to him when he was acting in Sanderson's absence. Lord Salisbury shared his assistant under-secretary's distaste for such interviews and commented: 'I am sceptical of the advantages of our connection with Reuters—so is Lord Kimberley to whom I spoke about it.'

son did not go out of his way to cultivate good relations with Fleet Street.

The Permanent Under-Secretary's views, as far as one can gather from the limited evidence, were very much in accord with those of Lord Salisbury.[1] He would have welcomed an agreement with Russia in China and in Persia but had become convinced that the Russian military authorities would block any such attempt.[2] He was frequently annoyed by the rough diplomatic tactics of the Germans, was suspicious of Holstein and found the Kaiser's erratic temperament an unwelcome factor in Anglo-German relations. Although he never let his personal irritation embitter his relations with Count Hatzfeldt, he did not trust the policy-makers in Berlin and even suspected the possibility of a Russo-German bargain in the Far East. As to France, Sanderson made every effort to prevent the numerous small clashes from developing into any major diplomatic crises. Here again, after Fashoda, his policy echoed that of his chief. Sanderson was the perfect second to Lord Salisbury. His moderation and conciliatory manner eased relations with diplomats sometimes perturbed by Salisbury's more caustic and enigmatic approach. Moreover, Sanderson was a master of the diplomat's greatest virtue, discretion, and Lord Salisbury completely trusted him. Sanderson's genuine conservatism somewhat masked the fact (as it masked it from Sanderson himself) that he was taking an active role in the making of policy. The very intimacy of his relationship to Lord Salisbury meant that specific proposals would be initiated by the Permanent Under-Secretary, even as that intimacy also meant that he would be hardly aware of his initiating role. Thus, in effect, Sanderson was expanding the powers of his office well beyond the confines envisioned by Lord Hammond.

A far more dramatic challenge to this confine came from Francis Bertie, the second son of the Earl of Abingdon.[3] Well placed in society, Bertie was a frequent guest at the Prince of Wales's table and a close friend of Sir Francis Knollys, the Prince's private secretary. 'The Bull', as he was later called, was shrewd, sharp and unsparing in his criticisms.[4] He was noted for his violent temper, his petulance and his caustic tongue. Unlike Sanderson, with whom he was far from popular, Bertie was inclined to express his

---

[1] There is only a small collection of Sanderson papers preserved in the Public Record Office but additional material will be found in the Hardinge, Lascelles and Spring-Rice correspondence.

[2] FO 60/648, minute by Sanderson, 23 April 1899; BD II, no. 73. Lascelles MSS, vol. III, pt 1, Sanderson to Lascelles, 12 and 29 April 1899.

[3] Bertie belonged to one of the oldest diplomatic families in England. The first Lord Abingdon represented Queen Elizabeth at the French court. Bertie's father, a country squire in Oxfordshire, gave his son the usual education of his class. Bertie had gone to Eton (where he had known Lansdowne) and then was sent abroad to perfect his languages. He was a member of St James's, Travellers', Brooks' and The Turf, where he frequently met Alfred de Rothschild, a useful connection for the Foreign Office.                                    [4] See pp. 180–1.

37

opinions freely and offered advice even when it was not sought. It is a striking fact that almost all the long policy memoranda of this period are written by him and not by Sanderson.

By chance, Bertie headed the African and Asiatic Departments, two of the most active areas during Lord Salisbury's last years. In neither area did Salisbury show that surety of diplomatic knowledge which characterized his dealing with other parts of the world. Much of the African business was not of first-class diplomatic importance and was left to Bertie and the head of the African Department, Clement Hill. In fact Hill, a man of much experience, dealt independently with the African protectorates and Bertie rarely intervened.[1] There were, however, an increasing number of African questions which involved the European powers, and in such disputes Bertie played a crucial role.[2] In a number of cases, particularly in the East African border conflict with France, it was Bertie who proposed the compromise solution which satisfied Joseph Chamberlain and yet gave some measure of freedom to the Foreign Office officials actually negotiating with the French.[3] The job of settling the details, drawing up the line, preparing the Niger transit regulations and calming the explosive head of the Royal Niger Company, Sir George Goldie, was left to members of the African Department.

The extent of Bertie's independence is well illustrated by the Anglo-Portuguese negotiations over Delagoa Bay during 1897 and 1898. Joseph Chamberlain played a very important role in these negotiations to which he attached far more importance than Salisbury.[4] Bertie's proposals provided the basis for Chamberlain's talks with the Portuguese minister and it was the Under-Secretary who persuaded a reluctant Alfred de Rothschild to consider a loan to the Portuguese Government.[5] The terms of the projected understanding with Portugal were suggested by Bertie and accepted without change by Salisbury and Chamberlain.[6] Obviously, these drafts were pre-

---

[1] See p. 11. Hill's correspondence with African consuls and the chartered companies was sent with Bertie's signature but were Hill's own drafts.

[2] In each of the African border discussions a similar procedure was followed. Clement Hill prepared the required information and attended the preliminary meetings with Colonial Office representatives while Bertie drafted with Hill's assistance suggestions for Lord Salisbury's final approval. In the case of the German south-western border claims, army officials and map experts were drawn into the discussions and a mixed commission was sent out to Africa to determine a new boundary line.

[3] See the East African delimitation discussions with France (FO 27/3411, Gosselin to Bertie, 1 February 1898; FO 27/3716, Bertie to Gosselin, 1 January 1898; Salisbury to Monson, 27 January 1898; FO 27/3713, Monson to Salisbury, 15 May 1898; FO 27/3412, minute by Salisbury, 24 April 1898; FO 27/3416, minute by Bertie, 23 May 1898; Salisbury to Monson, 4 June 1898).                [4] Grenville, *Lord Salisbury and Foreign Policy*, p. 185.

[5] FO 63/1359, memorandum by Bertie to Salisbury, 22 March 1897, 18 January 1898.

[6] *Ibid.* memorandum by Bertie, 10 March 1897.

ceded by discussions with the two Cabinet ministers but what should be noted is Salisbury's passivity and Chamberlain's dependence on Bertie's expertise. Salisbury had been content to allow the discussions to be conducted by the Colonial Secretary, until early in June 1898 the Germans intervened at Lisbon and in London. Despite Bertie's strong objections and Salisbury's own hesitations, the latter was soon involved in talks with the German ambassador. The Under-Secretary's two negative memoranda (30 June and 10 August) went far beyond a discussion of the specific agreement under consideration but had little influence on the subsequent proceedings.[1] Bertie felt that England could secure all she wished in Africa without German assistance or neutrality. He further argued that an African agreement would not pave the way for an alliance in the Far East. 'Germany is not likely to risk a quarrel or even an estrangement with Russia for our benefit unless we guarantee her against France and Russia.'[2]

Once talks were begun with Berlin, Bertie's role was restricted to providing the drafts needed to bring the agreement to its conclusion. The Assistant Under-Secretary's doubts were shared by Sanderson and even Chamberlain began to have second thoughts when he realized how much the Germans were demanding. Early in August 1898 Salisbury fell ill and went to the south of France. Balfour, far more enthusiastic about an accommodation, persevered and the agreement was signed on 30 August 1898. Subsequent problems were hammered out by Hatzfeldt's son and Bertie. The conversations were unpleasant; each demand and counter-demand became the subject of a dispute as Bertie and Sanderson tried to improve the British position. Bertie was openly annoyed and his clerks felt that England had lost more than it had won.

Other events tended to increase the Under-Secretary's hostility towards the Germans. During the Boer War, Bertie had to deal with questions of contraband and the problems raised by the seizure of German steamers 'about which the German Government are making themselves as nasty as they know how which is saying a good deal'.[3] In the Far East, Bertie was irritated by the failure of the Government to stand up to any opposition, Russian or German.[4]

The Germans as regards Shantung have lied with their customary awkwardness. I live in hope that we may succeed in putting them in the cart. I am convinced that if we show that we mean business we shall have very little trouble with our big

[1] BD I, nos. 72, 81.  [2] *Ibid.* no. 81.
[3] Satow Papers, Campbell to Satow, 2 January 1900. In fact, the British were wrong in this case; the German vessels were not carrying contraband and damages had to be paid.
[4] BD I, no. 24.

European friends. Unfortunately, France, Russia and Germany have got it into their heads that we shall never stand up to one First Class Power much less 2 or 3 even if we had little Japan with us.[1]

When the Boxer Rising (a movement which Bertie did not anticipate or understand) broke out, it was Bertie's responsibility to arrange the details of the allied intervention.[2] The Russians took advantage of the situation to occupy Manchuria and seize part of the British railway line there and Bertie's anger was directed both at Russia and at Germany, for the latter did not give him the backing he required.[3]

Bertie's mounting distrust of the Germans can be traced in the daily records of the Foreign Office. His views were clearly put in a memorandum opposing the Anglo-German Agreement of October 1900.[4] Like Salisbury and Sanderson, Bertie argued that Germany was not a suitable ally against the Russians. Instead, he was becoming more sympathetic to the idea of a Japanese agreement which might slow the Russian advance. If the Japanese did not secure British support, warned Bertie, they might settle directly with the Russians at England's expense.[5]

Even during Salisbury's last years at the Foreign Office, Bertie's contribution to the making of policy surpassed that of Sanderson, certainly in its self-consciousness. Both the African and Asiatic Departments gave Bertie ample scope for his abundant energies.[6] Though the Assistant Under-Secretary was not always particularly acute about the problems which arose in these contested areas, he was clear and tenacious in his views and had no hesitation about expressing them.[7] When Sanderson was absent, Bertie took over his responsibilities and departments.[8] There is little doubt that Sanderson took a wider and more moderate view of the diplomatic scene but Bertie was far more outspoken in his opinions. Although the two men had little in common personally, they took a similar negative view on the question of an Anglo-

---

[1] FO 64/1347, Bertie to Lascelles, 16 March 1898.

[2] Satow MSS, Satow Journal, 20 August 1900. FO 64/1496, Bertie to Salisbury, 8 August 1900.

[3] Hardinge Papers, vol. 3, Hardinge to Bertie, 15 November 1900. Hardinge congratulated Bertie for his firm stand against the Russians. For Bertie's complaints against Germany: Lascelles MSS, vol. III, pt 1, Sanderson to Lascelles, 7 November 1900, FO 64/1495, nos. 271, 275, Lascelles to Salisbury, 26, 31 October 1900.

[4] BD II, no. 12.          [5] FO 64/1496, minute by Bertie, 17 November 1900.

[6] Bertie and Campbell (the senior clerk in the China Department) dealt with many problems which did not even reach the foreign secretary. Bertie, as well as Campbell, dealt with the conflicting demands by concessionaires, met the deputations from the China Association, Chambers of Commerce, etc. Nathan Pelcovits, *Old China Hands and the Foreign Office* (New York, 1948), pp. 256 and 262.

[7] Ian Nish, *The Anglo-Japanese Alliance* (London, 1966), p. 154.

[8] Under-secretaries (including the parliamentary under-secretary) did each other's work during vacation times usually during the summer and early autumn. FO 366/391, St John Brodrick to Salisbury, 17 February 1899.

German agreement. Sanderson remained convinced that Salisbury's 'free hand' policy would prove adequate; Bertie impatiently pressed for a more energetic display of British power. Bertie's determination to make his personal voice heard was to have the most important consequences for the future development of the Foreign Office.

The other assistant under-secretaries were men of less distinction who shared Sanderson's limited view of the proper functions of his office. Francis Villiers, the fourth son of the Earl of Clarendon, had come to the Foreign Office from Harrow and like Sanderson had made his way up the hierarchy through a series of private secretaryships. His family had a long history of service in the Diplomatic Corps and Villiers hoped one day to replace Sanderson as permanent under-secretary.[1] His son entered the Foreign Office in 1903 to continue the family tradition. Martin Gosselin, the third assistant, had been educated at Eton and at Christ Church. A Catholic of great charm, good temper and musical interests, Gosselin had spent most of his life in the Diplomatic Service and had the unusual Foreign Office experience of having already served in a number of important posts abroad.

Villiers supervised the Consular Service and assisted Sanderson with the work of the Treaties Department. On the political side, his assignments were varied and covered a wide geographical area. From 1898 he was in charge of American affairs, first in the combined American and Asiatic Department and in the following year in the newly-created American Department. His contribution to the making of policy was not a negligible one and some of his summaries and policy explanations were circulated to the Cabinet. Although most of these were concerned with Anglo-American relations, Villiers also corresponded with diplomatists in Central and South America, thereby saving many a grateful minister from total oblivion. One of the most irritating minor questions which occupied the Assistant Under-Secretary throughout this period was the partition of the Samoan islands.[2] The division of 'this miserable archipelago' dragged on for four years until the King of Norway and Sweden made his arbitral decision in October 1902. Lord Salisbury was only too happy to leave this troublesome question to Villiers who often consulted with Sanderson before acting. There were disagreements about the future treatment of the King of the islands, the salaries of the chief justices and the expense of the adjudicating commissioners. 'All the delays and petty difficulties in this matter are due to the Germans', Villiers

[1] Villiers was offered and refused an under-secretaryship at the Colonial Office.
[2] FO 318, BD I, pp. 117-31.

complained.[1] Assisted by his senior clerk, Arthur Larcom, Villiers corresponded with the British ambassador in Washington and received Count Hatzfeldt.

Villiers helped Sanderson in the Western Department whenever pressure mounted. At various times he handled the correspondence concerning Newfoundland, Borneo and Morocco; complex and tedious disputes which consumed a great deal of Foreign Office time. For instance, in 1898 Villiers repeatedly intervened in the battle between the Newfoundland colonists and the French fishermen bordering on the Treaty Shore and worked with the Colonial Office in an attempt to settle this ancient struggle.[2] Disputes raised by the joint Anglo-French administration of the New Hebrides islands involved Villiers in talks with both the French and the Colonial Office.[3] He was also the recipient of complaints from numerous missionary groups who were protesting against the gun- and alcohol-selling activities of the French in these far-off islands.

As the most junior of the under-secretaries, Gosselin was used wherever his services were needed, in the Consular Department and then in the Commercial and Sanitary Department (all too naturally cast in a subordinate role). As he had been one of the British delegates sent to settle the West African border disputes with the French, he was also asked to assist Bertie with African affairs. Gosselin became the link between E. D. Morel and the Foreign Office during the early stages of the former's campaign for reforms in the Congo.[4] In 1898 Gosselin took over the Moroccan correspondence and Nicolson, the British minister at Tangier, used his letters to Gosselin to bring his views to the attention of an unsympathetic foreign secretary.[5] Like Villiers, Gosselin handled a great variety of political business. In 1899 he was responsible for Belgium, Denmark, Sweden, Norway and the Newfoundland dispute. In the case of the latter, Gosselin inherited Villiers' job of keeping the peace with France. He too saw the Colonial Office officials, reviewed, usually negatively, Chamberlain's proposals for a settlement and, in consultation with Sanderson, made alternative suggestions.[6]

1 FO 67/1507, Villiers to Sanderson, 12 August 1900.
2 FO 27/3443, Villiers to Sanderson, 18 July 1898; Villiers to Colonial Office, 3 October 1898; Memorandum by Villiers, 6 July 1898.
3 FO 27/1324, Villiers to Salisbury, 12 January 1899; Salisbury to Monson, 21 October 1899.
4 Wm. Roger Louis and Jean Stengers, *E. D. Morel's History of the Congo Reform Movement* (Oxford, 1968), pp. 93, 95.
5 FO 99/367, Nicolson to Gosselin, 18 May 1900, 22 May 1900; Nicolson to Salisbury, 26 May 1900. Salisbury vetoed Gosselin's attempt to support Nicolson's reforming activities at the Sultan's court. See A. J. P. Taylor, *Rumours of War* (London, 1952), pp. 140–1. Nicolson wrote regularly to Villiers and Gosselin.
6 FO 27/3443, memorandum by Gosselin, 26 April 1899, and other evidence in FO 27/3521.

Such issues made up the bulk of his daily activities. Responsibility remained limited, though the pressure of business did result in a more active role for the assistant under-secretaries than had been customary.

As suggested earlier, the real experts in the Foreign Office were the senior clerks. Clement Hill in the African Department was a special case but Larcom in the American, Campbell in the China, Maxwell in the Eastern and Hopwood in the Western were all thoroughly familiar with the disputes and diplomatists in their areas. All were called upon to prepare factual information on points at issue.[1] They summarized reports for the supervising under-secretaries and prepared first drafts. Their letters to diplomatists might contain explanations of technical transactions, complaints against the use of the diplomatic bags for personal parcels or the latest bit of official gossip. There was a regular exchange between Hardinge in Morocco and Hopwood with regard to customs regulations, transit duties and such matters. Francis Campbell, who became an assistant under-secretary in 1902, settled a number of minor issues ranging from commercial concessions and copyright laws to local border disputes. The senior clerks also dealt with delegations, with the continuous flow of letters from commercial groups, missionaries and would-be travellers. Campbell received the representatives of the China Association; Hopwood saw H. F. B. Lynch who had extensive interests in Persia.[2]

It is true for the most part, however, that these men remained clerks whose supervisory and clerical concerns took up the major portion of their day. Their assistants and juniors were, as before, scribes who wrote and filed and despatched without any real part in the policy-making process. Walter Langley, still an assistant clerk at this time, carried out a survey of the ports importing fish from Newfoundland and issued a memorandum on the History of the Negotiations on British Codfish Traps. But only an initial on the left-hand corner of the despatch gives any evidence for the existence of the remaining staff. Officials were willing to accept tedium for prestige, good hours, congenial company and predestined promotion. Complaints were rare and hardly welcomed.[3] Under Lord Salisbury the 'third room' was officially silent.

---

[1] Hopwood's commentaries on the Annual Newfoundland Fisheries reports were useful, as were his careful analyses of the points at issue between the Newfoundland colonists and the French. FO 27/3607, 3608 for similar illustrations.

[2] Satow Journal for 1900, entries for June and July; Hardinge MSS, Hopwood to Hardinge, 1 June 1897. Pelcovits, *Old China Hands and the Foreign Office*, p. 252. Hardinge MSS, Hopwood to Hardinge, 2 January 1898.

[3] The most notable exception was Arthur Ponsonby, son of Queen Victoria's private secretary,

It is clearly easy to overestimate the degree of change during these years. The Foreign Office continued to lag behind the domestic departments. There was a gulf between the Foreign Secretary and his staff which was scarcely altered in this period. The methods of dealing with daily business were not strikingly more efficient than in the days of falling ceilings. A few men carried a huge burden while the junior staff did work more competently performed elsewhere by secretaries and filers. Foreign policy did not emerge through a process of consultation within the Foreign Office. Lord Salisbury was the master of his house, he made his own decisions and expected them to be carried out. After 1898, however, the under-secretaries did have a larger share in the conduct of diplomacy. Sanderson and Bertie were careful to frame their instructions in accordance with Salisbury's views; the former in particular was exceedingly cautious. But Bertie openly criticized his chief's direction and already showed signs of that irritation and impatience which were to make him a leading voice in the reform of the Foreign Office. The divergencies between Salisbury and Chamberlain gave the Assistant Under-Secretary a unique opportunity to be heard.

*Note on Percy Anderson and Clement Hill*

Sir Percy Anderson was the most famous African expert of his day. He had been senior clerk in the Consular and African Department throughout its existence (1883–93) and then supervising under-secretary of the African Department until his death in 1896. He ruled a vast empire; his suggestions were rarely vetoed and his political chiefs took an active interest in his affairs only in moments of crisis. A recent article has shown that Anderson's anti-French attitude was crucial in the development of British policy in Africa during the 1880s and 1890s. Professor Louis has commented: 'His influence on African questions was tantamount to that of the Foreign Secretary' (W. Roger Louis, 'Sir Percy Anderson's Grand African Strategy, 1883–1893', *The English Historical Review* LXXXI, 308). Anderson was succeeded by Clement Lloyd Hill who had entered the Foreign Office in 1867 and was well versed in the problems of his new empire. When the African protectorates were separated from the African Department, Hill was made their superintendent. While less forceful than Anderson, Hill coped with every kind of

who was sorting private print by the age of seven. Ponsonby, a junior second secretary, despised the idle, social life of the diplomatist abroad and returned to the Foreign Office where he was soon equally disenchanted. In London he sent Sanderson a memorandum (dated October 1900) with detailed suggestions for improving the diplomatic service. Two and a half years later, having found life at the Foreign Office intolerable, he resigned from the Service and embarked on a political career. For the details of this memorandum and the acrimonious exchange of letters between Sanderson and Ponsonby, see Appendix 4.

problem ranging from the suppression of slavery and the preservation of game to the creation of the Uganda railway and the settlement of the Nandi revolt. He was in constant touch with the chartered companies and supervised a large staff of African officials including even Harry Johnston. Hill disliked and clashed with the latter and the difference in their views was in part responsible for Hill's general tour of inspection in 1900. According to A. T. Matson, who is doing a history of the Nandi, Hill's mission and his on-the-spot decisions marked a sharp departure in the traditional Foreign Office policy of leaving things in the hands of the local man. In any case, Hill seems to have interpreted his rather vague instructions in their broadest sense and Johnston, though special commissioner for this area, did not challenge his authority. The loose division of authority and the tremendous power of Hill, who, assisted by two or three clerks (including Harry Farnall and Eyre Crowe), controlled this huge overseas area is an interesting commentary on the late imperial period. See Tilley and Gaselee, *The Foreign Office*, p. 220. Louis, 'Sir Percy Anderson's Grand African Strategy, 1883–1893', *The English Historical Review* LXXXI, 292–314. I am indebted to Mr A. T. Matson for his account of Hill's tour in 1900, its background and consequences.

# CHAPTER 2

# Transition and reform, 1901–1905

### Lord Lansdowne takes over

Lord Lansdowne succeeded Salisbury at the Foreign Office when the Prime Minister reorganized his Cabinet in the autumn of 1900. This appointment paved the way for a departure in British policy and for a major upheaval within the Foreign Office. The new minister was well suited to his office both by temperament and background. Educated at Eton and Balliol, Lansdowne entered Gladstone's Cabinet at an early age and rose quickly to a position of eminence. At thirty-eight, he was made governor-general of Canada and five years later became viceroy of India. His clash with Gladstone over Irish questions (he had extensive holdings in Ireland) had brought him into the Conservative party and Salisbury was quick to make use of his administrative experience. Though judged by many as a failure at the War Office, he seemed the logical successor to Salisbury when the Premier was finally convinced that the double burden of office was too great.

Though lacking any outstanding abilities, Lansdowne proved to be an adroit foreign secretary at a particularly difficult period in British history. Salisbury's loyal support of him during the Boer War years made Lansdowne particularly anxious to recoup his reputation. 'I shouldn't call him clever,' Arthur Balfour commented, 'he was better than competent.' Modern commentators have varied in their judgements of Lansdowne's talents but all agree that he put his own stamp on the course of British diplomacy.[1] He had a limited but flexible approach to the problems of his day. He was willing to solicit and accept advice, to compromise and to accept temporary defeat without losing his balance. His tact, his very lack of brilliance or bellicosity aided his efforts to seek a *modus vivendi* with each of the great powers. He was skilful in handling diplomatists and an excellent negotiator. Though the new foreign secretary lacked Salisbury's knowledge and wit, Lansdowne

---

[1] Monger, *The End of Isolation*, and Nish, *The Anglo-Japanese Alliance*, both argue that Lansdowne was both shrewd and extremely able. Grenville, *Lord Salisbury and Foreign Policy*, is more critical. Francis Knollys' (the King's private secretary) comment is revealing. 'His mind I think moves slowly, he is ultra-cautious and undecided in character, besides being a long time in making up his mind.' 800/163 series A, Knollys to Bertie, 19 November 1902.

came to his post with a keen appreciation of imperial problems. He was used to making major decisions and, though cautious, was decisive at critical moments.

Lansdowne belonged to that group of Unionists who were alarmed at England's isolation. He was willing to pay a good price for better relations with other countries and was anxious to reduce England's commitments in the far corners of the world. Even when Britain's foreign position substantially improved with the ending of the Boer War, Lansdowne remained convinced that her resources were over-taxed and that she needed continental friends if not allies. Though the pattern of diplomacy was considerably altered by events over which Lansdowne had little control, a large measure of the credit for Britain's stronger continental position after 1904 was due to the Foreign Secretary's response to these occurrences.

Like Lord Salisbury, Lansdowne found that repeated efforts (in January and April 1901 and in October 1902) to come to an agreement with Russia failed. An overestimation of Russian strength and fears of a Russian advance in central Asia and in the Far East dominated the thinking of the Conservatives. To check the Russians, Lansdowne turned to Berlin but none of his attempts to lure the Germans into the Far East succeeded. The question was left pending and even when the need for German friendship diminished, Lansdowne sought to keep the line to Berlin open. It was the failure to achieve an agreement with Russia which led to an approach to Japan, though the coolness of the Germans towards a Far Eastern understanding was not without some importance.

The Anglo-Japanese alliance avoided the possibility of a Russo-Japanese bargain at British expense and allowed the British naval commitment in the Far East to be reduced. Naval considerations also played a role in the settlement with the United States. By signing the Hay–Pauncefote Treaty, the British recognized the supremacy of the Americans in Western waters and subsequent crises in Anglo-American relations never fundamentally upset this basic understanding. In a sense, the Anglo-French entente was but one more effort on the Foreign Secretary's part to eliminate the major sources of dispute and to adopt a policy more in keeping with England's available resources. It is paradoxical that Lansdowne is best remembered for the entente, a colonial bargain initiated by the French which, from the British point of view, had little to do with the balance of power in Europe.[1]

For the entente did not bring Britain into the European alliance system.

[1] Christopher Andrew ,*Théophile Delcassé and the making of the Entente Cordiale; a reappraisal of French foreign policy, 1898–1905* (London, 1968), p. 211. Monger, *The End of Isolation*, p. 135.

Though, with Delcassé's approval, talks with Russia were again resumed in the autumn of 1903 and in the spring of 1904, the Russo-Japanese War cut short this new approach. Far Eastern affairs dominated much of Conservative thought even at the time of the first Moroccan crisis.[1] The total collapse of Russia in this area took the Foreign Office by surprise. Consequently, the great importance attached by the Conservatives to the conclusion of the second Anglo-Japanese alliance in 1905.

Recent studies have shown that Lansdowne did not feel fully committed to France and had no intention of pursuing an anti-German policy. On the contrary, during 1904 he hoped Anglo-German relations would improve. But the European tensions created by the Russo-Japanese War during the winter of 1904–05 induced a mood of panic in Berlin and the possibility of an Anglo-German clash was discussed seriously in both countries. Despite the rising tide of anti-German feeling, Lansdowne remained detached and continued to believe in the vanishing possibility of an Anglo-German understanding. The German challenge in Morocco, therefore, came as a shock to many and strengthened the Anglo-French entente in an unexpected manner. Contrary to Lansdowne's intentions, the Anglo-German estrangement had become a fact of European diplomacy.

Like Lord Salisbury, Lansdowne was scrupulous in his relations with his Cabinet. Though he had the backing of the majority of the reconstructed Cabinet, there were times when his policies were checked or even vetoed by his colleagues. The offer of a Far Eastern agreement to Germany was delayed by Cabinet action in March 1901. The terms offered to Japan in 1902 and in 1905 were subjected to close scrutiny and took into account Cabinet objections. Even on minor matters, for instance the loan to Persia in 1901, Lansdowne consulted his colleagues before drafting his proposals. On one important occasion, on the eve of the Russo-Japanese War, Lansdowne was overruled by Balfour (backed by a majority of the Cabinet) and his attempt to intervene before the outbreak of war blocked. If it is true that, in the final analysis, Lansdowne was less sensitive to the checks imposed by public opinion than Lord Salisbury, he was at least equally conscious of his responsibilities to the Cabinet.

The Cabinet reshuffle had strengthened the position of those anxious to abandon Salisbury's policy and the appointments of St John Brodrick to the War Office and Lord Selborne (Salisbury's son-in-law) to the Admiralty gave the new foreign secretary important support. In addition to Lord Salisbury, only Michael Hicks Beach, the Chancellor of the Exchequer,

---

[1] Monger, *The End of Isolation*, pp. 194, 221–2.

opposed Lansdowne's overtures to Germany. When Lord Salisbury retired from public life, Hicks Beach left and Arthur Balfour, a sympathetic chief, turned the balance even further in Lansdowne's direction. Though the ministry was weakened and finally wrecked by Chamberlain's tariff fight, Lansdowne could afford to remain aloof from these dissensions and his policies were not seriously affected by the Conservative split. Domestic issues tended to overshadow foreign and Lansdowne had some difficulty in getting a proper allotment of time, but he was never seriously checked by his colleagues during his years at the Foreign Office.

Lord Salisbury, until his retirement, continued to carry considerable weight and his advice was solicited on a wide variety of subjects during 1901. Lansdowne worked with him on Persian and Chinese questions as well as on the more crucial problem of an understanding with Germany. It was probably Salisbury's intervention at the Cabinet which stayed Lansdowne's hand in March 1901.[1] The latter's memorandum of 24 May 1901, summarizing the German proposals, was first sent only to Salisbury and the Premier's hostile reply further slowed the pace of the negotiations.[2] Before approaching the Germans at the end of the year, Lansdowne again consulted the Prime Minister with identical results.[3]

Salisbury was also kept informed of the Anglo-Japanese talks and concurred, though without enthusiasm, with Lansdowne's proposed action. During the last weeks of these conversations, the two men were in constant communication and the Prime Minister rewrote one of the crucial clauses delaying agreement.[4] If Salisbury had opposed the treaty, Lansdowne would have had a most difficult time but in his last days the Prime Minister completely gave way to the new mood in the Cabinet. In the summer of 1902 the aged giant retired. 'I have contemplated this step for some time but as long as the war lasted I was apprehensive that it might be misconstrued to indicate some division in the Cabinet and therefore might have a prejudicial effect' he wrote to the Duke of Devonshire.[5] After vainly seeking to recover his health on the continent, he returned to Hatfield where he died on 22 August 1903.

Lansdowne and Balfour were on excellent terms and there was as much intimacy between them as could be expected between two such reserved individuals.[6] Lansdowne repeatedly referred to Balfour for support and

---

[1] *Ibid.* pp. 28–9.    [2] BD II, nos. 82, 84.    [3] *Ibid.* nos. 92, 93.
[4] FO 277, Lansdowne to Salisbury, 31 December 1901; Nish, *The Anglo-Japanese Alliance*, pp. 209–10.
[5] Devonshire MSS, Salisbury to Duke of Devonshire, 10 July 1902.
[6] Balfour had been Lansdowne's fag at Eton. Both belonged to The Club, a small informal dining club.

49

advice. The highly intelligent Balfour produced some of the most interesting foreign policy analyses of the period.[1] Bored by details, Balfour was always available for discussion and could see daily problems in their broader context. It is true that his judgements were not always sound and his tendency to abstraction sometimes clouded the realities of a given situation. For instance, he exaggerated Russian strength and erroneously predicted a Russian offensive in central Asia. He expected the Russians to emerge victorious, though not triumphant, from their Far Eastern struggle and predicted that this moderate victory over Japan might well be to Britain's advantage. He underestimated American isolation and was repeatedly disappointed in the American failure to play a more active role in the Far East.[2] Though far from infallible, Balfour gave Lansdowne loyal backing both in the Cabinet and in the Committee of Imperial Defence, a committee which was very much Balfour's creation.

In addition to the Prime Minister, only a small group of ministers was actively concerned with daily policy. Before the Cabinet split of 1903, Devonshire, Chamberlain, Hicks Beach, Hamilton, Brodrick and Selborne constituted a small inner group to whom relevant despatches were circulated. The Duke of Devonshire was the least active and important. Though he favoured an approach to Germany in 1901, it seems doubtful whether this old statesman kept abreast of foreign matters and it was generally assumed that his views could be discounted. Balfour superseded him as the head of the newly-reconstructed Defence Committee, now called the Committee of Imperial Defence. Devonshire was one of the few ministers who made no contribution to the discussions of the Anglo-Japanese treaty and he had to be instructed about its details for his House of Lords speech. Joseph Chamberlain, too, though he was of far more importance than Devonshire, played a less significant role than might have been expected after his bid for leadership during the Salisbury period. After his Edinburgh speech of October 1901, and negative German reaction to it, Chamberlain's attitude towards Germany veered sharply and during 1902 he was one of the most outspoken anti-Germans in the Cabinet.[3] Highly responsive to changes in public mood and often anticipating public attitudes, Chamberlain was partly responsible for the anti-German press campaign in 1903 which defeated Lansdowne's efforts to bring the British into the Baghdad railway combination. The rest of Lansdowne's policy had Chamberlain's full

[1] Blanche Dugdale, *Arthur James Balfour, First Earl of Balfour* (London, 1936), vol. I, pp. 376–8, 386–9.
[2] Monger, *The End of Isolation*, pp. 97–9, 147–8, 180–1, 233.
[3] FO 277, Chamberlain to Lansdowne, 5 January 1902

approval. The exposed position of the Empire weighed on the Colonial Secretary and he seconded Lansdowne's efforts to conclude an agreement with the United States. He also welcomed the first Japanese alliance despite the apparent inequality of the bargain. There is only limited evidence that the Colonial Secretary took any important part in the negotiations which resulted in the Anglo-French entente; he left for South Africa in November 1902 and did not return until March 1903 when he became preoccupied with the tariff question. It is true, however, that before this time he had tried to come to a settlement with France over Newfoundland, Siam and the New Hebrides and had been repeatedly frustrated in his efforts to conclude an arrangement. He was doubtlessly pleased when Lansdowne and Paul Cambon, the French ambassador in London, took these matters in hand during the summer of 1903.[1] Chamberlain was one of the few men in the Cabinet who saw in the entente an anti-German gesture.

Lord George Hamilton stayed at the India Office only until the tariff split. He was generally consulted about central Asian problems, one of the key trouble areas between Britain and Russia. Hamilton was in despair about the Russian advance into Persia, and Curzon's forward policy in Persia as well as in Tibet and Afghanistan was already causing discomfort before Hamilton resigned. Hamilton's fear of Russia was so great that he favoured joining the Triple Alliance and backed Lansdowne's moves in the German direction.[2] St John Brodrick, Hamilton's successor, though a close friend and admirer of Curzon's, was even more opposed to the Viceroy's activities and their partnership soon erupted. It was highly fortunate that Lansdowne and Brodrick (as well as Balfour) viewed the situation in central Asia in a similar light, though they differed on the way in which the Russian challenge could be met.[3] All three, in varying degrees, had accepted the judgements of the Committee of Imperial Defence that Britain could not block a Russian advance through military means. They therefore vetoed Curzon's demands for a more aggressive display of British power in the Middle East and, after a sharp clash, ultimately checked him.

The Viceroy was not the only thorn in Lansdowne's side. Michael Hicks Beach, an old political associate of Lord Salisbury's, proved to be an equally irritating and less remote colleague. The new foreign secretary soon understood Salisbury's comment 'It is rare to get a letter from Beach without a

[1] Monger, *The End of Isolation*, p. 108; C. Andrew, *Théophile Delcassé and the making of the Entente Cordiale*, pp. 196, 209.
[2] See Monger, *The End of Isolation*, pp. 87–8, 91–2, 109 for discussions of Lord Hamilton.
[3] Brodrick did not favour the discussions with France and subsequently retained his doubts about the entente.

"No, I will not" on the first page.' It is one of the ironies of the Conservative period that Britain was unwilling to use its financial powers to win the battle for imperial influence. Beach, a parsimonious country squire, brought up in the tradition of Gladstonian orthodoxy, viewed with horror the practice of guaranteeing foreign loans, a practice which he felt meant putting money into the pockets of the British financial houses. He had repeatedly vetoed guarantees for loans in Persia on these grounds.[1] Elsewhere, too, the Treasury exerted its power. For instance, Hicks Beach thought the presence of British troops in China after the Boxer rebellion an unnecessary expense. 'The Cabinet as a body seem to me to care little or nothing about this expenditure. We cannot go on like this', Beach complained to Salisbury.[2] Lansdowne insisted that these troops were a necessary counterweight to Russian activity in the north but they were withdrawn in the autumn of 1901. When the Foreign Secretary asked for another loan to underwrite the Yangtsze viceroys to avoid German intervention, the Chancellor flatly refused. 'We cannot keep foreign trade out of the Yangtsze or foreign settlements; I do not myself think it is in our interests to do so.'[3] If the business was so attractive to foreigners, Hicks Beach argued, both in the Persian and China cases, why were British bankers and investors so passive?

Hicks Beach's efforts to cut expenditure and to avoid the financial underwriting of British firms were due in part to the rising service estimates. The Boer War and the reforms instituted by the service chiefs had sent the budget soaring (in Hicks Beach's view) and 'Black Michael' engaged in a losing battle against further rises. The Chancellor of the Exchequer found himself in an increasingly isolated position and, once Lord Salisbury retired, left the Cabinet. A new fight was brewing over the Admiralty programme and Hicks Beach refused to face it alone. He, moreover, disliked Lansdowne's new course in foreign policy. He had supported Salisbury in the latter's opposition to an agreement with the Germans and had strongly criticized the Anglo-Japanese treaty both because of its secret clauses and its one-sided appearance.[4] He thought there was no necessity for such a departure from Salisbury's established policy. But his moral qualms carried little weight with the Cabinet and Lansdowne easily prevailed.

It was perhaps fortunate that the Foreign Office had never been an expensive department.[5] The permanent officials were extremely conscious

---

[1] FO 60/601, 17 May 1898. FO 277, Lansdowne to Hardinge, 19 November 1901.
[2] Hicks Beach, *Life of Sir Michael Hicks Beach*, vol. II, p. 149.     [3] *Ibid.* p. 126.
[4] FO 277, Hicks Beach to Lansdowne, 2 January 1902.
[5] For instance, in 1902, the estimated cost of the Foreign Office establishment was £79,515 (FO 366/754).

1*a* York House with Dorset House, one of the early homes (1786–93) of the Foreign Office, adjoining

*b* Lord Sheffield's private house, in Downing Street, the Foreign Office in 1793–1861, 'a thorough picture of disorder, penury and meanness'

2a Sir George Gilbert Scott's original Gothic design for the Foreign Office (1858)

b Sir George Gilbert Scott's Byzantine Structure—'a regular mongrel affair'

3 Edmund Hammond, permanent under-secretary (1854–73)

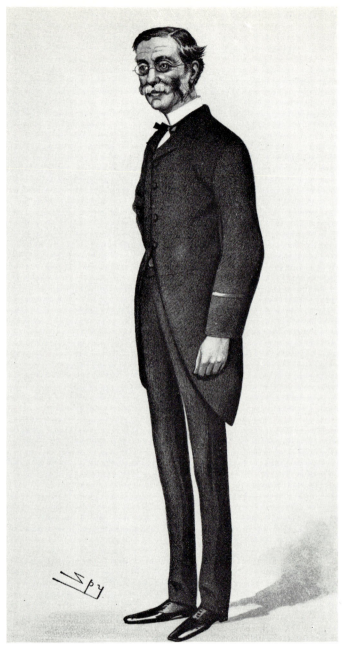

4 Thomas H. Sanderson ('Lamps'), permanent under-secretary (1894–1905)

of the Treasury's parsimony. With the Treasury in mind, diplomatic representation at some of the minor German courts was abolished and pleas for increases in consular staff dismissed. Wherever possible, the secret service fund under the Foreign Secretary's control was used for extra-ordinary expenditure, particularly in such places as Persia. As far as the Foreign Office was concerned, the Treasury interfered only in minor matters; on major issues Balfour (whom Hicks Beach disliked) and Lansdowne generally triumphed.

As might have been predicted, Lansdowne was more responsive to strategic considerations than Salisbury. The latter had often dismissed the fears of his army and navy advisers and rarely gave much heed to their warnings. Even in Salisbury's day there were important links between the Foreign Office and service ministries, and the reports of the Defence Committee were circulated both to Salisbury and the Queen. But Salisbury remained unimpressed; he 'very characteristically pooh-poohed the present naval and military Defence Committee as its members were all professionals and professionals were always narrow-minded'.[1] Obviously, there were occasions when strategic decisions were crucial to Salisbury's thinking (e.g. the Straits question in 1895) but the Prime Minister took only a limited interest in military and naval matters and not even the new mood created by the Boer War shocked him out of his general complacency.

The case was markedly different under Lord Lansdowne. His decision to curtail Britain's overseas responsibilities was backed by the judgements of his service chiefs who had become deeply conscious of the Empire's military weakness. In 1901, for instance, the Intelligence Department drew up a report 'The Military Requirements of the Empire in a War with France and Russia' and came to the conclusion that such a war would entail a period of humiliating disaster for all members of the Empire.[2] More important for immediate decisions, the service chiefs were in almost unanimous agreement that Russia could not be effectively checked in central Asia without a major war, too high a price to pay for British power in this area.[3] Having just come from the War Office, Lansdowne was fully aware of these deliberations and his subsequent policies bear their mark. It was, in part, Lord Selborne's arguments that British naval power was over-extended which enabled Lord Lansdowne to carry through the revised Hay–Pauncefote Treaty and it was

[1] Devonshire MSS, Goschen to Devonshire, 6 September 1895.
[2] FO 60/657, Report by Lt.-Col. Altham, Intelligence Division.
[3] *Ibid.* memorandum by W. R. Robertson, 4 October 1902; Lt.-General Sir S. Nicolson, 16 October 1902.

C

certainly naval considerations which encouraged him to pursue the talks with the Japanese.[1]

As in so many other respects, the Lansdowne period was one of transition. The Admiralty and War Office were rethinking their programmes and strategies; the machinery for service co-ordination was being improved and strengthened; the Foreign Office was slowly but markedly becoming more interested in the judgements of the Committee of Imperial Defence and the Intelligence Departments. The changes were just perceptible; in Edward Grey's period, strategic planning was to have a much more profound effect on the course of diplomacy. The growth of the German fleet, however, increased public awareness of defence problems and placed the Admiralty in a new position. Both the Admiralty and Foreign Office had been slow to respond to the German naval laws of 1898 and 1900. A naval attaché was appointed for Germany and a few experts began to enlarge on the theme of German naval power. But the head of the Admiralty thought the increase in the German fleet would bring about larger French and Russian fleets and only indirectly affect British naval strength. As late as April 1902 the British ambassador in Berlin denied that the new German naval law was aimed at the British, a denial which had to be retracted in a postscript after consultation with his naval attaché.[2]

In the spring of 1902 the professionals considered the possibility that Germany might join France and Russia in a war against England. In October of that year Lord Selborne reported to the Cabinet that the German navy 'is being carefully built up from the point of view of a war with us'.[3] A Cabinet decision was made to establish a new base in the North Sea. If France and Russia were still considered the powers to be watched, the head of the Foreign Section of the Intelligence Department thought that the possibility of an Anglo-German war must also be studied. From this time onwards, the Intelligence Department became markedly anti-German.

These changes had a limited effect on foreign policy. The settlement with France owed little to the German naval challenge. Until the middle of 1904, in fact, the Admiralty continued to think in terms of a three-power standard. It was only in the summer that plans for a war against Germany were prepared

---

[1] Nish, *The Anglo-Japanese Alliance*, pp. 174–8; text in Z. Steiner, 'Great Britain and the creation of the Anglo-Japanese Alliance', *The Journal of Modern History* XXXI (1959), 29–31. On service opposition to the Anglo-French entente, see Monger, *The End of Isolation*, pp. 103–2.

[2] Lansdowne MSS, Lascelles to Lansdowne, 25 April, 26 April 1902.

[3] A. J. Marder, *British Naval Policy, 1880–1905: the Anatomy of British Sea Power* (New York, 1940), p. 107.

and it was the destruction of the Russian fleet at Tsushima which fully focussed Admiralty attention on Berlin.

The Foreign Office did, moreover, increasingly operate against a background of rising Germanophobia which found a convenient centre in the naval question. In October 1904 Sir John Fisher returned to Whitehall as first sea lord and the popular campaign against Germany in the *Spectator* and *National Review* seemed to receive official sanction. Even if Fisher had never envisaged a war against Germany, his drastic references to 'copenhagening' the German fleet magnified German fears and became public catch-words.[1] Lansdowne, for his part, had no intention of cutting the line to Berlin because of this naval furore. He tried to reassure the German ambassador but his efforts to smooth relations with Berlin became increasingly difficult. The war scare of 1904-5 left a permanent scar on Anglo-German relations. If Lansdowne remained markedly detached from the public hysteria, the Moroccan crisis confirmed those who were certain that the real danger to European peace lay in Berlin. In 1905-6 the Admiralty, War Office and Committee of Imperial Defence were considering the implications of a possible Anglo-French war with Germany. Though the Foreign Secretary was still preoccupied with the Far Eastern situation, the rivalry with Germany had become the key factor in British diplomacy.

What effects did these considerations and deliberations have upon the Foreign Office? What role did the permanent officials play in the charting of this new course? To the casual observer Lansdowne's relations with his staff were not markedly different from those of his predecessor. 'Since Lord Rosebery was at the Foreign Office', J. D. Gregory wrote, 'I do not remember a single case of a secretary of state going the rounds of the departments on a voyage of inspection, save on one isolated occasion when one of them was reluctantly driven thereto by a nervous private secretary who in his turn had been prompted.'[2] In sharp distinction to Lord Salisbury, however, Lansdowne did almost all his work at the Foreign Office and, particularly in his first years, sought the views of his senior advisers. Most of Salisbury's staff remained to assist the new foreign secretary. Sanderson's expertise proved invaluable; Barrington assured a smooth transition abroad as well as in the office and Bertie, an old acquaintance from Eton, was only too anxious to advise his chief. Lansdowne, again in contrast with Salisbury, was interested

---

[1] *Ibid.* p. 111. Marder doubts whether the idea was ever seriously held by Fisher. *Ibid.* p. 113. For the history of German fears, see J. Steinberg, 'The Copenhagen Complex', *The Journal of Contemporary History*, I, no. 3 (July 1966), pp. 23–47.

[2] J. D. Gregory, *On the Edge of Diplomacy*, p. 25.

in administrative problems and took pains to discover how his office functioned.[1] He not only studied the problem of recruitment and discussed the question with various heads of Oxford and Cambridge colleges but in 1903 supported the formation of an inter-departmental committee to reorganize the Consular Service and place it on a more professional basis.[2]

During his first years, Lansdowne leaned heavily on the permanent under-secretary, for Sanderson was one of the few people left whose memory extended back to the mid-Victorian period and who had been a witness to most of Lord Salisbury's transactions.[3] When, for instance, the problem of the Straits was revived as a result of the pending Russo-Japanese clash, Sanderson was asked to review the history of the Mediterranean agreements, the background and details of which were little known. The texts of these agreements were kept in Sanderson's office and his memoranda provided an excellent summary of Salisbury's policy in 1887. Again in 1902 Sanderson was asked to explain the details of the Anglo-German agreement on China in order to clarify British intentions at the time.[4]

Sanderson handled a number of minor disputes on his own. As head of the Eastern Department, he continued to deal with Persian questions and gave Lansdowne ample guidance on this hopeless tangle. The Permanent Under-Secretary worked out the details of the proposed loan in 1901 and headed the inter-departmental conferences on central Asian defence problems held at the Foreign Office in 1902.[5] When Lansdowne

---

[1] Cmd. 7749, Q. 43, 509.

[2] This committee under Sir William Walrond included Lord Cranborne, the future Lord Inchcape and Andrew Bonar Law, the parliamentary secretary to the Board of Trade. As a result of its recommendations, this ancient service was finally placed on a professional footing. A system of limited competition for appointment was instituted, the Service was to be classified as to rank and pay and a system of inspection of consulates was tentatively introduced. Though most of the Committee's recommendations were implemented, the calibre of the recruits did not markedly improve and the committee's hope that men with business backgrounds might be attracted (the age for recruitment was put at twenty-two to twenty-seven) proved over-optimistic. The Service remained the Cinderella of the overseas branches, particularly the General Consular Service. In 1912 an intra-departmental committee (Algernon Law, C. Cartwright, Lord Dufferin and Ava, J. Tilley and H. Montgomery) made additional suggestions for improving the status, pay and training of consuls and vice-consuls. But less than two years later, the Mac-Donnell Commission still found the General Service inadequate both in terms of number and calibre and pressed for more radical changes (see pp. 169–70). Reform came slowly. In 1936 the areas services (Far Eastern and Levant) were merged with the General Consular Service but it was not until the Eden Reforms of 1943 that the Consular Service as a whole was brought into the amalgamated Foreign Service. The reports mentioned can all be found in full in Cmd. 7748. Other information can be found in Ward and Gooch, *Cambridge History of British Foreign Policy*, vol. III, especially pp. 620–4; Tilley and Gaselee, *The Foreign Office*, pp. 111–12, 247–51, and D. C. Platt, *Finance, Trade and Politics in British Foreign Policy*, Appendix 1.

[3] *The Times*, obituary, 21 March 1923.

[4] BD II, no. 38.

[5] FO 60/657. Sanderson was shown Curzon's letters to Lansdowne.

was absent, Sanderson competently dealt with unexpected crises. The Koweit dispute is typical. The Germans were anxious to secure a terminus for the Baghdad railway in Koweit and there were rumours that the Turks, supported by the Germans, had kidnapped the Sheikh who was under British protection. The case was a confused one. The Foreign Office had not declared a protectorate over this Persian Gulf territory but had demanded that Germany and Turkey recognize their special position there. The crisis came to the boil in September when Lord Lansdowne was on his estate in Ireland.[1] Sanderson quickly clarified the general issues involved, and after securing permission, vigorously lectured the German and Turkish ambassadors. Again, when a leakage in the Cambon–Lansdowne conversations on Morocco in 1902 prematurely upset the Sultan and his advisers, Sanderson and Nicolson, the minister in Morocco, took the immediate steps necessary to reassure the Sultan. It was Sanderson rather than Lansdowne who checked Kaid Maclean who was pressing for a more active British policy in Morocco.[2] Sanderson's cool response to Maclean's reform programme influenced the Foreign Secretary, though the decision to jettison the reform effort was made after the Cambon–Lansdowne conversations were started.

These were all minor matters but most daily business at the Foreign Office consisted of such problems. The same combination of knowledge, background and diplomatic skill enabled Sanderson to assist Lansdowne with the Baghdad railway discussions. When the possibility of British financial participation in this German enterprise became a real one, Sanderson not only supplied Lansdowne with all the back papers but tendered his own judgement of this delicate matter. In the early months of 1903 Lansdowne tried to associate some of the City firms with the project; Sanderson saw their chief representatives.[3] Together the two men worked out a formula which would assure the financiers of the Government's support without any direct pecuniary assistance. Much to their mutual disappointment, the talks failed, one of the few victims of organized public pressure.[4]

Sanderson was consulted on all the major diplomatic issues of the day in

[1] Lansdowne MSS, Sanderson to Lord Lansdowne, 2 September 1901. 'As to Kuwait I hope that the tension will pass but while I would give up nothing I would not insist on dotting the i's too much.'

[2] A. J. P. Taylor, *Rumours of War*, pp. 148–9; BD II, memorandum for Kaid Sir Henry Maclean, 24 October 1902, pp. 272–3. Nicolson, *Sir Arthur Nicolson, Bart., First Lord Carnock* (London, 1930), p. 147.

[3] BD II, nos. 207, 208, 216.

[4] The subject was again reviewed in the summer of 1905 when Sanderson saw the British representatives of the Imperial Ottoman Bank but nothing came of their discussions. BD VI, no. 212; Monger, *The End of Isolation*, pp. 222–4.

addition to the more immediate minor questions which crossed his desk. He prepared the draft of the proposed Anglo-German defensive alliance of May 1901. The proposal, an excellent example of Sanderson's drafting ability, was accompanied by a short note summarizing the difficulties of a project which did not find much favour in the Under-Secretary's eyes.[1] As Lansdowne was at Darien during this time, Sanderson was left to cope with Baron Eckardstein, whom even the patient Under-Secretary described as a 'horrible and portentous bore', engaged in a rather unsavoury diplomatic duel with the ailing German ambassador, Count Hatzfeldt. Sanderson assisted, though he did not have a major share, in the drafting of the Anglo-Japanese treaty, an agreement which he hoped would have 'a steadying effect' on Japan.[2] During the Tangier crisis, though Lansdowne was sole director of British policy, Sanderson was in full agreement with the Foreign Secretary's efforts to chart a middle course between assisting the French and yet avoiding a total identification of French and British policy.[3]

The parliamentary under-secretaries also participated in discussions of general policy, though their importance depended on their political positions rather than their official posts. Both Lord Cranborne (1900–3) and Earl Percy (1903–5) contributed to the diplomatic debates which went on within the Foreign Office. Cranborne had been appointed because it was thought useful to have a Cecil at the Foreign Office. He seems to have shared his father's views; his memorandum of October 1901 added weight to those at the Foreign Office who disliked the new approaches to Germany.[4] Cranborne emphasized the antipathy which existed between the two countries particularly on the German side. 'The feeling is bitter, is deeply rooted and is increasing. It is not in the least likely to be altered by an alliance for many years to come, and if its origin is commercial not even then.' Britain, he argued, in terms reminiscent of his father, could rely on the self-interest of the other powers to prevent the formation of a coalition against her. Moreover, Germany would not support the British in any extra-European quarrels with Russia while England might be drawn, because of her association with Germany, into a conflict in the Middle East or with America which would run counter to her real interests. Cranborne ended his memorandum on a pessimistic note: 'We do not quite trust the Emperor; he will not fully trust us. Herein other Powers will see their opportunity and after all peace will not be assured.'[5] It is difficult to judge how far Cranborne's negative

---

[1] BD II, no. 85, FO 277, Lansdowne to Sanderson, May 1901.
[2] BD II, no. 148. Nish, *The Anglo-Japanese Alliance*, p. 240.　　　[3] BD III, nos. 97, 105(a).
[4] FO 277, Cranborne to Lord Lansdowne, 18 November 1901.　　　[5] *Ibid.*

appraisal influenced the Foreign Secretary. It did not deter Lansdowne from seeking other ways of strengthening the line to Berlin though it must have underlined for him the problems involved in achieving an agreement. Cranborne's minutes suggest, moreover, that he was not enthusiastic about the Anglo-Japanese treaty. He preferred to see in the new alliance an adjustment of conflicting claims and a development of past policy rather than a new departure. His statement in the Commons 'It is not for us to ask for treaties: we grant them', though a diplomatic blunder, undoubtedly revealed his genuine feelings.[1] Nor was Cranborne totally sympathetic with the Anglo-French negotiations. In April 1903 he wrote to Bertie 'It looks from several symptoms as if we could have a very close understanding with France by holding up one finger, but that it would hardly suit even such a Germanophobe as yourself, or at any rate, me. I prefer the middle position, the "tertius gaudens".'[2] Cranborne succeeded to his father's title in 1903 and left the Foreign Office, though he entered the Cabinet as Lord Privy Seal.

Cranborne's influence on both general and specific issues derived not from his position but from his family connections and closeness to Arthur Balfour. He was succeeded by Earl Percy (Henry Algernon) a well-known expert on Middle Eastern problems. Percy, who had travelled extensively in Asiatic Turkey, was one of the leading Turcophiles on the Conservative side of the House. Both his speeches and books indicate that he was highly suspicious of Russian influence at Constantinople and in Persia.[3] He favoured a partnership with the Germans in these areas to check the Russian advance. It would have been surprising had he not thrown his weight in this direction between 1903 and 1905, when Lansdowne was so concerned with British policy in the Middle East.

Percy was friendly with both Cranborne and Balfour and, like his predecessor, was more important politically than his official position warranted. In addition to his Middle Eastern preoccupations, Percy was a warm supporter of the Anglo-Japanese agreement and urged that it be further strengthened by raising the legation at Tokyo to an embassy and making the Emperor of Japan a Knight of the Garter. More important, he was one of the first to press on Balfour the idea of renewing the alliance for an additional

[1] Nish, *The Anglo-Japanese Alliance*, p. 228; Hansard, 4th series, vol. CX, col. 734.
[2] Bertie MSS, series A, Cranborne to Bertie, 12 April 1903.
[3] Percy had written two books, *Notes from a Diary in Asiatic Turkey* (London, 1898) and *Highlands of Asiatic Turkey* (London, 1901) and had been parliamentary under-secretary at the India Office (1902–3) where he had a great deal to do with Lord Curzon's Persian problems. For information on Percy's attitude towards Persia see J. Plass, *England zwischen Deutschland und Russland, 1899–1907*, pp. 62, 91–2, 177.

five years. He argued that the peace terms which Japan would accept at Portsmouth would depend in part on whether she could count on the continuation of the British alliance and his arguments seem to have impressed both Balfour and Lansdowne.[1]

Though called on to give advice, neither Sanderson nor the parliamentary under-secretaries represented any major break with the general traditions of the Foreign Office. Lansdowne undoubtedly treated Sanderson with all the respect due to such an experienced colleague and far more than Salisbury relied on his advice and support. The parliamentary under-secretaries, though important figures in their own right, continued to be restricted both in their jurisdictions and influence. Nevertheless, the trends noticed during Lord Salisbury's last years were accelerated as Lord Lansdowne sought a different answer to the problems which the country faced at the turn of the century. Lord Lansdowne's search for new friends, a series of inter-office intrigues, and a new plan for reorganizing the work at Whitehall were to transform 'a cosy if sometimes rather tedious family party to that of a great and efficient department of state'.[2]

Lord Lansdowne not only discussed his problems with members of the Conservative Cabinet but also approached the senior permanent officials for their advice. His repeated efforts to court the Germans aroused little sympathy among these men and their general opposition led to expressions of dissent and considerations of general policy which were not common Foreign Office practice. Even Sanderson was deeply disturbed by the attempts to draw Germany into the Far Eastern situation. He warned his new chief that whatever was told the Japanese would be repeated to the Germans, who would inform the Russians and make capital out of the situation. A war between Japan and Russia would leave 'Germany dancing round the combatants and ready to bleed whichever is first stunned'.[3] The Permanent Under-Secretary was extremely cautious about Eckardstein's approaches in the spring of 1901 for a triple agreement in the Far East. Rather than an arrangement with Japan and Germany, Sanderson favoured a policy of non-intervention in the Far East, for he was convinced that the Japanese could not effectively check the Russians and that the Germans had no real interest in doing so.[4] In May, when asked to prepare the draft of an Anglo-German agreement, he wrote: 'However the Convention may be worded, it seems to

---

[1] Nish, *The Anglo-Japanese Alliance*, pp. 299–300.
[2] Rohan Butler, 'Beside the Point', *World Review*, April–May 1953, p. 9.
[3] Lansdowne MSS, Sanderson to Lansdowne, 10 March 1901.
[4] Lascelles MSS, vol. III, pt 2, Sanderson to Lascelles, 27 March 1901, 3 April 1901.

me that it will practically amount to a guarantee to Germany of the provinces conquered from France, and that is the way in which the French will look at it. I do not see exactly what Germany would guarantee us.'[1] Sanderson saw the fatal flaw in Lansdowne's hopes. Germany was fundamentally interested in her European position and not in the Far East while Britain's needs lay outside Europe. As the discussions continued during the last days of May 1901, it became clear that the gap between British and German interests was too great to bridge. German diplomacy was far from adroit and it was only with great effort that Sanderson maintained equable relations with the rival German diplomatists.[2]

But Francis Bertie was even more outspoken in his opposition to Lansdowne's pro-German orientation. Bertie's established position at the Foreign Office has already been described. The repeated crises in the Far East gave Bertie an opportunity to impress his views on Lord Lansdowne. During the Manchurian crisis of January 1901, Lansdowne tried to include the Germans in his stand against Russian land-grabs at Tientsin with negative results.[3] In March, as the crisis continued and the Japanese turned to Lansdowne for support against the Russians, the Foreign Secretary again appealed to Berlin to discover what role she would take in the Far East. On 18 March Bertie was asked by Lansdowne to draw up a possible agreement for joint naval assistance if any other power joined Russia in an attack on the Japanese Government.[4] All through these negotiations, Bertie argued that the Germans would not depart from their self-appointed role as 'the honest broker sitting on the fence'. Already in the autumn of 1900 he had drafted a strong memorandum arguing against an Anglo-German agreement and the German attitude in March 1901 confirmed his beliefs.[5] On 14 March, before Lansdowne's offer of an agreement was even sent, it was known that by 'benevolent neutrality' the Germans meant the 'strictest neutrality'. 'This amounts to very little', Bertie minuted Lascelles' despatch.[6] The coup de grâce was administered by Count Bülow in the Reichstag on 11 March when the German Chancellor repudiated all interest in the fate of Manchuria and denied that the 'Yangtsze agreement' of 1900 was in any way concerned with this area.

[1] BD II, no. 85.
[2] Lansdowne MSS, Sanderson to Lansdowne, 20, 27 May 1901. Lascelles MSS, vol. III, pt 2, Sanderson to Lascelles, 12, 15 January, 20 May 1902.
[3] Lansdowne MSS, Lansdowne to Lascelles, 17 January 1901.
[4] FO 46/547, Draft by Bertie, 12 March 1901. J. Grenville, 'Lansdowne's Abortive Project of 12 March 1901 for a Secret Agreement with Germany', *Bulletin of the Institute of Historical Relations*, XXVII, no. 76 (November 1954), 210–12.
[5] BD II, no. 12.        [6] FO 64/1524, Lascelles to Lansdowne, 14 March 1901.

Despite the diminishing possibility of an Anglo-German or even an Anglo-German-Japanese agreement in the Far East, both von Eckardstein, the first secretary at the German embassy, and Count Hayashi, each in his own way, continued to press these solutions. Bertie had little use for the German proposal, Eckardstein was a man whom he deeply mistrusted. He was, however, more sympathetic towards the efforts of Count Hayashi and it was on his suggestion that the British minister in Tokyo was recalled for consultations.[1]

As early as 11 March, when the proffered 'alliance' offer to Berlin was being prepared, Bertie pointed out the danger of a Japan hostile to British interests:

If we do nothing to encourage Japan to look to us as a friend and possible ally against Russia and France, we may drive her to a policy of despair, in which she may come to some sort of terms with Russia. I do not say that it is probable, but it is possible, and our interests would greatly suffer if she did.[2]

Bertie's attitude towards Germany was summed up in his comment to Lord Salisbury: 'The Germans' aim is to push us into the water and steal our clothes.'[3] His aim was to secure an accommodation with the Japanese.

On 20 June Bertie suggested that England should purchase Japan's share of the Chinese indemnity bond, thus breaking the deadlock at the Peking Conference over the Boxer rebellion claims and easing Japan's financial situation.

To satisfy Parliament that we get something for our purchase of the Japanese share of bonds (£5,000,000) we might enter into an understanding with Japan that neither Power will without consultation with the other enter into a separate Agreement with any other Power with regard to China ... We might perhaps enter into a *secret* agreement with Japan that we will assist by sea in resisting any foreign occupation of Corea, Japan undertaking to give us armed assistance in resisting any encroachment by any Foreign Power on the Yangtsze region and the South of China.[4]

Though Lord Lansdowne did not immediately act on Bertie's suggestion, the Assistant Under-Secretary returned to the point early in July and the Foreign Secretary's discussions with Count Hayashi, the Japanese minister in London, indicate that Bertie's views had taken root.

Bertie came to the heart of the dilemma in a memorandum first submitted to Lord Lansdowne on 22 July and then resubmitted when Lans-

---

[1] Nish, *The Anglo-Japanese Alliance*, p. 144. For Bertie's minutes see BD II, no. 54.
[2] BD II, no. 54; see the similar view in FO 64/1946, 17 November 1900.
[3] Grenville, *Lord Salisbury and Foreign Policy*, p. 213.
[4] FO 547, memorandum by Bertie, 20 June 1901.

downe returned from his Irish holiday in September.[1] This memorandum, 'Anglo-Japanese Agreement: reasons why one is desirable and why Germany should not be included', was crucial in shaping the British proposals which were laid before the Japanese later that year. On the assumption that Russian possession of Corea would result in British as well as Japanese action, Bertie proposed the formula which the agreement with Tokyo should follow.[2] It is interesting that Bertie stressed the importance of naval co-operation between the two. This feature, as well as the form of the alliance and the recognition of Japan's dominance in Corea, all found in this paper, were subsequently included in the final draft.

At the same time, Bertie repeated his reasons for not including the Germans in the negotiations. His tone was bitter; the product of his experience with German behaviour during the Manchurian crisis. 'Germany is not going to jeopardize her relations with Russia by entering into such an understanding and if advances were made to her she would only make use of them to make capital with Russia.' The Under-Secretary concluded: 'A reliable understanding with Germany in opposition to Russian designs in the Far East is not obtainable, recent experience of German policy in China proves this.'[3]

During September 1901, while the members of the Cabinet were considering the new possibility, Lansdowne asked Bertie to revise his earlier memorandum and carefully checked the under-secretary's proposals. Though it was probably Lord Selborne's naval arguments which were decisive in convincing the Foreign Secretary and Cabinet, the British draft treaty clearly reflects some of the Assistant Under-Secretary's views.[4] Lord Lansdowne continued to move with great caution. To the extreme annoyance of Bertie, he again took up the possibility of an Anglo-German settlement. Both Bertie and Cranborne registered their objections. Bertie wrote:

In our present position we hold the balance of power between the Triple and Dual Alliances. But there is little chance of a combination between them against us. Our existence as a great and strong state is necessary to all in order to preserve the balance of power, and most of all to Germany whose representations as to the disasters which await the British Empire if His Majesty's Government do not make an alliance with her have little or no real foundation.[5]

[1] FO 547, memorandum by Bertie, 22 July 1901; re-submitted after amendment, 22 September. For a full discussion of Bertie's role see my article 'Great Britain and the creation of the Anglo-Japanese Alliance', *The Journal of Modern History* XXXI, no. 1 (March 1959), 27–36, and the even more extended study in Nish's *The Anglo-Japanese Alliance*, particularly pp. 153–6.
[2] FO 547 memorandum by Bertie, 22 July 1901.
[3] *Ibid.*
[4] BD II, no. 91. This should be dated 27 October 1901. Selborne's memorandum was circulated to the Cabinet, Bertie's was not.
[5] BD II, no. 91.

According to Bertie, there were few common interests on which to build an agreement. Neither in China, Turkey, Morocco nor in Koweit were British and German interests identical, and on the naval issue Anglo-German interests were clearly contradictory. Instead of a defensive alliance, Bertie suggested an agreement limited to Europe and the Mediterranean along the line of the 1887 treaties. While Lansdowne dismissed many of his under-secretary's arguments, he did adopt Bertie's proposal for a limited agreement in a memorandum prepared for Lord Salisbury.[1] This feeler, like all previous ones, met with a negative response. When the question was reopened in a conversation with Count Metternich in December, Lansdowne declined to join the Triple Alliance and Metternich, not unexpectedly, refused Lansdowne's narrower offer.[2] But by that time the Anglo-Japanese talks were well under way and the Germans were not included in the discussions.

In addition to the talks with Berlin, a fruitless approach was made to the Russians, a key factor in Lansdowne's diplomacy. For it was the Russian threat and not the failure to conclude an understanding with Germany which lay behind the Anglo-Japanese alliance. As the Japanese were also hesitating, Bertie grew increasingly uneasy. He even suggested that the Wilhelmstrasse was responsible for the delaying tactics of the Japanese.[3] His fears, though groundless, were typical of Bertie's general view of German duplicity. The treaty was finally concluded on 30 January 1902; its terms had been carefully discussed in the Cabinet but the form and wording were left to Bertie and Francis Campbell. Members of the Cabinet were deeply worried by this new departure in British diplomacy and expected much hostile criticism.[4] Neither Lansdowne nor Sanderson expected a Japanese victory over Russia. Bertie was one of the few in the Foreign Office who fully understood that the Japanese alliance ended the need for German support and might have European implications for the future. It was Japan's unexpected defeat of Russia which was to transform the Far Eastern situation and effect the alignment of powers in Europe.

Few assistant under-secretaries could have intervened more decisively in the policy-making process. Bertie was one of the initiators and framers of the Anglo-Japanese alliance.[5] He was also partly responsible for the decision to exclude Germany from the Far Eastern talks. His analysis of the German

[1] BD II, nos. 92, 93.    [2] *Ibid.* no. 94.
[3] Goudswaard, *Some Aspects of the End of Britain's 'Splendid Isolation', 1898–1904* (Rotterdam, 1952), pp. 82–3.
[4] Nish, *The Anglo-Japanese Alliance*, pp. 204–5, 209–10, 223–4.    [5] *Ibid.* p. 370.

situation in the Far East proved to be correct. Given her exposed European position and her fundamental lack of interest in China, Germany could not risk antagonizing Russia in return for British friendship. Does this mean, however, that Francis Bertie was the 'eminence grise' of the Foreign Office? Baron von Eckardstein more than once suggested to the Wilhelmstrasse that Lord Lansdowne merely reflected his under-secretary's views.[1] There is no question that Bertie influenced Lansdowne and that the Under-Secretary contributed to the new but growing Germanophobia of the department. But Lord Lansdowne did not accept all of Bertie's conclusions and never shared his deep distrust of German activities. If the Under-Secretary's suggestions for an Anglo-Japanese understanding fell on more fertile ground after the failure of the German talks in the spring of 1901, Lansdowne never gave up hopes of improving relations with Berlin. In Lansdowne's eyes, the Anglo-Japanese alliance and an arrangement with Germany were not competing policies. It should be further noted that Bertie and Lansdowne were not personally close and, as will be shown, Bertie's subsequent promotions were pressed upon the Foreign Secretary by Edward VII. At the end of 1902 Bertie left the Foreign Office for the embassy in Rome. No other official at the office attempted to emulate Bertie and Lord Lansdowne increasingly charted his own course.

Bertie's interventions were crucial in yet another way. In the years after the conclusion of the Anglo-Japanese entente, his hostility towards the Germans became increasingly virulent. His experiences with German diplomacy in China and South Africa during 1902 added fuel to his general dislike for the Germans.[2] His opinions were shared by some of the younger and most able men in the diplomatic corps, Louis Mallet and William Tyrrell of the Foreign Office, Charles Hardinge and Reginald Lister, men of growing reputation in the Diplomatic Service. Bertie urged his views on his friends. His correspondence with Louis Mallet, an assistant clerk at the Foreign Office, reveals the depth of their mutual antipathy towards Berlin.

I am nervous about the visit [of the King] to Kiel . . . Entre nous, I do not think Mr. Balfour at all realizes what may be expected from the Anglo-French understanding, and would be ready to make an agreement with Germany tomorrow . . . the only terms on which I would make a treaty with them would be an understanding on their part to add no more to their fleet . . . The next ambassador to Paris will have a great role to play. It has never been so necessary before to have

---

[1] Hermann von Eckardstein, *Lebenserinnerungen und politische Denkwürdigkeiten*, vol. II (Leipzig, 1920), p. 310.

[2] See Bertie's conversations with Dr Stuebel with regard to German claims for compensation in South Africa, BD II, no. 81.

someone there with his eyes open and above all open to German designs. I hope it will be you.[1]

Bertie's answer was in the same tone. 'Your letter of the 2nd breathes distrust of Germany and you are right. She has never done anything for us but bleed us. She is false and grasping and our real enemy commercially and politically.'[2]

Unlike Lord Lansdowne, neither man was surprised by the German challenge in Morocco. Bertie hoped that it would remain an open sore between Germany and France and saw in the crisis an excellent opportunity to strengthen the entente.[3] In London Louis Mallet, now Lansdowne's assistant private secretary, encouraged his chief to give Delcassé the full support which the Frenchman sought. Mallet was sent to see Admiral Fisher about the possibility of ceding a port to the Germans. He reported to Bertie: 'He [Fisher] is a splendid chap and simply longs to have a go at Germany. I "abound in his sense" and told him I would do all I could with Lord Lansdowne.'[4] Once Edward Grey (the only Liberal whom Bertie and Mallet trusted) came into office the two men worked together to turn the entente into an alliance and attempted to block any efforts made to improve the tone of Anglo-German relations.[5] Even at this time their extreme view was shared (though for different reasons) by Eyre Crowe who, by 1904, though as hostile towards the Russians as he was suspicious of the Germans, was becoming a crucial figure in the moulding of British policy towards Berlin. Although Crowe was only an assistant clerk and not of the Bertie group, he was already marked for future promotion. By 1906, as head of the Western Department, he became the leading German expert in the Grey stable.

This change in attitude, particularly among the junior members of the Foreign Office, did not go unnoticed. Thomas Sanderson was nearing the age of retirement. Though ill and over-tired, he became increasingly conscious of the new mood in the Foreign Office and did his best to combat it. While he had little sympathy with Lord Lansdowne's efforts to conclude an alliance with the Germans, after 1902 the Permanent Under-Secretary felt that the balance had gone too far in the opposite direction. Already at the end of 1901 he had urged that the Prince of Wales be asked to go to

---

[1] Bertie MSS, series A, Mallet to Bertie, 2 June 1904. Bertie's papers have been reclassified. Wherever possible I have given new citations but occasionally, as in this chapter, have used the old.

[2] *Ibid.* Bertie to Mallet, 11 June 1904.   [3] *Ibid.* Bertie to Mallet, 31 March 1905.

[4] *Ibid.* Mallet to Bertie, 25 April 1905.

[5] *Ibid.* Bertie to Lansdowne, 1 May 1905; Mallet to Bertie, 2 March 1906; memorandum by Bertie, 4 March 1906.

Berlin despite the irritation created by the German reception of Chamberlain's speech.[1] In March 1902, when a fresh quarrel broke out over the respective British and German roles during the Spanish-American War, Sanderson warned Lascelles to minimize this and other diplomatic difficulties to counter the prevailing hostility.[2] In a most revealing letter, Sanderson wrote

whereas some time ago, I had to explain often enough that there were certain things we could not expect of the Germans, however friendly they might be, I have now, wherever they are mentioned, a labour to show that the conduct of the German government has in some material respects been friendly. There is a settled dislike of them—and an impression that they are ready and anxious to play us any shabby trick they can. It is an inconvenient state of things for there are a good many questions in which it is important for both countries that we should work cordially together.[3]

Sanderson remained deeply suspicious of Russian movements in Afghanistan and Persia and had strong doubts, based on years of past negotiations, whether an agreement could be reached with St Petersburgh.[4] 'I wish we could make the lunatics here who denounce Germany in such unmeasured terms and howl for an agreement with Russia understand that the natural effect is to drive Germany into the Russian camp and encourage the Russians to believe that they can get all they want at our expense and without coming to any agreement with us.'[5] During the Tangier crisis Sanderson backed Lansdowne's cautious policy towards France and tried to stem the anti-German tide.[6] One of Sanderson's final acts was to be the intermediary between the new foreign secretary and the naval and military authorities, who had begun discussions with their French counterparts.[7] Although Sanderson was instructed to authorize these consultations, his warning to M. Cambon about the future of Anglo-French co-operation sounds like a repetition of Lord Salisbury's arguments to Count Hatzfeldt many years before.[8]

[1] Lascelles MSS, vol. III, pt 2, Sanderson to Lascelles, 22 January 1902.
[2] *Ibid.* 19 March 1902.
[3] *Ibid.* 5 March 1902.
[4] Hardinge MSS, vol. 7, Sanderson to Hardinge, 19 September, 3 October 1905. For Sanderson's later support for the Anglo-Russian agreement, FO 800/241, Sanderson to Spring-Rice, 6 August 1907.
[5] Lascelles MSS, vol. III, pt 4, Sanderson to Lascelles, 3 January 1905.
[6] *Ibid.* 10 October 1905. Lansdowne MSS, Sanderson to Lansdowne, 9 October 1905.
[7] BD III, nos. 210(b), 211, 214.
[8] *Ibid.* no. 220. 'In the first place, in the course of my experience, which was a pretty long one, I know of no instance of any secret agreement by the British Government which pledged them further than if a certain policy agreed upon with another Power were in any way menaced, the two Powers should consult as to the course to be taken. This I thought was the limit to which the Government could properly bind itself without in some way making Parliament aware of the obligations it was incurring.'

It is clear that the ailing Permanent Under-Secretary was attempting without success to check Grey's pro-French policy.

Sanderson's analysis of the German position was one which appealed to Lord Lansdowne but found little sympathy with either Grey or his Foreign Office backers. Even before the first Moroccan crisis, Sanderson feared the consequences of the new emphasis on the naval rivalry between Germany and England and the general deterioration of relations between the two nations. He doubted whether sufficient allowance was being made either for the difficulties of Germany's diplomatic position or the seriousness of her naval inferiority.[1]

It is true that *France shows no sign of aggressive disposition but she has obstinately refused to be reconciled to her loss of territory . . . But it seems to me that quite irrespective of colonial ambitions Germany must feel it necessary to increase her navy* and that unless she can feel sure that we will not at some untoward moment throw ourselves on the side of France, she must as a matter of precaution cultivate the goodwill of Russia far more than is convenient for her to do. It is only natural that she should let us know this and endeavour to keep our friendship on terms as easy to herself as possible. But I *do not see that we can reasonably resent this and as a matter of fact a certain amount of friendship with Germany* would be valuable for us in any bargaining with Russia.[2]

On 1 January 1907 Eyre Crowe circulated his historic memorandum reviewing in the most negative light the course of Anglo-German relations.[3] His brilliant, if not entirely accurate, survey was sent to Lord Sanderson, already in retirement. Somewhat unexpectedly, Sanderson took up the cudgels for the Germans, and wrote an extensive commentary on Crowe's review.[4] In this, he made no effort to disguise his own personal dislike of the methods used by the German Foreign Office which he characterized as over-subtle and sometimes treacherous. But Sanderson, unlike his successors, carefully distinguished between means and ends. The crises created by an aggressive German diplomacy were more annoying than serious, and were best forgotten. The German Emperor's outbursts should be ignored; the blackmailing techniques of the German Foreign Office resisted but understood.

If one compares the two memoranda, it is clear that Sanderson's account is more accurate and balanced than Crowe's but less acute.[5] In effect, the

[1] Lansdowne MSS, Sanderson to Lansdowne, 20 January 1905.
[2] *Ibid.* italicization by Lansdowne (?).                    [3] BD III, Appendix A, see pp. 250–5.
[4] *Ibid.* Appendix B, pp. 420–4.
[5] Sanderson properly interprets French policy in Morocco whereas Crowe overstates the rectitude of the French position. The same is true about the Anglo-German dispute over Samoa. Salisbury made himself decidedly unpleasant about these islands and Crowe apportions too large a share of

Permanent Under-Secretary did not deny the substance of Crowe's indictments but rather saw this 'uncheckered record of black deeds' in another light. Mistakenly or not, Sanderson compared German experience to its British counterpart. Germany was a young power, striving for recognition as a world influence. It was inevitable that she should emulate the British and have colonial aspirations. It was unfortunate that everywhere Germany wished to expand 'she will find the British lion in her path'. 'It has sometimes seemed to me that to a foreigner reading our Press the British Empire must appear in the light of some huge giant sprawling over the globe, with gouty fingers and toes stretched in every direction, which cannot be approached without eliciting a scream.' Sanderson's conclusions were not strikingly dissimilar from Eyre Crowe's, though his tone reflected a mood of self-confidence which had begun to vanish with Lord Salisbury's departure. A policy of one-sided concession was foolish as well as impossible. But German sensitivity should be respected and her expansion not checked where it did not clash with major British interests. Sanderson's voice came from a period when colonial disputes still determined the more fluid relations between the great powers and where there were large areas in which to manœuvre. External events and Lord Lansdowne's policy had created a new distribution of European forces and imperial concerns were to play a subsidiary role in the years which followed.

the blame to Berlin. Sanderson's comments about the Anglo-German convention respecting the Portuguese colonies illustrate the difference of approach between the two officials. The retired Permanent Under-Secretary puts the agreement in its historical perspective. Crowe takes a narrow view of a transaction which was not just intended to buy off the Germans in an area important for South Africa but was to pave the way for a wider agreement or even an alliance. The Senior Clerk, because his information was restricted to what was printed, underestimates the pro-German feeling in the Cabinet and as a result views the agreement as one which the Germans extracted from the British. Sanderson knew that an important segment of the Cabinet (though not Salisbury) was most anxious to reach an accord though they tended to be niggardly when it came to settling the terms. Sanderson's and Crowe's accounts of the Yangtsze agreement do not differ in substance but the former shares Salisbury's view that the agreement was a poor one and that German behaviour, while hardly creditable, was not unexpected. At worst, it was just one more illustration of German bad manners. Crowe sees in the Manchurian crisis a perfect example of German blackmailing techniques. On the issue of German behaviour during the Boer War, Sanderson again has the better historical memory and his account is to be preferred to Crowe's. It is strange, however, that Sanderson should deny that proposals were made inviting England to take sides with the Triple Alliance as he must have known about these discussions in 1901. Finally, Sanderson denies Crowe's statement that during Salisbury's last two administrations all the most important business was transacted under the cover of 'private' correspondence. With two or three important omissions (including the 1901 negotiations with Germany cited by Crowe), Salisbury's official records for his last administration are more than adequate. It is true that Salisbury, like all nineteenth-century foreign secretaries, treated a number of official papers (including Cabinet memoranda) as private documents and simply removed these to Hatfield. But Crowe exaggerates the lacunae in the official records. Professor John Grenville checked these two memoranda for me and made many helpful comments.

## New men and new ways

The future lay not with Sanderson but with those who thought in terms of continental Europe and of its balance of power. The internal history of the Foreign Office reveals the rise of a group of men, led in the first instance by Francis Bertie and Charles Hardinge, who were committed to an anti-German policy and were anxious to strengthen Britain's links with France and Russia. Through a series of intrigues, promotions and transfers, these men succeeded to the most influential posts in London and abroad. Their views became the prevailing orthodoxy under Sir Edward Grey. The role of Francis Bertie is the key to any understanding of these changes which influenced the course of policy and gave the Foreign Office a new role to play in British diplomacy.

Between Sanderson and Bertie there was no sympathy and little personal liking. Commenting on Bertie's appointment to Rome in 1902, Sanderson wrote to his friend, Frank Lascelles, in Berlin: 'Between ourselves it is not to my mind an ideal selection but we must hope that in the Italian climate and with much less work to do some of the asperities from which we have suffered will disappear. I fancy the King pressed a good deal.'[1] At the same time, Bertie had become increasingly critical of the way in which Sanderson was running the Foreign Office and thought a radical reorganization long overdue. When Gosselin left for Lisbon in 1902 Bertie urged the appointment of Charles Hardinge, a good friend but also a successful diplomatist already known for his energy and efficiency.[2] After a slow start, Hardinge had been transferred from Teheran to St Petersburgh over the heads of seventeen of his seniors, a most unusual procedure in days when promotion by seniority was the general rule.[3] Hardinge's position was further improved by his wife's appointment as one of the Queen's ladies-in-waiting and by the monarch's active interest in his future. At both Teheran and St Petersburgh, Hardinge proved to be a far abler observer than either of his chiefs and Bertie

---

[1] Lascelles MSS, vol. II, pt 3, Sanderson to Lascelles, 31 December 1902. See also vol. II, pt 2, Sanderson to Lascelles, 10 April 1901. Others, beside Sanderson, suffered from Bertie's caustic tongue.

[2] Like many of his contemporaries, Hardinge was educated at Cheam, then Harrow and Trinity College, Cambridge. He knew both George Curzon and St John Brodrick; the Lytteltons were close friends. After Cambridge, Hardinge prepared for the Foreign Office examination by a few months in France and a final cramming at Scoones. He served for a short time at the Foreign Office in the German Department under Sanderson and then began the slow initial round of minor diplomatic posts. His ability was already recognized by Barrington and Sanderson and his royal connections marked him out for special consideration.

[3] Lord Hardinge of Penshurst, *Old Diplomacy, The Reminiscences of Lord Hardinge of Penshurst* (London, 1947), pp. 4–9, 68–9.

saw that his despatches were brought to the attention of the King.[1] But Bertie had ambitious plans for Hardinge. 'You know what my ideas are as regards your coming here as Assistant Under-Secretary . . . I think it would be a better preparation for your future than Paris. I do not at all know what Lord L. intends . . . You know the red tape of Sanderson, Villiers and Co.'[2] Hardinge thanked Bertie for his support which he attributed to the latter's concern for efficiency in the office.[3] But Bertie failed; the King could not intervene in a purely departmental matter and Francis Campbell was promoted to the vacated position. 'Lord L. is bound by the red taperism of this office' Bertie complained.[4]

In fact, Hardinge's opportunity came during the following year when, due to the intervention of Arthur Balfour and the King, Bertie was sent as ambassador to Rome and Hardinge recalled to take his place as assistant under-secretary. Lansdowne had acted with some reluctance and only the insistence of the King's private secretary saved the bellicose Bertie from the choice of a very minor post or retirement.[5] Once his own appointment was confirmed, Bertie set about assisting his friend. Here, again, the King's intervention was decisive for if Edward VII had little influence on Lansdowne's diplomacy, he could still persuade the Foreign Office to accept his nominees for the senior diplomatic posts. Hardinge's appointment was not a conventional one; it was most unusual for a diplomat to prefer a Foreign Office position to advancement in ambassadorial circles. But Hardinge was extremely ambitious and it was useful for him to return to London at this juncture.

Upon arrival, 'Capability' Hardinge immediately associated himself with those anxious to reform the Foreign Office. For him, as for Bertie, Sanderson and Villiers were the great stumbling stones. Villiers was not only identified with the methods of an earlier epoch, but was slow in his ways and unpopular with the juniors in the office.[6] Though he was conscious of the need to modernize the administration, he was considered Sanderson's ally and distrusted by the Bertie–Hardinge faction.[7] Hardinge made his views known to both Lansdowne and Sanderson; the former shared his estimate of Villiers' abilities and was not convinced that he should be appointed to

[1] Hardinge MSS, vol. 3, Bertie to Hardinge, 6 November 1901.
[2] Ibid. Bertie to Hardinge, 4 June 1902.
[3] Ibid. Hardinge to Bertie, 9 June 1902.
[4] Ibid. 25 July 1902.
[5] Bertie MSS, series A, Knollys to Bertie, 14 October; 5, 19 November; 22 December 1902. Bertie to Knollys, 27 December 1902.
[6] Ibid. series B, Hardinge to Bertie, 2 January 1904.
[7] Tilley and Gaselee, The Foreign Office, p. 153.

succeed Sanderson.[1] Hardinge's first positive step was to put through a new grading system in the Diplomatic Service which cut short long periods of duty at the same rank and pay scales. But he had more wide-ranging reforms in mind.

I hope before long to break down the trade unionism that reigns here and of which Villiers is the champion. I told Lord Lansdowne and Cranborne what I think of it all and I shall rub it into Lamps and Villiers when I get a chance. I hear that Balfour and some of the Cabinet are very sharp in their criticisms of the FO now and I think they are quite justified in what they say. There is now a scheme of reform for this office, which has been approved by Lord Lansdowne of which the principal features are

1. a Cypher room;
2. a blue book room;
3. the office keepers to make up bags.

This relieves the juniors to a certain extent, but the devolution of work which is the most important feature of the scheme remains entirely dependent on the under-secretaries and is not likely to be put in practice as long as Sanderson and Villiers reign here.[2]

Behind the subsequent pressure for Hardinge's appointment as permanent under-secretary was the knowledge that he would put the new reforms into operation. 'If I remain in this office any time', he wrote to Lascelles, 'I shall make a desperate push for second division clerks in the political departments and then chanceliers in our missions abroad would be the natural sequence but as long as Sanderson remains as Head of the Office it would be useless to suggest such a change.'[3]

For immediate purposes, Hardinge was placed in the Eastern Department where, in accordance with his past experience, he was responsible for Persia and central Asian affairs.[4] Lord Curzon, one of the key figures in central Asia, welcomed Hardinge in his new post and thought of him as an ally in pushing for a more active policy in Persia and Tibet.[5] Nevertheless, in

1 Villiers, under Lord Lansdowne, was primarily involved in American questions and was absorbed in the Newfoundland dispute with France (which continued to plague Anglo-French relations even after the entente), the New Hebrides conflict and clashing interests in Borneo. After Bertie's transfer to Rome, Villiers took over the African Department. In 1905 he collected evidence of a possible Franco-German African bargain. His major fear was that the French, for concessions in Africa, would give the Germans a free hand in some other part of the world, regardless of British interests. FO 64/1630. Memorandum by Villiers, 16 May 1905. Martin Gosselin had left the Foreign Office by 1902 to go to Lisbon and was replaced by F. A. Campbell.
2 Bertie MSS, series A, Hardinge to Bertie, 25 May 1903.
3 Lascelles MSS, vol. III, pt 4, Hardinge to Lascelles, 21 October 1905.
4 Hardinge MSS, vol. 3, Bertie to Hardinge, 14 January 1903. Hardinge also helped in the Western Department and supervised the Treaty and Consular Departments.
5 Ibid. Hardinge to Lord Curzon, 26 October 1903; Curzon to Hardinge, 21 November 1903.

November 1903, Hardinge met the Russian Ambassador at Windsor and re-iterated his hopes for an eventual agreement. He and Bertie were anxious to see the French agreement concluded and strengthened by a Russian agreement. It was natural, therefore, that both men wanted positions in which they could directly influence British policy in Paris and at St Petersburgh.

The British ambassadors in both countries were retiring. Hardinge and Bertie set to work. Bertie was bored in Rome and wished either to replace Sanderson as head of the Foreign Office or to be given the Paris embassy.[1] At the same time, Hardinge, after a Mediterranean tour with the King, became the royal choice for an appointment to Russia.[2] Edward VII and Lord Knollys urged his appointment on Balfour and Lansdowne.[3] The Foreign Secretary hesitated as Hardinge had just come to the Foreign Office and there were other diplomats in line for promotion. Once again, the King prevailed and Hardinge's appointment was confirmed for the New Year. During the same period, Hardinge pushed Bertie's candidature for Paris but met with rather formidable opposition amongst the higher officials in the Foreign Office.[4] Bertie wrote bitterly to Mallet, 'That little man Lord L. did not mean me to come here and he does not want me to go to Paris.'[5] It is interesting to speculate whether Lansdowne's opposition was political or personal, for even Bertie admitted that the 'Germans would not like me to be at Paris. Metternich I know considers me to be anti-German.'[6] Bertie's chances were not improved by his intemperate outbursts about the tedium of Rome and the inefficiency of the Foreign Office. Despite the opposition, Hardinge persisted. 'I had an hour's talk with the King a few days ago and I found him as strong as ever on the subject of your going to Paris and I drummed into him that there is *nobody* else'.[7] Lord Lansdowne's objection was overruled. The decision to appoint Bertie was made during the summer of 1904.

Neither Hardinge's nor Bertie's ambitions were restricted to their own posts; they were also anxious to gain control over the senior appointments in the Foreign Office and even in the Diplomatic Service where Charles Scott and Rennell Rodd were their particular targets. Even at the time of Hardinge's appointment to the Foreign Office, Bertie reported 'Farnall is

[1] *Ibid.* vol. 7, Valentine Chirol to Hardinge, 10 August 1904.
[2] *Ibid.* Knollys to Hardinge, 1 December 1903. FO 800/176, Bertie to Hardinge, 23 December 1903.
[3] Hardinge MSS, vol. 7, Knollys to Hardinge, 17 December 1903.
[4] Bertie MSS, series A, Hardinge to Bertie, 27 December 1903.
[5] *Ibid.* series A, Bertie to Mallet, 11 June 1904.          [6] *Ibid.*
[7] *Ibid.* series B, Hardinge to Bertie, 3 January 1907.

prepared to sulk . . . The next thing to do is to get rid of Hopwood or Cocker-
all, move Law into one of the places so vacated and force Farnall into the
Commercial Department.'[1] Both men were subsequently delighted when
Farnall, who was Sanderson's candidate, was not given Hardinge's post when
the latter went to St Petersburgh. Neither man knew the new appointee,
Eldon Gorst, who was the choice of the King, Lansdowne and Cromer.
But he was at least an outsider and not committed to the Sanderson–Villiers
faction.[2] As a matter of fact, Gorst did not live up to the expectations of
either his proposers or the reformers but was subsequently sent to Egypt
to replace Lord Cromer. Meanwhile, Louis Mallet had been made assistant
private secretary to Lord Lansdowne and this was a critical post for the
reformers and the anti-German group to have.

The final triumph for this faction came when Sanderson was taken
seriously ill during the summer of 1904 and Bertie was summoned back to the
Foreign Office to take his place.

It seems that he [Sanderson] has been strongly advised not to attempt to resume
work, and as he has only about two years to run anyhow, it would seem to be mere
ordinary prudence for him to make up his mind to retire now when he can still
save his sight rather than run the terrible risk of a relapse if he stays on. Bertie is
evidently very keen to get somebody from outside . . .

What I fear is that Sanderson has made the Foreign Office for so many years a
one-man show, that when he goes the rather obsolete and defective machinery he
has mainly kept going by his own motive power will collapse altogether.[3]

This view of Sanderson's rule was shared by other senior men (R. P. Maxwell
and Sir Edward Davidson) who were not of the Bertie persuasion. Various
names were suggested as possible replacements for Sanderson—Bertie,
Hardinge, Gorst and Sir A. Godley of the India Office.

Despite the weakness of his eyes, Sanderson was determined to return
to work in mid-December and Bertie was anxious to prepare the ground
before he left for Paris. In November Bertie saw Arthur Balfour and suggested Hardinge's name with a temporary substitute appointed until Hardinge could leave St Petersburgh.[4] November was a crucial month in Anglo-
Russian relations and Lord Lansdowne, faced with a bellicose faction in his
Cabinet and an aroused public, barely kept the Dogger Bank incident from

1 Hardinge MSS, vol. 3, Bertie to Hardinge, 14 January 1903.
2 Bertie MSS, Hardinge to Bertie, 21 February, 27 March, 4 April 1904. Bertie's candidate was not
  selected either but Bertie was pacified by Sanderson's defeat. Gorst had played an important part
  in the negotiations for the Anglo-French entente. Lord Cromer had sent him from Cairo to
  London to help Lansdowne during these talks.
3 Hardinge MSS, vol. 7, Valentine Chirol to Hardinge, 18 October 1904.
4 Ibid. Bertie to Hardinge, 28 November 1904.

resulting in a deep and lasting clash.[1] Bertie at the Foreign Office and Hardinge at St Petersburgh gave the Foreign Secretary their full support, and Lansdowne's success in handling the crisis must in part be credited to Hardinge's adroit handling of the matter in Russia.[2] This diplomatic crisis only intensified, in Bertie's eyes, the need to replace Sanderson with someone sympathetic to a Russian agreement. The new ambassador to Paris was sure that Sanderson would break down but for the moment 'he passes his time in writing offensive minutes and letters about the reorganization of the office'.[3]

During the summer of 1905 Lord Lansdowne made up his mind to find a diplomatic post for Villiers and to appoint Hardinge as permanent undersecretary before the pending general election.[4] It was at this point that Hardinge, for financial reasons, began to hesitate whether he could afford to accept this new position.[5] Louis Mallet urged Bertie to overcome his friend's doubts. 'Everyone hopes he will come here. There is much to be done in the way of reorganization and the importance of having someone who will keep the Liberals straight I thought is overwhelming.'[6] Bertie seems to have succeeded, for Hardinge's appointment was announced before Lord Lansdowne left office.

Mallet was not forgotten in the reshuffle. As early as 1904 Hardinge had suggested that Mallet might one day succeed Eric Barrington whose appointments rarely met with the approval of the Hardinge–Bertie group. On taking office, Hardinge was able to accomplish his aim.

He told me [wrote Reginald Lister to Bertie] in confidence that he had recommended Grey very strongly to take Mallet as his private secretary and give the vacant undersecretaryship to Eric for the 18 months he still has to serve. On his departure Mallet will be appointed to his place and trained to succeed Hardinge. I think this is quite right. Crowe is far too much mixed up with middle class Germans and far too uncouth a creature to be the Permanent Under-Secretary as I believe Tyrrell wished him to be.[7]

In April 1906 Barrington was appointed to the assistantship vacated by

[1] *Ibid.* Knollys to Hardinge, 15 November 1904. Selborne was particularly bellicose.
[2] *Ibid.* Bertie to Hardinge, 21 September, 11 November 1904.
[3] *Ibid.* Bertie to Hardinge, 28 November 1904.
[4] *Ibid.* Bertie to Hardinge, 5 July, 27 August 1905. Hardinge had already scented success a year earlier. 'If the Goose gets Vienna . . . Villiers will be shunted to Lisbon.' FO 800/176. Hardinge to Bertie, 9 June 1904.
[5] Hardinge MSS, vol. 7, Bertie to Hardinge, 5, 25 July 1905; Bertie MSS, series B, Hardinge to Bertie, 21 June 1905; series A, Hardinge to Bertie, 11 July 1905.
[6] *Ibid.* series B, Mallet to Bertie, 10 October 1905.
[7] *Ibid.* series A, Reginald Lister to Bertie, 12 December 1905.

Villiers, and Mallet, one of the most violent and outspoken anti-Germans in the Foreign Office, became Grey's private secretary.[1]

Thus, in a manner somewhat breathless and charged with personal intrigue, the personnel of the Foreign Office had been changed and its character altered. Sanderson was by nature modest, slow and cautious. All his personal traits favoured his belief in maintaining a free hand in Europe. He was replaced by an energetic diplomat, already predisposed towards the Dual Alliance, anxious for an agreement with Russia and deeply disturbed by the German naval threat. Moreover, Hardinge was already pledged to reform the Foreign Office. Sanderson thought of his establishment in terms of its nineteenth-century functions; Hardinge thought of it as a policy-making bureaucracy. Similarly, as a private secretary Eric Barrington took only the most minor role in the diplomatic business of the office; first Louis Mallet and then William Tyrrell thought it their function to advise their chief and to act as one of his key representatives. Mallet's anti-German feelings did not abate; during 1906 and 1907, key years in British policy, he constantly urged Grey to take a determinedly pro-French line.[2] In the chief European posts, only Frank Lascelles at Berlin represented the old Cecil persuasion. His views were increasingly discounted, particularly by the new head of the Western Department, Eyre Crowe.[3] In 1908 Lascelles was replaced by Edward Goschen. The Bertie–Hardinge political faction had triumphed and although the friendship between the two men was temporarily strained over administrative and political matters, their main goals had been accomplished by the time Sir Edward Grey took office.[4]

These key changes in personnel were accompanied by a major administrative reform which gave further power to the senior officials. The reforms of 1906 were the culmination of a series of steps taken by Lord Lansdowne to improve the status of his diplomatic establishment.[5] There were pressing problems within the Foreign Office. While some members of the Cabinet rarely read their despatches and others were notoriously careless or purposely

[1] In 1907 Mallet succeeded Gorst when the latter went to Egypt and Barrington's under-secretaryship was promised to W. Langley when Maxwell refused it. (Bertie MSS, Series A, Hardinge to Bertie, 27 May 1907.)

[2] *Ibid*. Mallet to Bertie, 2 March, 26 October 1906.          [3] BD VI, nos. 78, 81, 85, 88.

[4] Bertie MSS, series B, Hardinge to Bertie, 6 October; Bertie to Hardinge, 9 October; Hardinge to Bertie, 12 October; Bertie to Hardinge, 15 October 1906. Bertie was annoyed by the inefficiency of the Western Department and Hardinge answered sarcastically. At a later date, Bertie wrote 'The young gentlemen at the Foreign Office are too much occupied with "la haute politique" to attend to departmental duties', 21 September 1911. Bertie also found Hardinge less anti-German than he had hoped (*ibid*. series A, Mallet to Bertie, 24 August 1906; Bertie to Mallet, 25 August 1906).

[5] See above, p. 56.

indiscreet about their contents, there was a small group of ministers who repeatedly complained that they did not receive all the information they required. Despite measures taken by Sanderson and Barrington to improve the system of distribution, Arthur Balfour and a few others became openly dissatisfied and urged Lansdowne to modernize the Foreign Office machinery.[1] It became increasingly difficult to locate past papers, and an endless amount of time was consumed in searching for lost documents. The system of keeping records, initiated after the Ridley Commission of 1890, proved totally inadequate. By 1899 there were neither complete departmental indices nor any general index. A scheme of reform proposed by the librarian was rejected by Sanderson but two additional second-division clerks were added to the librarian's staff to compose a general index from the departmental indices.[2] Even these clerks were unable to keep up with the flow of business and as the departmental registries were inaccurate as well as incomplete, chaos resulted.[3] Worst of all, from the point of view of the department, at a time when all the political desks were extremely busy, the best men were bored and repelled by the routine. The entrance of a larger number of university men only increased the discrepancy between the training and the duties of the junior clerks. While Sanderson had little sympathy with their complaints, the rumblings of the staff could not be completely ignored.[4]

Although the documentary evidence is still incomplete, it seems to have been Francis Villiers who first brought pressure on Sanderson to reorganize the work of the department. Villiers and Sanderson, undoubtedly supported by Lord Lansdowne, worked out the first modest but important measures which were to lead to a greater division of responsibility among the first-division clerks. By May 1903 the first steps had been taken. C[ranborne], wrote Bertie, half in jest and half in sorrow:

We are proceeding with many minutes and much deliberation. The under-secretaries have been consulted semi-officially. The Permanent Under-Secretary has given a great deal of thought to it, the Secretary of State has at length been approached with carefully drawn general principles, he has been very sympathetic and has asked that these principles be crystallized in definite proposals. The Permanent Under-Secretary is now engaged in crystallizing. In the meantime a messenger is to tie up the bags instead of a first division clerk—but it is a shame to poke fun at him [Sanderson] for he is indeed overwhelmed in work. They tell me

[1] Bertie MSS, series A, Hardinge to Bertie, 25 May 1903.
[2] General, Librarian's Department, 1890–1918, vol. v, memorandum by Augustus Oakes, 22 November 1897; minute by Sanderson, 31 May 1898; minute by Sanderson, 20 October 1898.
[3] Two second-division clerks were added to the political departments in 1898 to prepare the indices from the registers.
[4] Cmd. 7749, Q. 39,394–7.

this spring beat the record for the abundance of work which has been supplied to the Foreign Office.[1]

In the summer of 1903 Sanderson appealed to the Treasury for additional second-division clerks and two assistant clerks, the latter to help with parliamentary papers in the proposed Blue Book department and to act as secretary to the Committee of Imperial Defence.

But there was pressure from within the Foreign Office for more radical reforms. Sanderson appointed an intra-departmental committee consisting of the librarian, chief clerk and the senior clerks (A. Oakes, W. C. Cartwright, R. P. Maxwell, W. Langley and H. Farnall) to inquire into the record-keeping operations of the other major government departments.[2] Most of the work was done by Farnall, the senior clerk whom Sanderson had vainly supported for Hardinge's Foreign Office position.[3] Acting on Farnall's findings and recommendations, the Committee reported in the spring of 1904.[4] They suggested that a Registry system be instituted and that the Colonial Office method of registering and filing papers be adopted for the Foreign Office. The change would involve a redistribution of work which would relieve the first division of almost all its clerical functions. Nothing was immediately done; Sanderson's illness and hostile reaction to the proposed reform certainly contributed to the delay. But even the Permanent Under-Secretary realized that some measure of reform was inevitable.

The poor old Eastern Department is a bit swamped again [Maxwell wrote to Bertie]. All the questions seem to have taken this opportunity to become extra troublesome. —Until we have a new system in operation and a good staff, whose time is not taken up with routine, we shall never be able to do the work properly. I have done my best to put this into Sanderson and he does not disagree.[5]

After some argument, Sanderson was finally convinced but difficulties with the Treasury delayed further action. A query went out to ambassadors in all European capitals asking for a description of the Foreign Office in their respective countries in the hope of supplying the reformers with additional models.[6] The Permanent Under-Secretary prevailed and on 29 December 1905 a memorandum explaining the new system was sent to the heads of all departments.[7] The reformers had won and the anti-German faction was in

---

[1] Bertie MSS, series A, C[ranborne?] to Bertie, 31 May 1903. See above, p. 72 for Hardinge's negative description.
[2] General 55/3, no. 8616, Report on Registration and Keeping of Papers in the Foreign Office, 18 May 1904.
[3] *Ibid.* Farnall's name is mentioned specifically in the committee's report.    [4] *Ibid.*
[5] Hardinge MSS, vol. 7, Maxwell to Hardinge, 28 November 1904.
[6] General 55/3, Inquiry to ambassadors in Germany, Italy, Russia, Austria-Hungary and France, 29 November 1904.
[7] *Ibid.* no. 8552, memorandum by Sanderson, 29 December 1905.

power. The appointment of Charles Hardinge as permanent under-secretary and the selection of Eyre Crowe as temporary head of the Central Registry assured the success of the new programme.

Although only a change in the keeping of papers, the introduction of the Registry system deeply altered the Foreign Office.[1] The role of the first-division clerks was transformed. From being clerks they became advisers engaged in the policy-making process. The functions of the Palmerstonian establishment were now taken over by members of the second division who staffed the Central Registry and three sub-registries. All incoming despatches were registered in the Central Registry and were then sent in 'jackets' to the appropriate sub-registry. Here, a second-division clerk summarized the despatch, collected all related material, and copied the entry into his register. The jackets containing the new despatches and old papers were then sent to the senior clerk of one of the political departments. He handed it over to one of his juniors who read the papers, looked up any additional information and in some cases recommended a possible course of action. At this point, the senior clerk could then settle about half the business which came to his desk. Unfinished questions were forwarded with his suggestions to the assistant under-secretary who settled the matter if possible. The same process was repeated at this level; only the most important issues went to the permanent under-secretary and finally to Sir Edward Grey.[2] The permanent under-secretary was relieved of his specific departmental responsibilities so that he could exercise a general supervision over the whole Foreign Office.

The despatch boxes which the foreign secretary received contained telegrams which he had already read and new correspondence. To each telegram was now attached a sheet giving the views of the subordinate officials. Each despatch, in turn, had 'a minute by the head of the department specially affected, another by the assistant under-secretary in whose group of departments this one is, and finally one by the permanent under-secretary'.[3] This was a far cry from the day when Lord Salisbury's despatches carried only a brief comment or query by the permanent or assistant under-secretary and at most an explanation by a senior clerk. Once the foreign secretary initialled his own or any other minute, 'the Office is authorized to carry it out, without any further reference to him'.[4] The final jobs of copying, printing, distributing and indexing, formerly done by members of the diplomatic

---

[1] For an excellent description of the Registry system, see Cmd. 7749, Q.36,917–931. R. Butler, 'Beside the Point', *World Review*, p. 9; Tilley, *From London to Tokyo*, p. 69, on the changes in the Foreign Office.

[2] Gosses, *The Management of British Foreign Policy*, pp. 73–4.

[3] Grey, *Twenty-Five Years*, vol. II, p. 260.     [4] *Ibid.*

establishment, were now performed by the Registry staffs.[1] Only telegrams were processed by a first-division clerk in the Eastern Department, a practice dropped in 1911. J. A. C. Tilley, a critical observer of the system, commented:

the actual effect was that in many cases the highest authorities had to accept and become responsible for the view of their subordinates, or else let the matter stand over till they had time for proper consideration. Moreover, when a subject had been thoroughly threshed out by a junior and then by a senior who knew their subject, it was often natural for the Secretary of State to accept their views and save an expenditure of time and thought which he could not easily afford.[2]

When it is remembered that the new senior officials were men with definite political aims and that Grey was relatively young and faced with a difficult Cabinet situation, it is not surprising that the senior hierarchy soon asserted its new power.

When and how Eyre Crowe became associated with the reform movement is not entirely clear. Though he was not a member of the 1903 committee, he soon became involved in the elaboration and implementation of the committee's recommendations.[3] Crowe was only an assistant clerk in the African Protectorates department (which was being disbanded during 1904) yet he soon became the real power behind the new regime. 'Crowe worked solidly for three years, if I remember right, at the reconstruction scheme; and, when it was launched, it was he who manipulated the transition behind the scenes and made it go through without a hitch.'[4] Crowe firmly believed that better methods for collecting, circulating and keeping papers would improve the calibre of British diplomacy. He also viewed the new minute-writing system as a training programme for future advisers.

We were soon given more interesting tasks—the writing of memoranda on special subjects or drafts of replies to despatches from abroad. Later we were promoted to deal with special areas or special subjects within the purlieu of the particular department to which we belonged. All correspondence relating to his particular area was sent to the junior official concerned, who studied it and sent it on to his immediate superior with comments and suggestions for action to be taken. Thus we had the advantage of earlier responsibility, wider scope and more initiative.[5]

---

[1] Cmd. 7749, Q.36,917.

[2] Tilley and Gaselee, *The Foreign Office*, pp. 160–1. For Tilley's negative view of the reforms and his somewhat critical opinions of Crowe, see his autobiography *London to Tokyo*.

[3] There is no reference to Eyre Crowe in General Volume 55/3, no. 8616, but see R. Butler, 'Beside the Point', *World Review*, p. 9; J. D. Gregory, *On the Edge of Diplomacy*, pp. 255–6; Tilley and Gaselee, *The Foreign Office*, p. 153. Crowe personally testified that he had examined the registries of all government departments before the new system was initiated (Cmd. 7749, Q.37,046).

[4] J. D. Gregory, *On the Edge of Diplomacy*, p. 250.

[5] Sir Hughe Knatchbull-Hugessen, *Diplomat in Peace and War* (London, 1949), p. 12.

Other contemporaries confirm Knatchbull-Hugessen's recollection. 'It soon became my duty', Owen O'Malley records, ' . . . to write opinions on the papers which reached us and to draft letters carrying out the instructions minuted upon them by the Secretary or Under-Secretaries of State and it was in this manner that the education of everyone who joined the Foreign Office was conducted.'[1] Crowe's intention was to encourage the juniors to train their intelligence 'by having a little say in high matters, however wide of the mark at first'.[2] Since the juniors were restricted to duties in which they could not easily go wrong, and since papers went up the Foreign Office pyramid, there was little danger of an irreparable error.

The omnipresent Crowe hoped that the accumulated knowledge of diplomats and officials could be collected and systematized so that the foreign secretary would always have available for his use a record of the relations of Great Britain with every foreign country, and of each foreign country with each other. Acting on Crowe's recommendations, the Foreign Office instructed the heads of missions to prepare annual reports for their countries; juniors were asked for memoranda on particular subjects of interest. Crowe hoped that promotion would be granted in the light of these records (a somewhat Utopian vision). In addition to these diplomatic reports, each department was to produce an annual Foreign Office summary. Some of these annual reviews make fascinating reading for the historian but few could have been of great interest to a foreign secretary with barely enough time to go through the most urgent despatch boxes. Lord Strang, a post-war recruit to the Foreign Office, was not the only one to state that Crowe 'believed overmuch in the virtue of papers for their own sake'.[3] The new innovation did not arouse much enthusiasm among Crowe's contemporaries and the temporary head of the Registry was forced to bully ambassadors into complying. 'We have had some excellent reports', Crowe wrote to the delinquent Lascelles in Berlin, 'and if you have time to look at one or the other, you will find those from Stockholm, Copenhagen, Tangier, Sofia, Washington (short) decidedly interesting.'[4]

Impelled by Crowe's driving energy and Hardinge's enthusiastic support, the Registry system was soon in full operation. Since the second-division clerks worked from 10.30 a.m. to 6 p.m., most of the Foreign Office staff was expected to be present during these hours. The earlier flexibility was disappearing and the pace of office life began to quicken. The long weekend was still normal and vacations were of a length which suited gentlemen. As late as

[1] O'Malley, *Phantom Caravan*, p. 35.    [2] Vansittart, *Mist Procession*, p. 98.
[3] Lord Strang, *Home and Abroad*, p. 308.    [4] FO 800/13, Crowe to Lascelles, 8 April 1907.

1913 Maurice Peterson was rejected for the Foreign Office because of his handwriting but this was considered an outrage and he was soon appointed. The 'good old days' had not yet vanished altogether. But the new reforms did push the office into the twentieth century. Telephones were placed in all departmental rooms and the number of typists was increased. Some degree of expertise was encouraged and men with special competence were used in an appropriate department. Some of those affected regretted the old regime but the future lay with men who looked ahead.

The 1906 reforms affected the Diplomatic Service only indirectly. Hardinge did encourage transfers and a more flexible system of grading and pay facilitated such exchanges. Nevertheless, an opportunity for reforming the Diplomatic Service was missed and diplomatists continued doing clerical work of the most routine order. 'The result is', Harold Nicolson reported in 1930, 'the Diplomatic Service is still to a large extent conducted on the system of 1842. And the energetic Civil Servant, when relegated to Diplomacy, is thus apt to resign.'[1]

The new internal organization of the Foreign Office did not fulfil the hopes of its initiators and more drastic changes were soon necessary. The increase in pay scarcely reflected the new pressure of work and responsibility. But the work of the diplomatic establishment at home had been permanently transformed. Young men became a part, however unimportant, of the policy-making process and senior men were officially encouraged to express their views. Future foreign secretaries did not always consult their advisers; they themselves were sometimes ignored. But never again were the permanent officials cut off from the nerve centres of political decision. The days of the Foreign Office as a department of scribes were past.

[1] Nicolson, *Sir Arthur Nicolson*, p. 326.

# CHAPTER 3

# Power and perplexities, 1905–1914

## *Sir Edward Grey in Whitehall*

Sir Edward Grey's appointment to the Foreign Office in December 1905 confirmed the new position of the permanent officials. This change of balance resulted from a number of interacting factors, though the most important was undoubtedly the personality and views of the new foreign secretary himself.

Grey remains an elusive figure. The stern portrait which prefaces his autobiography needs to be compared to the rather shy figure feeding the ducks at Fallodon. Though only forty-three years of age when he came to the Foreign Office, Grey was neither as indecisive nor as inexperienced as his critics subsequently claimed. Raised in the Whig tradition of political services, he was the direct descendant of the second Earl Grey of the Reform Bill. His father had been an equerry to the Prince of Wales and the son was sent to Winchester and Balliol to prepare for a political career. He had entered Parliament at twenty-three, was made Lord Rosebery's parliamentary under-secretary in 1892 and after 1895 became the recognized Liberal spokesman on foreign affairs in the Commons. When Lord Cromer refused the foreign secretaryship in 1905, the young Liberal Unionist seemed the logical alternative.

Grey was subsequently accused of being the most insular of foreign secretaries.[1] He disliked travelling, his French was poor and he was not at ease with foreigners. Though he enjoyed his work, he had little of that love of diplomatic manœuvre which made Salisbury such a master in the field. Even before he took office, his Liberal supporters knew he was a man divided between a strong sense of political responsibility and ambition and a deep desire to retreat from London politics to his rural preoccupations. 'Last night I saw Metternich, the Kaiser's favourite diplomat. He talked of E. Grey with great admiration as having a real talent for Foreign Affairs. You see that everyone says the same thing and you [Munro Ferguson] and Lady Helen ought to see that he spares a little time from his ducks to learn

[1] David Lloyd George, *War Memoirs of David Lloyd George* (London, 1933), vol. I, p. 98.

French', Spring-Rice wrote in 1898.[1] Grey was a passionate naturalist, birdwatcher and fisherman who repeatedly felt the need to escape from his London desk. As he was, moreover, the first foreign secretary since Palmerston to sit in the Commons, he had an even heavier load of work than his already over-burdened predecessors.

> One of his most depressing moments, [Grey wrote of his time as foreign secretary] is after a long Foreign Office debate in the House of Commons. The debate may have begun at four o'clock and ended at eleven. It will have been necessary for him to sit through it and speak, possibly to make a difficult and important speech. When the debate is over he enters his room at the House of Commons and sees the pile of red boxes that have accumulated. The minister sorts out the urgent work, condenses it into one or as few boxes as possible, and takes it home with him to work up at night . . .[2]

As time passed, Grey grew increasingly weary. He was never fully at home in the Foreign Office nor totally at ease in the House. 'The elections mercifully are over; we are confirmed in office, which is not so merciful. After five years of FO and H of C combined (and such years!), it would be hardly human not to wish for some relaxation.'[3] The Foreign Secretary left London as often as possible and even in moments of crisis his staff were reluctant to recall him. But total relief and isolation were impossible.

There are further contradictions about Grey which blur an accurate portrait. Contemporaries honoured his honesty, sincerity and loyalty. Even his critics portrayed him as a man of moral rectitude though a foreign secretary of limited vision and imagination. Arthur Ponsonby, one of Grey's most vocal back-bench opponents, wrote in 1913:

> To begin with he is a gentleman in the best sense of the word. Personal ambition and a desire to advertise himself I don't suppose he has ever felt for a single instant. This makes him a sharp contrast to many of his colleagues. His House of Commons manner has been a great service to him. It is very simple very sincere dignified and direct. He is rather aloof and unapproachable which makes a certain mystery that attracts. He is a liberal & capable of passionate devotion to a cause but he is over-cautious and not really very able. He trusts the opinion of his permanent officials more than his own judgment and is, therefore, capable of making rather serious mistakes. He is out of touch with the party. I don't suppose he knows more than a score of them by name . . . He has a great reputation in the country specially among Tories. His successes have been more due to chance his failures to want of per-

---

1 S. Gwynn (ed.), *The Letters and Friendships of Sir Cecil Spring-Rice* (London, 1929), vol. I, p. 325. See also p. 339.
2 Grey, *Twenty-Five Years*, vol. II, p. 262. Lord Morley and Haldane occasionally took over the Foreign Office to give Grey a complete break.
3 FO 800/98 Grey to Hardinge, 18 December 1910.

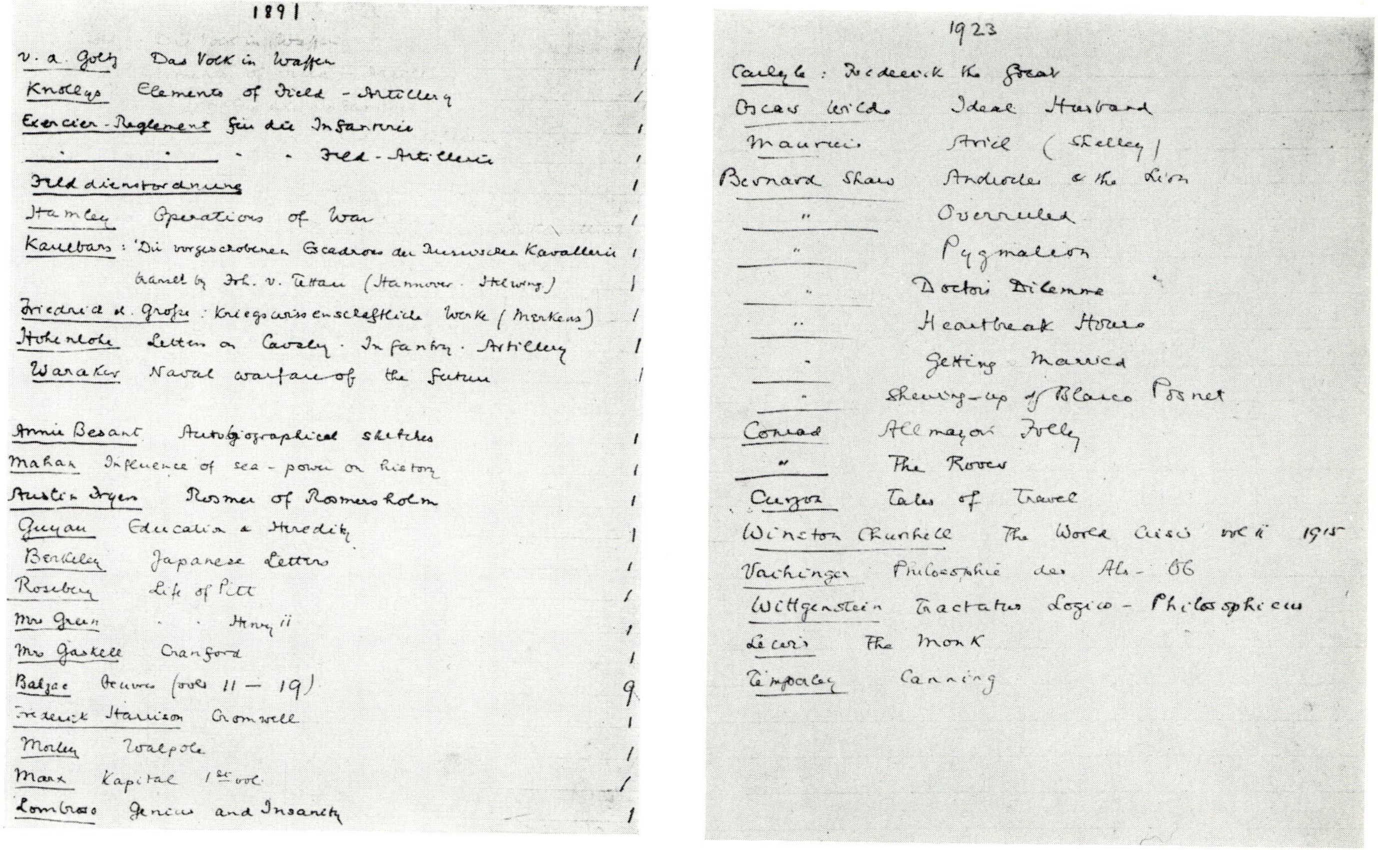

1891

v. d. Goltz Das Volk in Waffen 1
Knolleys Elements of Field-Artillery 1
Exercier-Reglement für die Infanterie 1
" " Feld-Artillerie 1
Felddienstordnung 1
Hamley Operations of War 1
Kaulbars: 'Die vorgeschobenen Escadrons der Russischen Kavallerie 1
transl. by Frh. v. Tettau (Hannover. Helwing) 1
Friedrich d. Grosse: Kriegswissenschaftliche Werke (Merkens) 1
Hohenlohe Letters on Cavalry. Infantry. Artillery 1
Waraker Naval warfare of the Future 1

Annie Besant Autobiographical sketches 1
Mahan Influence of sea-power on history 1
Austin Dryer Rosmer of Rosmersholm 1
Guyau Education & Heredity 1
Berkeley Japanese Letters 1
Rosebery Life of Pitt 1
Mrs Green " " Henry II 1
Mrs Gaskell Cranford 1
Balzac Oeuvres (vols 11 – 19) 9
Frederick Harrison Cromwell 1
Morley Walpole 1
Marx Kapital 1st vol. 1
Lombroso Genius and Insanity 1

1923

Carlyle: Frederick the Great
Oscar Wilde Ideal Husband
Maurois Ariel (Shelley)
Bernard Shaw Androcles & the Lion
" Overruled
" Pygmalion
" Doctor's Dilemma
" Heartbreak House
" Getting Married
" Shewing-up of Blanco Posnet
Conrad Almayer's Folly
" The Rover
Curzon Tales of Travel
Winston Churchill The World Crisis vol ii 1915
Vaihinger Philosophie des Als-Ob
Wittgenstein Tractatus Logico-Philosophicus
Le Caron The Monk
Temperley Canning

5 Specimen pages from Crowe's *Lesebuch*

6a Eyre Crowe as an assistant clerk (1904)

b Charles Hardinge, permanent under-secretary (1906–10, 1916–20)

c Arthur Nicolson, permanent under-secretary (1910–16)

d William Tyrrell, Grey's private secretary (1907–15), permanent under-secretary (1925–8)

7 Vansittart viewing his predecessors in the room of the permanent under-secretary. Portraits include those of Hammond, Sanderson, Hardinge, Nicolson, Crowe and Tyrrell

8 Sir Stephen Gaselee, librarian at the Foreign Office from 1920 to 1943, in proper Foreign Office dress (despite red silk socks), before the old safe containing treaties

ception. He would be a good friend for Lloyd George and Lloyd George would be a good friend for him.[1]

Grey had 'inherited something of Gladstone's moral earnestness',[2] and it was this quality which impressed his colleagues, both domestic and foreign. It was perhaps this reputation for righteous behaviour (a reputation which Grey sometimes consciously exploited) which explains the tremendous disillusionment in the post-war period.[3] For, as the public of the nineteen-twenties discovered, morality was often tempered by necessity. Grey was not always open in his dealings with either friends or opponents and his diplomacy was often more complex than was expected from 'a straight, North-country gentleman'. Grey was a composite of opposites and a man of some inner tension. He has been variously described as 'strong' and 'weak', 'stubborn' and 'open to persuasion', 'straightforward' and 'elusive', 'rigid' and 'flexible'. He could give the appearance of total calm and command and then suddenly collapse when the strain became too great. He was apparently almost child-like both in his firm moral convictions and in his emotional responses to moments of crisis. Yet he was often politically shrewd and showed considerable diplomatic acumen. A simple man could not have remained head of the Foreign Office during this period whatever his training or sense of moral responsibility. He was dealing with highly complicated problems which did not admit of simple solutions. There was an understandable gap between the public image and the private reality.

There were others beside Ponsonby who argued that Grey deferred too much to the judgements of his permanent officials. By disposition and temper, Grey was the kind of chief who solicited and welcomed advice and even encouraged adverse criticism. 'Grey was always tolerant of opposition', Algernon Law said of his former chief. 'He liked to hear and weigh arguments against a line of conduct which he was inclined to favour.'[4] The new foreign secretary, in sharp distinction to Lord Salisbury, had a deep respect for men who now fully merited the title of professionals. He was willing not only to learn from them but to give them responsibilities which he had neither the time nor the inclination to shoulder. As will be shown, those officials whom he trusted he treated as equals and was quick to appreciate where their

[1] Ponsonby MSS, notes by Ponsonby on the members of the Liberal Cabinet, January 1913.
[2] A. J. P. Taylor, *The Struggle for Mastery in Europe, 1848–1918* (Oxford, 1954), p. 436.
[3] Grey's reputation has survived the battering. See the comment in F. Gosses, *The Management of British Foreign Policy*, p. 117. 'Considering the great honesty and loyalty of especially this foreign secretary, one can hardly doubt his testimony.'
[4] G. Trevelyan, *Grey of Fallodon* (London, 1937), p. 168. See also Hardinge, *Old Diplomacy*, p. 192.

particular talents lay. The gulf between the foreign secretary and staff remained, but the senior officials were to provide a new bridge between the two. This is not to say that Grey was a cipher-minister directed by his officials. Though he sought advice, he made his own decisions even during his first years in office when his inexperience was more marked.

Another factor which influenced Grey's relations with the Foreign Office was his position within the Cabinet. During his first two years in office, the new foreign secretary enjoyed a large measure of freedom. The Liberal-Imperialist/radical split did not weaken Grey's power. On the contrary, the three Liberal-Imperialists—Asquith, Haldane and Grey—were in the key ministries and represented a powerful faction in the new Cabinet. Grey consulted the Prime Minister and Lord Ripon, the Lord Privy Seal and party's senior statesman, on all issues of importance, but neither man ever vetoed one of Grey's major decisions. Fortunately for the success of Grey's diplomacy, Lord Morley, the secretary of state for India, supported Grey's efforts to conclude an entente with the Russians.[1] Though Morley played a crucial role during the Anglo-Russian talks of 1907, he did not fully understand the general European implications of the new agreement and Grey did not enlighten him. Lord Tweedmouth was an isolated figure soon to depart under something of a cloud! The other radicals—Loreburn, Bryce, Lloyd George, Sinclair, Burns, Buxton and Harcourt—were all in domestic departments and in these early years took little interest in foreign affairs. When Asquith replaced Campbell-Bannerman, Grey's position was further strengthened, for the new prime minister was not only an old political ally but shared Grey's views on the European situation. Asquith was content to leave the direction of affairs in his colleague's hands.

In general, the Cabinet was far too involved in its domestic programme to give much time to foreign policy. In February 1908, for instance, Ripon was told that the Cabinet passed hastily over the Baltic and North Sea agreements (about which he had some doubts) to consider a Licensing bill.[2] Grey himself was drawn into the political and social problems of the day—the coal strike, the House of Lords debate and the elections. But in marked contrast to his immediate predecessors, Grey was far from open in his dealings with other ministers. Numerous documents, some of importance, were marked by Grey (or by his private secretary) for limited circulation

[1] Monger, *The End of Isolation*, pp. 284-7. Ripon MSS 43547, Grey to Ripon, 8 September 1907.
[2] Lucien Wolf, *Life of the First Marquess of Ripon* (London, 1921), vol. II, p. 294. Ripon opposed the North Sea Agreement. Ripon MSS 43640, Grey to Ripon, 13 December 1907.

only.[1] The most famous example of such an omission, the conversation with Cambon in January 1906 and the subsequent Anglo-French military conversations, has been repeatedly discussed. Grey consulted only Campbell-Bannerman and Ripon; no Cabinet meeting was held and only Haldane, Tweedmouth and possibly Asquith knew of their existence until the time of the Agadir crisis.[2] There were, however, other instances when Grey sent despatches only to the King, Prime Minister, Ripon and sometimes Morley and Haldane. It is clear that he repeatedly tried to omit involving the radical group in the Cabinet. 'Please regard it as secret since only a portion of it [Hardinge's conversation with Prince Bülow in Berlin in 1909] has been issued to the Cabinet. There is a good deal of leakage from the Cabinet at present, which shows itself in the Manchester Guardian, so we have to take special precautions . . .'[3] At a later date, 11 April 1911, a key despatch from Bertie in Paris was minuted, 'Prime Minister, Lord Morley, Lord Haldane, in first instance' and then follows a second notation by the private secretary, 'Sir E. Grey thinks this circulation sufficient'.[4] Previous foreign secretaries had also consulted a small inner group of interested ministers but neither Salisbury nor Lansdowne would have purposely avoided consulting their colleagues. Grey clearly preferred to keep his own counsel.

The Foreign Secretary knew that his beliefs, which he had formed even before he took office, were not shared by all Liberals. Even in 1895 Grey had been full of apprehension, 'feeling that we are dependent on Germany and yet had not Germany's good will and that we were drifting towards war with France or Russia or both'.[5] In the years which followed, Grey welcomed the French entente and acted on the assumption that Germany was the main threat to the peace of Europe. Once in office, he not only extended Britain's obligations to France but in settling with the Russians had the German threat very much in mind. The Anglo-Russian conventions did more than ease Britain's central Asian position; during the Balkan crisis of 1908–9 Grey gave British support to the Russian side thereby altering the European diplomatic balance. Unlike Lansdowne, Grey was not conscious of the Empire

[1] In 1906 the confidential print was rearranged. Papers were divided into categories of special and general interest and only the latter went to the King, Prince of Wales and such Cabinet ministers as the secretary of state might designate in addition to the Foreign Office heads of department and the embassies and legations abroad. See FO 371/167, 27 July 1906, and the discussion in Monger, *The End of Isolation*, p. 307.

[2] *Ibid.* pp. 253–6.     [3] Hardinge MSS, vol. 17, Hardinge to Bryce, 26 February 1909.

[4] BD VI, p. 460. This despatch was a report of a conversation between the British military attaché at Paris and General Foch and referred to the possibility of joint staff talks. For other examples of which there are many see the list in Monger, *The End of Isolation*, pp. 307–8.

[5] Grey, *Twenty-Five Years*, vol. II, p. 43.

and had little real interest in colonial affairs. The continent of Europe was the main focus of his attention. Within four years, a Liberal foreign secretary had committed his country to the diplomatic support of the entente powers.

Grey repeatedly failed to spell out his policy at the Cabinet table. When he could, he avoided consulting the radicals in the Cabinet who might have had serious doubts about the direction of his diplomacy. There were certainly ministers (and even more back-benchers) who would have opposed the military talks with France in 1906. Moreover, many radicals as well as Labour supporters looked upon the talks with Tsarist Russia with deep suspicion on ideological grounds. The King's visit to Reval caused a parliamentary division. Even those who accepted the Anglo-Russian conventions never found the agreement a palatable one. Russian misdeeds in Persia, revealed in a series of Blue Books and in a large number of newspaper reports, created a hostile chorus both in and out of Parliament which had repercussions in the Cabinet. For the most part, Grey could afford to ignore these critiques. But when, in October 1908, Isvolsky asked for a revision of the Straits convention to recoup his diplomatic reputation after the annexationist crisis, the radical section of the Cabinet baulked and the Russian minister had to be satisfied with a compromise formula.[1]

Grey was acutely aware of this lack of unanimity. Even his closest colleague, R. B. Haldane, did not share his assumptions about the nature of the German threat and the proper way to meet it. Haldane, particularly after the end of the Algeciras Conference, thought there was much to be gained from a rapprochement with Berlin. Grey was not totally averse to such an approach but feared that Haldane's visit to Germany in 1906 would rouse suspicions in France. It was, however, the battle over the naval estimates which, quite apart from Haldane, revealed the deep and lasting split over German policy in the Cabinet. The Liberals, involved in an expensive reform programme, were anxious to reduce defence expenditure. The possibility of a Franco-German naval combination (the basis of the previous two-power standard) had become a dead phantom and the economists forced through cuts in the Cawdor ship-building programme. British naval strength was now measured against the Kaiser's fleet and this decision, like the redistribution of the fleet, focussed all attention on Berlin.[2] A section of the party, represented by a strong group in the Cabinet, pressed for still further reductions in naval costs and hoped that the Hague Peace Conference would lead to general naval disarmament. There were others, however, who shared Grey's

[1] BD v, nos. 358, 364, 377, 389.
[2] Arthur Marder, *From the Dreadnought to Scapa Flow* (London, 1961), vol. I, pp. 125–8.

more pessimistic view of future naval relations between England and Germany. These ministers, somewhat dismayed but hardly surprised by the failure of the conference (which some radicals attributed to Grey's lukewarm support) and by German amendments to the 1900 law, began to agitate publicly for a larger navy.

The fight over the naval estimates preoccupied the Cabinet during the first two months of 1908.[1] The Admiralty brought in a revised estimate of a million and a quarter pounds which roused the radicals. The First Sea Lord was supported by Grey, Haldane and Asquith (who had already forced certain economies on the Admiralty) while the radicals—Harcourt, McKenna, Lloyd George, Crewe and Burns—demanded further reductions. The prime minister, Campbell Bannerman, hammered out an acceptable compromise but the division had important effects on Grey's policy. Those supporting economies pressed for an accommodation with Germany which Grey thought dangerous. Though the discussions with Metternich and the royal visit to Cronberg in the summer of 1908 represented an effort on Grey's part to limit the naval race, the Foreign Secretary's approaches to Germany were always circumscribed by his assumption of the ultimately aggressive nature of German ambitions.[2]

The real crisis came in the early months of 1909 when the false but widely-believed rumour spread that Germany was building dreadnoughts secretly and would, by 1912, have more ships of this class than Great Britain.[3] This time, McKenna, the first sea lord, was supported by Asquith, Grey, Haldane, Runciman and Crewe (the latter with reservations). The radical ministers—Lloyd George, Churchill, Morley, Burns and Harcourt—threatened to resign. Asquith was particularly annoyed with Lloyd George and Churchill. 'There are moments', he said, 'when I am disposed summarily to chastise them both. E. Grey is a great standby, always sound, temperate and strong.'[4] Asquith found the compromise formula but the public debate created an atmosphere of hysteria, which complicated Anglo-German diplomacy. Only Lloyd George's budget finally swept the story from the front pages. The 'big navy' group had succeeded in its major goals but Grey knew that an important section of his Cabinet would continue to argue that an agreement with Germany would lead to a reduction in the naval budget and ought to be pursued for this reason.

Despite the furore created by the naval debate, the Germans continued

[1] *Ibid.* p. 138.  
[2] *Ibid.* p. 143; BD VI, no. 117.  
[3] Marder, *From the Dreadnought to Scapa Flow*, vol. I, ch. VII, especially pp. 160–4.  
[4] Roy Jenkins, *Asquith, Portrait of a Man and an Era* (London, 1964), p. 195.

to press for an agreement. Prompted by Churchill and the other radicals, Grey was forced to consider the possibility of new talks during the spring and summer of 1909. The German proposals, presented by Bethmann Hollweg on 21 August, were disappointing and met with a cool response at Whitehall. Grey discussed the offer with Asquith and Crewe only; the dissolution of parliament and the elections gave him an excuse to postpone further exchanges. But neither the Germans nor the cabinet radicals were content and when the former returned to the charge in the summer of 1910, Lord Loreburn took the lead in insisting on a positive British response. Grey proposed that the Germans be asked not to increase their existing naval programme. He wrote, 'It was my view too that nothing which did not modify the fleet law in Germany would seem worth much to public opinion here but the cabinet thought it would be better than nothing and in that view I concur especially if it would be combined with an exchange of naval information to which I have always attached importance.'[1] It was now the Germans who delayed answering though the election crisis of 1910 again gave Grey a breathing space.

Early in the new year the pro-German radicals persuaded their colleagues in the Cabinet to set up a committee consisting of Grey, Asquith, Crewe, Morley, Runciman and Lloyd George to handle the talks with Berlin. The Foreign Office officials believed this committee, though mixed in its composition and views, was established to check Grey and to force through an Anglo-German agreement.[2] The naval costs, clashes with Russia in Persia and a general uneasiness about the loyalty of the French in Morocco continued to make such an approach attractive. Though preoccupied with the continuing constitutional crisis, the committee hammered out an answer to Berlin. Grey dropped his demand that a naval agreement precede any political bargain, but insisted that the two be concluded simultaneously and that any such formula be so worded as to avoid giving offence to either France or Russia. The final offer, made to the Germans on 24 March, represented a compromise between Grey and his radical critics. The German counter-proposals, not received until 9 May, were hardly encouraging yet the cabinet insisted that negotiations be continued. As Nicolson wrote to Lord Hardinge in India, 'Grey is perfectly sound on the whole matter but I am afraid there are in the cabinet several members who desire to come to what they term a friendly understanding with Germany at almost any cost and there

---

[1] BD vi, no. 392.
[2] *Ibid.* nos. 434, 440. Papers including some on non-German affairs which went to this committee were not usually seen by the rest of the Cabinet. The Committee seems to have disappeared by 21 July.

are no doubt sections of the Radical party who are still more emphatic on this point . . .'[1] Even in July it was rumoured that Grey and Asquith 'were not quite as strong in the cabinet as they are outside it'.[2]

The Agadir crisis brought these already languishing talks to an end but, as will be shown, the pro-German and anti-Russian groups were soon to make a strong joint attack on Grey's diplomacy and the British in 1912 were once more engaged in Anglo-German conversations. Grey's colleagues did interfere in the direction of affairs though their interventions were sporadic and sometimes fruitless. One can understand (without approving) why Grey restricted the circulation of contentious despatches and why he drew back from spelling out all the implications of his diplomacy. We know from these pre-Agadir talks and from the Cabinet blow-up after Agadir that an important group of ministers had serious doubts about Grey's proceedings. Until 1911 the Cabinet as a whole had not understood the full extent of the existing ties between Britain and France and never quite appreciated the European side of the Anglo-Russian entente. Part of its ignorance was due to lack of interest and domestic preoccupations but part was also due to Grey's reserve and reluctance to discuss policy questions in the Cabinet. Grey's high reputation in the country assured him a large measure of freedom in his office.[3] Unless openly challenged, he preferred to avoid open debate. Yet the radicals in the Cabinet knew far more about Grey's diplomacy than they later admitted. If they could not move the Foreign Secretary on fundamental issues, they could and did force him into unwelcome paths. Lloyd George's contention that the 'Cabinet as a whole were never called into genuine consultation upon the fundamental aspects of the foreign situation' is neither accurate nor just.[4]

## Hardinge's regime, 1906–1910

The knowledge that there might be difficulties in the Cabinet forced Grey to prepare his briefs carefully. Questions were fully examined in the Foreign Office and memoranda prepared for ministerial scrutiny which put forward a Foreign Office point of view. Grey had entered the Foreign Office when it was being transformed. The new administrative system resulted in a wider distribution of power among the senior officials. A group of extremely able men had come into the key positions of influence, men who had decided views and were all too anxious to make these views known. The permanent

---

[1] *Ibid.* no. 440.    [2] Hardinge MSS, vol. 69, Goschen to Hardinge, 15 July 1911.
[3] It was commonly thought that Grey's 'influence in all matters of foreign policy was almost unlimited' and his authority 'undisputed'. Prince Lichnowsky, *Heading for the Abyss* (New York, 1928), p. 67.    [4] David Lloyd George, *War Memoirs*, vol. 1, p. 28. See also pp. 50-1.

officials repeatedly tried to strengthen Grey's resolve in the battles with his radical critics. Between 1906 and 1910 Charles Hardinge, the new permanent under-secretary, was the key figure. It was clear from the start that Grey's official relations with Hardinge would not duplicate those of Thomas Sanderson with Salisbury or even with Lord Lansdowne. For Hardinge came to his post with all the advantages of a long career abroad. He was both older and more experienced than his chief. He was on friendly terms with most of his European counterparts and had dealt with some of the key conflicts of the day, both at Teheran and St Petersburgh. He had friends at Whitehall and abroad. The support of Lord Knollys and the King strengthened his position. Spring-Rice, a junior who had served under Hardinge, wrote 'Hardinge himself is not a courtier but is a good business man and perfectly fearless and decided'.[1]

Grey and Hardinge worked well together; their relationship was based on respect and on agreement. Though a commanding figure Hardinge was deeply loyal to his chief. The Permanent Under-Secretary knew that Grey had to face a divided Cabinet and was careful that the rumour-mongers never detected any split at the office. Moreover, Hardinge believed that Grey was steadily growing in stature and in political importance.

I am glad to say that Sir Edward Grey's position has recently become enormously strengthened and I think that no Liberal Party could now do without him. This has had an admirable effect on the confidence which it has given him, and I can assure you that he is worth now a great deal more than he was two years ago, owing to a greater decision of character and naturally to knowledge which he had acquired.[2]

Hardinge distrusted Asquith and had little sympathy with the radical wing of the Liberal party but his loyalty to Grey never wavered.[3] 'Altogether I am not very happy about the state of affairs, as although I am not a radical I am very anxious from a Foreign Office point of view to see the present regime go on as I think Grey's policy is better even than Lansdowne's or anybody else's.'[4]

Grey found Hardinge an invaluable adviser. Particularly in his first years, he leaned heavily on Hardinge's expertise and fully appreciated the acuteness and soundness of the latter's judgements. Hardinge's drafts repeatedly

1 Gwynn, *The Letters and Friendships of Sir Cecil Spring-Rice*, vol. 1, p. 400.
2 Hardinge MSS, vol. 13, Hardinge to Villiers, 19 November 1908.
3 For Hardinge's comment about the 'wildgoose schemes of social reform' and 'wild-cat legislation' see Hardinge MSS, vol. 21, Hardinge to Villiers, 6 January 1910. Hardinge's opinion of Asquith was shared by others at the Foreign Office, including William Tyrrell.
4 FO 800/24, Hardinge to Villiers, 20 February 1908.

became the basis for a key policy decision or important despatch. Though there were some disagreements, a good proportion of these were resolved in Hardinge's favour. In sharp contrast to Sanderson, Hardinge considered it his first duty to give advice and frequently discussed questions of general policy with Grey. The Permanent Under-Secretary's trips with the King to Reval, Ischl, Cronberg and Berlin did more than relieve Grey of an unwelcome burden of ceremony. They often proved to be occasions when the diplomatic climate could be tested or alternative possibilities explored on a semi-official basis. Hardinge's impressions were crucial factors in Grey's subsequent deliberations. The Foreign Secretary never seems to have resented Hardinge's royal friendship and personal intervention in matters of high diplomacy.

Our co-operation in the interests of the Foreign Office was so united and Sir Edward Grey's character was so frank and upright, that he never felt any jealousy of my close political friendship with King Edward . . . Before I left he wrote: 'I am grieved that our time together is over. I can't tell you what a comfort it has been to me in these years to have someone who could be a friend to work with.'[1]

The relationship between Grey and Hardinge was more one of peers than any previous partnership between a foreign secretary and his permanent under-secretary.

The sheer volume of work and the amount of time Grey, unlike Salisbury and Lansdowne, had to spend in the Commons, made it essential for the permanent officials to take a more initiatory role. 'My days are so full when the House of Commons is sitting that I have not written to you as I intended', Grey wrote to Nicolson in April 1907: 'I rely on Hardinge to keep you informed.'[2] The main task of writing to ambassadors and ministers was delegated to Hardinge though Grey supplemented his permanent under-secretary's letters with notes of his own.[3] As Grey explained to Spring-Rice when the latter complained of his isolation at Teheran:

As for the bag I have given up writing at all. This year I have to attend royal dinners and so forth and the result is that I sometimes work until 2 a.m. and begin work again at 7 a.m. My normal day begins at nine and ends at midnight . . . The weekend I spend alone out of London and that keeps me going.[4]

[1] Hardinge, *Old Diplomacy*, p. 192–3.
[2] Nicolson, *Diplomatic Narrative*, vol. I, Grey to Nicolson, 1 April 1907, p. 130.
[3] Some letters to Hardinge were circulated to the Prime Minister and other Cabinet ministers.
[4] FO 800/241, Grey to Spring-Rice, 15 April 1907. Spring-Rice had complained of Hardinge's tone. Grey defended his permanent under-secretary whom he wrote 'hasn't got a gift of circumlocution and I have come to the conclusion that anyone who did would be intolerable in the Foreign Office, there isn't time for it'. Hardinge's peremptory tone also irritated the Germans, particularly the Emperor. DGP XXVII, 791.

After 1906, moreover, the new system clearly concentrated responsibility in the hands of the permanent under-secretary who became the channel for almost all business coming to the foreign secretary. Rather to the annoyance of some members of the Foreign Office, Hardinge made full use of the potential of his position and within a very short time was the master of his domain.[1]

Hardinge's main areas of concern were Germany, Russia and Turkey, all key places of diplomatic activity. Both Grey and Hardinge took up office fearing the future direction of German policy. Both were committed to finding means by which German power could be contained. Thus, in 1905, Grey had urged the editor of the *Westminster Gazette* to combat the idea that a Liberal government would unsettle the understanding with France in order to make up to Germany.[2] Hardinge, too, was convinced that German strength represented a major threat to British security. 'It is generally recognized that Germany is the one disturbing factor owing to her ambitious schemes for a Weltpolitik and for a naval as well as a military supremacy in Europe.'[3] Hardinge rarely wavered in this view though he usually laid more emphasis on the naval threat than on any other aspect of this challenge. The strength of his conviction influenced the already uneasy Grey and gave a distinct focus to British policy.

During the Algeciras Conference, Grey went much further than Lansdowne in committing England to the French entente.[4] Hardinge, too, wished to maintain the entente but was anxious to give British policy greater power and independence by coming to terms with Russia. In the years which followed, Hardinge was more concerned with the line to St Petersburgh than to Paris. Thus, during the conference, he was more willing than either Grey or Bertie to bring pressure on the French and was anxious not to be tied too closely to the Quai d'Orsay.[5] Hardinge saw in a revived Russia the real continental check to German threats though he knew it would take some time for the Russians to build up their resources.

It was, in fact, to achieve an Anglo-Russian understanding that Hardinge

---

[1] FO 800/179, 27 September 1913, memorandum by Bertie. Like Sanderson, Hardinge attended meetings of the Committee of Imperial Defence and chaired one of its most important sub-committees on Neutral and Enemy Merchant Ships. The conclusions of the sub-committee were incorporated in a draft Order-in-Council which was actually used in August 1914. Lord Hankey, *The Supreme Command, 1914–18* (London, 1961), pp. 88–9.

[2] Spender MSS 46389, Grey to Spender, 19 October 1905.

[3] FO 55/3, memorandum by Hardinge, 30 October 1906; See also FO 800/91, Hardinge to Grey, 20 February 1906.

[4] Monger, *The End of Isolation*, pp. 268–80.

[5] BD III, no. 439; Monger, *The End of Isolation*, p. 274.

came back to the Foreign Office in 1906.[1] Apart from his own personal ambitions, he hoped to work closely with Arthur Nicolson, his successor at St Petersburgh, to bring this agreement to fruition. His key role in the creation of the entente was acknowledged by both Grey and Nicolson.[2] His knowledge of Russia and his experience with Russian officials proved invaluable. With Eldon Gorst's assistance, he was able to draft the Persian agreement and convince the India Office, if not the Indian Government, of its necessity.[3] He prodded Count Benckendorff, a frequent visitor to the Foreign Office, to stir the Russians when the talks threatened to lapse.[4] He was responsible for the form of the Afghanistan settlement and he explained to Grey the previous negotiations over the Persian Gulf and the Dardanelles.[5] He sat on the inter-departmental committees dealing with railways in Persia and Turkey and met with the financiers interested in these questions. Repeatedly, when discussions reached an impasse, Hardinge's suggestions for a solution enabled Nicolson to break the deadlock.[6] Late in 1909 Hardinge knew he might become viceroy of India and this gave him a special interest in central Asian problems.[7]

Like Grey, Hardinge fully appreciated the European side of the new agreement and once the entente was concluded became one of its staunchest supporters. The price, politically and diplomatically, was a high one, for the agreement was not popular with the radicals and actual Russian and British interests were far from identical. 'We have no pending questions with Germany except that of naval construction, while our whole future in Asia is bound up with the possibility of maintaining the best and most friendly relations with Russia. We cannot afford to sacrifice in any way our entente with Russia even for the sake of a reduced naval programme.'[8] The need to reduce tensions in the Middle East and the military burden on the Government of India was one reason for the new entente. The wish to check Germany was the other. Hardinge always feared that the Germans would

1 'I have been so imbued with the importance of an agreement with Russia that it was one of the reasons which induced me to give up the embassy at St Petersburgh since I felt that I could do more by impressing my views on people at home, and I promised Lamsdorff and the Emperor that I would do my level best to bring it about.' BD IV, no. 520.
2 Hardinge MSS, vol. 9, Grey to Hardinge, 27 September 1907.
3 BD IV, nos. 370, 389, 411 (additional evidence in nos. 320, 371 and 369).
4 Ibid. nos. 263 and 267.
5 Ibid. nos. 241, 426; FO 371/320/3227, Hardinge to Nicolson, 29 January 1907.
6 Ibid. 371/367/7661, memorandum by Hardinge, minute by Grey, 9 March 1907.
7 Esher, Journals and Letters of Viscount Esher, vol. III, p. 348. Esher claims a decision was still pending in the spring of 1910. Lord Kitchener was the other candidate and had the King's support despite the latter's friendship with Hardinge.
8 Hardinge MSS, vol. 17, Hardinge to Nicolson, 26 March 1909.

either try to destroy the new entente or, worse still, return to the old Bismarckian policy of the Dreikaiserbund. Both he and Nicolson were constantly reassuring the Russians. When Edward VII paid a state visit to Berlin in 1909, Hardinge told the Russian ambassador there was no cause for anxiety. While urging the British financiers to take a share in the Baghdad railway construction, Hardinge insisted that nothing be done without Russian participation as well. Hardinge's solicitude is even more striking when one considers the negotiations in fact taking place between Berlin and St Petersburgh.

Hardinge sought ways to strengthen the new understanding. One attempt at co-operation was in Macedonia where the two powers joined in pressing a reform programme on an unwilling Porte. 'It appears to me that it will probably result in the closing of our ranks, and will cement our agreement with Russia in the same manner as the action of Germany at Algeciras cemented our friendship with France.'[1] For both Grey and Hardinge, co-operation with Russia implied hostility to Germany. Despite a chorus of adverse comment from radical and Labour back-benchers, the Under-Secretary successfully urged Grey to permit the King to meet the Tsar at Reval. At the meeting Hardinge took the occasion not only to discuss the difficult Macedonian reform programme but to make a series of proposals to the Russians for joint action aimed at countering German advances in the Middle East and Balkans.[2]

Despite good intentions, co-operation with the Russians was a difficult task. The Macedonian reform proved to be a nettle and Hardinge was clearly relieved when the Anglo-Russian programme was dropped. There was, moreover, a contradiction between England's new friendship with Russia and her traditional support for an independent Turkey.[3] Hardinge very much wanted to prevent the dismemberment of this tottering empire, an aim which the Russians did not share. The contradictions in Grey's policy at Constantinople and even in the Balkans resulted in part from conflicting loyalties. Hardinge thought the maintenance of the Russian entente the primary goal and he generally pressed in this direction. But particularly in the Balkans the path was not an easy one and the annexation crisis of 1908-9

---

[1] M. B. Cooper, 'British Policy in the Balkans 1908-9', *The Historical Journal* VII (1964-5), 261; Hardinge MSS, vol. 13, Hardinge to de Salis, 29 December 1908.

[2] BD V, no. 195. I have had the advantage of reading Dr F. R. Bridge's unpublished thesis on Anglo-Austrian relations, which deals with Hardinge's and Grey's Balkan and Turkish policy in great detail. F. R. Bridge, 'The Diplomatic Relations between Great Britain and Austria-Hungary, 1906-12', University of London, 1966.

[3] Cooper, 'British Policy in the Balkans 1908-9', *The Historical Journal* VII, 264-70.

illustrated all the difficulties of working with St Petersburgh. Like Grey, Hardinge wanted to support Isvolsky but was equally unwilling to become involved in a Balkan war to satisfy Russian demands.[1] In the end British policy towards the Austro-German alliance appeared more rigid than Russia's and it was to Hardinge's deep annoyance that the Russians gave way completely to the German threat in 1909. Yet the Russian surrender saved both Grey and Hardinge (who had worked up endless proposals to solve the Serbian crisis) from an impossible situation.[2]

Co-operation over the Baghdad railway and in Persia proved to be even more troublesome than a joint policy in the Balkans.[3] 'It is extraordinary how difficult it is to get Russia to work honestly and loyally anywhere; one always had to be continually at them.'[4] Hardinge knew that the Russian entente was not popular; Russian policy in Persia had already created major difficulties for Grey before Hardinge left the Foreign Office. But if one started, as both Grey and Hardinge did, from an assumption of German expansion, it followed that the Russian entente was a necessary part of British policy. Hardinge believed that only the preservation of the entente would thwart German ambitions both in the Middle East and on the continent of Europe. A Germany hemmed in between Russia and France would be in a most unenviable position.

Unlike Nicolson who was strongly Russophile and had little concern with the fate of the Turks, Hardinge realized that there were limits to any agreement with St Petersburgh. Neither he nor Grey thought it desirable to turn the entente into an alliance. The Cabinet difficulties alone were insurmountable:

There is no hope of this while the present government is in office in this country. I am almost certain that certain members of the Cabinet assiduously spread a report that in the event of a general conflagration, England should stand aside; I mention this to show how impossible it is to hope for a step forward by the government to a closer entente or even alliance with Russia ... When Balfour comes into office it may be different, but we must hope that it may not be too late. This is not said in any party spirit as I have none, and I would sooner have Grey as my chief than anybody.[5]

Hardinge was under no illusions: 'If a promise to render material assistance in the event of war were invited by Russia and refused ... it is almost inevitable that Russia would be compelled by her military weakness to come

[1] BD v, no. 441, FO 800/341, Hardinge to Nicolson, 11 November 1908.   [2] BD v, no. 764.
[3] *Ibid.* no. 296, FO 371/374/41546. FO 371/399/4194, 5761 for examples.
[4] Hardinge MSS, vol. 13, Hardinge to Goschen, 30 June 1908.
[5] *Ibid.* vol. 17, Hardinge to Nicolson, 12 April 1909; see also Hardinge to Cartwright, 19 May 1909.

to terms with Germany and to modify her attitude towards the aims of the Central Powers.'[1] If Russia settled with Germany, France too might be forced into the German orbit. French policy during the Bosnian crisis and her successful negotiations with Germany over Morocco confirmed many of Hardinge's fears about the stability of the Anglo-French entente.[2] But it was far better to maintain the ententes, however precarious, than to accept the opposite alternative. An agreement with Berlin 'presented an even more serious and more insidious danger to England that must be carefully watched and avoided'.[3] In the final analysis, Britain might be left isolated and under such conditions her real strength and safeguard lay in her fleet. 'As long as we maintain our undoubted supremacy at sea, we need have no cause for alarm even if we find ourselves once more in a position of complete isolation but supremacy at sea is a condition which must be regarded as an absolute *sine qua non*.[4] Hardinge was one of the first diplomats to identify the naval race as the key factor in the Anglo-German rivalry.

Throughout 1906 and 1907 Hardinge watched the development of the German fleet with alarm. In 1908 both Grey and Hardinge read the detailed reports of the naval and military attachés in Germany who were taking seriously the possibility of a surprise German attack. 'It seems to be hardly credible that the German government can seriously entertain such an idea. My own opinion is that the enormous fleet which the Germans are building is intended rather to exert pressure upon us at a critical moment when we are involved in difficulties elsewhere than for the purpose of invading this country.'[5] Hardinge accepted Tirpitz's risk theory but he drew rather different conclusions than the German admiral hoped. Only an accelerated naval building programme which would clearly demonstrate England's overwhelming superiority would deter Berlin. Commenting on a temporary détente in Anglo-German relations at the end of 1908, Hardinge attributed the change in German attitude to Asquith's pledge to maintain a navy based on a two-power standard. The Permanent Under-Secretary was obviously pleased when Grey made the acceptance of the naval estimates a condition for remaining in the Cabinet in March 1909. Grey was in fundamental agreement with his under-secretary and it is difficult to distinguish between the views of the two men. The eventual triumph of the 'big Navy' group laid some of Hardinge's deepest fears to rest.[6]

[1] BD v, Appendix III.    [2] Hardinge MSS, vol. 17, Hardinge to Cartwright, 26 January 1909.
[3] BD v, Appendix III; BD vi, p. 311.
[4] Hardinge MSS, vol. 17, Hardinge to Bryce, 4 June 1909.
[5] *Ibid.* vol. 13, Hardinge to Goschen, 7 December 1908.
[6] *Ibid.* vol. 18, Hardinge to the King, 31 March 1909.

Hardinge's belief that the fleet was Britain's essential weapon coloured his views of Anglo-German relations. The erratic nature of German diplomacy, accompanied by the German naval building programme, convinced him of the correctness of his judgement. Yet he was not an extremist; he did not oppose a détente in Anglo-German relations which might lead to a solution of the naval problem. After the Algeciras Conference, Hardinge persuaded a reluctant Grey to permit a meeting between the King and the Kaiser at Cronberg. Hardinge not only accompanied the King but was hopeful that the Germans might renounce their idea of driving a wedge into the entente.[1] The discussions with the Kaiser were discouraging, to say the least, but this and other demonstrations of friendship worried the extreme opponents of any rapprochement—Bertie in Paris, Mallet and Crowe in London. Bertie and Mallet, in particular, viewed Hardinge's modest efforts with alarm.[2] Such fears were exaggerated. Hardinge disliked Haldane's visit to Germany and Haldane later lectured the Permanent Under-Secretary on his anti-German prejudices.[3] It was Hardinge, backed by Grey, who vetoed the rather harmless royal suggestion that the band of the Coldstream Guards be sent to Germany because it had not gone to France.[4] Such petty issues show the quality of Anglo-German relations.

Hardinge again intervened in 1907 so that Edward VII could invite the Kaiser to Windsor.[5] Hardinge thought this might reduce German ill-will while the Anglo-Russian talks were proceeding. But, like Grey, he was extremely nervous about the French reaction to the Kaiser's visit. He did not want the Kaiser to bring Count Bülow with him and was constantly checking the attempts of Sir Frank Lascelles, the British ambassador at Berlin, who was trying to lay the basis for a real understanding.[6]

The fight over the naval estimates and the increasing public alarm over the German navy made it clear that the state of tension between the two countries might well lead to disaster. The subject of British participation in the Baghdad railway was opened again and the possibility of an agreement canvassed in both countries during the first half of 1909.[7] Prodded by the Cabinet, Grey and Hardinge felt they must at least explore the German feelers. If the Germans modified their naval building programme, England would consider some kind of political arrangement. Von Schoen, the German

---

[1] FO 371–79, minute by Hardinge, 5 September 1906, quoted in Monger, *The End of Isolation*, p. 303.
[2] Bertie MSS, series A, Bertie to Mallet, 25 August 1906.
[3] FO 800/13, Haldane to Lascelles, 8 September 1906.
[4] Hardinge, *Old Diplomacy*, p. 180. Information in FO 371/262/33356.      [5] BD VI, no. 44.
[6] *Ibid.* no. 88; FO 371/261, minute by Hardinge, 19 June 1907      [7] BD VI, no. 308.

Minister for Foreign Affairs, made a proposal early in May and the German Chancellor initiated negotiations on 21 August.[1] Hardinge prepared the key memoranda which became the basis for the ensuing discussions. Grey was not without hope but neither man was sanguine. As he had in the past, Hardinge underlined the overriding importance of a naval understanding if the tensions between the two countries were to be resolved. He drafted for Grey's consideration a political formula which might be acceptable to Germany without irrevocably binding the hands of England.[2] Hardinge's draft agreement, as well as his subsequent minutes, indicate that he remained sceptical of a successful outcome. But his modest tone contrasts sharply with the far more hostile view of Louis Mallet, who feared both German trickery and a negative Russian reaction.[3]

When the detailed German offer was received in October 1909, it was apparent that the Germans, at best, would only accept a reduction in their rate of shipbuilding.[4] Hardinge found this offer unacceptable and referred to an earlier memorandum (May 1909) in which, while discussing Anglo-Russian relations, he had argued persuasively for an all-powerful fleet and had warned against any political agreement which might compromise relations with Paris and St Petersburgh.[5] Hardinge was obviously relieved when the question was postponed until after the election.

The German Chancellor is no doubt sincere in his professions of his desire for friendship, but his aim is to secure a political agreement entailing the neutralization of England in schemes where England blocks the way, and as an inducement or bribe, he makes to England a proposal which is neither one of disarmament nor even of limitation of armaments within the enormous programme already laid down by the German naval law.[6]

For political as well as diplomatic reasons, the door was kept open but Grey and Hardinge undoubtedly shared Eyre Crowe's pessimistic appraisal of the chances for success.[7] Hardinge never abandoned his belief that if the German fleet 'were strong enough to challenge us, we should be continually having to choose between war and diplomatic humiliation'.[8]

Hardinge did not leave London until the autumn of 1910; during the first half of the year he continued to take an active part in Foreign Office business. With a naval agreement ruled out, various other formulas for co-operation

[1] BD VI, nos. 179, 186. See Grey's comment in FO 800/91, Grey to Hardinge, 6 August 1909, that the situation was not hopeless.
[2] BD VI, no. 190.     [3] *Ibid.* no. 191.     [4] *Ibid.* no. 200.
[5] *Ibid.* minute by Hardinge, pp. 310–12.     [6] *Ibid.* p. 312.
[7] *Ibid.* nos. 207, 208, minutes by Crowe.
[8] Hardinge MSS, vol. 21, Hardinge to Cartwright, 11 January 1910.

were investigated. At the same time, Hardinge pressed for alternative policies which would serve to check German advances in central Asia. The British tried to secure new railway concessions from the Turks and Hardinge urged Grey to bring pressure on the Persian Government to refuse German demands for economic concessions in the south and Persian Gulf areas.[1] The Germans, for their part, still looked for a political agreement; this time the unsuccessful bait was the Baghdad railway consortium. The conversations continued only because neither the Turks nor the Persians proved amenable to British demands and because one wing of the Liberal Cabinet, antagonistic to the Russian partnership, thought a German agreement highly desirable.

Hardinge was more than an anti-German Sanderson. He had considerably expanded the advisory functions of his office. His successor, however, was Arthur Nicolson, a good diplomat but a poor choice for the chief Foreign Office position. Hardinge welcomed Nicolson's appointment.

The Germans have already sedulously disseminated stories of Nicolson's hostility to Berlin and Austria. Metternich, who has been in Berlin, even complained to Goschen ... this did not surprise me when I heard it as Metternich actually made a complaint on my own appointment to the Foreign Office five years ago ... Nicolson's only fault is that he has been pro-British, and not pro-German or anything else.[2]

'I fully believe', Hardinge wrote to his successor, 'in the theory of Germany's intention, if possible, to dominate Europe to which we are the only stumbling block.'[3] To counteract this, 'the only thing we can do is to go on building, and to make our position so absolutely secure that no sane man could ever dream that he would gain an advantage by attacking us'.[4]

As was customary, Grey gave Hardinge a free hand in dealing with purely administrative matters and the latter's appointments strengthened the anti-German tone at Whitehall. During 1907 Hardinge recommended Louis Mallet to Grey as private secretary.[5] When Eldon Gorst (one of those strange, brilliant Foreign Office figures who never found his right place either in London or in Egypt) left to take Cromer's place in Cairo, Mallet, again due to Hardinge's intervention, replaced him as assistant

[1] BD VI, nos. 318 344 351.
[2] Hardinge MSS, vol. 21, Hardinge to Cartwright, 28 June 1910; also Hardinge to Lister, 21 June 1910; Hardinge to Goschen, 28 June 1910. Nicolson's appointment had been quickly arranged to avoid outside intervention. FO 800/92, Hardinge to Grey, 11 June 1910.
[3] FO 800/92, Hardinge to Nicolson, 29 March 1911.
[4] Hardinge MSS, vol. 21, Hardinge to Bertie, 1 April 1910.
[5] Monger, *The End of Isolation*, p. 265

under-secretary. William Tyrrell, Grey's précis writer, who shared Hardinge's fears about German intentions, and was one of Hardinge's protégés,
took Mallet's place. G. S. Spicer, Hardinge's secretary, was also an active
member of the anti-German wing, as was C. H. Montgomery. In the
Diplomatic Service, too, Hardinge played an important role in determining
senior appointments. His special friendship with the King gave him a unique
influence; ambassadorial appointments were one of the few questions in which
the royal prerogative was still exercised. Lascelles was due for retirement
and Hardinge discussed with both the King and Grey his possible replacement. Though he favoured Cartwright (whom the Germans vetoed and who
went to Vienna), Goschen was also acceptable.[1] The Permanent Under-
Secretary was less impressed by Ralph Paget who went to the Court of
Bavaria at Munich and whose reports were less hostile than those of his predecessors. Paget was sent to Belgrade in 1910 and not brought back to
the Foreign Office until 1913 when Hardinge was in India. It was on
Hardinge's suggestion that Gerard Lowther was sent as ambassador to
Turkey, though he had subsequent doubts about the wisdom of his choice.[2]
When, on the other hand, the King pressed Hardinge to take the ambassador-
ship in Washington, Hardinge refused and the matter was dropped.[3]

Hardinge's correspondence abroad was extensive; he wrote and received
lengthy explanations of policy. Often he acted as a channel of communication between diplomats; for instance between Nicolson in Russia, Lowther at
Constantinople and Marling, the chargé d'affaires, at Teheran. Hardinge's
letters were far more frequent and contained detailed analyses of policy
which contrast sharply with the short notes sent by Sanderson. He expressed
views, moreover, which Sanderson would never have committed to paper.

Had Hardinge replaced Bertie as the 'real power' at the Foreign Office?[4]
In the *Review of Reviews* W. T. Stead, provoked by the failure of the Hague
Peace Conference, launched a full-dress attack on Hardinge, that 'Tchinov-
nik[5] of the Foreign Office' who 'at the intrusion of the fresh air of popular

1 Hardinge MSS, vol. 14, Hardinge to the King, 7 May 1908. Spring-Rice and de Bunsen were also
considered but were vetoed by Count Metternich, the German ambassador in London. 'Bülow
now regrets exceedingly that Nicolson could not have been sent. Ye Gods—When I remember
the language applied to him after Algeciras.' FO 800/241, Tyrrell to Spring-Rice, 16 July 1908.
2 Hardinge MSS, vol. 21, Hardinge to Lowther, 19 April 1910.
3 Hardinge, *Old Diplomacy*, p. 130–2. Hardinge MSS, vol. 9, King to Campbell-Bannerman, 23
November 1906. Hardinge recommended Lord Bryce for the post after Cabinet consultation.
4 For this view see Wilhelm Gall, *Sir Charles Hardinge und die englische Vorkriegspolitik, 1903–10*
(Berlin, 1939). For a similar contemporary comment see E. D. Morel's observation, 'The Hardinge crowd and I are fighting one another for the possession of Grey's mind.' W. R. Louis and
J. Stengers, *E. D. Morel's History of the Congo*, p. 218.
5 Tchinovnik = civil servant—bureaucrat.

aspiration into the musty and mouldy recesses of his lair, muttered through his teeth "I'll see them d--d first". And he was as good as his word.'[1] Stead contended that Grey had yielded too much power to his subordinate and that Hardinge had torpedoed the policies of the Liberal Government.

To conclude: Sir Edward Grey has now had a bitter lesson as to the consequences of acquiescing in the usurpation of the Tchinovnik. It is for him to justify the confidence which his country reposes in him to make himself master in his own house. A self-effacing modesty, a beautiful humility are admirable virtues in private life. They are out of place in the head of the Foreign Office. The task before him is simple and clear. The Tchinovnik is a good servant, but an abominable master. Let him reform the Foreign Office from roof to basement. Let him purge the diplomatic service from all the antiquated fossils and reactionary survivals from the Jingo epoch. And above all, let the country and foreign nations understand that Sir Edward Grey is master in his own office, and not Sir Charles Hardinge.[2]

Stead's attack oversimplified a complex personal relationship. Hardinge was not Grey's master but his partner. A genuine concordance of views, particularly in the vital matter of Anglo-German relations, bound them close. Without such concordance, neither Hardinge's strong personality nor the changing character of the Foreign Office itself could have prevailed. Because of this concordance Hardinge played a part such as no permanent official had played before.

Hardinge's colleagues and subordinates shared his views. Thus Grey received a continuous stream of minutes and memoranda all based on a suspicious if not hostile interpretation of German motives. The Crowe–Hardinge reforms had encouraged officials to record their opinions. Louis Mallet, William Tyrrell, G. S. Spicer, C. H. Mongomery, G. H. Villiers and the foremost German expert in the Foreign Office, Eyre Crowe, all argued in similar vein. Even Walter Langley and Francis Campbell, under-secretaries who had served many years under Salisbury, had become convinced that German hostility would be a perennial fact of diplomatic life and that the growth of the German fleet constituted a major threat to British power. Only Lord Edmond Fitzmaurice, the parliamentary under-secretary (1905–8), stood out firmly against this 'anti-German current in the Office'. As will be shown in greater detail, Fitzmaurice's sympathetic letters to Lascelles in Berlin underline his relative impotence and the isolation of the two men. On the whole, diplomatists in the major European embassies shared the fears of the London group. Lascelles was the exception and he was read critically. A few men like Cecil Spring-Rice in Persia, who had

[1] *Review of Reviews*, December 1909, p. 567.     [2] *Ibid.* p. 575.

to work closely with the Russians were more often irritated by St Petersburgh than by Berlin. This ultimately made Spring-Rice even more anti-German; if there had been no German menace, there would have been no Russian agreement.[1] The anti-Germans did not constitute a formal group. There were variations in their views and different degrees of intimacy between the men concerned. The impression of an organized lobby led by Charles Hardinge pressing the Foreign Secretary in an anti-German direction is a misreading after the fact.

In terms of Anglo-German relations Louis Mallet, the most avid anti-German at the office, was most influential during the first Moroccan crisis when, as Grey's private secretary, he did eveything possible to strengthen the Foreign Secretary's determination to support France.[2] He not only tried to block Haldane's visit to Berlin in the summer of 1906 but was deeply irritated by Hardinge's rather mild efforts to create a better atmosphere at Cronberg.[3] When Crowe's memorandum on German policy was circulated early in 1907, Mallet added further illustrations of German perfidy.[4]

In December 1907 he wrote William Tyrrell about the German-proposed North Sea agreement.[5] 'I am nervous about this German proposal and think that we ought to tell Cambon at once in confidence . . . The whole idea is a farce.'[6] Mallet was similarly worried about Russian reactions to the Anglo-German talks of 1909. On 26 August he warned Grey: 'If we fall into the trap the entente with Russia would at once fall to the ground, a great revivement of feeling would take place and the policy of the last few years would go by the board.'[7] On both occasions Grey followed Mallet's advice and the entente power was informed of the negotiations. Mallet both opposed a general political arrangement with Berlin and negatively minuted suggestions for more limited bargains in the Middle East.[8]

Nevertheless, Mallet's influence on major policy issues began to decline when he became assistant under-secretary in 1909. As head of the Eastern Department, Mallet was almost totally absorbed in the extremely difficult

[1] Gwynn, *Letters and Friendships of Sir Cecil Spring-Rice*, vol. II, pp. 101–2.
[2] Monger, *The End of Isolation*, pp. 270–1, 276. Z. Steiner, 'The Last Years of the Old Foreign Office', *The Historical Journal* VI (1963) 84.
[3] Monger, *The End of Isolation*, p. 303.  [4] BD III, Appendix B, enclosure 2.
[5] The North Sea agreement was a convention concluded between Germany, Denmark, France, the Netherlands, Sweden and Great Britain providing for the maintenance of the *status quo* on the shores of the North Sea and for the consultation between the signatories in case the *status quo* was threatened. It paralleled one for the Baltic Sea signed by Germany, Russia, Sweden and Denmark at the same time, 23 April 1908.
[6] FO 800/92, Mallet to Tyrrell, December 1907; Tyrrell to Grey, 5 December 1907.
[7] *Ibid.* Mallet to Grey, 26 August 1909; BD VI, no. 191.
[8] FO 800/92, 17 March 1910; BD VI, nos. 267, 342.

technical problems connected with Turkey, the Balkans and Persia. A large proportion of his time was taken up with such questions as Macedonian reforms, concessions in Mesopotamia, the Turko-Persian frontier and relations with the Emir of Afghanistan.[1] In both Balkan and Turkish matters, he did the same kind of work Villiers did in the Lansdowne period. In the absence of any monographic study of Grey's policy towards Turkey and the Balkans, one cannot adequately assess Mallet's role. But my impression is that he played an important part in daily decision-making where the issues were often so complex that Grey was forced to accept his proposals. It is perfectly clear that Mallet and Hardinge worked closely together and repeatedly hammered out the line which Grey followed. Mallet was often irritated by Russian behaviour but, driven by his fears of Germany, remained loyal to the policy of the ententes.

Even after Hardinge left the Foreign Office, Mallet's fears about German ambitions did not abate and he watched the successive attempts at an agreement and the growing German role in the Middle East with deep apprehension. Yet from 1912 onwards, when Balkan questions again came to the forefront of European diplomacy, Mallet's major concern became the preservation of the decaying Ottoman Empire. He knew that the Balkans represented the weak link in the entente system and that the British public would not support Russia in a Balkan war.[2] As Britain seemed unable to re-establish her position at the Sultan's court, Mallet pressed for a joint policy with all the other interested powers. After the outbreak of the Italian-Turkish War, Mallet feared the worst; his only hope was a rapprochement between Turkey and the Balkan states which 'would relieve us of any difficulties which might arise with Russia, if she pursued a policy hostile to Turkey'.[3] Such hopes proved futile and the Balkan states secured their independence leaving a stripped and vulnerable Turkey. In the negotiations which followed the Balkan Wars, Mallet tended to be more pro-Turk than Nicolson for he felt it was more important to preserve what was left of the Ottoman Empire than to further conciliate Russia.[4] In fact, though critical of British policy at Constantinople, Mallet offered few practical alternatives. In June 1913, when the Turks again approached Britain for an alliance, Mallet summed up the situation for the Foreign Secretary in a general memorandum.[5] A division of Asiatic Turkey would negatively affect Britain's European and imperial

[1] Evidence in FO 371/374/41204, 41016, 41209; FO 371/804/4708, 9578.
[2] BD IX(I), no. 355.  [3] Ibid. no. 383.
[4] See, for instance, Mallet's view of the Anglo-Russian clash on an Armenian reform programme. BD X(I), nos. 534, 535, 542, minutes by Mallet; see p. 135 n. 3.
[5] BD X(I), Appendix, pp. 901–2. A first approach had been made in 1911.

position and might bring about a European war. An alliance with Turkey or even an agreement between Turkey and the Triple Entente would be viewed by the Germans as a direct challenge. A purely negative attitude would throw Turkey into the arms of an eager Triple Alliance. Mallet's ultimate suggestion was a joint declaration by all the powers 'to respect the independence and integrity of the present Turkish dominion, which might go as far as neutralization, and by participation by all the Great Powers in financial control and the application of reforms'.[1] But the concert of powers consisted of states with opposing aims and right up to the outbreak of war British policy was vacillatory and indecisive.

Though a study of the Eastern question will show, I think, the importance of Mallet's contribution, he was not as close to Grey as his supporters had hoped. In the spring of 1913 the Foreign Secretary had decided to remove Lowther from the embassy at Constantinople and Mallet was sent to replace him.[2]

I have felt, ever since you left, that the chances of my succeeding Nicolson were not very secure. Tyrrell never really accepted the solution, or rather he accepted it because it seemed in the circumstances to be inevitable; and Crowe naturally thought himself the better candidate. Still, I do not know who is the chosen candidate ... However, it will no doubt be very interesting, and I am heartily sick of being an Assistant Under Secretary, especially under Nicolson with whom, however, my personal relations are excellent.[3]

There is little question that Mallet's ambassadorship (which came as a total surprise to the assistant under-secretary) was a 'second prize'. Nicolson had already written to Hardinge '. . . after two and a half years watching Mallet's work, I feel sure that Crowe would be far better as head of this office when I leave. It would be awkward to pass over Mallet and perhaps an Embassy might tempt him.'[4] Mallet was not to have an easy time in Turkey, though the difficulties were not of his own making and Grey loyally defended him both in 1914 and later in his autobiography.[5]

The remaining assistant under-secretaries confined their activities to their own departments. They expressed themselves more frequently and with

[1] BD x(1), Appendix, p. 902.
[2] FO 800/365, Grey to Nicolson, 12 April 1913. Grey admitted that Lowther had been asked to make bricks from straw and that he (Grey) had made many mistakes but clearly felt that Lowther was inadequate for the task. Hardinge MSS, vol. 93, Chirol to Hardinge, 2 June 1913. 'I think the appointment [Mallet's] may turn out a good one in itself. But there is the danger of his being as jumpy as Lowther was phlegmatic.'
[3] Hardinge MSS, vol. 93, Mallet to Hardinge, 11 August 1913.
[4] *Ibid.* Nicolson to Hardinge, 21 May 1913.
[5] Grey, *Twenty-Five Years*, vol. II, pp. 174–5.

more freedom than had Lansdowne's assistants but they do not afford the same striking contrast as between Hardinge and Sanderson. Eric Barrington was an official of the old school and his appointment as assistant under-secretary was a short one just prior to his retirement.[1] Eldon Gorst served at the Foreign Office for only a brief period. As supervising under-secretary of the Eastern Department, he quickly mastered many of the details needed during the course of the Anglo-Russian negotiations and his minutes suggest that here was a first-class mind at work.[2] But Gorst was entirely absorbed in the concerns of his department and seems to have had little contact with Grey before his departure for Egypt. Francis Campbell was the Foreign Office expert on Asiatic affairs and he ran the China Department with a minimum of interference. When major issues arose, Grey was, of course, consulted but on a whole range of minor, daily business, Campbell settled matters directly with the minister or ambassador concerned. Thus, he and John Jordan (Satow's successor at Peking) handled a wide range of local Chinese problems, concessions, customs officials, railway-line disputes without any further reference to Hardinge or Grey.[3] Campbell's independence was not only due to his expertise but to the secondary importance of Chinese affairs in the early part of this period. It was when commercial rivalries became involved with great power politics that Grey intervened; Japanese, American and Russian interests in China had to be considered in terms of England's ties to these nations and Britain's China policy could not be dictated by commercial interests alone.[4] Campbell did not leave many memoranda or minutes on general foreign policy issues. He shared the general pessimism about Anglo-German relations though his appraisal was a balanced one. 'We are not liked in Germany and there it is', he commented on a despatch in 1907.[5]

Walter Langley, an assistant under-secretary from 1907 until 1918, was primarily concerned with the Western Department though he occasionally substituted for Campbell and took over the China Department after Campbell's death in 1911. Assisted by Crowe, he handled the many disputes with France (Newfoundland fishing rights, Madagascar, etc.).[6] With regard to Germany, he usually deferred to Crowe and the brevity of his minutes

[1] Barrington supervised the Western and African Departments, but wrote very few minutes.
[2] FO 371/369/6339, 7661; FO 371/3627, 3628; 371/389/15761, 6339, 7661.
[3] FO 371/356/4, the whole volume is relevant.
[4] E. W. Edwards, 'Great Britain and the Manchurian Railways Question 1909–10', *The English Historical Review* LXXXI (1966), 740–89.
[5] FO 371/262/30724, minute by Campbell, 26 August 1907.
[6] FO 371/666/37887, minute by Langley, 13 October 1909.

provide a striking contrast to the detailed analyses of his junior. 'The naval question dominates the situation', he wrote, 'and Germany alone can provide a remedy.'[1]

The parliamentary under-secretary, Lord Edmond Fitzmaurice, was the one Foreign Office official who actively opposed the anti-German line of his colleagues. Fitzmaurice, who was Lansdowne's brother, was returning to the Foreign Office for a second time and was an acknowledged expert on Middle Eastern and Balkan problems. Unlike Grey, he retained an almost instinctive distrust of Russian policy in these areas and feared that the British would rely too heavily on the Russian agreement to the detriment of its relations with Germany.[2] Not only did he believe that the Russians would prove unable to control her agents in Persia but thought that the new Persian agreement would weaken England's position in the Gulf and alienate Mohammedan support in India. His anti-Russian views reflected an earlier era in British foreign policy as did his attempts to cultivate good relations with Berlin. Fitzmaurice had been distressed by the military conversations of January 1906; he warmly supported Haldane's visit to Germany in the summer and hoped that Grey would personally visit Berlin to reduce the existing tension. But Fitzmaurice, like his friend Lascelles, had little influence on Grey and it was through Lord Ripon, a close friend, that the parliamentary under-secretary reached Cabinet circles. Fitzmaurice had been born in 1846; he was reaching the end of his long career and was anxious to enter the Cabinet before retirement. In October 1908 he was made Chancellor of the Duchy of Lancaster and left the Foreign Office. Neither Thomas Mackinnon Wood nor Francis Dyke Acland, Fitzmaurice's successors, seem to have made any major impact on Grey's diplomacy.

Apart from Hardinge, two men in Grey's Foreign Office rose to positions of national prominence. Eyre Crowe and William Tyrrell were 'a fruitful and harmonious combination of opposites'. Lord Strang who worked with both men writes:

Crowe was forthright where Tyrrell was devious. Crowe was a bureaucrat, a skilful and luminous draughtsman, a creator and a powerful operator of the official machine. Tyrrell disliked putting pen to paper. He preferred to work by word of mouth, to be the astute and sagacious adviser behind the scenes, and as such I do not think he has ever been rivalled. Where Crowe would fearlessly confront a situation, Tyrrell would take avoiding action and let the thing blow itself out.[3]

[1] BD VI, no. 183.
[2] Lascelles MSS, vol. III, pt 5. Fitzmaurice to Lascelles, 31 May 1906, 21 September 1906; Monger, *The End of Isolation*, pp. 260, 290.
[3] Lord Strang, *Home and Abroad* (London, 1956), p. 308.

Harold Nicolson, in an acute double-portrait, makes another disti nction. 'Eyre Crowe was the perfect type of British Civil Servant—industrious, loyal, expert, accurate, beloved, obedient and courageous. Sir William Tyrrell, who was inspired by a deep personal devotion to Sir Edward Grey, concentrated his efforts on sparing his chief all unnecessary complications and worries.'[1] Crowe disliked and distrusted outsiders (even those from other government departments) and considered them intruders in a highly skilled craft. He had 'an unfortunate habit of indicating to the Foreign Secretary, and his colleagues in the Cabinet, that they were not only ill-informed but also weak and silly'.[2] Tyrrell was more eclectic; he enjoyed a wide circle of acquaintances, cultivated the press and enjoyed gossiping. 'Crowe supplied the industry', Vansittart recalled, 'and Tyrrell the flair.'[3] It is curious that these two men, one a passionate agnostic and the other a Catholic, should have been good friends though there were moments when their partnership was somewhat strained. Under Grey, they were rightly placed, Crowe as senior clerk and then assistant under-secretary, Tyrrell as Grey's private secretary from 1908 until 1915.

The life of Eyre Crowe provides material for a fascinating biography.[4] There was nothing conventional about this vivid figure. He was the third son of Sir Joseph Crowe and Asta, daughter of Gustav von Barby and Eveline von Ribbentrop. His father began as a journalist, joined the consular service and ended his life as commercial attaché for all of Europe (1882–96). In addition to these duties, Joseph Crowe had time to become one of the major art critics of his day, and his books were accepted as standard texts. The young Crowe was born in Leipzig and was educated both in Germany and in France. He did not come to England until 1881 when at the age of seventeen he went to live with the family of Colonel Lawrence at Wimbledon in order to cram for his Foreign Office examination. From the start of his career, Crowe never conformed in manner, dress or interests. For ten years (1885–95) he was resident clerk at the Foreign Office where, in addition to the usual routine business, he read all despatches entering or leaving the department and explored the past records of British foreign policy. In his spare time he made an intensive study of modern European history, and hence entered his career with an amazingly wide and deep knowledge of diplomacy. Throughout his life Crowe was an avid reader not only in the field of history

[1] Nicolson, *Lord Carnock*, p. 327.
[2] *Ibid*. pp. 327–8.
[3] Vansittart, *The Mist Procession*, p. 193.
[4] For the best sketch of Crowe, see R. Butler, 'Beside the Point', *World Review*, pp. 8–13.

but in economics (the whole of *Das Kapital*), philosophy (including Wittgenstein), the classics and contemporary fiction. His annual bibliographies of reading completed are astonishing in their range of subject and language.[1] Crowe was fluent in both French and German; some contemporaries claim that when he was angry he even spoke English with German guttural sounds. His special language facility was to prove of the greatest use both before the Hague Tribunal in 1911 and in Paris at the Peace Conference.

Crowe had little patience with the snobberies and social preoccupations of many of his contemporaries. He had two diversions: he played the piano exceedingly well and composed for that instrument, and he had an absorbing interest in military tactics, a passion shared with his brother-in-law, Spencer Wilkinson.[2] It was typical of this strange but engaging figure that he should become a lieutenant in the First Volunteer Battalion of the City of London Fusiliers, a battalion without any social pretences. He subsequently volunteered for active service in the Boer War but failed to pass the medical examination.

Contemporary sketches of Crowe make intriguing reading. Some stress Crowe's driving energy and bureaucratic pedantry. J. D. Gregory writes, 'Crowe was nothing if not violent . . . His mentality, his culture, his outlook, were to some extent Germanic; his methods often enough entirely Prussian.'[3] Yet Crowe seems to have been a man of great personal charm who despite his intellectual intensity was deeply sensitive to the feeling of others.[4] Harold Nicolson, in another brilliant description of Crowe, recalls

Immediate to me and incessantly controlling, this man of extreme violence and extreme gentleness almost became an obsession. He was so human. He was so superhuman. At one moment we would observe with alarm his outrageous insolence in face of M. Clemenceau or some other bully. 'Crowe', said Clemenceau (who had an eye for value), 'c'est un homme à part.' At the next moment one would observe his immense solicitude towards a typist who had a cold in her head. It is difficult to speak of Crowe without lapsing into the soft ground of sentimentality. Yet here, if ever, was a man of truth and vigour.[5]

Most of the reminiscences about Crowe are written in this tone. He was obviously a man who provoked strong feelings and images; at the Foreign

---

[1] I am indebted to Miss Sybil E. Crowe for this information and for permission to use Crowe's annual reading lists.

[2] H. Spenser Wilkinson, *Thirty-Five Years, 1874–1909* (London, 1933), p. 221. Wilkinson, a well-known military expert and great supporter of the Volunteer system, became the first professor of military history at Oxford in 1909. He was also a leader writer for the *Morning Post*.

[3] Gregory, *On the Edge of Diplomacy*, p. 260.

[4] Lord Strang, in a personal letter, recalled that even when Crowe was permanent under-secretary he took an interest in the junior members of the office and that he was always 'deeply kind'.

[5] Sir Harold Nicolson, *Peacemaking, 1919* (London 1933), pp. 210–11.

Office in particular he aroused deep loyalties and left indelible impressions.

The young Crowe made his mark very early. First in the Consular and then in the African Department, he rapidly acquired a reputation for brilliance and industry, a combination rare enough to be noticed. Even as a lowly junior, he had made suggestions for improving the clerical system at the office and though still only an assistant clerk was asked to join the group preparing the reform of the Foreign Office. Crowe's role in the reforms of 1905–6 have already been discussed; the successful introduction of the Registry system further enhanced his reputation and he was soon mentioned as a possible candidate for the post of permanent under-secretary.

But Crowe was much more than a first-rate administrator, he rapidly became the Foreign Office's chief authority on German problems. In 1906 he was made senior clerk and became the supervising head of the Western Department. Here, he was in an excellent position to follow and influence the course of Anglo-German relations. There were sound reasons, quite apart from the obvious ones, why he spoke with authority and was assured of a sympathetic hearing. He maintained his continental connections and spent his holidays either at his father's home in Paris or at Baden where his uncle, Professor Carl Gerhardt, a distinguished surgeon, was the centre of an impressive scientific circle. At Baden he met and married Clema von Bonin who was related to many key figures in the German establishment. Crowe knew and corresponded with Admiral von Holtzendorff, the commander of the German High Sea Fleet (1909–13) and one of Admiral Tirpitz's life-long critics; Captain Siegal, the German naval attaché in Paris and an important writer on German naval tactics was his brother-in-law.[1]

'My impression, gained from much personal intercourse with Germans of all classes', Crowe wrote in a minute, 'and from the study of German periodicals and literature, is that the necessity of an all powerful navy has become an act of faith with the whole mass of the German population including a large number of socialists.'[2] Crowe's interest in military matters led him to read and comment on almost all the reports of the service attachés in Germany. There is hardly one of these despatches which escaped Crowe's amplifications or corrections and his comments were read with interest and approval by both Hardinge and Grey.[3] Crowe's grasp of such issues made

[1] FO 371/463/39194, minute by Crowe, 24 January 1908; BD VI, no. 75.
[2] FO 371/457, minute by Crowe, 13 January 1908.
[3] BD VI, nos. 80, 81, 94. See Crowe's perceptive minute on the future military potential of 'flying machines'. FO 371/252, minute by Crowe, 4 February 1907. Crowe was also a member of Hardinge's Committee on Neutral and Enemy Merchant Ships. Hankey, *The Supreme Command*, vol. I, p. 88.

him a useful delegate both at the Hague Peace Conference and at the London Naval Conference of 1908 where the abortive Declaration of London was drafted.

No one who goes through the Foreign Office papers can fail to be struck by Crowe's industry. There is hardly a major despatch on any German question which does not carry one of his minutes and many French despatches contain briefer but equally penetrating comments by the senior clerk. His minutes were formidable pieces of writing, always clear and to the point. His memoranda, too, combined historical analyses with precise advice as to the course to be followed. Crowe 'concentrated his energies upon penetrating the matter in hand without regard to collateral contingencies'. These papers were read by Grey and a large number were circulated to the Cabinet and Committee of Imperial Defence. Apart from earlier heads of the African Department, Crowe was probably the first senior clerk to be active at this level of policy-making.

Crowe's views about Germany can be traced back to his childhood. His father had little use for William II and there must have been much discussion about the death of German liberalism in the Crowe household. On the other hand, Crowe was brought up to appreciate fully the enormous talents and capabilities of the Germans and he never underestimated the importance of the German contribution to many parts of European life. Crowe's admiration and fears are both reflected in his 'Memorandum on the present state of British relations with France and Germany', perhaps the only Foreign Office memorandum to have become a classic state paper.[1] After reviewing the events which led up to the creation of the Anglo-French entente, Crowe denied that it was an offensive combination aimed at Berlin. But it could have been predicted that the Germans would view such an understanding in these hostile terms as they would any similar Anglo-Russian bargain. For it had always been one of Bismarck's basic principles to preserve the preponderant position of Germany on the European continent by promoting antagonism between all third powers. Crowe pointed out that the Moroccan crisis resulted from a German effort to destroy the new en-

---

[1] BD III, Appendix A. Despite the historical importance of the memorandum, contemporaries did not consider it epoch-making. Grey showed it to the Prime Minister, to Ripon, to Asquith, Morley and Haldane but his own comments are low toned and Hirst, in his introduction to John Morley's *Memorandum on Resignation August 1914* (London, 1928), p. xvii, suggests that neither Morley nor Loreburn paid much attention to it. My own researches suggest that it was probably seen by Hardinge, Mallet, Tyrrell, Nicolson, Bertie and Cartwright but some of the evidence is indirect. See R. Cosgrove, 'Sir Eyre Crowe and the English Foreign Office, 1905–14', Ph.D. thesis, University of California, June 1967, for information on this point and for modern commentaries on the memorandum.

tente, an attempt which failed because of inept German statesmanship. But the deeper and more important question was whether this quarrel was an 'ephemeral incident or a symptomatic revelation of some deep-seated natural opposition between the policies and interests' of Germany and Great Britain.[1]

Crowe clearly defined England's basic interests. 'The general character of England's foreign policy is determined by the immutable conditions of her geographical situation on the ocean flank of Europe as an island State with vast overseas colonies and dependencies whose existence and survival as an independent community are inseparably bound up with the possession of preponderant sea power.'[2] Britain's naval domain had been tolerated because she had always attempted to preserve the independence of other nations and their rights to free trade and intercourse. If the independence of such states was challenged by the temporary political domination of a single power, it was almost a law of nature that Britain should oppose the aggressor. Like Sir Edward Grey, Crowe thought almost exclusively in terms of the balance of power and saw in England the policeman of Europe, a moral force among the European nations.

Was Germany 'aiming at a political hegemony with the object of promoting purely German schemes of expansion and establishing a German primacy in the world of international politics at the cost and to the detriment of other nations'?[3] To answer this question, Crowe reviewed the history of the rise of Prussia and Germany stressing the key role played by 'blood and iron'. He went on to argue that once Germany had become a great European power it was natural that she should want to become a 'World Power' with her 'own place in the sun'. Crowe claimed that the dream of a colonial empire had taken a deep hold on the German imagination and that this must be accepted as a fact of political life. Germany would expand but would this expansion be peaceful or would it upset the existing balance of power so essential to England's security?

The history of Anglo-German relations between 1884 and 1904 did not encourage an optimistic answer. In the long list of disputes which Crowe analysed, he found that German policy was dominated by hostility towards England and by a total 'disregard for the elementary rules of straightforward and honourable dealing'. There were two possible explanations for her behaviour. Either she was 'consciously aiming at the establishment of a German hegemony at first in Europe, and eventually in the world' or 'the great German design is in reality no more than the expression of a vague,

[1] *Ibid.* p. 402.   [2] *Ibid.*   [3] *Ibid.* p. 403.

confused and unpractical statesmanship, not fully realizing its own drift'.[1] Crowe clearly believed the latter explanation was correct and that Germany was pursuing at the same time a number of grandiose schemes, some of them contradictory in intent, without any clear or consistent purpose. In either case, she would have to build as powerful a fleet as she could afford and both alternatives posed special problems for England.

It is wrong to believe that Crowe was anti-German in the crude sense of the word. He admired the German achievement, if not the methods by which it had been accomplished. 'Germany represents in a pre-eminent degree those highest qualities and virtues of good citizenship, in the largest sense of the word, which constitute the glory and triumph of modern civilization. The world would be immeasurably poorer if everything that is specifically associated with German character, German ideas and German methods were to cease having power and influence.'[2] The senior clerk was always quick to criticize those who underestimated the Germans. No one at the Foreign Office was so deeply versed in German history, literature and philosophy and few were more conscious of the splendour of this achievement. But the tradition of German militarism and its current restlessness and lack of direction filled Crowe with forebodings for the future.

Crowe's advice was based on a suspicious appraisal of German intentions. British assent to any agreement with Berlin must depend on the circumstances of the moment. Germany must be treated with courtesy but with firmness on a *quid pro quo* basis. The Germans must be met

with unvarying courtesy and consideration in all matters of common concern, but also with a prompt and firm refusal to enter into any one-sided bargain or arrangements, and the most unending determination to uphold British rights and interests in every part of the globe. There will be no surer or quicker way to win the respect of the German Government and of the German nation.[3]

As argued earlier, the difference between Sanderson and Crowe was one of tone rather than substance.[4] Both men were conscious of German expansion but Crowe was fearful of its implications whilst Sanderson remained confident that England could find a peaceful way to meet the challenge. Crowe believed that Germany would, by accident if not by design, upset the existing balance of power. Sanderson thought that with careful treatment a place could be found within the existing state system for this nervous giant. In Crowe's view, Britain had to walk warily, for 'to give way to the blackmailer's

---

[1] R. Cosgrove, *op. cit.* pp. 414–15.
[2] *Ibid.* p. 406; see also BD VI, p. 13, 7 February 1907.    [3] BD III, Appendix A, 419–20.
[4] See above, pp. 68–9.

menace enriches him, but it has long been proved by uniform experience that, although this may secure for the victim temporary peace, it is certain to lead to renewed molestation and higher demands after ever-shortening periods of amicable forbearance'. Crowe saw the problem in moral terms which weighed the balance against the new state. Britain, being a naval and commercial power, had not and would not abuse her position of strength. Germany, being a military power, would behave in the future as she had in the past. The senior clerk was far more deterministic in his view than Sanderson. Sanderson hoped that the Germans would mature and settle down; Crowe believed little could be done to alter the pattern of German behaviour. Hindsight suggests that Crowe was the more realistic in his judgement.

Crowe was consistent; his views did not change between 1907 and 1914. Nor, in fact, did they alter in the post-war period. The entente with France was a necessity and during the Algeciras Conference he pressed for a promise of armed support.[1] On the whole he was pleased with the outcome of this major crisis. 'The policy of showing a firm front and asserting British rights has once again been successful in inducing other countries to treat us properly.'[2] In the years which followed he showed little sympathy for those who took a more lenient or optimistic view of German aspirations. Thus he discounted the advice of Lascelles and corrected any optimistic reports sent by the military attachés.

Crowe wrote William Tyrrell during the Second Hague Peace Conference: 'The dominating influence in the Conference has clearly been fear of Germany. The latter has followed the traditional course, cajoling and bullying in turn, always actively intriguing.'[3] In a similar vein, he wrote Charles Dilke: 'The most marked feature of the Conference to my mind has been the open hegemony exercised by Germany over the States of Europe; not only Austria and Italy, but also Russia almost invariably voted with her.'[4] Crowe had little faith in the success of the conference: 'Our disarmament crusade has been the best advertisement of the German Navy League, and every German has by now been persuaded that England is exhausted, has reached the end of her tether, and must speedily collapse if the pressure is kept up. You will find that this impression now prevails all over Germany.'[5] In November 1908 Crowe was appointed a delegate to the International Maritime Conference in London. Though Crowe worked closely with his

[1] FO 371/70, minute by Crowe, 13 January 1906.          [2] BD III, p. 341.
[3] *Ibid.* VIII, no. 254.          [4] FO 800/243, Crowe to Dilke, 15 December 1907.
[5] *Ibid.* Crowe to Dilke, 15 October 1907.

German counterpart, his experience at this time strengthened his conviction that the German navy was being built to ensure German domination of Europe. It is one of the ironies of history that Crowe's participation in this latter conference was used as evidence for his pro-German sympathies in the campaign of vilification launched against him in 1915.

Ruthlessly logical, Crowe was the most extreme critic of the numerous attempts at an Anglo-German understanding. Unlike Grey or Hardinge, Crowe was not primarily concerned with the naval race for he saw in the building of the German fleet only a single symptom of a much broader danger. As a result, he was unwilling to pay a high price for a German modification of its naval programme. The panic of March 1909 barely moved him. He was convinced that the Germans would not attack until assured of their own superiority. But he was deeply worried lest in return for a bogus compromise on the naval question, the British would bargain away their diplomatic position. In the spring of 1909 he criticized a German suggestion for a political agreement in a devastating minute which concluded 'The whole proposal does not merit serious consideration.'[1] Crowe argued that German naval offers were either insincere or of minimal benefit, whereas any political arrangement would endanger the French entente and British security. In the autumn of 1909 yet another proposal was considered. In Crowe's eyes the Germans had raised their price and were not only demanding a political bargain without a naval agreement but asking for a colonial settlement as an additional bribe.[2]

Despite Crowe's opposition, the pressure for agreement continued. The senior clerk never shared Grey's very modest hope that some kind of limited arrangement might be considered. During 1910 Crowe opposed all plans for an accommodation both in Turkey (over the Baghdad railway) and in Persia. These matters, though falling under the jurisdiction of the Eastern Department, were referred to Crowe, an indication of the special position he held within the Foreign Office.[3] In the spring of 1910, when the Germans made another set of proposals in return for a British promise of European neutrality, Crowe wrote with obvious distaste: 'It is difficult to understand how Great Britain could entertain such a scheme . . . But to ask us for such abandonment of France and make, in addition, onerous conditions about the Baghdad Railway and Persia, is a plan to characterize which it is really difficult to find the appropriate adjectives.' 'Mr Crowe puts the case in a very clear way', Mallet minuted.[4] Yet, before the year was over, new discussions were under way.

[1] BD VI, no. 174.　[2] Ibid. no. 204.　[3] Ibid. no. 343.　[4] Ibid. no. 344, minutes by Crowe and Mallet.

Both Grey and Hardinge paid great attention to Crowe's judgements and analyses of German policy; his intimate knowledge of German affairs and his forceful statements gave him a special place within the Foreign Office. It was in these years that the Anglo-German rivalry was at its height and Crowe's weight was thrown on the side of those opposing a settlement. Crowe did not believe the Germans could offer terms which would ultimately protect the British against a German bid for the domination of Europe. It is important to notice, however, that Crowe's views, though more clearly defined and argued than those of his colleagues, reflected the opinions of most of the senior hierarchy. He was in no way a voice in the wilderness. Secondly, Crowe's centre of concern was the continent of Europe.[1] He knew little about Russia, played no role in the creation of the Russian understanding and had little interest in the conflicts of the Middle and Far East where Anglo-Russian difficulties were of major importance. Crowe's vision was a narrow one though his preoccupation with Germany reinforced Grey's own order of priorities. Finally, though Crowe's German minutes were read with respect, his advice was not always followed. Hardinge's advice was generally more flexible and temperate in tone.[2] The Foreign Secretary did not accept Crowe's proposals during the Algeciras Conference nor did he cut off negotiations with Berlin, which Crowe found useless and dangerous. Frequently it was Hardinge who developed the line which best suited Grey's needs.

Grey fully appreciated Crowe's brilliance and energy but there was little intimacy between the two men. Grey's mind moved slowly and Crowe's ruthless logic must sometimes have appalled him. Crowe had an intensity of vision which the Foreign Secretary did not share.

What I remember best is not his sensibility and good nature though these were enough to make him a good friend; nor his intelligence and flawless integrity though this would have made him a valued member of any society. There was besides these things such a heat in his spirit that knowledge of history and contemporary politics, acute judgement and power of exposition ran together with a kind of incandescence which lit up everything on which his mind and feeling and words were directed.[3]

---

[1] Crowe's responsibilities went beyond Germany. As head of the Western Department, he was asked to consider the implications of Belgian neutrality, to prepare a diplomatic and strategic study of the passages into the Baltic Sea and to analyse the new position created by the North Sea agreement. He also handled some of the irritating disputes with France (e.g. Newfoundland). He shared Hardinge's concern over the loyalties of the French and repeatedly feared a possible Franco-German bargain. Crowe could be as scathing about French greediness as he was apprehensive about German ambitions.

[2] Notice the difference in their approach to the question of Belgian neutrality. BD VIII, no. 311.

[3] O'Malley, *Phantom Caravan*, p. 47.

Crowe urged decisive action, Grey drew back from final steps. Grey had to work within a political framework and had to consider, not always sympathetically, the reactions of his Cabinet and the public. He might give less attention to these factors than his predecessors but he could not ignore them. Crowe was a professional who hated self-deception and ambiguity and had little patience with the domestic implications of foreign policy. It was with good reason that Stanley Baldwin later called him 'the ablest servant of the Crown'.

Even while Hardinge was at the Foreign Office, William Tyrrell was rapidly becoming Grey's closest confidant. Tyrrell had not had an easy start at the Foreign Office. He was temperamental, a heavy drinker and not without enemies. But a number of the senior men, particularly Hardinge, recognized his unusual talents and pressed his claims to advancement.[1] After being Grey's précis-writer from 1905 to 1907, he became principal private secretary and thereafter grew increasingly intimate with the reserved and rather shy foreign secretary. To contemporaries, Grey was the stereotype of the straightforward, bluff, simple Englishman; Tyrrell, the embodiment of subtlety and wit.[2] Tyrrell's critics attributed his somewhat unconventional 'Levantine methods' to his Anglo-Indian ancestry but Grey found his private secretary's talents of the greatest use.[3] 'Tyrrell's power of understanding the viewpoint of the foreigners', Grey wrote in his autobiography, 'had been of the greatest value in making the British position both more intelligible and more acceptable to them.'[4] Grey was uneasy with people; Tyrrell's power lay in his ability to find the right tone with the widest variety of visitors.

Sir Lewis Namier, who worked with Tyrrell at the Peace Conference, described him as 'complex, versatile, talkative, but extremely secretive; he was humble and even yielding on the surface but a stubborn fighter

[1] Tyrrell had been Sanderson's private secretary from 1896 to 1903; was then secretary for the Committee of Imperial Defence, 1903–4, and subsequently went to Rome as second secretary. Hardinge seems to have been instrumental in bringing him back to London. Hardinge MSS, vol. 93, Hardinge to Chirol, 30 May 1915.

[2] J. A. Spender, *Life, Journalism and Politics* (London, 1927). 'When I wanted something a little more sophisticated I went from him [Grey] to Tyrrell, then his private secretary, who played over the same subject with a keen and brilliant wit and the surest eye for its personal equations.' Vol. 1, p. 171.

[3] For a negative comment on Tyrrell's 'Levantine methods', an indirect reference to Tyrrell's background, as well as his approach, see FO 800/93, Ponsonby to Grey, 20 April 1911. 'I begin to see that Tyrrell, for all his quickness and superficial intelligence is a really small man. He has no knowledge of reading or width of view. He has a sort of nimbleness of wits and likes negotiation and palavering and intellectual jig-saw work. But he could not grapple with big situations or make a good Ambassador.' Lord Curzon to Grace Curzon, 22 December 1922.

[4] Grey, *Twenty-Five Years*, vol. 1, p. xviii.

underneath'.[1] Whereas the Foreign Office archives tell us everything we need to know about Crowe's views, there are few papers written by the Private Secretary and no systematic expression of his opinions. Tyrrell preferred to rely on personal contacts and informal talks rather than on hard facts and sharp minutes. He hated putting pen to paper and was lazy about the bureaucratic routine which Crowe so perfected.[2] A warm, gay and even impish man who shone in conversation, Tyrrell disliked all the trappings of officialdom. He was as bored by reading papers as he was by writing them.

His correspondence, brief and disorganized as it is, indicates that he was a powerful private secretary who took a leading role in determining appointments and promotions. But Tyrrell's influence soon extended well beyond the walls of the private secretary's office. He was the official personally closest to Grey and the latter not only consulted him but was later to use him as an unofficial ambassador—an Averell Harriman of the pre-1914 world.

A Roman Catholic born in India, Tyrrell, like Crowe, had been educated in Germany and had spent much of his early life in the home of Prince Radolin who had married into his family. Again, like Crowe, Tyrrell spoke German fluently but his German affinities had sharpened his fears about German aims.[3] Prince Lichnowsky, the German ambassador in London, wrote: 'Sir William Tyrrell, Sir Edward's private secretary, possessed far greater influence than the Permanent Under Secretary Nicolson . . . At first he favoured the anti-German policy, which was then in fashion among the younger British diplomats, but later on he became a convinced advocate of an understanding.'[4] Scattered as the evidence is, it is clear that until 1912 at least Tyrrell shared the general Foreign Office suspicion of Berlin. In May 1906 Tyrrell wrote to Spring-Rice: 'The real cancer at Berlin is Bülow who lacks all moral sense in no ordinary degree. I despair of decent relations with Germany as long as he has a finger in the pie.'[5]

Fundamentally, Tyrrell shared Hardinge's impression that 'The race in naval armaments is the disturbing factor. To get rid of this should be the main object in view. Political relations will improve automatically after that. . .'[6] Tyrrell did not favour the post-Algeciras talks with Berlin for he feared a

[1] L. B. Namier, *Avenues of History* (London, 1952), p. 87.
[2] O'Malley describes him as '. . . a little man as quick as a lizard with scintillating eyes and wit and a great aversion to any work not transacted orally.' O'Malley, *Phantom Caravan*, p. 45.
[3] Like Crowe, Tyrrell knew many German leaders including Admiral Holtzendorff and spent some of his holidays with the Radolins where he must have met other German diplomatists.
[4] Prince Lichnowsky, *Heading for the Abyss* (New York, 1928), p. 70.
[5] FO 800/241, Tyrrell to Spring-Rice, 1 May 1906.
[6] FO 800/92, Tyrrell to Grey, 27 August 1909.

negative reaction from Paris and St Petersburgh. Like others at the Foreign Office he welcomed the agreement with Russia and thought the Persian settlement a realistic one given the weakness of the British position. There were sound grounds for the German belief that Sir Edward Grey's secretary was generally unsympathetic to their cause.[1]

I cordially agree with what you say [Tyrrell wrote Spring-Rice, a good friend] as to the determination of the German nation to settle with us someday or other. What would you expect from the training in that school which it has had ever since the days of Frederick the Great, who accepted our subsidies and diverted these to his own purposes and to justify the proceeding was driven to vilify us.[2]

Tyrrell's modest hopes for peace lay in Emperor William, 'a man of words' and in the increase and spread of wealth in Germany which was bound to have the same 'deteriorating effect which it has had here and help to put off the crash'.[3] While Hardinge remained at the Foreign Office, however, Tyrrell's voice was just one more in the chorus pointing out the dangers of any bargain with Berlin. After 1910 he was to assume a much more important role.

By the time Hardinge left London for Delhi, Grey had served his apprenticeship at the Foreign Office. Although he had definite views about British diplomacy, he had been willing to solicit and follow the advice of his senior officials. Hardinge was the most important of these; his general analysis of the European situation coincided with that of his chief and England's Russian policy was in part shaped by the Permanent Under-Secretary. Among the assistant under-secretaries, Louis Mallet was the most ambitious but both he and his associates were far more influential within their areas of special competence than in the general areas of policy-making. Although these men did the kind of work and made the type of decisions Lord Salisbury would have reserved to himself, a large proportion of their recommendations were seen and approved by Hardinge and Grey, particularly where the matter involved great power relations. There was a similar increase in the responsibilities of the senior clerks and the number of memoranda and minutes in their hands rose steadily. Eyre Crowe was in a special position; he was the acknowledged expert on German affairs. Yet, as has been shown, his advice was not always followed and his role in the forming of policy has been somewhat exaggerated. If he had been in charge of the Foreign Office, there would have been no talks with Berlin in these critical years. R. P. Maxwell (who had refused promotion), the senior clerk in the Eastern

[1] DGP XXVIII, 219.  [2] FO 800/241, Tyrrell to Spring-Rice, 11 December 1907.
[3] *Ibid.* 15 April 1908.

Department, was an acknowledged master in his own area. Beilby Alston in the Far Eastern, John Tilley in the African, and Gerald Spicer, first as Crowe's assistant in the Western and then as the efficient and outspoken head of the American Department, were all establishing their reputations as experts. Among the younger group of clerks, both Eric Drummond and Alwyn Parker were marked for future promotion. Drummond was making his way up the ladder through a series of private secretaryships. Parker was already a specialist in the complex field of railways and concessions in the Middle East and was later, as assistant clerk, to be given an almost free hand in the discussions with Turkey and Germany over the Baghdad railway question.

The youngest men at the Foreign Office were no longer anonymous though their minutes were short and only occasionally initiated a line of action.[1] Those written by the members of the Western Department show how widespread was the feeling that Germany was the main enemy and the system of ententes essential to British security. But, as might be expected, men like Vansittart and Oliphant were still low on the ladder and their opinions carried little weight. Between 1906 and 1910 the Foreign Office became an effective organization and Grey was served by an exceptionally able and cohesive elite. Quite apart from the normal diplomatic correspondence, the Foreign Secretary had an additional professional source of information and advice. In the end, the decision and responsibility were fully his.

### Arthur Nicolson's permanent under-secretaryship

From the point of view of talent and of increased professional authority, Whitehall ought to have been at its zenith in the last years of European peace. In fact, the contrary was true. Hardinge's departure marked a downward turn both in personal relations and in administrative structure. Sanderson would never have imagined possible the extent of the gulf between Grey and his permanent under-secretary. Lloyd George and the realities of a world war were to sap the prestige and importance of the Foreign Office but the process was already under way.

Arthur Nicolson came back to London in October 1910 at the age of sixty-one, physically ill-prepared to face the long and sedentary hours of an

[1] Calvert, *The Mexican Revolution, 1910–14* (Cambridge, 1968), p. 149. There is an excellent illustration of Foreign Office procedure during the Mexican Counter-Revolution of 1912 when Knatchbull-Hugessen, a new entrant to the Foreign Office, gave his views on the recognition of Huerta. The despatch and minute is checked by Spicer, head of the American Department and then by Mallet, the supervising assistant under-secretary before it is sent to Grey for a final decision.

office position.[1] He had come with reluctance and his hesitations about his suitability for this civil servant's post were soon justified. His son has written:

He was overwhelmed with a mass of subsidiary questions—some of them trivial, all of them exacting, and for most of which he had but little appetite or interest. He would labour onwards increasingly, cursing the fate which had condemned him to so cruel a penitentiary . . . They [the despatch boxes] filled him with nausea and despair. Never had any man so cordially disliked being Permanent Under Secretary of State.[2]

Nicolson was a poor administrator, disliked interfering in personnel problems, and had little interest in bureaucratic details.[3] Eighteen months after taking office, Nicolson begged Grey for his release. He first pressed for the embassy at Vienna and then for Constantinople, but for reasons which are not really clear both requests were refused.[4] In February 1913 Grey promised him the Paris embassy when Francis Bertie retired. But Bertie was not to be dismissed so easily; he checked on the ages of previous British ambassadors in his post and demanded an additional year on the Faubourg St Honoré. Nicolson was again put off, this time until the end of 1914.[5] The war intervened; Bertie stayed in Paris until his abrupt dismissal by Lord Curzon and Nicolson continued to serve in the Foreign Office until June 1916 when he retired.

During his years at Whitehall, Nicolson failed to establish any kind of close relationship with Grey. The position of permanent under-secretary in itself gave its holder an important voice in the direction of affairs. Like Hardinge, Nicolson saw all papers of importance, had a voluminous correspondence with diplomats abroad and was extremely close to the French ambassador, Paul Cambon. Many of the letters which Nicolson received were important enough to be circulated to Grey, to Asquith and even to other members of the Cabinet. Yet despite his experience and contacts, Nicolson did not ultimately impress his views on Grey. There was little sense of partnership between the two men and relations deteriorated rather than improved.[6] The creation

---

[1] There was a sharp contrast between the upright, rather jaunty, Hardinge and the arthritic, frail, stooped Nicolson which made a strong impression on the clerks. Vansittart, *The Mist Procession*, p. 99.

[2] Nicolson, *Lord Carnock*, p. 334.

[3] Yet see FO 800/271, Nicolson to Spring-Rice, 10 October 1910. 'I find the post very hard work but none the less it agrees with me—and I feel light-hearted.' Disillusionment came quickly.

[4] Nicolson, *Lord Carnock*, p. 362; FO 800/93 Nicolson to Grey, 14 August 1912.

[5] Nicolson, *Lord Carnock*, p. 401; FO 800/93 Nicolson to Grey, 21 October 1913; FO 800/188, memorandum by Bertie, 25 July 1914. For further details see pp. 153–4.

[6] Hardinge MSS, vol. 93, no. 195, Chirol to Hardinge, 15 April 1914. One must be careful not to overstate the case, as Chirol and Bertie are the main sources. There are some, though relatively

of a Cabinet committee in 1911 (though it seems to have met infrequently) to deal with the Anglo-German talks further curtailed Nicolson's influence. 'I am sorry for Nicolson's position under the new system' Hardinge commented. 'He will practically have no power at all.'[1] During 1912 the Permanent Under-Secretary found that he did not always see Grey as frequently as he wished and found Grey so preoccupied with domestic matters that their meetings were perfunctory. This would have mattered little if the two men were agreed on fundamental issues but this was no longer true. Chirol wrote to Hardinge early in that year 'Unfortunately, I am afraid his [Nicolson's] personal influence over his Chief is not as great as it ought to be.'[2]

Some of Nicolson's differences with Grey stemmed from the former's distrust of the Liberal Government. He was openly opposed to the radicals and had little use for the pro-German, anti-Russian factions in the Cabinet and Commons. He always feared that Grey was too weak to withstand the pressure from his close friend Haldane and, until Agadir, the Lloyd George–Winston Churchill combination. He made no attempt to disguise his misgivings and openly acknowledged his dislike and forebodings. He wrote to Hardinge

I am afraid that the tendency of the present day is to avoid taking any responsibility whatsoever, or indeed of adopting any policy which has an element of vigour and foresightedness. This I see evidenced not only in China but throughout the whole of the world. I suppose it is a malady which attacks every Government who is in power for any length of time and feels that its future tenure is somewhat uncertain.[3]

Nicolson felt that the Liberals were both weak at home and inept abroad. 'My views are so entirely divergent with those of the present government', Nicolson wrote in January 1914, 'that I think it better to limit myself to talking on those matters which are strictly within my province.'[4] Tyrrell went so far as to accuse Nicolson of disloyalty and of 'criticizing his chief's policy in conversations with foreign diplomatists'.[5] Though Nicolson often

---

few, warm letters from Grey to Nicolson in the Carnock papers (FO 800/365, Grey to Nicolson, 16 April 1913; 800/366, Grey to Nicolson, 4 May 1913; 800/370, Grey to Nicolson, 3 October 1913).

[1] Hardinge MSS, vol. 92, Hardinge to Chirol, 5 April 1911.
[2] *Ibid*. Chirol to Hardinge, 15 February 1912. See the much earlier comment to the same effect in a letter of Lady Helen Munro Fergusson to Hardinge, 12 July 1911.
[3] *Ibid*. vol. 93, Nicolson to Hardinge, 18 July 1912.        [4] *Ibid*. 15 January 1914.
[5] *Ibid*. Chirol to Hardinge, 18 April 1913. FO 800/188, memorandum by Bertie, 30 July 1914. Murray Elibank and Tyrrell worked on Asquith to veto Nicolson's appointment to Paris. 'Nicolson continued his abuse of the Government about Ulster and had lately spoken ill of them to Lord Cowdray who had expressed his astonishment to Murray his partner.' Nicolson also publicly opposed the Arbitration Treaty with the United States.

exempted Grey from his general strictures about the Liberals, his political antipathies complicated their relations and Ulster completed the breach.[1]

What were the policy differences between Grey and Nicolson? Nicolson remained loyal to those ideas which had dominated the Foreign Office between 1906 and 1910. Germany was the only threat to the European balance of power and England's security lay in her ententes with France and Russia. Nicolson had already defended his belief that the ententes should be turned into alliances. Even while he was at St Petersburgh, he had been checked by the Foreign Office for using the term 'Triple Entente' in his official correspondence. He had pressed Grey repeatedly, though without success, to strengthen and extend the understanding with Russia, an understanding which he regarded as his special responsibility. At Whitehall he continued to argue that the existing situation would lead Germany to count on British neutrality and would encourage Russia, if not France, to settle their differences with Berlin, leaving England isolated and at German mercy. Both the entente ambassadors in London found in Nicolson a strong if ineffectual friend.

But Nicolson soon realized that these views were unpopular and that Grey was unwilling to define the diplomatic situation more clearly. When the Permanent Under-Secretary first came to the Foreign Office, a section of the Cabinet was urging Grey to continue his talks with the Germans. Nicolson had the strongest doubts about reopening discussions in the autumn of 1910. He disliked the idea of a visit of the German Emperor in the spring of 1911 and viewed the activities of the Anglo-German Friendship Society under Lascelles' patronage with deep suspicion.

I am keeping a very close eye upon the drafting of the instructions and am continually impressing upon Grey that it is essential that we should not move too far from our original position, which was that in any case reduction of armaments was a vital point, even if it did not precede the question of any political agreement . . . Personally, I do not see how it is possible that we should ever arrive at a satisfactory agreement.[2]

These talks, however, were being conducted under the general aegis of the newly formed Cabinet committee and Grey was obviously trying to steer a middle course between those pressing for an arrangement and his own wish to remain loyal to the policy of the ententes. When these 1911 talks failed to produce concrete results, Nicolson wrote:

I hope that our Government now fully realize that the aim of Germany in these

[1] Hardinge MSS, vol. 93, Chirol to Hardinge, 22 May 1914.
[2] *Ibid.* vol. 69, Nicolson to Hardinge, 2 March 1911.

negotiations is to smash up as far as she is able to do, the Triple Entente and that her chief object is to isolate France as much as possible. I am not completely at ease in my own mind that she may not succeed in this respect to a limited extent as it is known at the present moment there is a wave in many circles here towards a friendly understanding with Germany . . . I look forward to a troublesome time during the next few months, but as far as my voice is heard it will always be in favour of a firm maintenance of our understanding with France and Russia.[1]

Nicolson was 'not at all sorry that the Agadir incident has occurred, as I think it will open the eyes of all those who have been so clamorous of late for an understanding with Germany'.[2] The Permanent Under-Secretary forwarded and warmly supported Cambon's suggestions that a ship be sent to Agadir and was distressed by Grey's lack of enthusiasm and the Cabinet's veto.[3] While Grey sought concessions in Morocco or in Africa which might mollify the Germans, Nicolson, backed by Crowe at home and Bertie in Paris, thought only in terms of a united front with the French.[4] During the early summer, Grey tried to chart a course which would both maintain the entente and yet settle the dispute. It may have been the Foreign Secretary's various suggestions for compromise which prompted Nicolson to underline his point in a rather sharp letter to Grey.

'Were she [France] to come to distrust us, she would probably try to make terms with Germany irrespective of us while Germany who would soon detect our hesitations would be inclined to impose far harder terms than may be the case at present. In any case, France would never forgive us for having failed her, and the whole Triple Entente would be broken up. This would mean that we should have a triumphant Germany, and an unfriendly France and Russia and our policy since 1904 of preserving the equilibrium and consequently the peace of Europe would be wrecked.[5]

Nicolson continued to press unsuccessfully for a policy of all-out support for France.

After Lloyd George's Mansion House speech, a majority of the cabinet supported a firmer line towards Germany, and during August and September a small group of ministers (Grey, Asquith, Lloyd George, Churchill and Haldane) joined to consider possible action in case of a Franco-German war.[6]

[1] BD VI, no. 461.       [2] BD VII, no. 359.       [3] *Ibid.* nos. 343, 354.
[4] Carnock MSS, 1911, Nicolson to Goschen, 24 July 1911; Nicolson even modified a despatch to improve the tone of Anglo-French relations at the height of the crisis. BD VII, nos. 375, 376, 377.
[5] BD VII, no. 409.
[6] There was a special meeting of the CID on 23 August 1911 with Asquith, Grey, Haldane, McKenna, Lloyd George and the service chiefs present. Churchill, the home secretary, was invited to join but Morley, Crewe, Harcourt and Esher were either not informed or were away. In other words, the radical ministers who might have opposed co-operation with France were conveniently absent. The meeting revealed serious differences between the military and naval

The defection of Lloyd George and Churchill from the ranks of the pro-German radicals was warmly received by the Foreign Office. For once, Nicolson was well satisfied with the firm and even war-like mood of these earlier 'doves'.[1] But this 'fit of political alcoholism' soon passed. A reaction set in and Grey was soon faced with the most serious back-bench revolt of his administration and a further Cabinet intervention in his management of foreign affairs. 'There is rather a revolt against Grey's foreign policy among a section of the Ministerial sympathizers', Sanderson reported to Lord Hardinge in December 1911.[2] Opposition in and out of the House mounted. 'There is a considerable amount of discontent against Grey in the Liberal party', Sanderson again wrote to Hardinge. 'But part also arises from want of information. There has been a call for Blue Books and the Foreign Office has really given none for the last three years except a collection of Persian papers.'[3] Two of the most outspoken of Grey's critics, Arthur Ponsonby and Noel Buxton, urged that a committee be created to improve Anglo-German relations. The whole liberal press, except the *Westminster Gazette*, attacked Grey during November and December. A series of articles appeared and a number of public speeches were made, all critical of Grey's policy and methods of diplomacy. Due to this public campaign, the Government agreed to a debate on foreign policy, for even the publication, on 24 November, of the text of the Anglo-French agreement failed to quiet the critics. The attack continued and Grey was forced to defend his conduct.[4] 'Grey is hated by the Liberals and ought to go', a colleague wrote to Ponsonby. 'Our foreign policy is based on an alliance with Burglars. How can true Liberals follow?'[5]

plans for assisting France. Both Lloyd George and Churchill, in the weeks which followed, were enthusiastically planning for a war while Harcourt and Morley recoiled in horror. Asquith disliked the Anglo-French military conversations in September but Grey, despite his wish to follow a middle course, refused to have them stopped. Hankey, *Supreme Command*, pp. 78–84; Sir C. E. Callwell, *Field Marshal Sir Henry Wilson* (London, 1927), vol. I, pp. 98–100; FO 800/100, Asquith to Grey, 5 September 1911; Grey to Asquith, 8 September 1911.

[1] Hardinge MSS, vol. 92, Nicolson to Hardinge, 17 August 1911. Nicolson was forced to admit he 'was struck by the determination of both of them, not to permit Germany to assume the role of bully and at their belief that the present moment was an exceedingly favourable one to open hostilities'.

[2] Hardinge MSS, vol. 92, Sanderson to Hardinge, 15 December 1911; Esher, *Journals and Letters of Viscount Esher*, vol. III, pp. 74–5.

[3] Hardinge MSS, vol. 92, Sanderson to Hardinge, 26 January 1912.

[4] Grey, *Twenty-Five Years*, pp. 231–2. Compare the discussion in A. J. P. Taylor, *The Trouble-Makers: Dissent over Foreign Policy 1792–1939* (Bloomington, Indiana, 1958) with John A. Murray 'Foreign Policy Debated: Sir Edward Grey and his Critics, 1911–1912', in L. P. Wallace and W. C. Askew, *Power, Public Opinion and Diplomacy, Essays in Honour of E. M. Carroll by his Former Students* (Durham, North Carolina, 1959), pp. 140–71.

[5] Ponsonby MSS, C. A. Nicole to Ponsonby, 1 August 1912.

The revolt produced few concrete results in Persia but both the Haldane Mission and the renewed conversations with Berlin were moves meant to satisfy the 'Grey-must-go' group. Nicolson defended his chief. 'The movement is most unjust', he wrote to Buchanan at St Petersburgh, 'as no one has pursued a straighter or more moderate line of action.'[1] As might have been predicted, Nicolson strongly disliked Haldane's trip and opposed the political and naval talks which followed. 'I do not myself see why we should abandon the excellent position in which we have been placed, and step down to be involved in endeavours to entangle us in some so-called "understandings" which would undoubtedly, if not actually, impair our relations with France and Russia, in any case render the latter countries somewhat suspicious of us . . .'[2] It is not entirely clear how far Grey shared the general desire for some sort of détente or whether the accommodationists in the Cabinet forced his hand, but the talks went on. As Asquith and Grey were preoccupied with the coal strike, Nicolson inherited the unwelcome task of providing material for Haldane's discussions. The search for a suitable political formula took months; the German offer was a temporary suspension or modification of their naval law. To the enormous relief of the permanent officials, Grey, despite great pressure from Harcourt, McKenna and Loreburn, refused to consider a 'neutrality' clause. Basic disagreements and a Berlin decision to introduce a supplementary naval bill ended the matter.

The whole history of these recent German discussions is an extraordinary episode, and I have never seen any discussions conducted in such a strange manner. I am doing my best to get us out of this quagmire . . . into which we are plunged, and into which we have been led by our unscrupulous adversaries and our singularly naïve and feeble negotiators.[3]

Goschen congratulated the Permanent Under-Secretary on the collapse of the talks: 'You have been foremost in this good work.'[4] Three months later, though Nicolson believed that a naval agreement had passed out of the realm of practical politics, he still feared a possible political arrangement.[5]

Grey was genuinely relieved when the search for a political formula ceased but he gradually came to support the efforts made to conclude

[1] FO 800/353, Nicolson to Buchanan, 17 January 1912.
[2] FO 800/171, Nicolson to Bertie, 8 February 1912.
[3] FO 800/171, Nicolson to Bertie, 6 April 1912. The whole letter is relevant. FO 800/355, Nicolson to Goschen and Hardinge, 16 April 1912.
[4] *Ibid.* Goschen to Nicolson, 20 April 1912.
[5] Hardinge MSS, vol. 92, Nicolson to Hardinge, 18 July 1912.

more circumscribed bargains. After Agadir, the Foreign Secretary was forced to be more careful in his treatment of the radical wing of his Cabinet. Morley, Loreburn and Harcourt were particularly outspoken.[1] Grey, moreover, felt local arrangements outside Europe would not affect the grouping of powers on the continent while a friendly Germany would be a positive asset.[2] Nicolson not only had little sympathy with these later *pourparlers* but felt that Grey should have made a more determined stand against the pro-German mood in his Cabinet. The plans for a future division of the Portuguese colonies, Nicolson characterized 'as the most cynical business that I have ever come across in my whole experience of diplomacy'.[3] He left the Foreign Office part of the negotiations to Eyre Crowe. 'I consider the whole transaction to be most discreditable', he wrote to Hardinge, 'and I desire to have as little to do with it as possible.'[4]

Nicolson deplored any step in the German direction and would have preferred an open declaration in favour of the entente. Grey shared his belief that if France were attacked by Germany, Britain would be forced to intervene. But he knew the Cabinet would not make such a declaration and argued that the existing policy of the ententes provided the best protection against such an eventuality arising. Nicolson appreciated his chief's political difficulties but they frustrated and angered him. The French had watched the Anglo-German talks of 1912 with growing alarm and in April, Cambon, prompted in part by Bertie in Paris, came to the Foreign Office for a clarification of British obligations to France. Nicolson, though in total sympathy with his French friend, warned the ambassador that any attempt to turn the entente into an alliance would be rejected by the Government and by a large section of the British public.[5]

I would far prefer to see our entente with France developed into an alliance, but I think this is too strong a measure to take in the present temper of the British

---

[1] When news of the secret Anglo-French military conversations leaked, Morley (despite some previous knowledge of these talks) raised the whole question in a Cabinet meeting held on 1 November 1911. The Cabinet split with fifteen ministers against the talks with France and only five (Grey, Asquith, Haldane, Lloyd George and Churchill) in favour. Once again, the skilful Asquith found a formula which allowed the talks to go on but safeguarded the cabinet's future freedom of action. A strong cabal was formed against the entente led by Harcourt and the size of the anti-French majority undoubtedly had some influence on Grey's subsequent willingness to negotiate with Germany. It is interesting that Haldane who had supported Grey became with Harcourt the leader in the subsequent Anglo-German talks. Esher, *Journals and Letters of Viscount Esher*, vol. III, pp. 74–5.

[2] FO 800/62, Grey to Metternich, 9 May 1912.

[3] Hardinge MSS, vol. 92, Nicolson to Hardinge, 21 November 1912.

[4] *Ibid.* 9 January 1913; FO 800/353, Nicolson to Grey, 13 February 1912; FO 800/355, Nicolson to Goschen, 23 April 1912. Nicolson was not kept in touch with the Harcourt/Kühlmann proceedings.                                                                 [5] BD VI, no. 576.

public, and there is perhaps no real urgency as our relations are sufficiently intimate to enable us to co-operate quite cordially together without any precise Convention embodying our mutual obligations.[1]

Grey himself authorized Nicolson to inform the French embassy 'that there is no question of our hands being tied if Germany forces war upon any ally or friend of ours'.[2] But Nicolson was not as sanguine as his assurances to Cambon suggest. 'Those who were well acquainted with recent history would hardly regard Germany as an injured innocent—but there were many here who did—and of late there has been a very critical propaganda by financiers, pacificists, faddists and others, in favour of closer relations with Germany, and the propaganda has made considerable headway', Nicolson warned Lord Morley who was in temporary charge of the Foreign Office while Grey was on vacation.[3]

The Permanent Under-Secretary was trying to reassure Cambon without misleading the French ambassador as to the real mood of the present Government. Nicolson's contemptuous remarks about 'this radical socialist cabinet' and his scathing description of the pro-German forces were a genuine reflection of his own feelings.[4] But though an alliance was impossible, Cambon and Nicolson did have some measure of success. As a result of the German Novelle of 1912, the Admiralty decided to redistribute its fleet and concentrate more of its forces in home waters. Such a redistribution raised the question of the size and role of the British navy in the Mediterranean.[5] The Committee of Imperial Defence decided to maintain only a one-power standard in that sea. Nicolson fought for a larger commitment but evidently Grey had difficulties in securing a fleet equal in size to that of Austria. Proceeding from a masterly memorandum by Eyre Crowe, Nicolson argued that if the Mediterranean fleet had to be reduced, an arrangement with France was essential.[6] This was the moment to press for an alliance. 'An understanding with France, whereby she would undertake in the early part of a war, and until we could detach vessels from home waters, to safe-

---

[1] *Ibid.*                                   [2] FO 800/355, Grey to Nicolson, 5 April 1912.
[3] *Ibid.* Nicolson to Morley, 15 April 1912.
[4] DDF, 3rd series, II, no. 363. FO 800/165, Nicolson to Bertie, 23 April 1912. 'Our people are so blind. We are not very strong props on which to lean and I always fear that some day we will be left alone.'
[5] Churchill's proposals to withdraw the British fleet from the Mediterranean and concentrate it in the North Sea provoked a Cabinet crisis. McKenna, Morley and Harcourt opposed the scheme because they feared it would result in an alliance with France to which they were violently opposed. Haldane and the War Office also disliked the proposal though for different reasons. Asquith finally drew up an acceptable formula based on a one-power standard in the Mediterranean. The question was discussed throughout the spring and summer of 1912.
[6] BD x(2), nos. 385, 386.

guard our interest in the Mediterranean. She would naturally ask for some reciprocal agreement from us which it would be worthwhile to give. This to my mind offers the cheapest, simplest and safest solution.'[1]

The French asked for just such a declaration but neither Grey nor the Cabinet were willing to commit the Government in this way. Though Churchill welcomed the proposed naval exchanges, both he and his colleagues were anxious to preserve England's future freedom of action. In sharp distinction to 1906, the Cabinet discussed the naval arrangement throughout the summer of 1912.[2] In the end, the British undertook to safeguard the security of the northern coasts of France while the latter, with the help of the remaining British Mediterranean force, would safeguard British interests in the Mediterranean. In October the Cabinet demanded a further clarification of these obligations and in the exchange of notes between Cambon and Grey on 22 November a preamble was added by the British Cabinet to the effect that 'consultation between experts is not and ought not to be regarded as an engagement that commits either Government to action in a contingency that has not arisen and may never arise'.[3] Though this was a step in the right direction, it was not the declaration of support which Nicolson had desired. Britain's obligations to France were restricted to consultation; Parliament was later assured that Britain was free from commitment. The radicals in the Cabinet seem to have assumed that they were free to act as they wished when the moment of crisis came.

Nicolson retained his doubts. The wobbly position of the Cabinet on the naval agreement convinced him that little could be expected from the Liberals.

Were it possible to conclude a naval arrang[emen]t both with Russia and France, I am sure that our position would be more secure—and it is probable that Germany, in view of such a strong naval combination, would be disposed to slacken her rate of construction . . . I fear, however, that we are precluded from entering into any such understanding owing to our unfortunate parliamentary exigencies.[4]

Nor did Nicolson think that the military links between London and Paris were adequate for the defence of either power. 'I am afraid that should war break out on the continent', he wrote to Buchanan in 1914, 'the likelihood of our despatching any expeditionary force is extremely remote and it was on such an expeditionary force being sent that France at one time was basing her military measures.'[5]

---

[1] BD x(2), no. 385. Though Crowe wrote the memorandum it was phrased so that it represented a general Foreign Office view.
[2] *Ibid.* no. 383; For the 1906 military talks see Monger, *The End of Isolation*, chapter 9, especially pp. 248–56. The subject needs further investigation.
[3] BD x(2), nos. 416 and 417; Marder, *From the Dreadnought to Scapa Flow*, vol. I, pp. 278–311.
[4] BD x(2), no. 407.          [5] FO 800/373, Nicolson to Buchanan, 7 April 1914.

In every direction Nicolson thought that the crucial decisions were being avoided.

There is no doubt that the party in favour of intimate relations with Germany has increased and strengthened of late in this country [he wrote in the spring of 1913]. I am afraid, personally, supposing a collision did occur between France and Germany, that we should waver as to what course we should pursue until it was too late. It is unfortunate that the Government will not lay the state of the case frankly and openly before the country and endeavour to stimulate the public to follow the example of every country in Europe and be ready to make certain sacrifices for their own defence.[1]

The pro-German movement gathered force during the following winter; many sections wished 'to go over to Germany and throw over our present friends'.[2] Despite Grey and Asquith's loyalty to the policy of the ententes, Nicolson feared the Germanophiles would gain the upper hand and that his worst nightmares would become realities.

In the end, it was Nicolson's extreme pro-Russian orientation which weakened his position within the Foreign Office. His differences with Grey seemed at the start of his regime minimal but the gap grew in the last years of peace. Both men, but particularly Nicolson, had an exaggerated respect for the power of Russia. Throughout his years at the Foreign Office, Nicolson feared that a breakdown of the Anglo-Russian agreement would antagonize the Russians and lead them to take the offensive against England, either alone or with German assistance. In central Asia, he argued, the British were the weaker party. 'Her friendship is really of more importance to us than that of France and I am continually urging, even at the risk of being considered an infatuated Russophile, that we should put up with perhaps occasional annoyances in Persia in order to remain on the best footing with Russia.'[3] Ultimately, Nicolson feared Russia more than Germany. The latter 'would give us plenty of annoyance but it cannot really threaten any of our more important interests, while Russia especially could cause us extreme embarrassment and, indeed, danger, in the Mid-East and on our Indian frontier, and it would be most unfortunate were we to revert to the state of things which existed before 1904 and 1907'.[4] It is doubtful whether Grey would have made such a statement.

'Occasional annoyances' in Persia tried Grey's patience more than any other question.[5] The Russian take-over on Persia roused a continuous storm of protest at the Foreign Office, in the Commons and in the press. Grey,

[1] Nicolson to Hardinge, 29 October 1913, quoted in Nicolson, *Lord Carnock*, pp. 402–3.
[2] FO 800/372, Nicolson to Goschen, 19 January 1914; to Hardinge, 15 January 1914.
[3] FO 800/365, Nicolson to Buchanan, 22 April 1913.
[4] FO 800/355, Nicolson to Goschen, 15 April 1912.     [5] Grey, *Twenty-Five Years*, vol. I, p. 164.

prodded by his own legation at Teheran as well as by his back-benchers, became increasingly embarrassed by the open intervention of the Russians at Teheran. In the struggle between the Shah and the Constitutionalists, Russian and British sympathies were differently engaged. There was a continuous stream of complaining letters from Teheran. 'I have not read this document' Nicolson minuted a bulky memorandum on Russian violation of the Convention. 'But if, as I assume, it contains criticism of Russian procedure in Persia, it is largely based on prejudices and false assumptions.'[1] Nicolson felt, even when the Anglo-Russian convention had been negotiated, that a Russian absorption of northern Persia could not be avoided and that central Persia was not worth the price of a quarrel. Grey, too, had made his basic decision but he was made acutely uncomfortable by Russian behaviour in Persia and felt he could not allow the Russians to disregard totally their agreement.

This is not the place to go into a detailed account of the tangled situation in Persia and in the Gulf.[2] Matters came to a head during 1911 when Grey, contrary to the wishes of his legation, decided that Morgan Shuster, the American financial adviser to the Persians, had to be dismissed as the Russians demanded. When, however, the Russians threatened to occupy the whole north of Persia, Grey warned Benckendorff that he would be forced to resign unless the Russians kept to their part of the 1907 convention. Even Nicolson felt that the Foreign Secretary had been unduly pressed, and that Russia was 'a somewhat difficult partner'. He insisted that the Persians be forced to accede to Russian demands but did wish that the latter could be moderated. 'The whole question has greatly preoccupied, and is greatly preoccupying, us here', Nicolson wrote, 'and we shall be thankful if the ultimate issue enables us to emerge without any serious alteration having been produced in our mutual relations.'[3] The Persian difficulties threatened, in Nicolson's eyes, the whole fabric of Anglo-Russian relations. It was, for instance, doubly unfortunate that St Petersburgh raised the problem of the Straits just when the parliamentary rebellion against Grey was coming to a climax.[4] Nicolson was left so physically exhausted that he was ordered abroad for a six-week rest.[5]

Persian questions continued to plague Grey until the outbreak of war. Though Nicolson's recommendations for a forward policy in southern

[1] Nicolson, *Lord Carnock*, p. 354.
[2] The subject has been covered in a whole series of recent books. See, for instance, B. Busch, *Britain and the Persian Gulf, 1894–1914* (Berkeley, 1967).
[3] BD x(1), no. 898.　　　　　[4] FO 800/353, Nicolson to Buchanan, 19 December 1911.
[5] Hardinge MSS, vol. 69, Nicolson to Hardinge, 20 December 1911.

Persia in 1912 were vetoed by the Cabinet and Government of India, his extreme sensitivity towards Russian feelings did leave a mark on Britain's Persian policies. 'We must submit to these little difficulties', he repeatedly told Hardinge, 'sooner than permit a dissolution of the partnership.'[1] More than once Nicolson intervened 'to moderate, if not altogether to prevent' representations at St Petersburgh and the Permanent Under-Secretary warned Grey that the British were lecturing their friends 'a little too much'.[2] But Russian action in northern Persia, particularly the bombardment of Meshed, aroused not only the members of the Persia Committee but the fears of the India Office and Government of India.

When Sazonov and Grey met at Balmoral in September 1912 Persia was to be the main subject of conversation. Yet no concrete decision was made at the Foreign Office and matters were allowed to drift.[3] Grey was relieved to find Sazonov anxious for peace in the Balkans; mutual differences in Persia, Tibet and Afghanistan were discussed in a friendly manner. It was agreed that Persia should not be partitioned and that Russian troops should be withdrawn as soon as order was restored in the north.[4] Despite a generally optimistic response to these conversations, both Grey and Nicolson knew this was not a solution to their problems in Persia. There were public demonstrations against the Russian minister, and Nicolson, with Grey's permission, suggested to the King that he write privately to the Emperor expressing his warm feelings and general sympathy.[5]

As was anticipated, the Persian situation continued to deteriorate all through 1913 and the Russians consolidated their hold on the north. It was becoming clear that the Russian convention would soon have to be renegotiated. In the interval, Nicolson strongly supported the Russian demand for a Trans-Persian railway despite Indian opposition and tried to get Grey to moderate his many complaints about Russian action at Teheran. Given his personal distaste for the situation, domestic pressures for change and the forceful complaints of Lord Hardinge from India, Grey remained surprisingly loyal to the entente. But he was deeply irritated by Russian behaviour and, as the German danger receded, became somewhat less certain that it was necessary to pay such a high price for Russian support. Difficulties in Persia were compounded by problems in other parts of central Asia and China—Afghanistan, Tibet, Outer Mongolia and Turkestan—and the Foreign Office

[1] FO 800/356, Nicolson to Hardinge, 18 April 1912.
[2] *Ibid*. Nicolson to O'Beirne, 8 May 1912; Nicolson to Grey, 22 April 1912. Nicolson to Buchanan, 23 April 1912.
[3] Hardinge MSS, vol. 70, Chirol to Hardinge, 5 and 10 September 1912.
[4] BD IX(1), no. 803.      [5] *Ibid*. nos. 806, 807.

prepared to open discussions at St Petersburgh on a wide variety of claims. With each British complaint at St Petersburgh, Nicolson's despair about the future of the entente increased. More pessimistic than Grey about the future, both in the Middle East and in Europe, Nicolson set a higher value on the Russian understanding and was more willing to pay the necessary price for loyalty.

Problems in the Balkans raised issues of a different magnitude. Here again Grey was caught between conflicting aims, and Nicolson's advice was shaped by his fears for the future. As in Persia, the Permanent Under-Secretary pressed for stronger links with St Petersburgh than Grey was willing or able to consider. When the Balkan situation erupted, the marginal differences between the two men gradually became more apparent and Nicolson's Foreign Office position correspondingly weaker. Nicolson felt that a Turkish collapse could only be postponed temporarily and that a Russian advance into south-west Europe could not be blocked. 'The determination of Russia, now that she has got her finances in splendid order and reorganized her army, is to reassert and re-establish her predominant position in the Balkans' he warned the British ambassador in Vienna in 1912.[1] Nicolson's assumption of Russian recovery was generally accepted but there was less unanimity about his conclusions and the policies to be followed. Despite his prognosis, Nicolson wished to preserve the existing Turkish state and the peace in the Balkans. Both he and Grey, for instance, sought to insure British neutrality during the Turco-Italian War and intensely disliked Russian attempts to take advantage of Turkish weakness both in the Straits and in the Balkans.[2]

Nicolson fully shared the general Foreign Office concern over Sazonov's sponsorship of the Balkan League. He knew it was a dangerous game which could only lead to disaster. When the Balkan War broke out, therefore, Nicolson gave his full support to Grey's containment policy.[3] During the London ambassadorial conference of 1913, Grey's prestige soared; even Nicolson praised his chief with only minor qualifications.[4] Although Grey

[1] Nicolson, 'Diplomatic Narrative', Nicolson to Cartwright, 8 July 1912 (an unpublished manuscript written by Arthur Nicolson after his retirement from the Foreign Office).

[2] FO 800/173, Nicolson to Bertie, 29 September 1911. FO 800/351, Nicolson to Grey, 18 October 1911. FO 800/352, Nicolson to Hardinge, 2 November 1911. FO 800/355, Nicolson to Hardinge, 18 April 1912.

[3] Nicolson sometimes substituted for Grey and took the latter's share of the daily work load while Grey was in conference. For instance Nicolson saw the representative from Montenegro, heard the complaints of both the Austrian and Russian ambassadors and tried to keep the various British diplomats in the Balkans abreast of the negotiations.

[4] FO 800/365, Nicolson to Goschen, 16 April 1913.

tried to work loyally with the Russians, he was delighted to find that the Germans were conciliatory and anxious to achieve a peaceful settlement. The flare-up in the Balkans provided an excellent opportunity for Anglo-German co-operation (often at Austrian expense) and it was this working partnership which filled Nicolson with alarm. 'What Nicolson is concerned at', Chirol told Hardinge, 'is not so much, therefore, that actual policy hitherto adopted with regard to the different phases of the Balkan War, but the undercurrents which have accompanied it.'[1] If Grey was cheered by the possibility of an Anglo-German rapprochement and anxiously sought ways to strengthen it, Nicolson deplored and feared it. So the gap between the Permanent Under-Secretary and Grey widened.

Nicolson feared a negative Russian reaction to Grey's self-appointed role of 'honest broker'. At the height of the Scutari dispute, for instance, Nicolson told Buchanan (the British ambassador in Russia) that he did not care who got the port as long as the British supported the Russian position. Similarly, when the Austrians had been forced to compromise on the eastern frontier of Albania, it was suggested that the British bring pressure on St Petersburgh to compromise on Scutari. Nicolson rejected this proposal. 'We have promised the Russians our diplomatic support and we cannot now withdraw. Moreover, were we to abandon the Russian standpoint we should be heading straight towards a serious breach in our understanding with Russia, and this would be simply disastrous to us. Scutari is not worth running such a risk.'[2] The traditional Anglo-Russian divergence over the future of Turkey lay behind their clash over an Armenian reform programme. Louis Mallet, as head of the Eastern Department, urged that the Russian proposals for reform be rejected as their aim was to hasten the disruption of the Turkish Empire. Nicolson agreed with Mallet in principle but cautioned Grey that the matter must be handled with the greatest delicacy if the entente were not to be irreparably strained over a question not of secondary importance for British interests.[3] Discussions about Armenia were still going on when war broke out; only Buchanan's great tact had prevented a first-class crisis over the issue.

Nicolson felt that an open declaration of support for Russia would ultimately have been preferable to the careful balancing act which characterized British policy. He, like Cambon, would have preferred Grey to be a little less neutral in his Balkan attitudes.[4] Repeatedly, though not often with

[1] Hardinge MSS, vol. 71, Chirol to Hardinge, 10 April 1913.     [2] BD IX(2), no. 431.
[3] BD X(1), nos. 531, 535. Contrast Nicolson's advice with that of Louis Mallet's and also Norman's in the minutes. *Ibid.* nos. 507, 528, 531, 542, particularly the last for other differences.
[4] See Grey's suspicions about Cambon's position, *Twenty-Five Years*, vol. I, p. 264.

full success, he urged Grey to sacrifice the point at issue to the interests of maintaining the Anglo-Russian entente. It was the German side of the situation which made Nicolson increasingly uneasy. 'I have noticed of late', he wrote to Goschen on 11 February, 'that the German government have on more than one occasion endeavoured to induce us to co-operate with them in what would really be isolated action in matters in which they must know we should, were we to conform to their views, come into conflict with the desires of Russia.'[1] Nicolson was convinced that the Germans were using the Balkan situation to win the British while at the same time they were courting the Russians, a policy which would result in total British isolation.

We are on the whole convinced that the best means of preserving European peace is to maintain unimpaired the present grouping of the Powers, and I always tell the friends of Germany in this country that were we to abandon our understanding with France and with Russia, the peace of Europe would be in a most precarious state, as were Germany to be convinced that we at any rate would remain neutral in the event of a European war, I think that before long her western neighbour would very shortly find extreme pressure put upon her, and her position rendered almost intolerable.[2]

During 1913 the difficulties in the Middle East mentioned earlier placed further strains on the already stretched partnership in the Balkans. The Russians obviously felt they were stronger internally and could afford to take a more aggressive line. Nicolson gloomily predicted that the entente would collapse or worse still lead to a Russo-German bargain. Each of these questions raised the larger problem of Anglo-Russian relations. When the perennial issue of the Dardanelles was again raised, Nicolson pressed Grey to take a sympathetic line. 'To my mind it is of the very highest importance that in all these south-eastern questions, as in other matters, we should maintain a perfect harmony of views and action with her.'[3] But the tide was turning against Nicolson.

Both Nicolson and Grey, as well as observers all over Europe, were highly conscious of the revival of Russian strength. Nicolson believed that for the

[1] Carnock MSS, 1913 (1), Nicolson to Goschen, 11 February 1913.
[2] BD IX(2), no. 632. German sources suggest that Nicolson's interpretation of German actions was close to the mark, and that his suspicions were well-founded. See F. Stern, 'Bethmann Hollweg and the War: The Limits of Responsibility', in L. Kreiger and F. Stern (eds.), *The Responsibility of Power, Historical Essays in Honor of Hajo Holborn* (New York, 1967); George von Müller, *Der Kaiser: Aus den Tagebüchern des Chef des Marinekabinetts Admiral George Alexander von Müller*, ed. W. Gorlitz (Göttingen, 1965). I am indebted to John Röhl of the University of Sussex for information in the diaries of Admiral von Müller, who was chief of the German Naval Cabinet from 1906 to 1918.
[3] Nicolson, 'Diplomatic Narrative', Nicolson to Goschen, 2 April 1913.

British she was 'a most formidable factor in European politics'.[1] He warned that if the entente were not tightened the Russians would desert. 'The Russians could be exceedingly awkward in the Mid and Far East and could seriously shake the British position in India. This is to me such a nightmare that I would at almost any cost keep Russia's friendship.'[2] It was reported from both Berlin and Vienna that the Austrian Empire was rapidly disintegrating and that the Germans had serious doubts about the future place and utility of their only real ally. Nicolson argued that if the Dual Monarchy broke up, Germany would look to Russia for support and the British would be left isolated.[3] There was another possibility which disturbed Grey far more. The Russian army was being reformed and strengthened and would soon be the most formidable force in Europe. It was generally known that Germany was beginning to feel the strain of her armaments programme. In the long run, given the weakness of Austria-Hungary, she could not compete with Russia. The Germans believed that, even without British intervention, Russia and France could, within three years, defeat an Austro-German combination. If such a war could not be averted, there was much to be said for a decision before the Russian armies were ready to fight.[4] Grey, influenced no doubt by German co-operation in the Balkan crisis, was acutely aware of the mounting anxieties at Berlin and the possibility of a preventive war.[5] He knew there were two factions in Berlin and very much wanted to strengthen the 'peace' party. Nicolson, pursued by the nightmare of a Russo-German combination, wished to tighten the links with St Petersburgh. Grey, hoping that Germany would remain a conservative force in south-eastern Europe, attempted to reassure Berlin about Russian intentions.[6] Nicolson pressed for a clear statement of support for Russia; Grey preferred to maintain the ententes but to conciliate Berlin. The Foreign Secretary thought these policies complementary; Nicolson believed them to be contradictory and disastrous.

[1] FO 800/365, Nicolson to Goschen, 8 April 1913.
[2] See also the letter written by Nicolson to de Bunsen, 27 April 1914, quoted in E. T. S. Dugdale, *Maurice de Bunsen* (London, 1934), p. 284.
[3] FO 800/373, Nicolson to de Bunsen, 30 March 1914.
[4] FO 800/365, Buchanan to Nicolson, 14 April, 17 April 1913.
[5] FO 800/161, Bertie memorandum, 16 July 1914. 'Grey says that whereas hereto Germany has feigned alarm at the encircling policy against Germany falsely attributed to His Majesty's Government under the inspiration of King Edward, and made it an excuse for largely increasing her navy, she is now really frightened at the growing strength of the Russian Army, and may make another military effort additional to the recent large expenditure to meet which the special capital tax was instituted, or bring on a conflict with Russia at an early date before the increases in the Russian Army have their full effect and before the completion of the Russian strategic railways . . .'
[6] FO 800/171, memorandum by Bertie, 27 June 1914.

The situation between Russia and Germany deteriorated during the winter of 1914. The Liman von Sanders incident once again involved the British in the protection of Russian interests.[1] Though the Germans stepped down, a sharp Russo-German press war broke out which kept diplomatic nerves on edge. Just as the British Government were preparing to discuss a number of mutual problems with the Russians in central Asia, the latter, frightened by the German appearance at Constantinople, began to repair their diplomatic fences and pressed for a defensive alliance. Sazonov's proposal met with a mixed reception at the Foreign Office. Nicolson, who realized that the Anglo-Russian agreement had been seriously strained, was delighted. Though an alliance was impossible, he urged Grey to follow up subsequent Russian suggestions for strengthening the entente. Grey was cool, 'we had better postpone discussion of anything as long as we can'.[2] The Cabinet's reluctance to take a stand infuriated the Permanent Under-Secretary, particularly as the Germans did a volte-face at St Petersburgh and appeared to be again courting the Russians. 'I do not know', Nicolson wrote to Buchanan, 'how much longer we shall be able to follow our present policy of dancing on a high rope and not be compelled to take up some definite line or other. I am also haunted by the same fear as you—lest Russia become tired of us and strike a bargain with Germany.'[3]

Grey moved slowly and cautiously. Due to French prodding at Paris, he agreed to naval talks with Russia along the same lines as the 1912 naval conversations with France. The Liberal Cabinet felt that these talks committed the Government to little. Grey refused, however, to consider the possibility of a military engagement, however hypothetical. The British dragged their feet; the talks had hardly begun before Grey raised the question of Persia. Sazonov was furious and eventually replied to the British complaints in a memorandum which the Foreign Office found weak and childish.[4] 'I have never read a flimsier document', Crowe minuted, 'and it seems useless to take any notice of it.'[5] Again Nicolson intervened to check the hostile tone of the despatches coming from Teheran.[6] More important and even more distressing to the Permanent Under-Secretary, Grey tried (unsuccessfully) to mitigate the negative effects created in Berlin by leaked

---

[1] At first Nicolson urged Grey to take a strong stand against Germany but complications forced him to moderate his stand and he admitted that 'we should look rather foolish if we took the question up warmly and then found that Sazonoff more or less deserted us. In fact there is a certain disinclination on our part to pull the chestnuts out of the fire for Russia'. (BD x(1), no. 393.)

[2] BD x(2), no. 537. Crowe supported Nicolson.

[3] FO 800/373, Nicolson to Buchanan, 21 April 1914.

[4] FO 800/374, Buchanan to Nicolson, 11 June 1914.　　　　　　[5] BD x(2), no. 561.

[6] FO 800/372, Nicolson to Buchanan, 7 April 1914.

reports of his naval talks with St Petersburgh. He not only reassured the German ambassador that Britain had no binding engagements but warned the Russians: 'The persistent reports about a naval convention and Straits agreement would do great harm in Germany. They might lead to a new Novelle in connection with the German fleet and they might impair our good relations with Germany, which had improved very much during the last Balkan crisis, and which I wished to maintain.'[1] On 9 July 1914 Grey tried to secure German moderation at Vienna by reassuring her about future Russian policy.[2] On 14 July Nicolson wrote to Buchanan 'It seems to me that our relations with Russia are now approaching a point when we shall have to make up our minds as to whether we should become really intimate and personal friends, or else diverge into another path.'[3] Persia, despite the agreement on the trans-Persian railway, remained a prickly thorn. Nicolson's hopes lay in a Russian proposal on 18 July for a Triple Alliance with Japan in the Far East.[4]

But well before this date, Nicolson was completely alienated by the Ulster policy of the Liberal Government and its indecisive foreign diplomacy. 'What has been recently passing in this country, and for which I think the Government are entirely to blame, has been perhaps most disastrous for our position and influence abroad', Nicolson wrote to Goschen in Berlin in March 1914.[5] Convinced that despite the temporary calm, a clash was inevitable, Nicolson was appalled by the Government's failure to prepare the country for the coming struggle. Yet Nicolson's isolation was complete. His relations with Grey were strained over Ulster.[6] William Tyrrell openly mistrusted him and found him far too pro-Russian to give wise counsel, an opinion shared by Francis Bertie.[7] Nicolson seems even to have clashed with Eyre Crowe, a man whose views he fully accepted and for whom he had great respect.[8] As a result, he was extremely anxious to leave London for the Paris embassy, which he had been promised. Grey, too, was looking forward to

---

[1] BD x(2), no. 588.    [2] BD XI, no. 41.    [3] BD x(2), Appendix I.    [4] *Ibid.*
[5] FO 800/373, Nicolson to Goschen, 30 March 1914.
[6] Hardinge MSS, vol. 93, Chirol to Hardinge, 22 May 1914. See, however, the letters exchanged earlier, cited in pp. 122–3, n. 6.
[7] Hardinge MSS, vol. 93, 10 April 1913; 23 May, 20 June, 4 July 1913; Chirol to Hardinge on Tyrrell's dislike and distrust of Nicolson. 'What I regret most of all—quite between ourselves— is his bitter antagonism now towards Nicolson, whom he charges in so many words with grave disloyalty towards Grey. If what he tells me is not an exaggeration, Nicolson would seem to have been woefully indiscreet, to say the least. Nicolson talked to me very freely, but that is quite a different thing from criticizing his chief's policy in conversations with foreign diplomatists—if he really has done so.' *Ibid.* Chirol to Hardinge, 10 April 1913. For Bertie's view, *ibid.* Bertie to Hardinge, 19 February 1914.
[8] *Ibid.* Chirol to Hardinge, 15 April 1914.

Nicolson's departure, both on personal grounds and for the sake of the Foreign Office.[1] In the early summer of 1914, Arthur Nicolson was Grey's chief adviser in name only.

In the Nicolson Foreign Office, Eyre Crowe too was to have less influence than he had formerly exercised. Though appointed assistant under-secretary in 1912 (an overdue promotion) he was increasingly caught up in the minutiae of policy and had less time to devote to general considerations of power politics. In the autumn of 1913 when Louis Mallet went to Constantinople, Crowe was made supervising under-secretary of the Eastern as well as the Western Department. In addition to carrying this double load, Crowe was seriously ill during much of 1913 and had still not recovered in the winter of 1913–14.[2] His reputation grew steadily during these years; his masterly handling of the Savarkar case against France before the Hague Arbitration Court (1911) brought him to the attention of a wide circle outside the Foreign Office. Unlike Nicolson, Crowe was above all a superb civil servant. His capacities in this respect were such that his assistance was required even when his advice was disregarded. He was completely loyal to his chief and carried out Grey's wishes even when they ran counter to his own inclinations. Crowe's name was repeatedly mentioned as a likely replacement for Nicolson when the latter would leave the Foreign Office. But though Crowe advanced in rank and reputation, his influence on the general pattern of diplomacy diminished.

Crowe did not alter his views in the years between 1910 and 1914. He continued to oppose efforts to conclude an arrangement with Berlin. This shrewd analyst understood that the German naval building programme was just an outward symbol of a general restlessness and an indication that her enormous energies could not be absorbed internally. 'The building of the German fleet is but one of the symptoms of the disease', he wrote. 'It is the political ambitions of the German government which are the source of the mischief.'[3] The talks of 1910 confirmed Crowe's suspicions. 'The allusions to the contents of the proposed political agreement are as vague as the rest of the suggestions. But we know from the former correspondence that what Germany wants is both precise and unacceptable.'[4]

---

[1] FO 800/179, memorandum by Bertie, 25 July 1914. According to Bertie, Grey was anxious 'to get rid of Nicolson from the Foreign Office as he stands in the way of something better, viz. Crowe'.

[2] Crowe was absent from the Foreign Office from March until the middle of August 1913, due to an appendectomy and serious gallstone trouble. He recuperated slowly and even in the early months of 1914 was often forced to be absent from Whitehall.

[3] BD VI, pp. 534–5.

[4] *Ibid.* no. 399.

While Grey was encouraged by the German willingness to discuss alternatives, Crowe argued that the Germans could not offer anything concrete and were not to be trusted.

Though no progress was made and there were few grounds for optimism, the Germans continued to press for a political agreement and discussions proceeded. Crowe repeatedly warned the Foreign Secretary that it was 'the openly avowed policy of Germany to make herself so strong that in all matters in which she considered German interests to be involved, she will have her own way'.[1] In his memorandum reviewing the course of the Anglo-German naval negotiations from 1909 until May 1911, Crowe emphasized the many examples of German duplicity and the special problems thereby faced by the British Government.[2]

But it was the Moroccan crisis and not the opposition of the Foreign Office which brought these talks to a halt. Until the Germans intervened, Crowe had deplored French activities in Morocco and was suspicious of their ultimate intentions. 'It is to be feared that the present instance is only a more flagrant example of the vicious policy which the French Government are pursuing in Morocco, whereby, trading on the friendliness of this country, they are ready to make important political bargains with Germany at our expense.'[3] When it became apparent that the Germans would demand a price for such a bargain, Crowe took a very different view of the situation and became an active supporter of the French. The Senior Clerk rightly predicted that the Germans would first display indifference and then at the crucial moment demand material concessions for keeping quiet. Talks were already under way between Paris and Berlin when the Germans decided to make their dramatic gesture at Agadir. Crowe attributed the German decision to the general improvement in Anglo-German relations which had encouraged Berlin to believe that the British would stand aside in any Franco-German dispute.[4]

Like the rest of the Foreign Office, Crowe could not understand what the Germans wanted. England's total exclusion from the whole affair (there was no reply to a British note for seventeen days) created a state of panic in the office which seems to have engulfed Crowe as well as Nicolson. He clearly shared Nicolson's fears that either Berlin would successfully blackmail the French or conclude a bargain with the French in Morocco at British expense.[5] When the German demands for much of the French Congo became

---

[1] *Ibid.* no. 464.
[2] *Ibid.* no. 468. This was written at Grey's request for the Cabinet committee handling Anglo-German relations.
[3] BD VII, no. 179.      [4] *Ibid.* no. 352.      [5] *Ibid.* no. 383.

known, Crowe minuted the relevant despatch 'This is a trial of strength, if anything. Concession means not loss of interests or loss of prestige. It means defeat, with all its inevitable consequences.'[1] Crowe had no doubts that the defeat of France was a matter of life or death for England. He was to return to this same position in July 1914.

The German silence continued. Crowe joined Nicolson and Bertie in urging full support for France but their advice was only partially adopted. Crowe told Bertie that he 'was sorry beyond words at the line we are taking . . . It seems to me our cabinet are all on the run and the strong hints we are giving to France that she must let Germany into Morocco make me ashamed as well as angry.'[2] Though Crowe continued to be active until September (when there are few minutes in his handwriting), the real decision-making was done in the Cabinet or by the small inner circle of ministers who conducted British policy during the late summer.[3] It was not until October when the war scare subsided that the Senior Clerk took the matter up again.[4] Crowe suspected that M. Caillaux (a minister for whom he had little respect) might well have planned to sacrifice the entente for a bargain with Berlin. Crowe's uneasiness about the loyalty of the French increased when *Le Temps* revealed the secret clauses of the Anglo-French declaration of 1904, a break of diplomatic trust which appalled the civil servant in him. In a long review of the crisis early in 1912, Crowe erroneously argued that Caillaux and the Germans had concluded an arrangement prior to July 1911 and that the 'spring of the Panther' represented a planned step in their collaboration.[5] In Crowe's view, it was French public opinion which had forced their government to repudiate Caillaux, leaving the Germans furious and cheated of their promised rewards. Crowe feared the possibility of German revenge far more than French duplicity and repeated the ideas elaborated in his 1907 memorandum that these unsatisfied German grievances were the real dangers to the peace of Europe.

In the last resort our quarrel with Germany arises not from the peculiar methods of German diplomacy . . . although these have done much at all times to cause trouble and difficulties . . . but from a conflict of policies. German policy seeks the fulfilment of many ambitions, territorial, idealistic, and other, through the acquisition of a general ascendency in Europe . . . or, rather the world—such as will make it impossible for any other State to oppose whatever wishes or designs she may consider herself justified in entertaining.[6]

Crowe argued that only England could block German aggressive designs.

---

[1] BD VII, no. 392.  [2] FO 800/160, Crowe to Bertie, 20 July 1911.
[3] Crowe may have been on holiday for part of this time.  [4] BD VII, no. 619.
[5] BD X(2), Appendix III, memorandum by Crowe, 14 January 1912.  [6] *Ibid.* p. 825.

England stands for the maintenance of existing rights and liberties so far as they are not incompatible with the orderly progress of the world. She is a strong supporter of the existing balance of power as most conducive to the continuance of independent States, on whose inter-action and peaceful rivalry the progressive evolution of highest social ideals seems to depend . . . It is England's paramount duty to hold fast to the *entente* with France and Russia in order to maintain the balance of power.[1]

Crowe was deeply disturbed by the radical campaign against Grey in the winter of 1911 and had little sympathy with the decision to send Haldane to Berlin. He undoubtedly included Haldane and Harcourt among those 'amateur diplomatists, peace mongers and meddlesome busybodies' whom he so abhorred.[2] He deplored the talks initiated by Haldane and during the spring of 1912 pointed out to Grey in numerous minutes the dangers of the search for a political formula and the one-sided nature of the German colonial proposals.[3] He did not believe that the peace party in Berlin was strong enough to prevail against Tirpitz and, unlike Grey, was to find von Jagow no better than any of his predecessors at the Wilhelmstrasse. Even when the search for a 'formula' failed, Crowe remained uneasy about the pro-German trend of the Government's policy; he believed all negotiations with the Germans were bound to be 'indecisive, vacillating and highly dangerous'. But despite the strong feeling in the Foreign Office, Grey favoured local agreements which would lower the diplomatic fever chart and encourage a rapprochement with Germany.[4] This feeling grew as the Balkan crisis erupted but it was one that Crowe could not share. Nevertheless, a good civil servant carries out his minister's orders, and Crowe himself was soon involved in the search for a colonial bargain which would cement the détente with Berlin. As he had served earlier in the African Department and had become its supervising under-secretary, Crowe prepared a memorandum summarizing the historical background of the Portuguese colonial question and suggested the course Britain should follow. Though far from enthusiastic about the talks, Crowe, assisted by John Tilley, prepared the drafts used by Lulu Harcourt and criticized the countless drafts and counterdrafts submitted by the Germans.[5] He was always jealous of the prerogatives of the Foreign Office and fruitlessly urged Grey to intervene with the Colonial Secretary.[6]

[1] *Ibid.*          [2] Nicolson, *Lord Carnock*, p. 239.
[3] BD x(2), pp. 429–34.          [4] BD VI, nos. 527, 529, 564.
[5] *DGP* XXXVII, no. 73. Von Kühlmann to Bethmann Hollweg, 19 August 1913. 'Sir Eyre Crowe is the only official in the Foreign Office, who has had sufficient legal training and knows the German language well enough to be able to perform the task of an adequate translation of the Portuguese Colonial Treaty.' BD x(2), no. 299.
[6] BD x(2), no. 285. Grey first moved reluctantly but then swung to Harcourt's support. 'I am to

For Grey had agreed to the discussions and left Harcourt a free field even when it had become clear that the latter had 'given away a great deal and has received very little in return'.[1] Bertie recorded his impressions, 'Crowe, whom I saw at the Foreign Office today, told me Grey had allowed Harcourt to negotiate with the German Embassy and had taken no heed of Foreign Office warnings in regard to Germany.'[2] Crowe did successfully back his demand that full records be kept in order to safeguard his country against future misrepresentations.[3]

Under Crowe's prodding, the British insisted that the Germans consent to immediate publication and also proposed that the original Anglo-German and Anglo-Portuguese treaties of 1898 and 1899 be made public at the same time.[4] This was one of the few cases where Crowe urged the use of publicity to gain his point. The Wilhelmstrasse baulked; if the Portuguese knew of the bargain they would take steps to avoid such a partition of their colonial empire. It is true that Grey was somewhat relieved when the matter was dropped at German insistence, for the discussions were hardly creditable to Britain.[5] But the Foreign Secretary had fulfilled his major aim. 'The most important motive', he wrote to Goschen on 3 March 1914, 'had been the improvement of relations with Germany.'[6] Though the treaty remained unratified, the conversations underlined the détente with Berlin. Crowe, despite his objections and distaste for the proceedings, had carried out these lengthy and technical exchanges with a skill matched only by the very best of his clerical predecessors.

The same is true of the Baghdad railway negotiations. Though Alwyn Parker, the Foreign Office expert in these matters, conducted the talks with both the Turks and the Germans, he had the backing and support of Crowe.[7] Originally, Crowe had opposed the idea of an Anglo-German bargain but after the Potsdam agreement between Germany and Russia realized that British participation in the building of the railway was the only alternative to total exclusion.[8] The convention which was signed on 29 May 1914 was

meet Harcourt next month and study the map of Africa with him in a pro-German spirit; then the Cabinet will review the situation.' *Ibid.* no. 266. Grey gradually came to support the negotiations; notice the sharp change in tone in his communications to Bertie between 1912 and the summer of 1913 when he defended the agreement on the grounds that 'Portugal is unfit to administer anything and that she ought to renounce her colonies'. FO 800/176, memorandum by Bertie, 29 June 1913.

[1] FO 800/176, memorandum by Bertie, 23 June 1913.
[2] FO 800/188, memorandum by Bertie, 17 February 1914.    [3] BD x(2), no. 323.
[4] *Ibid.* nos. 270, 281, 299, 320-22, 331.
[5] FO 800/188, memorandum by Bertie, 19 February 1914.
[6] FO 800/176, Grey to Goschen, 3 March 1914.    [7] BD x(2), nos. 156 and 225.
[8] *Ibid.* no. 23. This despatch with Parker's and Crowe's minutes was circulated to the King and

the kind of arrangement with Berlin which Crowe tended to favour for both sides secured almost equal advantages. Crowe quickly mastered the details of these complex discussions and played an active if supporting role in their successful conclusion.

After Crowe made a partial recovery from his illness, he was plunged into the heart of the Balkan conflagration. Here he was less concerned than Nicolson over the Russian side of the question and concentrated on three vexed issues—the disposition of the Aegean islands, the boundaries of the newly constituted state of Albania, and the recurrent but difficult question of Armenian reforms. Italy, Greece and Turkey all claimed the Aegean islands and the question had been submitted to the mediation of the great powers. Crowe was anxious that England should work in harmony with the concert of powers and backed Grey's efforts to avoid isolated action.[1] But the concert rarely acted in unison; Grey was pressed in opposite directions by Russia and Turkey, and the Assistant Under-Secretary accused Berlin of deserting the Anglo-German partnership for the sake of fomenting discord so that she could acquire a special position of influence at Constantinople.[2] It was as if Crowe was trying to underline for Grey's information all the evidence that the Germans could not be trusted even in the Balkans.

With regard to Albania and Armenia, Crowe did the kind of work a foreign secretary traditionally expected his under-secretaries to perform.

Cabinet committee 23 March 1911. Alwyn Parker of the Eastern Department had established his reputation as the office expert on Turkish and Persian affairs. He worked out all the agreements connected with the Baghdad and trans-Persian railways, irrigation works in Mesopotamia, oil concessions in Persia and knew far more about these subjects than any man at the Foreign Office. 'This paper has been referred to me for observations by Mr Mallet; I minute it with some diffidence, partly because I am so much occupied in getting up other important questions (e.g. the Declaration of London and the Flushing Fortifications) in my own Department that I cannot follow in detail the Middle East negotiations; and principally because I do feel very strongly indeed that our policy in regard to these negotiations should not be merely passive and expectant, —but since my previous minutes to this effect have not been approved, I am not sure whether insistence from my subordinate position will be welcomed.' (BD x(1), no. 664, minute by Parker, 31 January 1911.)

Parker's advice on the question of British participation in the Baghdad railway (which implied negotiations with Berlin) was finally accepted. Both the major railway agreements (with Turkey and Germany) were negotiated by Parker and all the attendant commercial and financial issues were also settled by him. Grey gave him a free hand and other Foreign Office officials (though not always Mallet) and diplomats deferred to him. Grey's praise (BD x(2), no. 183) of Parker's work and the tributes to his knowledge and skill were more than fully warranted. At one point Parker wrote to Hardinge that he had been working twelve hours a day for five weeks (Hardinge MSS, vol. 70, Parker to Hardinge, 9 July 1912) and the archives fully bear out Parker's laments. Parker's case is an excellent illustration of the competence of the staff of the pre-war Foreign Office. For details, see Edward Mead Earle, *Turkey, the Great Powers and the Baghdad Railway* (Northampton, Mass., 1948). There is also a review of British policy by Parker in the *Quarterly Review*, October 1917.

[1] BD x(1), no. 212.    [2] *Ibid.* no. 223. Grey MSS, no. 41, Grey to Mallet, 12 March 1914.

Grey was at Fallodon when the Austrian ultimatum to Serbia in October 1913 threatened to turn the Albanian question into a major conflict.[1] Though Crowe, like Nicolson, deplored the Serbian action which had precipitated the crisis, he was distressed by Austria's independent intervention and, once again, accused the Germans of encouraging her ally to break up the concert.[2] The whole Albanian tangle was further complicated by the attempt of the great powers to establish a decent government for the newly created state. Crowe believed that it was England's duty to take a part in this settlement. But as Austria and Italy were soon using the international commission to further their own aims, Crowe urged that the British withdraw before their own reputation for moral behaviour was compromised. 'My own inclination is in accord with Sir E. Crowe's minute', Grey wrote, 'and I would come to that decision and act upon it at once, if Russia and France had not to be considered.'[3] The Austrian intrigues continued. 'To remain in the concert on these terms is neither useful nor dignified', Crowe minuted. 'If we were to retire it would not be so much laying down our flute, as calling attention to the fact that we are not admitted to the orchestra.'[4]

The perennial problem of Armenia also occupied Crowe's attention.[5] Here Crowe feared that the entente with Russia might be permanently injured over the dispute. The question was so complicated that Crowe had one of his juniors draw up a summary précis but even the most ingenious civil servant could not find a formula which would satisfy the Russians and yet preserve Turkish amour propre.[6] In the von Sanders case, Crowe found the Russian demand excessive and was somewhat less sympathetic to their cause than Nicolson.[7] Crowe worked closely with Grey and provided the Foreign Secretary with a multitude of proposals on each of these questions.

During 1913 and 1914 Crowe was immersed in the detailed work of his department: 'his abilities as an administrator eclipsed his role as Cassandra'.[8] Quite apart from his illness, there was a notable decrease in the number of memoranda in Crowe's hand. This is not because he had changed his views about Germany. Even in 1914 he deplored the demand for a reduction of naval expenditure and had little doubt that German naval policy was still motivated by hostility towards England however irrational such a policy might appear. 'I feel confident that if we make a "definite

[1] BD x(2), no. 38.
[2] *Ibid*. nos. 12, 54, 57.    [3] *Ibid*. no. 100.    [4] *Ibid*. no. 123.
[5] *Ibid*. no. 567, minute by Crowe.    [6] *Ibid*. no. 586.
[7] *Ibid*. no. 452, minute by Crowe, circulated to King and Cabinet.
[8] Cosgrove, 'Sir Eyre Crowe and the English Foreign Office, 1905–14', Ph.D. thesis, p. 163.

proposal" vis-à-vis a naval holiday we shall not be treated straightforwardly in the negotiation, and I regard any such negotiations with so unscrupulous an adversary as highly dangerous.'[1] Perhaps to counterbalance Grey's general impression that Berlin would be a useful partner in the Balkans, Crowe repeatedly emphasized German disloyalty in this area. It was against Crowe's better judgement that Grey sought ways to conciliate the Germans and lent his support to the 'doves' in Berlin. It was against his advice that nothing was done to strengthen the Anglo-French entente in a decisive manner and he was undoubtedly as alarmed as Nicolson by the failure of the Government to press preparations for war. Crowe's hammering logic did not suit the temper of the times and he was strangely silent. He did not, moreover, appreciate the new problems being created by Russia's re-emergence in Europe and said little about this most important aspect of Grey's policy during 1914. But the Assistant Under-Secretary was a skilled draftsman and an able negotiator and there was more than enough business to absorb his abundant energies. Nicolson's weaknesses as an administrator placed an additional burden on Crowe and during Grey's absences from the Foreign Office it was often Crowe who received foreign ambassadors and met visiting diplomats. 'The main purpose of Mallet's appointment is, I fancy, to clear the way for the Crowe Bird when Nicolson goes and that is quite sound', Chirol informed Hardinge.[2] Nicolson himself believed that Crowe was the right man to succeed him. Hardinge, however, had his reservations. 'Much as I admire Crowe's ability, I shall be sorry if he becomes head of the Foreign Office. It will lower the prestige of the office, as he is so palpably German . . . Further, I mistrust the soundness of his judgements.'[3] Hardinge's snobbery was deeply marked; his social sensibilities were offended by this 'outsider' achieving such a position.[4]

There was another contender. After 1910 it was William Tyrrell who gradually emerged as the key figure at Whitehall. It must be remembered that Tyrrell was not in an official position of power; no previous private secretary (with Mallet's exception) had intervened in questions of high policy. Yet both English and foreign contemporaries have remarked on Tyrrell's pre-eminent role in the pre-war Foreign Office. At the time of Agadir, Clemenceau is reputed to have said, 'Je voudrai savoir ce qu'en

[1] FO 371/1987/6310, minute by Crowe, 11 February 1914.
[2] Hardinge MSS, vol. 93, Chirol to Hardinge, 11 August 1913.
[3] *Ibid.* Hardinge to Nicolson, 18 June 1913.
[4] FO 800/243. Typescript report of conversation with Lord Curzon, 15 October 1919; 'In the service', Crowe said, 'I had always been made to feel that I had come in as an outsider.' See also Bertie MSS, series A, Lister to Bertie, 12 December 1905, for a view similar to that of Hardinge's.

pense le petit Japonais au bord de la Tamise.'[1] 'In talking to Sir William', Colonel House wrote to President Wilson in 1913, 'we were practically talking to Sir Edward Grey and I thought it would be foolish not to utilize the opportunity in order to bring about a better understanding with England regarding Mexico.'[2] Despite the many references to Tyrrell's power, one must piece together an account from scanty and even unreliable sources.

Throughout the Agadir crisis, Tyrrell shared the general Foreign Office alarm about German efforts to wreck the entente. In July 1911, when Bertie was summoned back to London, Tyrrell hoped the ambassador would convince their chief to stand firmly with France. Grey's private secretary was delighted with Lloyd George's Mansion House speech.

Don't forget to teach your children to keep alive the memory of Lloyd George [Tyrrell wrote to Spring-Rice] who by his timely speech has saved the peace of Europe and our good name ... His co-operation with the Chief is delightful to watch ... From yours and my point of view he is as sound as a bell and it hardly needed the Germans to undeceive him.[3]

But during 1912 Tyrrell supported a somewhat more flexible approach to the German problem. As he believed that the naval race was the key to Anglo-German relations, he may well have thought that once this issue had been decided in England's favour, Germany's real threat had lost its sting. Or perhaps, being more sensitive to public opinion than the majority of his Foreign Office colleagues, he may have responded to the back-bench revolt against Grey's foreign policy and have been anxious to protect his chief from unjust criticism. Even in the spring of 1912, members of the German embassy thought him sympathetic to the idea of a colonial agreement. It was at this time, while Grey was away, that the German counsellor, Richard von Kühlmann, suggested various ways that Anglo-German relations might be improved if the search for a political formula failed.[4] There is no evidence, on the British side, for Kühlmann's story that in October 1912 Tyrrell approached him privately with 'a serious and decisive proposal' which involved co-operating with Germany in the Balkans, China, Persia, Turkey and Africa.[5] Even Kiderlen, writing from Berlin, expressed his scepticism about the seriousness of such an offer and though

1 *Dictionary of National Biography*, quoted by F. Ashton-Gwatkin; Oppenheimer, *Stranger Within*, p. 206. 'Sir William Tyrrell, who was rising to the position of the Grey Eminence in the Foreign Office...' (date, October 1911).

2 E. M. House, *Intimate Papers of Colonel House*, arranged as a narrative by C. Seymour (Boston, 1926), vol. 1, p. 198.

3 FO 800/241, Tyrrell to Spring-Rice, 1 August 1911.

4 FO 800/55, Tyrrell to Grey, 3 April 1912.

5 DGP XXXIII, 12284–12287. See also 12240, 12278 and the account in Nicolson, *Lord Carnock*, 384–6.

Kühlmann saw Grey on 7 and 14 October, the matter was not raised. Grey spoke only of the need to prevent the great powers from being pulled into the imminent Turco-Bulgarian War. When Kühlmann retold the story in his memoirs, his account was so garbled and inadequate that it can hardly be admitted as evidence.[1] Nevertheless, there is some substance to the German diplomatist's assertion that Tyrrell thought the Russians were becoming increasingly difficult and that an improvement in Anglo-German relations might serve as a useful corrective to the Russian Government. Tyrrell might well have been testing possibilities with Kühlmann which Grey was not yet prepared to formulate or to discuss through the usual official channels. Equally plausible was Kühlmann's telegraphic report of Tyrrell's subsequent warning that he had been merely expressing Grey's personal opinion and that neither Nicolson nor Goschen had been informed.[2] Sazonov's recent visit and Foreign Office fears about Russian action in the Balkans could explain Tyrrell's approach.

The outbreak of the Balkan War in October 1912 shifted the centre of European diplomacy to that area in which the links between allies were most subject to strain. As we have seen, Nicolson found himself increasingly isolated and during the London Conference of ambassadors, Grey did work out a more satisfactory relationship with the Germans. In the spring of 1913 Tyrrell was more optimistic about the possibilities of peace than he had been a year ago.

William Tyrrell is very perky indeed—thinks that all is for the best of all possible Europes and paints our own position as absolutely *couleur de rose*. He seems to think that we can now snap our fingers at the Triple Alliance and at France and Russia, upon the latter of whom he has gone back in a most astonishing way . . .

I confess I am rather alarmed at the extraordinary change which his views seem to have undergone in the course of the last six months. Nico, I think, to some extent shares my alarm, for though he does not believe that William Tyrrell has any real confidence in the benevolent sentiments of which Germany is so profuse towards us, the course which William Tyrrell welcomes must, he is convinced, bring us once more, and is now already bringing us, into the orbit of German policy.[3]

Chirol confronted Tyrrell and sought an explanation. 'He is convinced however, that we are relieved, at least for a long time to come, from the

---

[1] Richard von Kühlmann, *Erinnerungen* (Heidelberg, 1948), 339–41, 343, 373. Kühlmann dates this meeting September 1911 but this seems impossible. The more likely date would be 1912, though here again (as with many of Kühlmann's accounts of conversations with Tyrrell) there are internal contradictions which cast doubt on Kühlmann's veracity or memory. See Louis Namier, *Vanished Supremacies* (London, 1958), 103–4. There is an interesting account of Grey's warnings about this German diplomat during the Baghdad railway negotiations by Alwyn Parker in *The Times Literary Supplement*, 7 October 1949.

[2] DGP XXXIII, 12285.  [3] Hardinge MSS, vol. 93, Chirol to Hardinge, 10 April 1913.

German menace and can therefore take up a somewhat firmer line with Russia without compromising the Entente.'[1] Tyrrell went on to argue that Russia was following a cynical policy in Persia and China while hoping that the British would fight Russian battles in the Balkans, a role scarcely acceptable to Grey.[2]

What in his opinion compromises the Entente is the cynical selfishness of Russian policy in Persia, Mongolia, Pekin ... and in fact to save the Entente he holds Russia must be brought to her bearings—That this can be done without estranging her, he considers to be proved by the success of the firm front shown towards her throughout the Balkan crisis by Sir Edward who had kept her to her engagements by telling her straight out that he was not prepared to repeat what happened in 1908 when we went far beyond the demands of British interests to support Russian policy, and then were left in the lurch.[3]

Tyrrell believed that once the Balkan crisis subsided, the British should take a sharper line with the Russians in Persia, Mongolia and China and 'bring her to her senses'. Hardinge was very much alarmed by Chirol's report 'since I know well the influence he enjoys with Edward Grey, who temperamentally is quite ready to listen to German blandishments influenced as he is by Haldane in his views'.[4]

As might be expected, Tyrrell's views led to a sharp clash with Arthur Nicolson 'who still, as Tyrrell put it, wanted to leave the Russians to pipe the tune and us to dance to it what ever it may be'.[5] The personal enmity between the two men was barely disguised. Grey's private secretary wanted Nicolson to retire 'and his (Tyrrell's) influence with Sir E. Grey is growing greater and greater—perhaps too great'.[6] The two men gave contrary advice on the policy to be followed towards Russia in the Balkans, in Armenia, in Asiatic Turkey and in Persia.[7] Paul Cambon, the French ambassador in London, warned the Quai d'Orsay in March 1914 that Tyrrell's complaints about Russian policy in Persia should not be taken too seriously. 'C'est à Sir E. Grey et Sir A. Nicolson que revient le soin de diriger la politique britannique à l'égard de la Russie'.[8] Cambon was misled by his closeness to Nicolson and his natural isolation from the gossip of the Foreign Office.

It was a sign of the times and of Tyrrell's growing power that Ralph

[1] Hardinge MSS, vol. 93, Chirol to Hardinge, 18 April 1913.      [2] *Ibid.*
[3] *Ibid.* vol. 71, Chirol to Hardinge, 18 April 1913.
[4] *Ibid.* vol. 93, Hardinge to Chirol, 30 April 1913.
[5] *Ibid.* vol. 71, Chirol to Hardinge, 23 May 1913.
[6] *Ibid.* vol. 93, Chirol to Hardinge, 2 June 1913.
[7] *Ibid.* 23 May, 4 July, 9 July 1913 for some of the evidence. FO 800/241, Chirol to Spring-Rice, 30 July 1913.
[8] DDF, 3rd series, vol. IX, no. 414, Cambon to Doumergue, 8 March 1914.

Paget, a diplomat of known pro-German sympathies, was brought from Belgrade to become assistant under-secretary in 1913.[1] In November of the same year, Tyrrell was sent to Washington as Grey's private ambassador and discussed a wide range of diplomatic problems with the Americans, extending from the Panama Canal tolls and Wilson's Mexican policy to the general questions raised by Colonel House's scheme for armament reduction.[2] Cecil Spring-Rice (the British ambassador in Washington) was ill and Tyrrell took over the embassy for about six weeks, making an excellent impression on both House and Wilson. His sojourn in Washington added considerably to his reputation; thereafter his name was increasingly mentioned as the next ambassador to Germany or as a replacement for Nicolson when the latter would go to Paris in the autumn of 1914.[3]

It was through his personal closeness to Grey that Tyrrell could out-influence everyone else. He went with his chief to Paris and subsequently did everything possible to lighten Grey's load of work. The Foreign Secretary's eyes were beginning to trouble him seriously and the political difficulties of the Liberal party in the spring and summer of 1914 pre-occupied him. 'Grey is absorbed, not unnaturally, with domestic politics and leaves things (perhaps a great deal too much) in Willie Tyrrell's hands, who is overworked and over-wrought', Chirol reported to Hardinge in the early summer.[4]

How influential Tyrrell was and to what extent Grey followed his advice must remain open to question. British diplomacy towards St Petersburgh did not follow a well-defined path and it is not at all clear that Grey had decided to take the firmer line being pressed by Tyrrell. One is not even sure how far Tyrrell supported a rapprochement with Germany.[5] He may well have believed, as I think Grey did, that a détente had to be limited in scope and the existing pattern of European alignments maintained if peace were to be preserved. But the Private Secretary seems to have felt that the Russians, if not called to order, might disturb this balance and force the Germans into an even more aggressive position. The evidence thus far shows that Tyrrell was recommending a line of policy which differed sharply from that favoured by Nicolson and, to a lesser extent, by Crowe. 'Nicolson and Tyrrell were both away,' Austin Lee wrote Bertie, 'I am told

---

[1] Paget took over the American Department.
[2] *Intimate Papers of Colonel House*, vol. I, p. 242.
[3] Hardinge MSS, vol. 93, Mallet to Hardinge, 11 August 1913; Chirol to Hardinge, 15 April 1914.
[4] *Ibid*. Chirol to Hardinge, 22 May 1914.
[5] Tyrrell was to visit Jagow in the spring of 1914 but his trip was postponed and never took place. Count Bernstorff, *Memoirs*, trans. by B. Sutton (London, 1936), 137.

the latter is in high favour and is everything to Grey. Both are now very Germano-phile.'[1] Hardinge confirmed this impression. 'Tyrrell practically runs the policy and . . . Nicolson is now of no account. The latter has played his cards very badly and his heart is not in his work.'[2]

In assessing Tyrrell's influence, it must be remembered that Grey was now at the peak of his reputation. His masterly handling of the London ambassadorial conference enhanced his prestige in every European capital. If he continued to seek advice and delegate authority, he was no longer a 'new boy' and did not need the kind of support formerly offered by Charles Hardinge. Tyrrell seems to have been the bridge between this shy man and the outside world; the private secretary could have influenced but did not shape Grey's view of the European world. In the Cabinet, though old divisions and suspicions persisted, the Foreign Secretary had won his major battles. The entente with France was firmly established. The understanding with Russia might have to be re-negotiated but Grey did not share Nicolson's alarm or sense of urgency. The naval conversations with France and the proposed talks with Russia had been approved by a majority of Grey's colleagues. Neither the Prime Minister nor the Foreign Secretary could be pressed into a fuller examination of Britain's continental obligations. Moreover, the sting had been removed from the radical-Labour opposition to Grey's diplomacy. As has been suggested, Grey was less adverse to an accommodation with Berlin as long as such agreements did not touch Britain's naval superiority or alter relations with France and Russia. The Baghdad railway agreement was initialled in June 1914; the naval question simmered but did not boil.[3] The Cabinet had more immediate domestic problems to consider.

Looking back at these last years of peace, a major conclusion emerges. The new Foreign Office was one in which very gifted men played roles more significant, complex and, at times, difficult to define than had their predecessors. This meant that differences of personality and diplomatic inclination were coming into the open and becoming relevant to the actual making of policy. These differences, as we have seen, reflected the larger ambivalence of England's position in Europe. Even if such men as Nicolson, Crowe and Tyrrell had been unanimous in their reading of the world map, England's role between and towards Berlin, Paris and St Petersburgh would

[1] FO 800/188, Austin Lee to Bertie, 14 April 1914.
[2] Hardinge MSS, vol. 93, Hardinge to Chirol, 11 June 1914.
[3] Churchill's proposals for a naval holiday were neither pressed by Grey nor openly rejected by the Germans. In January 1914 there was a new Cabinet split and public dispute about the naval estimates. The 'economists' were again defeated.

have been an intricate and unstable one. The changing position of Russia was the new factor which complicated relations in 1914. But this general diplomatic instability was underlined by those differences of tone and vision inside Whitehall which I have been outlining. If the ultimate responsibility for policy-making rested with Sir Edward Grey, the counsel which he was receiving was no longer unanimous and the role of the Foreign Office was thereby altered.

## The July crisis

In the spring of 1914 there was only one issue—Ulster. The Cabinet had little time for foreign policy; even the Anglo-Russian negotiations were pushed to the side.[1] Fortunately for the Liberals, the European scene was unusually peaceful. Grey's visit to Paris had been a great personal success. Balkan problems were no more pressing than usual and Anglo-Russian conversations had begun. Relations with Berlin were better than they had been over a decade. 'Since I have been at the Foreign Office', Nicolson wrote early in May, 'I have not seen such calm waters.'[2] To the outsider, the Foreign Office seemed to be operating effectively in its usual remote and secretive manner. Though there were recurrent demands for a more demo-cratic approach to diplomacy, there was no repetition of the concerted attack of 1911–12. Yet at its senior level the Foreign Office was ill-prepared for a major crisis.

In May 1914 Chirol wrote to Hardinge

The way in which things are going at the Foreign Office causes me much concern ... Nicolson's position seems to me quite impossible. For some reason or other ... perhaps because he talks too much about Ulster and his wife still more ... he has absolutely lost Grey's confidence and he does not conceal the fact that he is sick of it all.[3]

The difficulties of the situation were compounded by Grey's procrastination. Though he wished to 'be rid of Nicolson', he had to find a place for him and Bertie did not wish to leave the Paris embassy. Nicolson anticipated his chief by asking Bertie in June 1914 how much of his furniture the Ambassador was willing to sell. Right in the middle of the July crisis, Bertie mounted a counter-campaign which included pressure on the Prime Minister and the

[1] B. de Siebert and G. A. Schreiner, *Entente Diplomacy and the War* (New York, 1921), pp. 717, 719. The Cabinet discussed the question on 13 May.
[2] See the letter by Nicolson in FO 800/374, 4 May 1914.
[3] Hardinge MSS, vol. 93, Chirol to Hardinge, 22 May 1914.

outcome was very much in doubt.[1] Moreover, Grey had not decided who should replace Nicolson in London. 'The majority regard Crowe's success as certain. I feel there may be a battle of giants between him and Tyrrell', Mark Oliphant wrote early in 1914.[2] Valentine Chirol complained to Hardinge,

The Foreign Office, as far as I can gather, seems to be just as much at sixes and sevens as the Cabinet. I have not yet seen any of my friends there, but apparently the feud between Crowe and Nicolson is again very bitter; and though some little time ago it seemed to be quite settled that Nicolson was to go to Paris, this is by no means so certain . . . Who is to succeed him [Nicolson] at the Foreign Office, Crowe or Tyrrell? And if Tyrrell is put over Crowe's head, will Crowe remain? There has been a great deal of talk lately of Tyrrell going as ambassador to Berlin but he himself has gone out of his way to contradict it.[3]

Grey did nothing to resolve this difficult internal situation, and others in Whitehall shared Bertie's opinion that Grey was too weak to make up his mind.[4]

There were other administrative difficulties. The office machinery was already under considerable strain before war broke out. Between 1906 and 1913 the volume of Foreign Office business increased some 36 per cent while the number of staff employed barely rose. These problems were compounded by a dramatic increase in paperwork within the department. Nicolson's difficulties were not all of his own making. 'Hardinge's innovation of *everything* passing through him to the Secretary of State instead of each of the Assistant Under Secretaries having direct access to the Secretary of State has been an egregious failure. No one man can properly do the work which Hardinge's system entailed.'[5] John Tilley, who became chief clerk in 1913, later commented adversely on the 'ominous increase in paperwork', a tendency encouraged by Crowe's predilection for the written word and the opportunities given to juniors to air their views. The Registry system seems to have collapsed under the strain. A departmental sub-committee in 1909 had already found the sub-registry indices incomplete and badly organized. The Central Registry had become a giant bottleneck and by 1913 the whole mechanism of keeping, recording and binding papers threatened to break down completely.

[1] Bertie MSS, FO 800/188, Nicolson to Bertie, 28 June 1914, Bertie to Tyrrell, 30 June 1914, memorandum by Bertie, 25 July 1914. This memorandum is about Grey's failure to find a suitable berth for Hardinge, who had been promised Paris, and his hesitation about Nicolson, who expected Paris. Memorandum by Bertie, 30 July 1914.
[2] Hardinge MSS, vol. 93, Oliphant to Hardinge, 23 February 1914.
[3] *Ibid.* Chirol to Hardinge, 15 April 1914.
[4] FO 800/188, memorandum by Bertie, 2 July 1914.
[5] FO 800/163, memorandum by Bertie quoting Tyrrell's view, 19 December 1914.

The second-division staff, whose numbers had risen after the Crowe–Hardinge reforms, grew increasingly dissatisfied. Though they dealt with all kinds of documents, their chances for promotion and salary increases were severely restricted. When one of the last supplementary clerks used in the Treaty Department retired, a first-division clerk was appointed to his position. The second-division staff (with the exception of those employed in the Chief Clerk's Department) rose in revolt and petitioned Grey against this action.[1] Grey refused to act or to reconsider the question and the matter came before the 1914 Royal Commission. A great deal of hard feeling was created and neither Grey's reply in 1913 nor Crowe's subsequent testimony before the Commission served to soothe relations. The Sarajevo crisis could not have occurred at a more inopportune moment.

The July crisis took the Foreign Office by surprise. The early summer had brought no new alarms. Though everyone anticipated that the next blow-up would be in the Balkans, all appeared calm. The British fleet was making a visit to Kiel; Grey was considering a journey to Germany to consult a famous oculist about his eye condition. At the British Foreign Office it was generally thought that the assassination of Francis Ferdinand on 28 June would have few major repercussions.[2] The press treated the matter calmly; other matters, including the death of Joseph Chamberlain on 2 July, crowded the news off the front page. On 6 July Nicolson wrote to the British ambassador in Vienna that apart from Albania, 'We have no very urgent and pressing question to preoccupy us in the rest of Europe.'[3] Warned by Prince Lichnowsky on 6 July about the possible German reaction to the assassination, Grey was far more apprehensive than his officials and discussed the implications of the shooting with both the French and Russian ambassadors. The Foreign Office expected some action on the part of the Austrian Government but neither Nicolson nor Crowe believed Vienna would proceed to extreme measures.[4] Grey apparently did not tell Nicolson of the warnings he

[1] Cmd. 7749, Appendix LXXXVI. The second-division staff in 1914 consisted of fifty-nine clerks. In 1905 there had been eighteen. Crowe was a key figure in this dispute. It was on his suggestion that the Treaty Department was upgraded so that its status, in terms of the salary of its heads, equalled that of the chiefs of other departments. Crowe, after consulting with the Chief Clerk, Mallet and Langley, decided to appoint a first-division clerk instead of a second-division clerk to the vacated position of head of department. The previous incumbent had been one of the old supplementary clerks. See FO 800/366, 1913 (vol. v), Crowe to Nicolson, 12 May and 27 May 1913. Crowe was convalescing at Tyrrell's country house at this time.

[2] BD XI. All documents unless otherwise noted are from this volume, no. 340. For an exception see the minute, written by Vansittart, no. 40.

[3] No. 33.

[4] No. 40. Notice Crowe's minute, 'Consul Jones seems to look upon the assassination . . . in the spirit of an insurance broker,' FO 371/1989/2558.

had received from the German ambassador. While the Foreign Secretary was urging M. Cambon to press for moderation at St Petersburgh should the Austrians act, Nicolson was assuring his close friend that there was little cause for alarm.[1] Grey moved on his own, without the assistance of the Foreign Office or the knowledge of the Cabinet. He consulted only Asquith, Haldane and Churchill. It was only with the passing days that the permanent officials began to realize that a major crisis was brewing.[2] 'Lichnowsky knew that "something very strong" was being cooked and one could smell it', Vansittart recalled.[3]

The Foreign Secretary hoped that he could work with Berlin and that the latter would restrain the Austrians. To further calm the Germans, he urged the Russians to take a conciliatory line at Berlin. When the Germans did not seem to respond to his prompting, he suggested direct Austro-Russian talks. This possibility was vetoed at St Petersburgh. When, in turn, the Russians proposed a joint intervention at Vienna, Crowe cautioned his chief that it was up to the Germans to restrain their ally.[4] Nicolson supported Crowe and no action was taken. Crowe, moreover, did warn Grey that the Germans knew what the Austrians were going to demand and had undoubtedly promised them full support should complications ensue.[5]

The diplomatic scene dramatically altered when the terms of the Austrian ultimatum became known on 23 July. Grey was now forced to raise the matter in the Cabinet for the first time on the twenty-fourth.[6] Eyre Crowe, in a key minute, argued that the question had taken on a new form. The merits of the Austrian charges against Serbia were irrelevant. 'The moment has passed when it might have been possible to enlist French support in an effort to hold back Russia', he wrote. 'France and Russia consider that these charges are the pretext and the bigger cause of the Triple Alliance versus the Triple Entente is definitely engaged.'[7] Crowe urged that as soon as Austria or Russia mobilized, the British fleet should be immediately mobilized for war to warn Germany that England would participate in any general war. 'Our interests', he argued, 'are tied up with those of France and Russia in this struggle which is not for the possession of Serbia, but one between Germany aiming at political dictatorship in Europe and the Powers who desire to retain individual freedom.' Crowe had thus restated the position which he had taken in 1907, the German threat to the continent of Europe. Nicolson, impressed as he was with the strength of Russia and always

[1] DDF, 3rd series, vol. x, no. 483.                    [2] Nos. 38 and 39
[3] Vansittart, *The Mist Procession*, p. 122.
[4] No. 76.            [5] No. 77.            [6] No. 91.            [7] No. 101.

fearful of the consequences of a rupture with her, seconded Crowe's advice though from a different point of view. 'Our attitude during the crisis will be regarded by Russia as a test and we must be most careful not to alienate her.'[1]

But Grey did not see the situation in such extreme terms. 'Mr Churchill told me today that the fleet can be mobilized in twenty-four hours, but I think it is premature to make any statement to France and Russia yet.'[2] Orders were given to keep the fleet together at Portsmouth as a warning to the central powers but nothing further was done. The Foreign Secretary still hoped that the dispute could be localized and continued to make a distinction between the Austro-Serbian dispute and the broader conflict between Austria and Russia which he was trying to avoid. The Cabinet urged mediation and then scattered for the weekend; Grey left London for his fishing lodge. On the twenty-sixth, Nicolson went to the Foreign Office and learnt that the Austrians had found the Serbian answer inadequate. Having received news from St Petersburgh that the Russians would not oppose international action, Nicolson proposed, and Grey accepted, the idea of a conference of disinterested powers in London.[3] Nicolson was anxious to make some kind of gesture towards the Russians though Grey was hesitant and pessimistic. His policy of moderation had been weakened by the harshness of the Austrian stand. From the twenty-fourth on, Nicolson and Crowe became increasingly suspicious of the German role at Vienna. 'Berlin is playing with us. Jagow did not really adopt your proposal to intervene in Vienna, and to be backed by us and France, but simply "passed on" your suggestions', Nicolson commented.[4] He was further agitated by news (erroneously reported) that Prince Lichnowsky was convinced that Britain would remain neutral in a European dispute. Both Nicolson and Crowe had their eye on Berlin and pointed out on almost every possible occasion that the Germans showed no inclination to check their ally.[5]

These officials wanted a clear declaration of support for the entente powers. Nicolson wished Grey to meet the Russian demand for a statement that Britain would not remain neutral in a general European war.[6] The Permanent Under-Secretary seems to have given an assurance to the French embassy though without authorization.[7] On the twenty-sixth the Austrians

---

[1] *Ibid.* For Nicolson's fears and opinion of Russian power, see BD x(1), p. 821. Herbert Butterfield, 'Sir Edward Grey in July 1914', *Historical Studies*, v (1965), 1–25.

[2] No. 101.

[3] Nos. 139, 239. Nicolson pressed the suggestion because it came from Sazonov.

[4] No. 144.     [5] Nos. 174, 185.     [6] Nos. 149, 158, 160, 185.

[7] DDF, 3rd series, vol. XII, no. 117.

rejected the Serbian reply and Austrian military preparations began. 'The outlook is bad', Crowe minuted, 'all now depends on what line Germany may be prepared to take.'[1] Crowe felt that the time of decision was approaching, 'within twenty-four hours His Majesty's Government will be faced with the question whether, in a quarrel so imposed by Austria on an unwilling France, Great Britain will stand idly aside, or take sides'.[2] If England abandoned her partners, Crowe warned, she would be the next victim of German aggression.

By 27 July Grey, too, wanted the Cabinet to declare itself, though for different reasons. He redoubled his own efforts to localize the conflict only to be met with checks from both his own partners and from the Germans. The Russians increased their pressure on London for an open declaration of support. Yet on 25 and 27 July Bertie reported from Paris that neither the French Government nor public would support the Russians in a struggle for the Balkans.[3] At a full Cabinet meeting on the twenty-seventh Grey asked for a decision; would the Government support France in a war between France and Russia against Austria and Germany? He knew he could not get a declaration in support of St Petersburgh; the French case was different and such an assurance would still help him vis-à-vis Russia. He needed time and diplomatic leverage at St Petersburgh. The Cabinet split; the opposition wing was powerfully placed and Grey's hands were tied.[4]

The Austrian declaration of war on 28 July and the subsequent bombardment of Belgrade made war inevitable for both Nicolson and Crowe.

What has preoccupied and I confess has troubled me very much [the former wrote to Buchanan on the twenty-eighth] is satisfying Russia's very natural request as to what we should do in certain eventualities... We, of course, living under such conditions as we do here, when no Government practically can take any decided line without feeling that public opinion amply supports them, are unable to give any decided engagements as to what we should or should not do in any future emergencies; but I think we have made it perfectly clear that in any case neither Germany nor Austria could possibly rely with any certainty upon our remaining neutral... There is no doubt whatsoever that were we drawn into this conflagration we should be on the side of our friends.[5]

Nicolson was a little premature in his assurances 'that we should not

[1] No. 175.    [2] No. 170.

[3] Nos. 129, 134, 192; Lord Bertie, *The Diary of Lord Bertie of Thame, 1914–18*, edited by Lady Algernon Gordon Lennox, vol. 1, p. 1–4. Bertie was anti-Russian and pro-French; this accounts in part for his dislike of Nicolson.

[4] Jenkins, *Asquith*, p. 325. Additional information from Michael Ekstein who is preparing a paper on this subject. Telegrams were sent to all naval, military and colonial stations and a 'precautionary period' initiated.

[5] No. 239.

hesitate to do our duty'.[1] Grey, faced with a divided Cabinet, continued his efforts to bring Austria and Russia together in the hope of deterring further military action.[2] The idea of a London conference *à quatre* had been vetoed by Berlin on the twenty-seventh.[3] The British Foreign Secretary, prompted by Goschen and Crowe, agreed to ask the Germans to outline their proposals for intervention should the direct Austro-Russian conversations, finally begun, fail.[4] On the twenty-eighth Crowe, backed by Nicolson, advised that the Government should not issue the usual declaration of neutrality.[5] By the following day, it seemed to Nicolson that 'the resources of diplomacy are, for the present, exhausted'.[6]

Military considerations were now forcing the pace. Crowe summed up the dangerous consequences of Austrian mobilization which would result in the calling up of all the armies of Europe.[7] When the Cabinet met on the morning of 29 July, the Austro-Russian talks had failed and Russian mobilization seemed imminent. Though Grey pressed for a Cabinet declaration of support for France, his colleagues were unable to agree and the Cabinet broke up without a decision. Grey took matters in his own hands. He warned Prince Lichnowsky on the afternoon of the twenty-ninth that the latter should not be misled by the friendly tone of their conversation into believing that England would stand aside should Germany and France enter the conflict.[8] He also told Cambon that England would not be drawn into a war over a Balkan question. Even should Germany and France join the dispute, 'it was a case that we should have to consider . . . We were free from engagements, and we should have to decide what British interests required us to do'.[9] On the same day, Grey assured Ponsonby 'We are absolutely free and working for peace.'[10] After 27 June Grey's hopes began to fade but his freedom to act was curtailed by the Cabinet. From 27 July until 2 August, Grey walked a diplomatic tight-rope; partly because he still hoped this path might preserve the peace but also because of the uncommitted stand of Cabinet and public.[11] Though he again tried to intervene both at Berlin and St Petersburgh, by the twenty-ninth the Foreign Secretary must have known that war was inevitable. The question remained whether Great Britain would intervene.

On 30 July the Foreign Office received news of Bethmann Hollweg's bid for British neutrality. Crowe was disgusted. 'The only comment that need be made on these astounding proposals is that they reflect discredit on

[1] *Ibid.*    [2] Nos. 188, 223.    [3] No. 185.    [4] Nos. 215, 223.    [5] No. 250.
[6] No. 252.    [7] No. 170.    [8] No. 286.    [9] No. 283.
[10] Ponsonby MSS, minutes on meeting with Grey, 29 July 1914.    [11] No. 303.

the statesman who makes them . . . It is clear that Germany is practically determined to go to war, and that the one restraining influence so far has been the fear of England joining in the defence of France and Belgium.'[1] Grey pressed the Germans to make some proposals of their own for mediation. But he had already told Lichnowsky on the afternoon of the twenty-ninth that England would not remain neutral in a European war and on the thirtieth formally rejected the German bid.[2] Despite Russian mobilization and increasing pressure from Paris, Grey still could not give the open declaration of support his entente partners were demanding.[3]

Though the Cabinet had sanctioned the preliminary measures for mobilizing the fleet (Churchill was to go much further on the thirtieth and on the first with the support of only a part of the Cabinet) and had discussed the question of Belgian neutrality, it remained divided on the ultimate question of support for France. On the thirtieth Grey recommended his version of a 'halt in Belgrade' to St Petersburgh and again avoided giving firm commitments to France and Russia.[4] Bertie from Paris counselled caution[5] and even on the thirty-first Crowe, in a most uncharacteristic minute, spelled out the choice before the Government. 'What must weigh with His Majesty's Government is the consideration that they should not by a declaration of unconditional solidarity with France and Russia induce and determine these two Powers to choose the path of War.'[6] News of the Russian mobilization and the German Kriegsgefahr order really ended any kind of continental diplomacy. Arthur Nicolson wrote bluntly under the impact of these measures: 'It seems to be most essential, whatever our future course may be in regard to intervention, that we should at once give orders for mobilization, of the army . . . Mobilization is a precautionary and not a provocative measure and to my mind is essential.' 'There is much force in this', Grey agreed. 'We ought to prepare and I think it should be considered early tomorrow.'[7]

Yet as late as 31 July Grey was still temporizing. He warned Lichnowsky that England would be drawn into any war in which France and Germany were involved, but refused to give Cambon any pledge of support. The Cabinet was to take action with regard to Belgian neutrality but did not think that 'any treaties or obligations of this country were involved'.[8] Cambon pressed for another Cabinet meeting. While these discussions were going on within the Foreign Office, Valentine Chirol, who fully supported the interventionist

[1] No. 293.   [2] Nos. 286, 303.   [3] No. 283.   [4] Nos. 319, 352.
[5] No. 320 (written by Bertie, 30 July) but see no. 373.   [6] No. 318, 31 August.
[7] No. 368.   [8] No. 367. DDF, vol. XI, no. 459.

campaign in *The Times*, exchanged bitter words with William Tyrrell who felt that Grey was pursuing the best policy possible.[1]

Crowe believed that there was a real danger that England might not stand by her obligations to France. If England remained aloof from war, all that he had feared and foretold would come to pass. With great diffidence, Crowe prepared a memorandum for Grey arguing the case for intervention.[2] 'Nothing is further from my mind than to trouble you needlessly or add to your grave perplexities at this moment', Crowe wrote. 'The theory that England cannot engage in a big war means her abdication as an independent state.'[3] It meant the end of British influence, the defeat of British interests, and the collapse of the balance of power on which her whole policy was based. Erroneously, Crowe attributed the panic in the City to the deliberate acts of the German financial houses. To him it was but one step in a preconceived German plan for war. But Crowe was not only certain that Germany was planning war, he believed there was no point in rejecting the German bid for neutrality if England were then, in fact, to remain neutral. 'The argument that there is no written bond binding us to France is strictly correct. There is no contractual obligation. But the Entente has been made, threatened, put to the test and celebrated in a manner justifying the belief that a moral bond was forged.' Both in terms of moral principle and political expediency, 'I feel confident that our duty and our interest will be seen to lie in standing by France in her hour of need. France has not sought the quarrel. It has been forced upon her.' Crowe's fears were genuine; he was not at all sure that Grey or the Cabinet would accept his arguments.

Nicolson, too, was in a state of panic. Sir Henry Wilson urged the Permanent Under-Secretary to bring pressure on Grey and in fact tried unsuccessfully to involve him in a political intrigue against his chief.[4] By the first the situation had deteriorated sharply. Mobilization orders were issued almost simultaneously in Germany and France and the Germans declared war on Russia in the evening of the same day. In London the Foreign Office ceased to have any role to play. On the first there was a Cabinet meeting. 'You will no doubt have read the White Paper' Nicolson later wrote to Hardinge, 'but I may tell you *quite* privately that . . . the Cabinet were not prepared to stand by France.'[5] Grey told Cambon 'that France must take her own decision at this moment without reckoning on any assistance that we are not

[1] Hardinge MSS, vol. 93, Chirol to Hardinge, 4 August, 5 November 1914. See also Ponsonby MSS, Tyrrell to Ponsonby, 31 July 1914: 'The "new style" and line *The Times* takes makes me fairly sick.'
[2] No. 369.     [3] *Ibid.*     [4] Nicolson, *Lord Carnock*, pp. 418–19.
[5] FO 800/375, Nicolson to Hardinge (copy), 5 September 1914.

now in a position to promise'.[1] Encouraged by Nicolson, Cambon raised the question of Britain's obligations to protect France's northern and western coasts under the 1912 agreements.[2] Grey promised to raise the question with the Cabinet, though it was the question of Belgian neutrality which was becoming the decisive issue.

Nicolson was distraught. After each meeting with Grey, Cambon reported to his close friend in the room below. On 1 August, after one such highly emotional scene with Cambon, Nicolson saw Grey. 'He found him pacing his room, biting at his lower lip. Nicolson asked whether it was indeed true that he had refused to support France at the moment of her greatest danger ... "You will render us", Nicolson said angrily, "a by-word among nations." '[3] It would be surprising if Grey did not resent Nicolson's tone and the partnership between his own senior official and the French ambassador. On the second, on receipt of news of a German invasion of French soil, Nicolson wrote, 'We should mobilize today so that our expeditionary force may be on its way during next week. Should we waver now we shall rue the day later.'[4]

Crowe, too, despaired of his inability to press the Government to declare themselves. Vansittart has probably exaggerated Crowe's distress but his portrait is not without foundation. 'Going to Crowe's room for an outlet of pent emotions, I found the dry man dissolved; tears glistened down the furrows of his face and all that he could say was "the poor French"...'[5] O'Malley, another contemporary, recalls, 'Crowe's face was white and drawn and he told me that he felt that his advice was falling upon the reluctant ears of a man—Sir Edward Grey—not qualified by upbringing or study to understand what was going on in the sinister depths of the German mind.'[6]

The permanent officials were of little importance; it was in the Cabinet that the fight for intervention had to be won. Though the 'peace party' was strong, it did not present a united front and on the morning of the second, a compromise solution was accepted.[7] Grey was authorized to tell Cambon that the German fleet would not be allowed to attack the French northern coast though he was to give no further pledge. It was also decided to make a

[1] No. 426.  [2] No. 424; Nicolson, *Lord Carnock*, pp. 419-20.
[3] *Ibid.* See also Hardinge MSS, vol. 93, Nicolson to Hardinge, 5 September 1914. Nicolson supported Steed's campaign for intervention in *The Times*.  [4] No. 446.
[5] Vansittart, *The Mist Procession*, p. 127.  [6] O'Malley, *Phantom Caravan*, p. 46.
[7] The 'peace party' was hardly a party at all. The ten men listed by Roy Jenkins in his biography of *Asquith*, p. 325 (Burns, Morley, Simon, Beauchamp, Harcourt, Lloyd George, Pease, Samuel, McKinnon Wood and Runciman) agreed only that Britain should not go to war to defend France. There was no leader: each man was motivated by different considerations. Pease had supported Grey at a previous Cabinet meeting and eight of the ten men listed seem to have agreed to Samuel's compromise formula. Only Burns resigned over the guarantee to France. The rest, though shaken, were probably willing to fight to preserve the independence of north-west Europe.

German violation of Belgian neutrality a *casus belli*. When the Cabinet disbanded its future seemed in doubt. Yet during a luncheon at Lord Beauchamp's house, it was clear that most of the waverers would accept the formula suggested in the morning. Though individuals continued to waver, by the evening the ministerial crisis was over. A majority supported the view that the British could not acquiesce in a German violation of Belgian neutrality. But the issue was decided at the last possible moment. On this same day, Bertie (who had now swung over to the side of the interventionists) wrote he was 'sick at heart' over the Government's indecision,[1] while Buchanan too was anxiously waiting for word from London. It was the German ultimatum to Belgium and the Belgian reply which enabled Grey to carry the Cabinet with him.

On the morning of 3 August Asquith received four resignations—Burns, Morley, Simon and Beauchamp. The latter two were prevailed upon to stay and the unity of the Cabinet was preserved. While Grey was in the Commons presenting his most effective dry recital of the case for war, Nicolson was in 'an agony of suspense' until the news of the Foreign Secretary's success reached him. But when he went to congratulate his chief, Grey could only groan 'I hate war, I hate war'.[2]

The divisions and inefficiencies of the Foreign Office made little difference to the course of events. Neither Nicolson nor Crowe had influenced Grey's policies during these critical days. Nicolson had minimized the importance of the assassination but both he and Crowe were subsequently quick to understand that the terms of the Austrian ultimatum had transformed the diplomatic situation. From 23 June onwards, both men had pressed for an open declaration of British support for the entente powers and then for intervention. Nicolson did so because he feared a hostile, embittered Russia almost as much as he feared Germany. Crowe argued that, without English assistance, the entente powers would be defeated and Germany would turn on England. He was scarcely concerned with the Balkans; he cared about Germany and the balance of power in Europe. But throughout the month of July Grey pursued his own line of policy. He was quick to realize that the crisis would be a major one. At first he tried to reassure Germany so that she would follow a moderate course at Vienna. Even when this policy failed, the Foreign Secretary looked for possible ways of containing the conflict well after Nicolson and Crowe thought such action hopeless.

[1] *The Diary of Lord Bertie of Thame*, vol. I, p. 8.
[2] Nicolson, *Lord Carnock*, p. 422; H. W. Steed, *Through Thirty Years, 1892–1922* (London, 1925), vol. II, pp. 26–7.

Though Nicolson and Crowe were appalled by the lack of decisive action and haunted by the possible desertion of France, there was nothing they could do. The lack of intimacy between Grey and Nicolson made the situation more difficult but did not alter the course of events. Grey was probably more isolated than he would have been if Nicolson had been less open in his opposition to the Cabinet. But even William Tyrrell, who was close at hand during these critical last days, could do little more than assist his chief and defend his policy. He was present during some of the critical conversations with key Cabinet ministers; he was sent to conduct the final discussions with Prince Lichnowsky. But Grey had to make his own decisions; he had to convince the Cabinet and then the House of Commons. On 4 August Grey despatched the ultimatum to the Germans. At 11 p.m. Germany and England were at war.

### Administration under stress

The impact of war failed to produce a change either in the state of the Foreign Office or in the morale of its occupants. Nicolson was asked to remain in London. Bertie commented in December 1914: 'In Nicolson's case the result has been that he neglects what he is supposed to do, and accepts without enquiry what others suggest. Under his rule the office is in a state of chaos. There is no discipline and the tail waggles the dog.'[1] Though the Permanent Under-Secretary disliked the 'crudities of wartime politics and the hysteria of belligerent patriotism' this did not prevent him from pressing for an extreme solution of the German problem.[2] The outbreak of war did temporarily restore relations between Grey and Nicolson and for a short time at least the Permanent Under-Secretary had a share in the making of British policy in the Balkans. It was not long, however, before Nicolson was again eclipsed and left to deal with the more routine matters in the office. 'I don't think the Foreign Office is going at all well', Ronald Graham reported to Hardinge in January 1915. 'Tyrrell and Crowe try to run everything and quarrel, while the former is anathema to diplomatists.'[3]

William Tyrrell, in particular, suffered from the strains and disasters of war. Overworked and overwrought, Tyrrell seems to have had a complete breakdown and in the spring of 1915 was forced to leave the Foreign Office.[4]

[1] FO 800/163, memorandum by Bertie, 19 December 1914.
[2] Nicolson, *Lord Carnock*, p. 427.
[3] Hardinge MSS, vol. 93; Graham to Hardinge, 7 January 1915; also G. B. Allen to Hardinge, 1 April 1915.
[4] Hardinge MSS, vol. 93, Chirol to Hardinge, 3 May 1915. 'I am afraid Willie Tyrrell's breakdown has been a terribly bad one ... It had begun a long time ago. His boy's death precipitated the debacle.' See also Chirol to Hardinge, 24 May, 23 June 1915 and Hardinge to Chirol, 31 May.

His younger son was killed in 1915 and his elder boy early in 1918.[1] Given the strained relationships between the two men, Nicolson treated him most generously until Grey found him a less taxing position at the Home Office.[2] Tyrrell returned sometime during 1916 and was made head of the newly-created Political Intelligence Department.[3]

Eyre Crowe was placed in charge of the War Department which bore the immediate brunt of the transition from peace to war. It was the Assistant Under-Secretary who drafted the plans for placing the Foreign Office on a war-time footing. 'All correspondence respecting the war should continue to be submitted to me', Crowe wrote in his memorandum of 7 August 1914, 'so as to preserve unity of direction.'[4] The Assistant Under-Secretary was given his own private secretary, Lord Drogheda, to relieve him of 'a multitude of details which I could not otherwise shake off'. But Crowe seems to have been driven to distraction by the failure of the Government to mobilize its resources effectively and he became increasingly frustrated in his own efforts to press forward. He quarrelled with Grey. Bertie records: 'Crowe has completely lost his head. His Prussian blood came out and he was insubordinate and insolent to Grey, who has decided that his appointment to succeed Nicolson is impossible. He has no judgement, tact or sense of proportion. His ability is undoubted.'[5] Hardinge was relieved, 'I always knew that Crowe would be impossible . . . He is one of those who can be a good second, but would be a bad head.'[6] Crowe was not only passed over for the top Foreign Office post; an attempt was made to remove him from the centre of Foreign Office business. Nicolson replaced him at the War Department (hardly a move calculated to strengthen the Foreign Office) and Crowe was made head of a new division created to deal with wartime commerce and trade.[7] It was in part

[1] Hardinge also lost a son who did not recover from his war wounds.

[2] Hardinge MSS, vol. 94, Chirol to Hardinge, 21 May 1915.

[3] Tyrrell was the co-author with Ralph Paget of a memorandum dated 7 August 1916 on the subject of British war aims and the future of the Austro-Hungarian Empire, so he must have been back at the Foreign Office before this date, perhaps on an unofficial basis.

[4] FO 366/768/40089, memorandum by Eyre Crowe. Crowe proposed that the Eastern and Western Departments be amalgamated under the headship of Mr Clerk and that this War Department deal with the 'general political, naval and military questions connected with the war', censorship, current work of eastern Europe, problems connected with the laws of neutrality, treatment of British armed merchant vessels and aliens in Britain, in the colonies and in the dominions. The Treaty Department was to be expanded and both the Commercial and Consular Departments were to assume new responsibilities. The staffs of the China and American Departments were to be reduced to release men for these more pressing tasks. I am indebted to Michael Ekstein who found this memorandum and called my attention to its importance.

[5] Bertie MSS, memorandum by Bertie, 19 December 1914.

[6] Hardinge MSS, vol. 94, Hardinge to Nicolson, 17 May 1915.

[7] O'Malley, *The Phantom Caravan*, pp. 46–7. Tilley and Gaselee, *The Foreign Office*, p. 178. George Clerk, Crowe's second in command, stayed on to help Nicolson.

due to Crowe's energy and resourcefulness that this small Contraband Department grew into the Ministry of Blockade under Lord Robert Cecil and became a vital, if contentious, factor in the prosecution of the war. Crowe was, moreover, as mentioned earlier, the victim of a wave of blind Germanophobia (like Haldane) which made it impossible to advance him while the war continued. As long as the war lasted, Crowe was somewhat roughly handled within the Foreign Office. It was only at the Peace Conference that he fully re-established his position; for in Paris he became the indispensable leader and co-ordinator of the official British delegation.[1]

In June 1916 Nicolson was allowed to retire and Hardinge brought back from India to take up his former position. Hardinge's reappointment did not substantially improve morale. He was far too conservative to alter the department radically and had little sympathy with those within the Foreign Office who wanted to extend the scope of their responsibilities.[2] Grey was ill during these years and frequently absent from his desk. As he believed that diplomacy must give way to military considerations in wartime, he did not attempt to fight for the prerogatives of his office in the Cabinet and the Foreign Office case was often lost by default. At times, the Foreign Secretary was strangely inactive as if physically exhausted and somewhat stunned by the realities and horrors of war. Identified with Asquith, Grey shared his leader's loss of prestige and this too weakened his position both in the Cabinet and in the country.[3] Diplomatic defeats in Turkey and the Balkans as well as difficulties over blockade procedures (particularly with the United States) further discredited the Foreign Office. The permanent officials, according to their critics, had not only failed to preserve the peace, they were unable to win the war. Even before Lloyd George defeated Asquith in December 1916, the Foreign Office was in eclipse. Once the new prime minister turned his attention to foreign affairs, this eclipse was to become a permanent feature of the British political scene.

Outsiders knew little about the personal feuds and administrative difficulties within the walls of the Foreign Office. Since 1911, however, there

[1] Oppenheimer, *Stranger Within*, pp. 353, 365; Nicolson, *Peacemaking*, p. 211. Charles Hardinge was the official head but Crowe the effective one.

[2] For a devastating attack on Hardinge, who it is claimed 'was as race conscious as any German Junker could have been', see Oppenheimer, *Stranger Within*, p. 321. Oppenheimer claims that it was Hardinge who turned down a plan for a new Foreign Trade Department which would have considerably strengthened the Foreign Office in its economic capacity.

[3] Hankey, *Supreme Command*, vol. 1, p. 184. Grey was also identified with Kitchener and this did not help his political position. An effort was made to push him out of the Foreign Office early in 1915. Jenkins, *Asquith*, pp. 339, 356. S. E. Koss, 'The Destruction of Britain's last Liberal Government', *The Journal of Modern History*, June 1968, pp. 271–2.

had been an increasing number of attacks both on Grey's diplomacy and on the role of the Foreign Office and Diplomatic Service. The books of Morel, Hobson, Brailsford and Angell (*The Great Illusion* was particularly influential) had attracted public attention and the complaints of the radicals were repeated in the columns of the *Manchester Guardian*, in the leaders of *The Economist* and in the letters to *The Times*. Though the attack on Grey's foreign policy somewhat diminished after 1912 (due in part to the rapprochement with Germany) the radicals continued to criticize the methods by which foreign policy was conducted. Not only did they argue that Parliament had little opportunity to hear or question the Foreign Secretary but they believed that Grey was dominated by his officials, who in turn were recruited from a narrow, isolated and self-perpetuating clique whose actions could not be controlled through any democratic means. The proper balance between political chief and civil servants had been altered to the detriment of democracy and peace.

Who, then, makes war? The answer is to be found in the Chancelleries of Europe, among the men who have too long played with human lives as pawns in a game of chess, who have become so enmeshed in formulas and the jargon of diplomacy that they have ceased to be conscious of the poignant realities with which they trifle. And thus will war continue to be made, until the great masses who are the sport of professional schemers and dreamers say the word which will bring, not eternal peace, for that is impossible, but a determination that wars shall be fought, only in a just and righteous and vital cause.[1]

E. D. Morel, Noel Buxton and Arthur Ponsonby, as well as other members of the Liberal Foreign Affairs Group, wished to make the foreign secretary more responsible to Parliament and the Foreign Office more representative and effective. They sensed but did not explore the contradiction in these two goals; a democratically controlled and recruited Foreign Office would automatically be more efficient. 'I am quite convinced that our Service is less efficient than that of other countries, and I believe that the wealth test and the society test is one of the principal causes', Buxton wrote in a characteristic letter to Ponsonby.[2] Even Lord Esher, hardly a radical, wrote at the end of 1913: 'It is stated, and I hear it on all sides, among foreign diplomatists as well as in "Government circles" that the personnel of the Diplomatic Service is at the moment weak in all its branches.'[3]

Many of these charges were repeated before the Royal Commission on the Civil Service which was constituted to consider the condition of the Foreign

[1] *The Times*, 26 November 1912, quoted in D. Collins, *Aspects of British Politics*, p. 115.
[2] Ponsonby MSS, Noel Buxton to Ponsonby, undated but either 1913 or 1914.
[3] Esher, *The Letters and Journals of Viscount Esher*, vol. III, p. 146.

Office, the Diplomatic and Consular Services. From 29 April until 18 July 1914, that is during the early stages of the July crisis, the commission heard testimony from officials and examined outside witnesses who pointed out the various weaknesses of the foreign service. The critics stressed the lack of proper publicity and press information, the aristocratic bias of the selection process, the limitations of the General Consular Service and the inadequacies of the commercial attaché system. 'The Foreign Office suffers', Trevelyan told the commissioners, 'from the misfortune of being practically removed from criticism.'[1] Francis Hirst, the editor of *The Economist* and one of Grey's most persistent critics, gave similar testimony, 'if the Foreign Office would give out a little more daylight, then they might deserve a little more sunshine, but he had not obtained enough information from them very often'.[2]

The arguments of the critics have a modern ring. 'The British Foreign Service was the second most expensive in the world and the most snobbish. It was clearly recruited from too narrow a social basis. There were too many peers' sons, too many Etonians, no non-conformists, no Scottish or Ulster Presbyterians and no one with radical or socialist leanings.'[3] It was not surprising that such a service was inadequately performing its proper functions. Reporting was weak and the subjects covered inconsequential. 'I think you would find a tendency in the Diplomatic Service today to really restrict their vision very much to a narrow area', Arthur Ponsonby testified, 'and intercourse with commercial classes, or political movements, is certainly not encouraged.'[4]

Representatives from various Chambers of Commerce urged the Foreign Office to take a more aggressive attitude in the struggle for markets. Both the Commercial Department and the Commercial and Consular Services abroad needed expansion and strengthening. James Bedford, vice-president of the Leeds Incorporated Chamber of Commerce, contrasted the roles of the British and German Consular Services. 'The competition of the world seems to be getting keener and keener every year, and in many cases England is being ousted from many profitable trading centres, and we can only believe that it is through the greater industry of those Germans, and the fact that the German Emperor encourages them to look after the commerce of Germany.'[5] It was a generally held opinion that British officials had a reputation for greater snobbery and 'less energy and activity than those of Germany and France'.

The commissioners pressed for fundamental changes in the existing

1 Cmd. 7749, Appendix LXXXVII, p. 320.  2 *Ibid.* Q.40,191.
3 *Ibid.* Appendix LXXXVII, p. 321.  4 *Ibid.* Q.39,381.  5 *Ibid.* Q.43,476.

system. The Foreign Office and Diplomatic Service were to be merged into a single foreign service and steps taken to eliminate the social and financial barriers to such a merger. The property qualification for attachés and the two-year honorary attachéship should both be abolished. Suitable entertainment and living allowances were to be offered and archivists employed to relieve diplomats of their purely clerical tasks. The commissioners urged that a departmental committee be created to improve the training of diplomats with an eye to increasing their efficiency and reducing their number. It is interesting to compare these suggestions with those made by Arthur Ponsonby fourteen years earlier.

It was rumoured that the Foreign Secretary was dependent not on the top men of his services but on a small personal clique, a 'camarilla' led by the Private Secretary. Judging from the way in which the commissioners pressed William Tyrrell, it is clear that they thought he had too much personal say in questions of appointment, promotion and transfer. They suggested that interviews for candidates come after and not before their examinations and that the Board of Selection be broadened to include public members. The examination was to be the same as for Class 1 entrance into the Home Civil Service and though special language competence was still demanded, candidates would also be eligible for one of the Home Departments. The commissioners wanted to see a Promotion Board established under the permanent under-secretary and urged that transfers be made according to set principles rather than by virtue of personal whim.

A great deal of attention was given to the question of commercial reporting and representation. The Commission members rejected the claim that British officials were less active than their foreign counterparts in promoting British trade and investment. They did, however, propose a number of changes in the General Consular Service which would make recruitment easier and its staff better equipped to serve the needs of the commercial community.[1] The Commission also found that the commercial attaché system could be considerably improved.[2] In 1914 there were only eight such appointments, one man covered Germany, Holland, Denmark, Sweden and Norway, and

[1] The MacDonnell Commission decided that attempts to recruit business men were doomed to failure and suggested instead recruiting young men (eighteen or nineteen) straight from school and then sending them for a two-year period to industrial and commercial firms as well as for further training at the Board of Trade and at the Foreign Office. It is interesting that the Commission did not recommend amalgamation and decided to preserve the dual system of paid and unpaid consuls. They did urge, with regard to the latter, that preference should be given to British subjects (over 40 per cent of the unpaid consuls were foreign) and that they should be supervised by salaried officers of higher rank.

[2] The commercial attaché system dated from 1880 when Joseph Crowe (Eyre Crowe's father) was

there was not a single commercial attaché on the whole American continent. Various suggestions were made both for increasing the number and the usefulness of this service.[1] All the witnesses examined agreed that the Government would have to pursue a more resolute policy if British trading interests were to be adequately informed and supported.

Though the war delayed innovations, a series of departmental committees were created to consider and implement the Commission's recommendations. In April 1918 a committee from the Foreign Office and Diplomatic Service presented its report and in the following year the two services were amalgamated.[2] Staffs became interchangeable, the property qualification was dropped and appropriate pay scales, still absurdly low, were introduced. The examination and interviewing system was revised and an enlarged Board of Selection appointed.[3] A second committee considered the reorganization of the registry system and measures were adopted to end the clerical chaos which had existed before 1914 but which had been aggravated by the war.[4] Finally, various committees and inter-departmental groups considered the question of trade promotion and commercial representation. In the Foreign Office, a committee under Eyre Crowe, backed by those who were working on blockade problems, strongly urged that the Foreign Office retain its newly-acquired responsibilities for overseas trade.[5] These men had found in their work 'a more satisfying field of activity and a more tangible touch with realities and personalities than had been afforded by the political moves and counter-moves of an older diplomacy; and they wished ardently to keep their place in the field'.[6] There was a fierce battle between the Foreign Office (led by a 'somewhat bewildered Grey') and the Board of Trade during which

made commercial attaché at Paris. The system was critically reviewed in 1906 when it was found that commercial attachés were doing the routine commercial work at their diplomatic missions and had no time to keep in touch with home needs. At that time it was decided to keep the European commercial attachés (though not those in more distant posts) in London while regular members of the diplomatic staff, commercial secretaries, were to handle routine work abroad. The system proved to be unsatisfactory at both ends.

[1] The Royal Commission suggested that commercial attachés again be attached to diplomatic missions but that they be freed from the ordinary commercial business at their posts. They were to spend a maximum of three months a year in England for consultation with the Foreign Office, Board of Trade and interested commercial enterprises.

[2] General 55/4, Foreign Office Organization, Discipline, 1844–1952, memorandum dated 29 April 1918.

[3] For specific reforms see *Hansard*, vol. CXVI, col. 524 ff. and for special post-war methods of recruitment, see Lord Strang, *Home and Abroad* (London, 1956), p. 49.

[4] General 55/4, no. 189672.

[5] Cmd. 8715, memorandum by the Board of Trade and Foreign Office with respect to the Future Organization of Commercial Intelligence. This includes the report of Eyre Crowe's 1916 committee. For further information see Sir Victor Wellesley, *Diplomacy in Fetters* (London, 1944), and Tilley and Gaselee, *The Foreign Office*, pp. 246–56.

[6] Lord Eustace Percy, *Some Memories* (London, 1958), p. 147.

many of the proposals made for strengthening the commercial and financial side of the Foreign Office were defeated. The creation of the Overseas Trade Department, though a compromise, tended not only to weaken the Foreign Office in its economic capacity but encouraged future diplomats to leave these problems to others at a time when commercial questions were at the heart of international relations.

The Foreign Office emerged from the war reformed but weakened in prestige and power. The changes of 1919 were not substantial enough to satisfy the innovators at the Foreign Office. Under the conservative leadership of Curzon and Hardinge, questions of recruitment, promotion, training, specialization and exchanges with other departments of state were left pending or were ignored. The 'old guard' soon re-emerged and the Diplomatic Service returned to its old ways though in a very different world. The moment for a radical transformation of the diplomatic apparatus was lost. Nor did the new measures dispel the fears of outside critics. The Union of Democratic Control made little headway in its efforts to extend the scope of parliamentary control while the specific reforms urged by writers in *The New Europe* were swallowed up in a general denunciation of the 'old diplomacy'.[1] Myth overcame reality and plots were proved where there were none. Lloyd George's contemptuous treatment of both the Foreign Office and Diplomatic Service was in part a response to the radical dislike and distrust of professional diplomacy. It is no exaggeration to claim that in the next decade a large section of informed opinion believed that 'secret diplomacy' was the principal cause of the war. The professionals were not to be allowed a second chance. The diplomats themselves suffered from a loss of nerve from which they never fully recovered. In the inter-war years the Foreign Offices of Europe were to play the minor parts.

[1] G. Craig and F. Gilbert, *The Diplomats* (Princeton, 1953), p. 22.

# CHAPTER 4

# The world outside

One cannot conclude a story of the Foreign Office without some consideration of the outside forces which affected decision-making within the department. I have already commented in the text on the respective contributions
of the prime minister and members of the Cabinet. We still need more
detailed studies of the relations between the Foreign Office and the Treasury,
the India and Colonial Offices (particularly in the Salisbury and Grey
periods), the service departments and the Committee of Imperial Defence,
on a scale which cannot be attempted in this monograph. There is also,
however, a wider public frame which must be considered. The foreign
secretary and his officials prided themselves on their detachment from the
changing moods of public opinion. Diplomacy was the concern of diplomats
and the professionals took a very restricted view of the boundaries of their
caste. Yet the Foreign Office could not be a self-contained institution.
The foreign secretary depended upon the information sent by diplomats who
in turn reported on the opinions and press of their host countries. Whatever
their social snobberies and inherited prejudices, diplomats and officials knew
that policy decisions could not be made in total isolation. They turned to
the columns of the London press not only for elucidation but for the views
of a highly articulate public. They received delegations from pressure groups
and commercial houses. They were forced to defend themselves against
attacks in the Houses of Parliament. Ultimately, the foreign secretary was a
politician, responsible to the Cabinet, to Parliament and to the electorate.
However weak these checks were, they did serve as an ultimate barrier to
autocratic rule.

It has only been in recent years that diplomatic historians have begun to
recognize the role of Parliament, the press, the military establishment and
the commercial world in the shaping of opinions and policies.[1] It is easy to
generalize but difficult to define the exact relations between each of these
institutions or groups and the Foreign Office. The material is either elusive

[1] See the recently published study on the commercial aspect of this subject, D. C. Platt, *Finance, Trade and Politics in British Foreign Policy* (Oxford, 1968).

or too voluminous to collect and systematize while the accuracy of one's readings depends very much on an ability to sense the nuances and balance of forces in the Edwardian age. In the following pages I have dealt with only four such topics—the diplomats, the press, Parliament and the sovereign— and have tried to show how each contributed to the context in which foreign policy was made. These summaries give only indications of how the diplomatic archives can be used to shed light on these themes. Not only must more be said on each subject but the whole outside framework in which the Foreign Office operated requires more extensive treatment than is offered here.

### The diplomats

The Foreign Office was dependent on its diplomats both for information and for the execution of much of its policy. The role of the ambassador was changing; his independence had been sharply curtailed but his general responsibilities were not markedly different from those of his predecessors. In a telegraphic age, communication between Whitehall and even the most remote mission presented few problems. The daily flow of telegrams and official despatches was supplemented by letters from the foreign secretary and the permanent under-secretary. For the most part, decisions were made in London. There were differences of opinion but few diplomats acted with complete independence or in direct contradiction to their instructions. There is no parallel to the situation before the Second World War and no pre-First World War equivalent to Neville Henderson. The Edwardian diplomat was expected to report intelligently, represent his country's interests and conduct whatever negotiations the foreign secretary deemed necessary. Though there were many pressures for change, diplomacy remained essentially conservative both with regard to its form and practitioners.

The Diplomatic Service was a small, socially homogeneous body of men known to each other and to their European counterparts. The service had been slow to develop its professional character.[1] Until 1822 the foreign secretary selected his own agents and they in turn named their own staffs. The Government paid only the salary of the head of the mission and his secretary; the rest of the staff were considered friends and formed part of the ambassador's family. In 1856, due to the general pressure for reform, a 'qualifying test' was introduced though this had little effect on the kind or

[1] Most of this information comes from Cmd. 7748, pp. 2–7; see also Tilley and Gaselee, *The Foreign Office*; and Ward and Gooch, *Cambridge History of British Foreign Policy*, vol. III.

quality of men recruited. In 1869 the costs of the Foreign Service were transferred from the Civil List to the Consolidated Fund, an action which made the service subject to parliamentary scrutiny. In 1872, after a Select Committee report, only candidates with University degrees were to be exempt from a formal examination in a variety of subjects and even these were to be tested in French, précis and handwriting. At the same time salary scales were introduced for third and second secretaries. Though the examination was made competitive under Lord Granville, the diplomatic service never attracted as many candidates as the Foreign Office. Even when the same papers were set for both competitions, this balance was not altered; financial considerations seem to have been a decisive factor.

By Lord Salisbury's time it was a general procedure that all candidates secured the Foreign Secretary's nomination before entering the competition. The prospective diplomat was assumed to have an income of over £400 although this seems to have become a formal requirement at a later date. Candidates often secured nominations at eighteen or nineteen and took their examinations four or five years later. The Foreign Office decided when the candidate would be permitted to compete. Three or four men were allowed to take the examination for each vacancy so there was an element of real competition.

The only subsequent change was the creation of a Board of Selection in 1907 which functioned in the same way for the Diplomatic Service as for the Foreign Office. Candidates could apply at an early age but were permitted to take their examinations only if they were within the age limit (twenty-two to twenty-five) and had secured official nomination. David Kelly suggests that there was a sharp difference in the standard set for the Foreign Office and Diplomatic Service competitions and that the latter was getting the weaker men. 'I presented myself at the Foreign Office in an ordinary suit, and saw to my horror that the other ten or twelve candidates (for that was all there were) were all in tail coats! When my name was called, as I went to the board room I heard an awed whisper of "Good Lord, he got a First . . ."'[1] Competition was restricted to a narrow elite. Even in 1914 there were less than 150 career diplomats. Many of these were the sons of peers and the number of old Etonians seems to have risen in the years before the war.[2] It was natural that diplomacy remained the occupation of gentlemen; few men could have lived on the salaries they were paid. Attachés were not paid

[1] D. Kelly, *The Ruling Few* (London, 1952), p. 77.
[2] Cmd. 7748, p. 15. 48 of 86 unsuccessful candidates for the Diplomatic Service also came from Eton.

at all for two years; third secretaries were given £150 a year.[1] Harold Nicolson claims that in 1919, after ten years, his actual salary after tax deduction was £86 annually.[2] The highest salary was reserved for the Paris embassy but given the costs of maintaining that building and conducting a social life fitting the position of British ambassador, neither Monson nor Bertie could have found their salaries of £11,000 and £11,500 generous.[3] It is a curious commentary on the times that only the ambassador at Berlin among the European embassies could live within his income.[4]

The Foreign Office reforms of 1906 barely touched the work of the Diplomatic Service. Most diplomats were still engaged in secretarial work which could have easily been handled by secretarial staff. R. J. Bruce writes about pre-war Vienna '. . . we just did the work which came along, decyphered telegrams when they came and had an occasional busy day, mostly when the Foreign Office bag arrived'.[5] A diplomat reported to the 1914 Commission 'the principal duty of an attaché from the point of view of the chancery is typewriting'.[6] It was not without reason that a vast majority of the diplomatic memoirs of this period concentrate on the social life of the capitals of the pre-1914 world. The real work of the embassy was done by two or three men though occasionally a junior would prepare a special report for the Foreign Office or contribute a section of the annual report sent to Whitehall. The diplomat's career was very much in the hands of the private secretary who determined promotions and transfers. Ambassadors were, of course, consulted though their preferences were not always the deciding factor. Senior appointments were made by the foreign secretary and permanent

---

[1] Permanent attachés     —Nil for two years
   24 third secretaries     —£150 per annum
   21 second and first secretaries—£300—£20—£500
   13 counsellors        —£500—£1000 (varied according to post)
   Grades and salaries for members of the Diplomatic Service in 1914 below the ranks of minister and ambassador. Cmd. 7748, p. 14.                [2] Nicolson, *Peacemaking*, p. 230.
[3] There were nine embassies, thirteen missions of the first Class, seventeen missions of the second Class and two ministers resident in 1914:

| | |
|---|---|
| Paris | —£11,500 |
| Washington | —£10,000 |
| Vienna | — £8,000 |
| Berlin | — £8,000 |
| St Petersburgh | — £8,000 |
| Constantinople | — £8,000 |
| Rome | — £7,000 |
| Madrid | — £5,500 |
| Tokio | — £5,000 |

The salaries of ambassadors and heads of missions covered not only their personal remuneration but also the 'frais de representation'. Income tax was paid on salaries. Cmd. 7748, p. 14.
[4] Bertie MSS 800/177, Tyrrell to Bertie, 31 January 1907.
[5] R. J. Bruce, *Silken Dalliance* (London, 1946), p. 101.         [6] Cmd. 7749, Q.39,562.

under-secretary; as has been shown, both the sovereign and prime minister were consulted and often intervened decisively.

By the turn of the century the age of the great independent ambassador was over. The diplomats were a very mixed group and it was usually only the men in remote places or those engaged in complex, local negotiations who were given real freedom. As London was the key post for most foreign nations, a great deal of British diplomacy was conducted at home. A closer examination of some of Lord Salisbury's ambassadors suggests that a number were men of mediocre ability. Neither Sir Edmund Monson at Paris nor Sir Charles Scott at St Petersburgh were noticeably successful. Monson failed to come to terms with Delcassé and suffered from the latter's extreme reserve. He was often forced to rely on newspaper reports for his own information and was sometimes treated with scant respect by his chiefs.[1] Sir 'Venturesome Scott', as his detractors dubbed him, was far too trusting to be useful and could not always be relied on for accurate reporting. Apart from Sanderson, few officials at the Foreign Office had much faith in his judgements and tended to rely on his first secretary, Charles Hardinge, for information and correctives.[2] The ambassadors in Turkey had more scope for action and were a stronger group. Salisbury worked closely with Philip Currie, who had been his permanent under-secretary, and the latter seems to have exhausted himself at this post.[3] Lord Lansdowne, for his part, depended heavily on the advice of Nicholas O'Conor, Currie's successor, particularly during the Macedonian crisis of 1903.[4] O'Conor was anxious to bring into operation a more active reform programme in Macedonia and influenced the Foreign Office in this direction. He also took an active interest in the strengthening of British commercial interests in Turkey and was deeply disappointed when the Baghdad railway negotiations failed both in 1903 and 1905. Even under Grey, when Turkish policy took a rather different turn, O'Conor tended to write his own instructions and often suggested rather than implemented the line of diplomacy followed at Constantinople. O'Conor died in Turkey and the next ambassador, Gerard Lowther, was a less dynamic figure who was not considered an able adviser even by those responsible for his selection.[5] But the conditions at Constantinople were such

[1] Lansdowne MSS, Monson to Lansdowne, 16 November 1900; this is only one of many examples.
[2] Hardinge MSS, vol. 3, Bertie to Hardinge, 6 November 1901.
[3] Grenville, *Lord Salisbury and Foreign Policy*, pp. 14, 93.
[4] Lansdowne MSS, O'Conor to Lansdowne, 23 October, 3 November 1902, information from unpublished thesis. F. R. Bridge, 'The Diplomatic Relations between Great Britain and Austria–Hungary, 1906–1912', University of London, 1966.
[5] Hardinge MSS, vol. 21, Hardinge to Lowther, 19 April 1910. BD x(2), no. 513.

as to make the British position increasingly difficult and situations were created over which the ambassador had little control.[1]

Among the remaining ambassadors who served Salisbury and Lansdowne, Julian Pauncefote in Washington and Frank Lascelles in Berlin require special mention. Pauncefote was one of the ablest men in the Service; he had gone from the Foreign Office to Washington with an already established reputation as an international jurist. He played a key role in cementing the Anglo-American 'connection' and though he failed to carry a general arbitration agreement did manage to settle a number of irritating disputes.[2] His successor was his young, able, second, Michael Herbert, who died only two years after taking charge. For some inexplicable reason, Mortimer Durand was sent as his replacement. Fortunately for Anglo-American relations, his term was a short one and on Hardinge's recommendation James Bryce arrived in 1908 to continue Pauncefote's work.

Sir Frank Lascelles served at Berlin from 1895 until 1908, a key period in Anglo-German relations. An ambassador in the old style, Lascelles succeeded in establishing some kind of personal relationship with the Kaiser which was a testament to his patience and goodwill. The Kaiser delighted in long semi-official talks which were as distressing to the Wilhelmstrasse as they were sometimes annoying to Salisbury. But Lascelles always persevered and the Emperor's not infrequent critiques of British policy rarely aroused him. During Salisbury's last years Lascelles apparently shared the views of the Chamberlain group and at one point, in August 1898, raised the question of a defensive alliance without Salisbury's approval.[3] Even when these bids for German friendship failed, Lascelles remained loyal to his convictions and continued to work for an agreement.

His correspondence with Lansdowne is both extensive and informative. The two men were in basic agreement and both thought that some kind of arrangement remained possible. Though Lascelles did not disguise the difficulties involved in reaching such an understanding, he never really understood or explained the nature of the German antagonism nor the fundamental causes of Anglo-German tension. He was sometimes slow in his reactions and even unwittingly indiscreet.

[1] FO 800/365, Grey to Nicolson, 12 April 1913. 'I am very conscious in these last five years that I have made several mistakes about Constantinople . . . but that doesn't alter the necessity in the public interest for a change.'
[2] For Pauncefote's role: John Grenville, 'Great Britain and the Isthmian Canal, 1898–1901', *The American Historical Review* LXI (October 1955), 55–7. Lansdowne MSS, memorandum for Cabinet, 8 July 1901. C. S. Campbell, *Anglo-American Understanding, 1898–1903* (Baltimore, 1957), pp. 35–6.
[3] Grenville, *Lord Salisbury and Foreign Policy*, pp. 173–5.

Though Lascelles' stay in Berlin was prolonged into the Liberal period, there was little sympathy between him and the Grey Foreign Office. As has been shown, the Foreign Office thought he seriously underestimated the importance of the naval race and accused him of repeatedly trying to soften the tone of his Foreign Office communiques. In November 1907 Hardinge told the King that Lascelles (who had reached retirement age) would retire the following October. Grey and Hardinge then looked for a man more suited to their own views. Hardinge wanted to appoint Fairfax Cartwright, the Minister at Munich, but the Emperor objected and after much discussion Edward Goschen was sent from Vienna.

Distance and disturbed local conditions sometimes gave ministers more scope for initiative than ambassadors. This was true, for instance, at various moments, for men in Peking, Tokyo, Morocco and Persia. Ernest Satow, who first served at Tokyo and then at Peking, was an exception to almost all the generalizations about the Diplomatic Service. He came from a commercial, non-conformist background and was educated at London University. An excellent linguist, Satow entered the Diplomatic Corps from the Consular Service and first went to Japan as an interpreter. When he returned years later as minister, he knew a number of the senior men in the Government and helped develop those links necessary for future diplomatic co-operation. Though unusually acute and accomplished, Satow did not expect the Japanese to win their war with the Russians and Bertie seems to have been misled by Satow's judgement.[1]

The minister was subsequently sent to the Peking Conference to settle the European claims arising out of the Boxer Rebellion. He was an excellent delegate and settled many of the most difficult questions on his own initiative. There were months when he seems to have been without Foreign Office instructions and occasions when the Foreign Secretary found himself committed to an unwelcome position.[2] In general, however, Satow's work at the conference won Sanderson's approval[3] but Salisbury seems to have lost confidence in his ministers.

Claud Macdonald (minister at Peking and then at Tokyo) was, like Satow, an outsider. He was a military man who had successfully served under Lord Cromer and had been appointed a governor in West Africa. Macdonald proved to be an obstinate and hard fighter at Peking and during the famous

[1] Lansdowne MSS, Satow to Lansdowne, 10 March 1901. Even experts could be wrong. See John Jordan's comment that Sun Yat-sen was no more than a 'windbag'. FO 350/4, 11 November 1911.
[2] *Ibid.* Satow to Lansdowne, 25 December 1900. Satow had no instructions between the end of August until well into December. See Salisbury's temporary anger at Satow's actions in Lansdowne MSS, 13 December 1900.      [3] BD II, note p. 58.

'battle of concessions' in 1898 managed to secure a larger share of the spoils than the British community could exploit. He rapidly became one of the favourite sons of the China Association (the pressure group of the Far Eastern business interests) and the British merchants protested against his transfer to Tokyo, a reward for his heroism during the Boxer uprising. In Japan, though he continued to be an energetic and driving figure, Macdonald played only a minor role in the alliance negotiations. He was less able than Satow and seems to have lacked the diplomat's traditional finesse and tact. But the major decisions were made in London and Macdonald's limitations were of secondary importance.

The smaller countries were often excellent assignments for rising younger men though they might also be graveyards. Here the problem was less one of distance than of the weakness of the governments involved. When Arthur Nicolson was sent to Morocco, for instance, he tried hard to force a reform programme on the Sultan and favoured an anti-French line.[1] Though Lord Salisbury gave him little encouragement, Lansdowne was more sympathetically inclined until the French offer to include Morocco in a more general agreement brought an end to this independent policy. But Nicolson's activities in Morocco brought him to the attention of the Foreign Office. Mortimer Durand, on the other hand, though a Persian scholar, had a difficult time in Persia. His analyses of the Persian situation did not lack acuteness but he was unable to stir Salisbury and failed to make an impression on the Persian Government. By 1900, owing to his wife's illness, he had practically withdrawn from all social life and the legation was in a generally depressed and disorganized state when he finally left.[2] His successor, Arthur Hardinge, was clever, tenacious, active and moderately successful. Supported by Lansdowne, he was able to improve the British position at the Persian capital though he could not in fact check the Russian advance. Hardinge's tactics were not always in the best traditions of the Service and even Lansdowne admitted that his minister was often too fond of using the Persians' own methods to gain his ends.[3] In the long run, in Persia as in Morocco, British policy was decided in London. The Anglo-Russian convention of 1907 placed a great strain on British ministers in Teheran and each in turn suffered under the necessity of working with the Russians to support a policy which they intensely disliked.

[1] Taylor, *Rumours of War*, pp. 141–4; FO 99/367, no. 55, Nicolson to Salisbury, 22 April 1900; minute of Salisbury tel. no. 9; Salisbury to Nicolson, 28 April 1907; Lansdowne MSS, Lansdowne to Nicolson, 20 March 1901; Lansdowne to Monson, 2 January 1902.
[2] Gwynn, *The Letters and Friendships of Sir Cecil Spring-Rice*, vol. I, p. 318.
[3] Lansdowne MSS, Lansdowne to Curzon, 24 April 1903.

The key changes in the Diplomatic Service, like those in the Foreign Office, took place during the last years of Conservative rule. The appointment of Francis Bertie to Paris and Charles Hardinge and Arthur Nicolson to St Petersburgh were crucial in creating and cementing the ties of England to the Franco-Russian alliance. Edward Goschen's appointment to Vienna (1905–8) and then to Berlin represented a further victory for the new school of diplomats. Cartwright, who was sent to Vienna (1908–13), tended to be more sympathetic to the Austrians than London appreciated and his counsel was not always heeded.

Paris was the great prize and Bertie the most outstanding of Grey's ambassadors. 'We called him the Bull because the only way to handle him was to wear him down early by junior picador and banderillo before the Matador or Counsellor finished him with the day's signatures. We tamed him, too, by telephone', Vansittart recalls in *Mist Procession*.[1] Bertie was a colourful figure, a dynamic personage and a passionate fighter. He was a rough taskmaster, caustic in his comments about his colleagues and fearless in his relations with his seniors. He bombarded Grey, Hardinge and Nicolson with advice not only on Anglo-French relations but on all aspects of European diplomacy. He never shrank from an unpleasant despatch and always made his views perfectly clear. He believed that Germany would destroy the peace of Europe and that the entente with France was the key to England's safety. Bertie never accepted Nicolson's view that the Russian agreement was of greater importance than the Anglo-French entente and thought the Under-Secretary had his priorities wrong. He not only took steps to preserve the entente but repeatedly pressed the French to strengthen it. During both Moroccan crises, the British ambassador urged Grey to take a more extreme position than the Foreign Secretary thought possible or desirable.[2] Particularly during the summer of 1911, Bertie opposed and even attempted to thwart Grey's efforts to find a compromise in Morocco which would break the diplomatic deadlock. Like Nicolson and Crowe, Bertie feared that unless the French were given full support, they would desert and settle with the Germans on the latter's terms. The ambassador was summoned back to London towards the end of August for explanations and discussions.[3] Though undoubtedly pleased by the warlike stand of both Lloyd George and

1 Vansittart, *The Mist Procession*, p. 54. Bertie used to charge into the Chancery 'like a bull entering the arena' (*ibid.* p. 182).
2 Monger, *The End of Isolation*, pp. 271, 277–9; BD VII, nos. 372, 375, 377; Bertie MSS, Bertie to Eyre Crowe, 21 July 1911. FO 800/171.
3 FO 800/161, memorandum by Bertie for an interview with Grey, Asquith and Lloyd George on 25 July 1911.

Winston Churchill, Bertie continued to press for military and naval arrangements with Paris which would give teeth to the entente.

Bertie's fears that the entente was too weak to provide an effective check to German ambitions were intensified as the pro-German movement gained ground during 1912. Despite his personal intervention with the King, Grey and other members of the Cabinet, Bertie could not block new efforts at an agreement with Berlin.[1] He supported and strengthened French protests in the winter of 1912 and was deeply relieved when the search for a political formula was abandoned in the spring. But Bertie's real opportunity to restore the balance came during the summer of 1912 when the Anglo-French naval agreements were being negotiated. Once again, like the permanent officials at the Foreign Office, the ambassador hoped that the Cabinet would offer a real *quid pro quo* in return for the North Sea/Mediterranean redistribution of naval forces. As during the Moroccan crises, Bertie's basic aims were frustrated both by the Foreign Secretary and by the Cabinet for neither wished to see the entente turned into an alliance. The final form of the arrangement did not create the binding commitment sought by Poincaré, Cambon or Bertie. Nevertheless, the acceptance of a formula which did commit the two countries to consultation was due to the persistence of the French and the continual prodding of the British ambassador.[2] Bertie's determination undoubtedly strengthened Grey's stand in a cabinet which, with few exceptions, tended to be strongly anti-French at this particular time.

Further studies will, I think, show that Bertie's reputation and influence were greater in Paris than in London. Though Grey appreciated his ambassador's unique position in the French capital, he did not always agree with Bertie's views and, at critical moments, rejected Bertie's advice as unsound or politically untenable. The 'Bull' was neither an easy chief nor colleague and from the start of his diplomatic career, had made powerful enemies. Even during his first years at the embassy, there were a number of intrigues against him. Bertie's royal connections (both with Edward VII and to a lesser extent with George V with whom he had a number of inconclusive interviews) and meetings with individual Cabinet ministers created suspicion. His relations with Nicolson were complicated during 1914 by their differences over Russia and quarrels over the future of the Paris embassy. Though Bertie succeeded in staying at his post throughout the war, Lloyd George was anxious to replace him. A first effort in 1917 failed, but in April 1918, under

[1] Bertie MSS, FO 800/171, memoranda by Bertie, 16 February 1912, 19 February 1912; FO 800/186, memorandum by Bertie, 17 February 1912.
[2] FO 800/187, memorandum by Bertie, 25 July 1912; BD x(ii), nos. 404, 405, 409, 413–16.

rather unpleasant circumstances, Lord Derby was appointed to this most coveted position.[1]

Hardinge was only at the St Petersburgh embassy for a brief period (1904–6) but stayed long enough to keep the peace during the Dogger Bank panic and to open the door for future conversations. The real work of negotiating the Anglo-Russian conventions was done by Arthur Nicolson (1906–10) and they were a tribute to Nicolson's skill and patience. The Ambassador's close relationship with Isvolsky was not without influence in the many crises which followed. Nicolson repeatedly tried to stiffen the Russian foreign minister's back against both the Germans and Austrians and at the same time urged Grey to support Russia in the battle for the spoils of the Turkish Empire. In partnership with Hardinge, Nicolson was certainly responsible for the pro-Russian orientation of British policy both in the Balkans and in the Middle East. Yet, as in the case of Bertie, Grey felt he could not go as far as Nicolson wished and the latter's correspondence is full of complaints against the Government's policy of 'half-hearted' friendships. When Nicolson returned to the Foreign Office, he was replaced, on his own and Hardinge's recommendations, by George Buchanan, a man who shared Nicolson's fears and hopes. Buchanan did extremely well and was given a good deal of latitude. Under ordinary circumstances his tact and common sense might have been sufficient, but the war-time situation ultimately proved too difficult for such a traditionalist.

George Goschen was not in the same category as either Bertie or Nicolson. Already at Vienna he had become convinced of the hostile intentions of the German Government and fully believed in the total subordination of Vienna to Berlin. Neither Bertie nor Hardinge had a high opinion of his ability. He never thought an agreement with Berlin feasible or desirable and did his best to check the pro-German current particularly after 1912. Goschen failed to make any real contact with the members of the German Government and tended to be baffled by the cross-currents in the Kaiser's entourage. During his ambassadorship the Emperor came to the embassy only once, on the occasion of King Edward's death. It is true that Goschen opposed the Nicolson–Crowe line both at the time of the Agadir crisis and in the spring of 1914. But though he did not wish to see the ententes turned into alliances, he thought Grey's hopes for a real détente with Berlin illusory and doubted whether the civilians could prevail over Tirpitz and the military. On the whole, he was a loyal servant and carried out Grey's

[1] Hardinge, *Old Diplomacy*, pp. 214, 216.

instructions.[1] 'I am too old a hand', he said to Oppenheimer, the British consul-general in Germany, 'at this game to ask for instructions. I am here to receive them and carry them out'.[1] It is doubtful whether even a more able diplomat would have been able to influence the highly complex mood which pervaded imperial Germany but Goschen did not really attempt to guide his superiors through the labyrinth.

Fairfax Cartwright at Vienna was a writer and poet, highly intelligent and courageous. A recent student of Anglo-Austrian relations has concluded that though Cartwright was an excellent reporter, he was unable to convince Grey that Austria could be encouraged to take a more independent line towards Berlin and his tendency to exceed his instructions did not endear him to the London office.[2] The so-called 'Cartwright interview' in 1911 ended his usefulness and the Austrians repeatedly pressed for his withdrawal. Though he stayed on two more years, he was *persona non grata* at court and could do little to capitalize on the détente which developed after the 1908–9 crisis.

Even a short and incomplete survey of the leading figures of the pre-war Foreign Service clearly shows that the foreign secretaries permitted their diplomats only a minor share in the making of policy. Though particular men could still alter the diplomatic atmosphere or take an active role in the negotiating process, with but few exceptions the Edwardian diplomats followed instructions from London. Moreover, whereas in Salisbury's day the diplomats provided a unique source of information and counsel, during Lansdowne's and Grey's tenures of office their advice was checked and even overruled by the professionals at Whitehall. 'At Downing Street one can at least pull the wires whereas an ambassador is only a d—d marionette', a frustrated Bertie wrote from Rome.[3] Even before the critics of the 'old diplomacy' mounted their attacks, the embassy circuit was losing its effective power.

There was a great deal of substance to the charges of the radicals— E. D. Morel, Noel Buxton and Arthur Ponsonby. British diplomats were recruited from an exceedingly narrow social base; even in 1914 there were few exceptions. Embassy life did not attract the ambitious or the energetic. Promotion was slow and the social life at most posts could have offered little variety. Able men wrote verse or plays or travel books. Only the rare individual sensed there were new forces, both political and economic,

[1] Oppenheimer, *Stranger Within*, p. 229.
[2] I am indebted to Mr F. R. Bridge for the following assessment. Hardinge's letter of rebuke, Hardinge MSS, vol. 17, Hardinge to Cartwright, 2 April 1909.
[3] Hardinge MSS, Chirol to Hardinge, 10 August 1904.

stirring in the countries to which they were accredited. Though the traditional disdain for 'trade' and 'traders' was diminishing, there were but a few diplomats—Arthur Hardinge, Claude Macdonald, John Jordan, Nicolas O'Conor and Gerard Lowther—who found themselves engaged in battles for concessions and spheres of economic influence.[1] Despite the Foreign Office awareness and response to the new competitive spirit abroad, its general attitude, even in the twentieth century, was best expressed by Claude Macdonald, the most active concession-hunter in the Service: 'British enterprise in China must be independent and self-reliant. The moment it ceases to be this and leans too much on state assistance, it ceases to be enterprise, indeed I may say it ceases to be British.'[2] There were some transfers from the Consular Service (usually one of the area services) to the Diplomatic Service —William White, Ernest Satow, John Jordan. But the former suffered from the condescending attitudes of their diplomatic colleagues and even on the eve of the war the gulf between these two overseas branches was a wide one. Ambassadors took only a marginal interest in the commercial affairs of their embassies. Bruce Lockhart claimed there was a letter from a certain British ambassador in the archives of the Moscow consulate: 'Dear Mr ——, Please remember that I am not here to be bothered with questions about trade.'[3] Members of the Consular Staff did not mingle with embassy personnel; as late as 1923 commercial attachés were 'not asked to dine at the Embassy'.[4]

It is true that in the period before the war foreign secretaries were becoming increasingly involved in the protection of British trade and in the use of concessions and foreign loans for political purposes.[5] But the Foreign Office

1 D. C. M. Platt, *Finance, Trade and Politics in British Foreign Policy, 1815–1914*, was read after this section was concluded but takes up the following points in much greater detail and with much more authority. See also H. Feiss, *Europe, The World's Banker, 1870–1914* (New Haven, 1930).
2 Quoted in Pelcovits, *Old China Hands and the Foreign Office*, p. 220.
3 Sir Robert Bruce Lockhart, *Memoirs of a British Agent* (London, 1932), p. 78.
4 L. E. Jones, *Georgian Afternoon* (London, 1958), p. 109. There are many other examples. See Oppenheimer, *Stranger Within*, pp. 305, 321. G. Campbell, *Of True Experience* (London, 1949), pp. 20, 22.
5 Both Salisbury and Lansdowne were conscious of the efforts made by German diplomats to help their traders though both tended to credit German commercial victories to the vigour of their firms. Satow MSS, Salisbury to Satow, 3 October 1895. 'I think you should give great attention to the commercial part of your duties. In recent years the old doctrine of entire abstention from any succour or support to particular English firms has become antiquated especially in view of the actions of the Germans . . . But while trying to be fair among various English rivals, it is of the highest importance to prevent contracts going to Germany which might go to England'. Satow later complained to Lansdowne that while Belgium, France and Germany were building railways, 'our people do nothing. The press alleged for them that it was because they were not properly supported by His Majesty's Government. My despatch is intended to put the blame on the right shoulders.' Lansdowne MSS, Satow to Lansdowne, 27 March 1902. 'Nothing annoys me more',

moved with reluctance and within very restricted confines. Only a few people at Whitehall, Eyre Crowe being the most notable example, understood the value of commercial reporting and the need for a more extended system of commercial representation. Though Hardinge had friends in the leading commercial houses, neither he nor Nicolson sensed that economic problems would soon become one of the central concerns of twentieth-century diplomacy. As indicated in the previous chapter, war-time efforts to equip the Foreign Office for an expanded economic role were defeated and some of the men involved left the office in disgust. The Diplomatic Service was even more conservative than the Foreign Office and firmer in its prejudices. Inherited attitudes proved difficult to displace.[1]

Even by the standards of pre-war Europe, the British Diplomatic Service was unduly restricted in its attitudes and interests. The Foreign Office would have been better informed had its agents been drawn from a wider circle of recruits. But while the reformers were justified in their complaints, they exaggerated the importance of their targets. Though there was still room for the powerful personality or 'grand eccentric' there was only limited scope for independent action abroad. The Foreign Office placed men in the leading posts who would loyally serve the foreign secretary and even the most independent ambassador or minister was always conscious of the checks on his initiative. Moreover, European diplomacy was still in the hands of a small social circle who spoke a common language and accepted similar standards of behaviour. All the foreign offices of this period operated in a rarified atmosphere and an examination of the other European diplomatic services will undoubtedly reveal similar prejudices and narrowness of vision. As far as the diplomats were concerned, the room for manœuvre was small and the post-war debate about the responsibility of the diplomats for the outbreak of war has a curiously artificial air about it.[2]

Lansdowne answered on 17 May, 'than the comparative inactivity of our own people in regard to these enterprises.' Grey was to have similar complaints about British financial houses in Turkey and Persia. Investors preferred settled countries whereas the Foreign Office, partly for political reasons, was concerned with weak or disintegrating empires.

[1] These questions still remain unsolved not only in Great Britain but also in the United States. Both the Foreign Office and the State Department have tried with only limited success to make commercial and economic assignments as important and attractive as political ones. Compare the British *Plowden Report* with the earlier *Wriston Report* on the State Department and Foreign Service. *Report of the Committee on Representational Service Overseas* (Cmd. 2276), 1964. *Report of the Secretary's Public Committee on Personnel*, May 1954 (later published under the title *Toward a Stronger Foreign Service*). For commentary on the latter (the Wriston Report), see Z. Steiner, *The State Department and the Foreign Service* (Princeton, 1958); *Present Problems of the Foreign Service* (Princeton, 1961).

[2] For a brief comment on the roles of those 'supra-diplomatists', Lord Curzon and Lord Cromer, see Appendix 6.

## The press

A second link between the Foreign Office and the outside world was through Fleet Street. This was a two-way process. The Foreign Office was aware of the usefulness of the press and periodically tried to influence it through private contacts or public pronouncements with varying degrees of success. For their own part, the foreign secretary and his staff read the leaders in the dailies and quarterlies and often found reports from special correspondents more informative than the despatches of their own diplomats. It must be remembered that foreign coverage in the period was extensive and that readers of the quality papers (many of whom may well have been the same men contributing to the boom in overseas investments) were probably better informed than their modern counterparts. Certain papers were considered more well disposed than others and some editors given preferential treatment either because of the importance of their journals or for reasons of a more personal nature.

There were no official contacts between the Foreign Office and Fleet Street. No press bureau existed. The foreign secretary occasionally received an editor but it was more often his private secretary or one of the senior officials at the office who dealt with editors and correspondents. In 1898 Francis Bertie suggested steps to bring order into a very chaotic system of communication.[1] He recommended that all journalists be admitted to the Foreign Office before 4 o'clock. Inquiries for the private secretary should be submitted in writing from the Front Hall waiting-room. An hour later, the private secretary would send down any items of intelligence. Editors waiting to see the private secretary could wait upstairs. There appears to have been an official list of newspapers to whom diplomatic news was circulated and papers could be punished by omission. Though a good deal of this press business was handled by the private secretary, the permanent under-secretary and the assistant under-secretaries often received visitors, particularly the foreign editors of the London journals.

No direct control over the press could be exercised though judicious hints were often given. *The Times*, regarded abroad as a semi-official paper, was in a special position, as was the *Westminster Gazette* during Sir Edward Grey's tenure of office. But the relations between *The Times* and the Foreign

[1] FO 366/391, Bertie to Salisbury, 10 September 1898. See the claim made in Kennedy Jones, *Fleet Street and Downing Street* (London, 1920), p. 97, that at the time of the Fashoda crisis Fleet Street was invited to the Foreign Office and a *Daily Mail* representative informed by Sanderson of the policy which the Government proposed to follow. 'The Fashoda incident', he writes, 'marked the breaking down of the barriers of Downing Street.'

Office were not always smooth and attempts at interference were often unsuccessful. There is little doubt that Moberly Bell, of *The Times*, was determined to publicize the German menace and the reports of Valentine Chirol and George Saunders constantly underlined the German menace. The Emperor and Count Metternich repeatedly complained to the foreign secretary and a number of efforts were made to quiet *The Times*. The most famous case occurred in January 1898 when the Queen herself intervened.[1] At the height of the Bundesrath crisis at the time of the Boer War, Sanderson received Valentine Chirol, then the foreign editor of *The Times*. Chirol came 'to have his head washed' but little was accomplished. 'As to Buckle and Moberly Bell, I believe them to be much worse. I don't think Lord Salisbury regards them as being at all friendly to him—and he every now and then warns me when I tell him of a conversation with Chirol, "Remember you are talking to a critic".'[2] The Germans asked Eckardstein and Alfred de Rothschild to see Moberly Bell in June 1902, again without positive results.[3] The climax in the press campaign came in April 1903 when members of Parliament supported by *The Spectator* and *National Review* forced Lansdowne to abandon the Baghdad railway talks with Germany very much against his will.

In addition to their suspicious attitude towards Berlin, *The Times* editors were also highly critical of Russian domestic and foreign policy. Once again Chirol came to see Sanderson, this time about Russian atrocities in Tientsin.

He asked whether I thought they were true—I said I could certainly not contradict them, but that I should suggest his not publishing them—as they would certainly hurt the Emperor of Russia's feelings, they would give the Chinese some handle for excusing their misdeeds—and I did not see that the publication would serve any useful purpose. He seemed to agree—and I noticed—they have not appeared—but *The Times* has got today a very scathing and sarcastic article about Russian proceedings in Manchuria.[4]

*The Times*, moreover, kept up its campaign against Russian internal abuses and, in 1903, because of a series of articles by their correspondent on the pogroms, the latter was expelled from Russia. Nothing was done by the Foreign Office but Lansdowne appealed to Buckle and Hardinge wrote from St Petersburgh to Chirol urging the paper to modify its angry tone.[5]

[1] G. E. Buckle (ed.), *The Letters of Queen Victoria*, 3rd series (London, 1930), vol. III, p. 253.
[2] Lascelles MSS, Sanderson to Lascelles, 28 March 1900.
[3] The Times *History of The Times, The Twentieth Century Test, 1884–1912*, vol. III (London, 1947), pp. 306–9.
[4] Hardinge MSS, Sanderson to Hardinge, 10 October 1900.
[5] *Ibid.* Hardinge to Lansdowne, June 1904; *History of The Times, The Twentieth Century Test*, pp. 320–1.

The Foreign Office placed reports to aid its diplomacy. Some of the leaks during the Newfoundland negotiations with France in the winter of 1900–1 seem to have been intentional.[1] On 20 December 1900 Barrington asked the *Daily Telegraph*, 'a well-disposed' paper, to publicize, at the request of the Shah, recent Persian concessions to British firms. The Foreign Office sometimes asked for help. In the summer of 1902 Lord Lansdowne approached Buckle for assistance on a Chinese issue:

I have just received a private telegram from Mackay in which he tells me that the Chinese are hearing by press telegrams of the favourable reception which his proposals have met with here, and are coming to the conclusion that they have yielded too much and they had better hold their hand. Mackay asks me whether it would not be possible to publish something to the effect that the prospects of the treaty being accepted by H.M. Government are less hopeful.[2]

Individual correspondents were men of great influence. In the foreign capitals, contacts with journalists could be extremely useful. Walter B. Harris, *The Times* correspondent in Morocco, became a close companion of Arthur Nicolson (the British minister). The former brought Nicolson into the Shah's circle and encouraged him to take up an anti-French reform programme.[3] Mackenzie Wallace, another correspondent friend of Nicolson's, was a close companion both at the Algeciras Conference and later in St Petersburgh where Wallace's sources of information were more extensive than those of the ambassador's. Wickham Steed had gained George Goschen's confidence at Vienna and established such a position for himself in the Austrian capital that the Foreign Office later accepted his judgements rather than those of their own ambassador.[4] Not infrequently, correspondents, because of their wider local knowledge, secured news which the Foreign Office needed. It was G. E. Morrison, the anti-Russian but extremely knowledgeable Far Eastern correspondent of *The Times*, who provoked Curzon's remark about 'the intelligent anticipation of facts even before they occur'. Morrison repeatedly despatched information about Russian activities in China well before they were reported by the British diplomats and Francis Bertie in London kept a close eye on this correspondent's reports. George Washington

1 *Westminster Gazette*, 27 December 1900; *St James Gazette*, 4 January 1901.
2 Lansdowne MSS, Lord Lansdowne to John Buckle, 1 August 1902.
3 Taylor, *Rumours of War*, p. 148; FO 99/395, tel. no. 16, Lansdowne to White, 23 September 1902. But see Nicolson's later difficulty with Harris in 1903. The relevant letters are in FO 800/22. Nicolson was sorry *The Times* retained him as half of his news was invention (27 April 1902). Stirred by a cry from Nicolson, 'Was Harris born to haunt the autumn of my life?', Sanderson spoke to Chirol 'and he promised to persuade Buckle and Moberly Bell to propose to Harris that he should take a holiday'. *Ibid.* Sanderson to Nicolson, 13 July 1903.
4 I am indebted to Dr F. R. Bridge for this information.

Smalley, another correspondent of the same paper, played a not inconsider able role during the Hay-Pauncefote negotiations of 1901 though not in a direction desired by the British ambassador.[1] Correspondents provided information for the local diplomatists as well as news for the readers at home.

Editors, too, cultivated their friends in the Diplomatic Service. Leo Maxse, the editor of the *National Review*, saw and corresponded with both Charles Hardinge and Cecil Spring-Rice. His important A.B.C. article in the November 1901 issue proposing an agreement with Russia was based on information from Hardinge though it was understood that the first secretary at St Petersburgh was in no way responsible for the views expressed.[2] Strachey of *The Spectator* and the editors of the *Quarterly Review* found Cecil Spring-Rice a particularly good source of information. The article in the latter review which so embittered Anglo-German relations in the autumn of 1908 owed a great deal to this source.[3] But of all the journalists of this period, Valentine Chirol was probably the most successful in penetrating both diplomatic and Foreign Office circles. Chirol was an old Foreign Office man who left the office rather abruptly after four years of service. Having embarked on a second career for which he was not entirely suited, he became one of the most able representatives of *The Times*.[4] He kept his old friend-ships, was intimate with Lascelles and Spring-Rice (whom he met at Lascelles' home) and later with Hardinge and Nicolson. He was a frequent visitor at the Foreign Office, saw Sanderson regularly, knew Tyrrell well and even met Eyre Crowe occasionally. It was Chirol who sounded Hardinge out about the possibility of a Russian rapprochement with England in the autumn of 1901. 'We are so sick over the slipperyness of our German friends that I think there would be a much greater disposition over here to respond to any such desire on the part of Russia than at any time within my memory almost. Even Joe Chamberlain is losing faith in Berlin'.[5] When Hardinge came back to the Foreign Office as permanent under-secretary, Chirol, then foreign editor of *The Times*, had an excellent source of information, for the two men were more than professional acquaintances, as their subsequent intimate correspondence indicates. Chirol, who was away from England during 1910 and 1911, resigned from his newspaper at the end of that year. Nevertheless, for various reasons, he continued to frequent the Foreign Office, managing to retain his links with both Tyrrell and Nicolson even

1 Campbell, *Anglo-American Understanding*, pp. 214–15, 245.
2 Hardinge MSS, Maxse to Hardinge, 31 October 1901.
3 Gwynn, *The Letters and Friendships of Sir Cecil Spring-Rice*, vol. II, p. 144.
4 *History of The Times, The Twentieth Century Test*, pp. 764–5.
5 Hardinge MSS, Chirol to Hardinge, 11 October 1901.

when these two men quarrelled. His letters to Hardinge during this period are one of the only sources for the story of the intra-office difficulties which plagued the department.

Newspapers could create or destroy a particular mood but they rarely caused any concrete change in Foreign Office thinking and both Salisbury and Lansdowne remained aloof from any press campaign to alter the course of British diplomacy. Cases of capitulation to popular pressure were rare but swings in opinion did sometimes complicate the diplomatic process.[1] The situation did not really alter in Grey's period. Grey made little effort to cultivate the press though William Tyrrell possessed the kind of sophistication, wit and love of talk which must have been a boon to journalists. In fact Grey was faced with a very hostile Liberal press during much of his time in office. *The Times*, of course, remained in a very special position. Despite repeated disclaimers from the Foreign Office, it was treated, both at home and abroad, as a semi-official paper. 'The Foreign Office seems to confide in The Times alone so we may get a little illumination from that quarter during the next few weeks', Ponsonby wrote to Lloyd George at the time of the Grey-Sazonov Balmoral meeting.[2] Grey was personally closest to J. A. Spender, the editor of the small but influential *Westminster Gazette*, and there were financial connections between the paper and Liberal Cabinet. Before coming to the Foreign Office, the newly appointed foreign secretary sought Spender's assistance in combating the idea that the Liberals would be less pro-French than their Conservative predecessors.[3]

Both the Foreign Secretary and his officials read the press regularly and followed much of the debate in the quarterlies. Even Eyre Crowe read his *Times* daily and through his brother-in-law, Spencer Wilkinson, had a link with Fleet Street. But in general, Grey was impervious to both blame and praise. Only the Liberal–Radical campaign against his Russian policy in the winter of 1911 pierced the Foreign Secretary's usual detachment. This attack, which was carried on in the press as well as in Parliament, enlisted the support of C. P. Scott of the *Manchester Guardian*, H. W. Massingham and H. N. Brailsford of the *Nation*, A. G. Gardiner of the *Daily News* and F. W. Hirst of *The Economist*. Even the Conservative *Daily Telegraph* joined in the hostile chorus. As indicated earlier, the effects of this public campaign were limited and the subsequent changes in Grey's policy were due to the

---

[1] The Venezuelan and Baghdad railway cases are examples, and Lansdowne's efforts to smooth relations with Germany were made more difficult by the press campaign even before the Moroccan crisis.

[2] Ponsonby MSS, Ponsonby to Lloyd George, copy, September 1912.

[3] Brit. Mus. Add. MSS 46389, Grey to Spender, 19 October 1905; see also, 24 September 1912.

divisions in the cabinet and diplomatic factors rather than to public pressure.[1]

Even when this polemic subsided, much of the Liberal press remained in opposition. Scott was invited to London where various ministers tried to conciliate him but his most important Cabinet contact was Lord Loreburn, one of Grey's strongest opponents.[2] Hirst also continued to criticize the policy of the ententes, opposed British entrance into the war and wrote scathing war-time leaders on Grey and the Foreign Office. While *The Economist* opposed the Foreign Secretary because he had involved the nation in the concerns of France and, worse still, Russia, *The Times*, using information supplied by Nicolson and Cambon, criticized Grey and the Cabinet for failing to support France at the critical moment. Relations between the Foreign Office and Printing House Square deteriorated sharply during the July crisis and after a blow-up over Turkey in the winter of 1914–15, there was a complete break between the two institutions.

As under the Conservatives, the Liberal Foreign Office did intervene in Fleet Street at certain critical moments. Hardinge persuaded the *Daily Mail* not to publish the Kaiser's interview with William Bayard Hale, though the Germans could not prevent a synopsis of the conversation from appearing in New York. When Wickham Steed's reports from Vienna grew increasingly hostile during the annexation crisis, Count Mensdorff complained to Tyrrell who intervened with only limited success. When, however, Tyrrell heard that *The Times* was considering Steed as a possible Berlin correspondent, he acted more decisively. Chirol, who had little sympathy for Steed, reported:

Tyrrell came to see me yesterday morning. He had heard from Buckle that Steed was going to Berlin, and he is much exercised about it, as he thinks Steed (whom he knows) would be the wrong man there in the interests of the paper, and in those of Anglo-German relations. His arguments impressed me, and I asked him to go and see you and talk it over with you. I have great confidence in his judgment and he has been a most valuable friend to me, and to the paper too.[3]

Steed was left in Vienna and Tyrrell, at least, thought he was responsible for this decision. As he wrote Spring-Rice, 'My observation to Chirol about Berlin was in reply to his congratulating me on having persuaded Moberly Bell of Steed's unfitness for the post. I never felt more pleased. It would have been a disastrous appointment both for *The Times* and for us.'[4] Steed's critical reports from Vienna continued. In 1909 Count Mensdorff again

---

[1] See pp. 127, 138–9, 143–4.
[2] J. Hammond, *C. P. Scott of the Manchester Guardian* (London, 1934), pp. 155, 158–61.
[3] *History of The Times, The Twentieth Century Test*, p. 646.
[4] FO 800/241, Tyrrell to Spring-Rice, 16 July 1908. For other examples of Tyrrell's activities see FO 800/93, 23 February 1912 and the correspondence with Chirol.

complained to Tyrrell and the latter promised to see *The Times* editors. But the Austrian complaints did not prevent Steed's eventual promotion to foreign editor.

The Foreign Office again acted with some vigour during the Turco-Italian war of 1911. Nicolson wrote to Cartwright (ambassador at Vienna) that he was 'exceedingly vexed at the tone of our press here towards Italy'.[1] Almost the whole of Fleet Street was pro-Turk in their reports and editorials.

The line taken by the English press (with some exceptions) is deplorable [Nicolson wrote] and I think serious endeavours should be made to induce them to observe neutrality. It ought to be possible to induce some of the less unreasonable Editors to maintain a decent neutrality and they might be reminded that their hysterical outburst against Austria five years ago did not improve matters.[2]

Pressure was exerted and the tone of the press, with the exception of the *Daily Mail*, did improve in the direction Nicolson indicated.

Such interventions were rare. Given the structure of the press in England, there were few retaliatory weapons in the private secretary's hands and the Foreign Office as an institution was barely aware of the potentialities of this kind of public diplomacy. It was only during the First World War that a News Department was established. Almost everything in the way of press relations depended on personal contacts and individual friendships. If press opinion did not substantially alter the views of the Foreign Office, there were few editors who would accept Whitehall direction.

### Parliament

By its very nature, Parliament is debarred from an executive role in foreign affairs.[3] Dependent on the Government for its information, it can only seek elucidation, criticize past policy and indirectly influence the future. Though no foreign secretary can commit the country to war without parliamentary support, he can create the most far-reaching obligations which must be honoured. Lord Salisbury, for instance, was far more conscious of the limitations imposed by a parliamentary regime than his successors but even he concluded secret treaties. Lord Lansdowne, too, was not averse to secret arrangements, and eventually concluded an entente whose secret clauses

[1] Carnock MSS, 1911 (v), Nicolson to Cartwright, 2 October 1911; BD x(1) 256.    [2] *Ibid.*

[3] For instance, parliamentary sanction is not needed for signing or ratifying treaties unless they involve expenditure or the cession of territory in time of peace. F. Flournoy, *Parliament and War* (London, 1927); N. Greaves, *Parliamentary Control of Foreign Affairs* (London, 1934); A. Ponsonby, *Democracy and Diplomacy—a Plea for Popular Control of Foreign Policy* (London, 1915); D. Bishop, *The Administration of British Foreign Relations* (Syracuse, 1961) have proved useful on the theoretical side.

were not revealed until printed in *Le Temps* in November 1911. Sir Edward Grey sanctioned military talks with the French without the knowledge of the Cabinet and later the Cabinet agreed to naval conversations with both France and Russia which created ties which were specifically denied in the House of Commons. Even on the most fundamental issues of foreign policy, the powers of Parliament were restricted.

But even within a narrower framework, neither House proved a real stumbling-block for the foreign secretary. Though there were many opportunities for debates on foreign policy, none of these occasions was adequately utilized. Since the 1880s no general election had been held on a foreign policy issue. A single seat might be lost as in the summer of 1898 when the radicals gained a victory in Lancashire on the Far Eastern situation but such occasions were rare enough to merit press comment. The parties tended to exclude foreign affairs from the arena of active debate and there was a tendency, particularly in 1906, to stress the continuities rather than the breaks in foreign policy. Within Parliament, the pressure of domestic business cut down the time available for parliamentary discussions. As the time-table was tightened, the opposition concentrated on domestic politics, and debates about diplomacy were restricted both in the numbers of speakers and listeners. All these trends were intensified during the Liberal period.[1] The debates in the Lords were often more informative but even before the reforms of 1911 the Upper House could do little more than provide an additional platform for public discussion.[2]

There were rarely more than one or two important debates in a year and few lasted longer than two days. Attendance was poor; during a discussion of the China situation in June 1898, there were only forty members present and much more enlightenment came from the columns of the London press.[3] The Lords' debates were no better attended despite the presence of a number of senior statesmen. Nor did matters improve after 1906. Some Liberal sessions passed without even a debate on the Foreign Office estimates (1910) and in 1914 only one and a half days were devoted to the Foreign Office vote and this only by chance.[4] In the Conservative period, apart from the official spokesmen in the Commons, Curzon (the

---

[1] *Hansard*, Parliamentary Debates, 4th series, vol. CIV, p. 789; 5th series, vol. XXIV, p. 540.
[2] The debate on the Anglo-Russian conventions in the Lords was far more important than the discussion in the Commons. *Hansard*, 4th series, vol. CLXXXIII, p. 999 ff. (Lord Curzon's speech). The Lords did reject the Naval Prize Bill in 1911 despite Foreign Office pressure. On the other hand, the Upper House was not even given a chance to debate the war crisis on 3 August. *Hansard*, 5th series, vol. XVII, Lords, cols. 318–20, 423.
[3] *Hansard*, 4th series, vol. LVIII, p. 1409.
[4] Bishop, *The Administration of British Foreign Relations*, p. 142.

parliamentary under-secretary) and Balfour for the Government and Vernon Harcourt, Charles Dilke and Edward Grey for the Opposition, there were a group of back-benchers who made foreign affairs their speciality and spoke repeatedly. T. Gibson Bowles (King's Lynn) and E. Ashmead-Bartlett (Sheffield) were the Government's most persistent questioners. The 'Pigtail Committee' was well represented and dominated the debates on Far Eastern and Russian affairs. Led by R. A. Yerburgh, a Conservative member from Chester, and Joseph Walton from York, there must have been at least a dozen members of the House who supported the China Association or its more radical branch, the China League.[1] There was also a Persian group, consisting of men with commercial interests in Persia or of men especially involved in Indian or Turkish matters.[2] Later, in Grey's period, a Persia Committee was formed and this powerful pressure group, active both in Parliament and outside, launched the impressive but unsuccessful campaign against the Foreign Secretary's Persian policy in the autumn of 1911. In 1903 a Balkan Committee was founded to watch over events in Macedonia.[3] This committee, which was anti-Turk and inclined to be pro-Bulgarian, found Lansdowne sympathetic with its aims but Grey more difficult to influence. The Foreign Office, particularly in the years before the war, showed little enthusiasm for the activities of these so-called experts and disliked their interventions in Balkan politics.

Question time provided the most useful daily check on the Foreign Office. The number of questions soared. In mid-century, 129 questions were asked; by 1901 the number had reached 6,448. In 1906 Grey was to complain bitterly that the new members had acquired the art of asking questions and raising debates.[4] But question hour was only a limited weapon for the parliamentarians. The Foreign Office had to be notified three days before a question was put and it generally prepared one or two questions daily. Naturally members raised issues which were topical or which specifically concerned their constituents. Most questions were highly specific—the burial of the Mahdi after the battle of Omdurman, the closing of the Armenian orphanages in 1898, the expulsion of an English missionary from the New Hebrides by the French. Even when Grey was present in the House (twice a week) no supplementary questions were permitted so that it was difficult to press the minister. From the Foreign Office point of view, the most difficult

[1] Pelcovits, *Old China Hands and the Foreign Office*, pp. 267, 278.
[2] J. Plass, *England zwischen Deutschland und Russland*, pp. 196–7, 210–12.
[3] Conwell-Evans, *Foreign Policy from a Back Bench*, pp. 3–8, 10, etc.
[4] Bishop, *The Administration of British Foreign Relations*, p. 150. Grey MSS, FO 800/72, Grey to Nicolson, 3 October 1906.

requests were demands for information involving negotiations with great powers. The parliamentary under-secretary's response was composed with great care and with far more concern for the diplomatic repercussions than for the information of Parliament. There were a number of convenient phrases which might save the Government from embarrassment. In 1901, for instance, Ashmead-Bartlett tried to draw Cranborne on the subject of the Russo-Chinese Manchurian agreement. Not only was the subject a highly sensitive one but the Foreign Office had received most of its information from *The Times* correspondent. Sir Ellis's efforts were cut short by Cranborne's polite refusal to answer: 'In the opinion of His Majesty's Government any statement or discussion on the subject at the present moment would be inexpedient.'[1] The subject was closed.

Such treatment sometimes confirmed the worst suspicions of the questioner and press. Early in 1902 Henry Norman, an M.P. who had formerly been the American correspondent of the *Daily Chronicle*, raised the question of the British ambassador's role in Washington on the eve of the Spanish-American War. Cranborne's reply on 20 February created great difficulties for it was only partially accurate and resulted in an angry exchange between the Wilhelmstrasse and the Foreign Office which reverberated in the newspaper columns of both countries. The Foreign Office refused to lay papers; its silence confirmed the impression that the German case against Lord Pauncefote was a good one.[2]

The parliamentary under-secretary had to take particular pains not to commit the Government to future action; such answers were carefully prepared by the head of the relevant department, the supervising under-secretary, the parliamentary under-secretary, and even by Cabinet ministers. The preparation of Blue Books too was a major task. The material was collected by the head of the department assisted by his second. The results were reviewed by the under-secretaries. The first revises, containing many papers which were not printable, were sent in duplicate to British ambassadors who noted what words, phrases or despatches they wished to eliminate. One of the duplicates, properly prepared, was then presented to the other country's foreign minister for his approval. When the revises came back, a final pruning took place and the results checked by the parliamentary under-secretary and foreign secretary.[3] As in the case of parliamentary questions,

---

[1] FO 83/1901, question by Ashmead-Bartlett, minutes by Cranborne, Lansdowne and Balfour.
[2] FO 5/2515, correspondence on H. Norman's question, 8, 22, 25 March 1902. Minutes by Cranborne and Sanderson. Further discussion in Campbell, *Anglo-American Relations*, pp. 246–50.
[3] This description comes from FO 83/1791, Bertie to Salisbury, 22 May 1899. Bertie complained that Charles Scott showed the whole revise to Witte.

papers were always published with an eye to foreign response. The threat of publication was a useful weapon for Lord Salisbury during the Fashoda crisis.[1] In general, however, every effort was made to comply with the objections of other states and to avoid arousing public hostility towards any one country. Lord Lansdowne curtailed the correspondence on the evacuation of Shanghai to meet Count Metternich's wishes and in November 1902 again excluded despatches which might stimulate the anti-German press.[2] The North Sea Blue Books were also carefully edited to prepare the way for an improvement in Anglo-Russian relations.

There is no doubt that despatches were particularly written for publication purposes and that deletions and changes were common practice. 'The incisions I have proposed in the Blue Book perhaps seem rather extensive', Satow wrote to Lansdowne. 'But I looked to keep our friends the Viceroys from harm, and to avoid if possible showing disagreement with Germany and Austria.' The same procedures were used under Sir Edward Grey. The Liberal foreign secretary was particularly careful to omit or alter despatches which might reveal differences between Britain and her entente partners. This was certainly true of the Persian Blue Books which were published to quiet criticism from Grey's own backbenchers.[3] Hardinge's advice to Barclay in 1908 underlined the Foreign Office view.

As regards to the Armenian Blue Book, we have to publish these things at certain times; there are several members of Parliament who take a very keen interest in Armenian affairs, prompted, no doubt, by some of the Armenian societies in London. We do not mind how much you bowdlerize the Blue Book as long as we are able to publish something; with us it is really the quantity and not the quality that are wanted for the House of Commons.[4]

Whenever possible, the Foreign Office tried to avoid laying papers. Parliament was told nothing of the approaches to Russia and Germany in 1898 or about the Anglo-German discussions of 1901. The Japanese treaty was laid twelve days before ratification and came as a complete surprise to the public. Tremendous care was taken with its presentation—'No splash, not even a statement in both Houses until we are asked.'[5] The abbreviated Anglo-French treaty was laid with a covering despatch but with no correspondence, a well-established practice which helped the diplomats but did not increase Parliament's understanding of foreign affairs.

[1] BD I, no. 197. Salisbury, after the Fashoda crisis was resolved, published a number of Blue Books on the subject.
[2] BD II, nos. 22, 166.     [3] FO 800/354, Buchanan to Nicolson, 22 February 1912.
[4] Hardinge MSS, 1908 (III), Grey to Barclay, 19 May 1908.
[5] FO Japan/560, Cranborne to Barrington, 10 February 1902.

There were times when the Foreign Office could not ignore requests for information. Sir Charles Dilke repeatedly asked for papers on the Muscat quarrel with France in 1900. Sir Thomas Sanderson admitted that he 'had earnestly hoped that we might get out of laying papers at all'. The Parliamentary Under-Secretary agreed that some brief papers would have to be printed. 'The only other alternative', he commented, 'is an appeal to Dilke on public grounds not to ask for them but this is a doubtful recourse.'[1] Parliamentary pressure could overcome diplomatic scruples, but only when it suited the foreign secretary's purpose. After the Bülow–Chamberlain recriminations in the autumn of 1901, Lansdowne warned the German ambassador that he might be obliged to produce the despatches in which their conversations were recorded:

He demurred however to their publication saying that all our conversations were unofficial. I replied that if this was so, any 'assurance' as to Chamberlain's intentions ought not to have been officially quoted . . .
   It ended in my promise to avoid publication if I could but there were any number of questions down already although the leaders of the Opposition have very much to their credit left the matter alone.[2]

No papers were published but questions were answered. Some delays in publication were genuinely unavoidable. A foreign minister might stall and printing schedules had to be abandoned. The burden on a department might be particularly heavy; the Blue Books involving multiple translations were usually late. But for the most part, the Foreign Office and not the members of Parliament decided when papers should be laid and what should be published.

Parliament had neither the interest, the information, nor the time to influence the course of diplomacy. Important decisions were made in secret, parliamentary questions could be avoided and Blue Books carefully edited. Travelling politicians were considered a nuisance and not much help was given to the inquiring visitor. The attitude of the Foreign Office official to members of Parliament was apt to be one of contempt: 'What a nuisance they are with their ill-timed questions! they know nothing about foreign affairs: it is our business not theirs'; and to the general public one of pity: 'If only you knew what we know you would think as we do.'[3] Though the number of pressure groups and the demand for information increased during the Liberal period, Grey did not attach great importance to public

[1] FO 83/1783, minutes of Sanderson, St John Brodrick and Lord Salisbury, 24 April 1900.
[2] FO 277, Lansdowne to Lascelles, 17 January 1902.
[3] Ponsonby, *Democracy and Diplomacy*, p. 47.

opinion and was even less generous in his treatment of Parliament than his predecessors:[1]

Judged by a Blue-book test Sir Edward Grey took the public into his confidence very much less than did Palmerston . . . It is literally true to say that as Parliament became more democratic its control over foreign policy declined, and while Blue-books on domestic affairs expanded and multiplied at the end of the century, those on foreign affairs lessened both in number and interest.[2]

We still need a detailed examination of the Blue Books, debates and question periods of the Grey administration.[3] But the evidence collected so far suggests that the members of Parliament were poorly served.[4] As Britain's relations with the European powers became more involved, the Commons knew less about them. Grey's answers to those who pressed him on England's obligations to France and Russia were neither direct nor totally honest. It was because they felt that the Foreign Secretary was too remote, too secretive and too dominated by his permanent officials that a group of radicals created the Foreign Affairs Group of the Liberal party and the short-lived Foreign Policy Committee. But there was little that such men as E. D. Morel, Charles Trevelyan or Arthur Ponsonby could do against the united front of both the Liberal and Conservative leadership and their demand for a wider parliamentary role went unheeded.[5] Even on that famous 3 August when Grey put the case in the Commons for participation in the war, he did not reveal all the conditions which tied England to France. Ultimately the

[1] Conwell-Evans, *Foreign Policy from a Back Bench, 1914–18*. Taylor, *The Trouble-Makers—Dissent over Foreign Policy, 1792–1939*, pp. 112–26. Cmd. 7749, Appendix LXXXVII.

[2] H. Temperley and L. A. Penson, *A Century of Diplomatic Blue Books, 1814–1914* (Cambridge, 1938), p. ix.

[3] See the discussions in H. Temperley, 'British Secret Diplomacy from Canning to Grey', *Cambridge Historical Journal*, VI (1938), pp. 1–32. L. Penson, 'Obligations by Treaty: their Place in British Foreign Policy, 1898–1914' in A. Sarkissian (ed.), *Studies in Diplomatic History and Historiography in Honour of G. P. Gooch* (London, 1961), pp. 76–89.

[4] It is true that with regard to such humanitarian questions as the conditions of the natives in the Congo, in Portuguese West Africa and the interior of Peru Grey was both generous with Blue Books and more responsive to public pressure than Lansdowne. For Roger Casement and E. D. Morel's complaints against Lansdowne see W. R. Louis and J. Stengers, *E. D. Morel's History of the Congo Reform Movement*, pp. 174–6, 185–6. Though the Foreign Office, in Grey's period, listened to Morel with respect, it could not accept his extreme demands and it was during his campaign for reform in the Congo that Morel turned against Grey and began his general attack on Grey's diplomacy and his long public campaign for the reform of the Foreign Office, that 'antiquated fossil'. *Ibid.* pp. 268–9, 201.

[5] The question of the role of Parliament was raised by Ponsonby and others before a Select Committee on House of Commons procedure in 1914. Ponsonby argued that the way in which foreign policy was conducted was both undemocratic and misguided. Both party leaders denied his allegations and Balfour, in particular, claimed that Parliament had ample opportunities for inquiry and criticism. Material in Ponsonby, *Democracy and Diplomacy*, pp. 121–7, and Gosses, *Management of British Foreign Policy*, pp. 84–5.

Government could not go to war without the support of the Commons and Grey appeared before that body with some sense of trepidation.

It is absolutely impossible for any government to contemplate war unless it feels certain that when the moment comes the House of Commons would be prepared to endorse the policy of the Government, by voting the supplies which are necessary and without which it would be absolutely out of the power of the Government to go to war at all.[1]

Yet the discussion in the Commons was put off until the last possible moment and the members opposed to war (led by Arthur Ponsonby) knew that the real trial of strength was in the Cabinet. It is true that up until the final clash, Grey's reluctance to turn the ententes into alliances was based in part on his knowledge that neither the Cabinet nor the party would accept such a departure from traditional policy. But within these ultimate limits Grey had a large area of independence which he exploited to the full. Though the general isolation of the Foreign Office from political and economic pressures was far from absolute, the Foreign Secretary retained a freedom of action shared by few of his political colleagues.

Apart from the Cabinet, it was through the press and parliament that the foreign secretary became aware of the general feeling in the country. Salisbury, Lansdowne and Grey were all conscious of the role played by public opinion in their diplomatic deliberations. Salisbury, in particular, believed that the public was the final arbiter in the realm of foreign affairs and argued that no English Government could agree to alliances which would restrict the government's freedom of action at some future time. Lansdowne felt less bound by such restrictions and was less adverse to alliances and secret understandings. Yet even he moved cautiously and found it difficult, both in 1903 and in 1905, to pursue a policy in the face of a hostile public. Grey, too, despite his willingness to engage in military and naval conversations with his entente partners, fully recognized the limitations on his ultimate freedom of action. He repeatedly warned the French, for the last time before July 1914 during his visit to Paris, that whether Britain engaged in a continental war or not would depend on the mood of the public when the time for decision came. Nor were these mere words. In the autumn of 1911, and again in 1912, the cabinet had taken steps to reserve its independence vis-à-vis the French, and in July 1914 this freedom and the divided state of public opinion shaped Grey's diplomacy. As to Russia, Grey always knew and warned his diplomats that the British public were unlikely to enter a war for the sake of this unpopular partner. These were the checks imposed by

[1] *Hansard*, vol. XXIV, 12 April 1911, cols. 538-9.

a parliamentary and democratic form of government. In terms of daily decision-making, public protests could be ignored but when it came to questions of peace or war or entering obligations which predetermined the decision to go to war, no foreign secretary could act with similar independence. Yet the public in general took only a limited interest in foreign affairs and even in the final moment of crisis did not speak with a clear or undivided voice. What is public opinion at any one time? How does it make itself felt and how do foreign secretaries assess the mood of a country? Even for the pre-1914 period, these questions remain the subject of historical debate.

## The Crown

The democratic checks on the freedom of the foreign secretary were limited and often ineffective. But the older forms of royal interference also diminished in this period. Traditionally, the crown could conclude treaties, declare war, make peace and even cede territory without the consent of Parliament. By 1895 most of these powers had been absorbed by the Cabinet and the monarch acquiesced in the decisions of her ministers. Queen Victoria had jealously guarded those prerogatives still left her and there had been, during her long reign, numerous clashes between Windsor and Whitehall over her remaining rights. Under Lord Salisbury harmony had been restored, for the Prime Minister was on the best of terms with his sovereign and shared many of her strong moral and religious convictions. The Queen knew that she could not alter the course of Salisbury's diplomacy but she wished to be informed and consulted and the Prime Minister fully complied with her demands. Salisbury, for his part, found his correspondence with the Queen both useful and instructive.

The Prime Minister not only wrote to Victoria after each Cabinet meeting but at the end of each day when the afternoon's interviews were over. In theory, Victoria received all incoming despatches and the drafts of all outgoing instructions. In practice, Salisbury selected those papers which he thought she should read. Many handwritten despatches marked 'Draft' were copies of letters already sent. Despite this selection process, the Queen did see a large proportion of the daily Foreign Office correspondence and was even sent papers not circulated to the Cabinet. The Foreign Office was very conscious of its special relationship to the sovereign. All copies and drafts sent for her perusal had to be written in a special ink, dried carefully near the fire to bring out the colour of the ink and then blotted with sand. As late as 1898 the Queen complained to Salisbury that she was receiving some despatches a month late.[1] It was at this time that she finally agreed to read some papers in print instead of insisting on written copies.

Although the Queen's judgements were often impulsive and emotional, Salisbury did not disregard her advice. Time and experience had sharpened her wits and the Prime Minister found that her views often gave him 'an indication of the thought and feelings of the great mass of the English people'.[2] The Queen did in fact read the contents of her despatch boxes and kept Salisbury amply supplied with advice and criticism. There were numerous letters about the behaviour of British diplomats abroad, the attitudes of other monarchs (usually the Queen's relatives), the necessity for a new policy in Persia and critiques of Salisbury's diplomacy in the Far East. The Queen's impressions were often well-founded. For instance, she warned Salisbury that Scott was too inclined to accept Russian assurances of peaceful intentions and reminded him that Durand had shown a certain haughtiness and want of tact with the Persians when it was suggested that the latter go as ambassador to Turkey.[3] Victoria could also be extremely critical of Salisbury's Cabinet colleagues. Particularly during the Boer War, she was inclined to blame Lansdowne for the obvious mismanagement of the army administration and wanted to be consulted about his replacement at the War Office.[4] She could be raised to high indignation, as during the Dreyfus affair, or she could show amazing restraint as in her treatment of the Kaiser.

In assessing the Queen's role in the realm of foreign policy, it must be remembered that she was related by blood or marriage to most of the ruling houses of Europe. The Kaiser's relations with 'his most beloved Grandmother' were of some importance in this period. 'Your Majesty's personal influence over the Emperor William is a powerful defence against danger in that direction' Lord Salisbury wrote to her, 'as is shown by the great effect of the letter which you wrote to him.'[5] After the Kruger telegram, the Queen urged that 'oil be poured into the waters' and suggested that hints be given to the respectable press against printing inflammatory articles. She acted as a brake on the impetuous William and generally turned a deaf ear to his complaints against Salisbury. Only once, after the Emperor had roundly criticized Salisbury's policy in Samoa, did the Queen retort sharply:

[1] Sanderson MSS, Salisbury to Sanderson, 14 November 1898.
[2] Grenville, *Lord Salisbury and Foreign Policy*, p. 333.
[3] Buckle, *Letters of Queen Victoria*, 3rd series, vol. III, Salisbury to Queen, 16 August 1899. Salisbury MSS, The Queen, 1892–6 (copy). Queen to Salisbury, 13 January 1892.
[4] Balfour MSS, Balfour to Salisbury, 19 December 1899.
[5] Buckle, *Letters of Queen Victoria*, vol. III, Salisbury to Queen, 16 August 1899, p. 392.

'The tone in which you write about Lord Salisbury I can only attribute to a temporary irritation on your part, as I do not think you would otherwise have written in such terms to another Sovereign, and the Sovereign his own Grandmother, about their Prime Minister.'[1] When the Emperor suggested in March 1900 that he intervene between England and the Boers, the Queen urged Salisbury to send him a friendly but '*very firm*' reply.[2] Her own private message was a model of the diplomatic rebuke.

Salisbury knew how to make the best use of the Queen's special position in Europe and her personal correspondence abroad brought him additional information. Though the Queen could be exceedingly obstinate Salisbury generally managed to prevail when their wills clashed. Though he complained of his responsibilities to Windsor, his exchanges with the Queen relieved his own isolation and he seems to have benefited from her detailed interest in international affairs. The Boer War saddened the last year of Victoria's life and during 1900 she aged considerably. Care was taken to protect her from the hostile tone of much of the European press and despatches were carefully selected.[3] Her eyes had begun to fail and though the Foreign Office copied out her despatches in huge letters she could no longer read Salisbury's handwritten messages.[4] Yet despite her age and failings, the Queen's death was a great personal blow to Salisbury and created a gap which the new king did not fill.

Edward VII inherited his mother's personal view of the European scene but his impact on the course of British diplomacy was far less important. He was fifty-nine years of age when he came to the throne and had suffered a long tutelage. It was not until 1886 that he was allowed to see the Foreign Office despatches (a practice not permanently established until 1890) and it was only in 1892 that he began to receive the prime minister's reports. With all due allowance for his mother's dictatorial behaviour, the future king had neither the inclination, the industry nor the ability to play a decisive role in international affairs. A man of limited intelligence with a distaste for reading, the heir apparent soon shook off the restraints of his home and rapidly developed into the royal playboy whose exploits still entertain the grandchildren of his subjects. He was more frequently seen at the races or at the gaming tables than at his desk. He was a fine host, a good mixer and a lover of conversation and soon collected about him a varied and cosmopolitan group of friends.

[1] Buckle, *Letters of Queen Victoria*, vol. III, Queen to Kaiser, 12 June 1899, p. 381.
[2] *Ibid.* Queen to Salisbury, telegram, 10 March 1900, p. 507.
[3] Esher, *Journals and Letters of Viscount Esher*, vol. I, p. 214.
[4] Grenville, *Lord Salisbury and Foreign Policy*, p. 332.

It is interesting that even in his lifetime exaggerated accounts of his role at the Foreign Office were spread and widely believed both in London and abroad. On his accession, he did demand that he be as well-informed as his mother. Although Balfour disliked letter-writing, his short reports on Cabinet meetings kept the sovereign abreast of current happenings. There were few ties between the clever and dry-humoured Balfour and the rather slow-thinking King. Lansdowne, too, dutifully sent him the despatch boxes each day. But Balfour, Lansdowne and Grey all strongly denied that the sovereign made any important suggestions or had any major influence on British diplomacy and the papers bear out their contention.[1]

It was well known at the Foreign Office that the King did not read despatches too carefully and that he could not give his attention to any one problem.[2] He tended to be impetuous in his judgements and often repented of his first thoughts. Roused by the Dogger Bank incident he first insisted that the Russian admirals be punished. After a good night's sleep and calmer reflection, the King sent a second telegram cancelling his first.[3] He tended to be inconsistent in his views, even on major questions such as the agreements with Russia or a rapprochement with Germany.[4] His opinions were determined by the events of the moment or the judgements of his personal entourage. He often thought of Anglo-German relations in terms of his personal feelings towards the Kaiser, a practice hardly conducive to rational diplomacy.

The King's comments on despatches and letters were on the whole short and rarely illuminating. 'Satisfactory', 'gossipy letter', or 'interesting despatch' were among his frequent phrases. Like his mother, he sometimes checked his diplomats. He found Arthur Nicolson too lukewarm in his anti-French stand at Morocco and repeatedly chided Lascelles (whom he found hopelessly pro-German) for not combating the Emperor's false ideas more vigorously.[5] As has been shown, through his private secretary, he had an important voice in the matter of diplomatic appointments, particularly to embassies in the 'inner circle'. His special interest in the careers of Francis Bertie and Charles Hardinge enabled both men to rise to their high positions and other appointments, too, were dependent on royal approval. The royal friendship with Hardinge, cemented by their tours abroad, was a useful link for the Foreign Office. The bi-weekly correspondence between the two

[1] Newton, *Lord Lansdowne*, pp. 292–3; Grey, *Twenty-Five Years*, vol. I, pp. 197–8.
[2] Notice the contrast between the King's minute and the contents of the despatch in BD II, no. 103.
[3] Sir Sidney Lee, *Edward VII: a biography* (London, 1927), vol. II, pp. 303–4.
[4] Monger, *The End of Isolation*, pp. 262–3.
[5] FO 277, Nicolson to Lansdowne, 11 February 1902, Lansdowne to Lascelles, 17 January 1902.

men is a rich source of information for those who can read the royal hand-writing. When the King was in London Hardinge visited him regularly, for the King could be more easily influenced in conversation than by letter. Grey, for his part, had some contact with the monarch but there was no parallel to Salisbury's relationship with the Queen.

In addition to diplomatic appointments, the King also took an interest in ceremonial questions and in the reception of foreign ambassadors. The granting of the Garter to non-Christians created endless difficulties for the Foreign Office. In the case of the Shah of Persia, the King proved so obsti-nate in his opposition that Lansdowne threatened to resign and both Balfour and the Duke of Devonshire had to intervene before the King would give his consent.[1] Similar problems arose with the King of Siam and the Crown Prince of Japan. The King had to be consulted before a new foreign ambas-sador was appointed. For instance, the brother of the newly-designated Turkish ambassador had been involved in a rather unsavoury abduction scandal and the King refused to have his residence turned into a 'refuge for disreputable Levantines'.[2] Though his veto was overruled, the ambassador was never made welcome. M. de Soveral, the Portuguese ambassador, on the other hand, was always welcomed at court even when there were diffi-culties over his position in Lisbon. The South American ministers were beyond the pale and no amount of Foreign Office persuasion could convince the monarch that their inclusion in a royal party was a boredom worth enduring.

In addition to these traditional forms of intervention, the King was the 'first diplomatist' of his country. He enjoyed travelling and was a frequent and engaging visitor at other royal courts. The King usually spent some weeks at Biarritz in early spring and then took a Mediterranean cruise in May. Later in the summer, he returned to the continent for his annual cure at Marienbad. Each journey involved a visit to one or more crowned heads and many were subsequently reciprocated. For the most part these royal per-ambulations were highly successful, for the King made an excellent goodwill ambassador and could swing even a hostile public to his side. His famous visit to Paris in 1903 was more than a personal triumph. It convinced Del-cassé and others that the time was ripe for an approach to the English and undoubtedly paved the way for the entente.[3] In 1902 Edward began a series of successful meetings with Franz Joseph which continued until the Bosnian

---

[1] Newton, *Lord Lansdowne*, pp. 236–7.
[2] FO 277, Knollys to Barrington, 25 November 1902; Barrington to O'Conor, 29 November 1902.
[3] C. Andrew, *Théophile Delcassé and the making of the Entente Cordiale*, p. 209.

crisis led to a sharp deterioration in the relations between the two countries. Already as Prince of Wales, Edward had visited the Russian court and soon became a convert (though with some reversals) to the idea of an Anglo-Russian rapprochement. Royal conversations with the Russian ambassador in London and with M. Isvolsky strengthened this support and the meeting with the Tsar at Reval was both successful and useful. The King took equal pains with lesser royal personages and visited the Kings of Italy, Spain, Portugal and the Scandinavian countries. The monarch was particularly interested in the separation of Norway and Sweden in the summer of 1905, for Prince Charles of Denmark, his son-in-law, was one of the candidates for the Swedish throne. Belgium was the one country assiduously avoided; Edward was deeply repelled by Leopold's private life and colonial policy, 'a blot on Christian civilization'.

Except for the visit to Paris, these visits had enormous popular appeal but only limited political significance. Neither Salisbury, Lansdowne nor Grey travelled like their modern counterparts; the sovereign generated the goodwill supposedly created by today's periodic gatherings of foreign statesmen. Charles Hardinge rather than a Cabinet minister accompanied the King on a number of these visits in the Grey period, a practice which aroused dispute and was stopped. There were also other clashes between the Cabinet and the sovereign.[1] The former was reluctant to sanction a visit to the Pope in 1903 and the King, supported by Hardinge and Bertie, fought hard to prevail. At Reval, the King proclaimed the Tsar an admiral of the Fleet without permission and thereby created a minor Cabinet crisis. Such independent actions and special royal interests created problems for the Foreign Office but few of these were of major importance.[2] On the whole, Edward's warm personality was an asset to his country's diplomacy and it was most unfortunate that the Germans saw in these visits a hostile plan to offend and encircle them.

For the King and Kaiser failed to strike a harmonious chord. The two men were temperamentally antagonistic. Neither could stand the other's company for any length of time; both were relieved when respective visits ended. Numerous small disputes of little importance aggravated this personal incompatibility. Early in 1902 the King wished to cancel a visit of the Prince of Wales to Berlin because of the Bülow-Chamberlain recriminations. An unfortunate reply, a lost letter and a royal insult all added to this comedy of errors. It was only after violent protests from the Emperor and a good deal

[1] Newton, *Lord Lansdowne*, pp. 308-9.
[2] The problem of the Norwegian succession was particularly difficult for the Foreign Office.

of effort on the part of Salisbury and Lansdowne that the visit finally took place.[1] 'The King talks and writes about his Royal brother in terms which makes one's flesh creep, and the official papers which go to him, whenever they refer to *him*, come back with all sorts of annotations of a most incendiary character.'[2] The Kaiser's minutes and letters to the King were no less irritating and hostile. Though Lansdowne dismissed them as exhibitions of ill-humour, the King was deeply affronted by his nephew's didactic tone.

It is curious that just as the Germans were becoming convinced that the British sovereign was intriguing against them, Edward tried to improve the tone of Anglo-German relations. The meeting with the Kaiser in the summer of 1906 was a success and the King warmly supported Haldane's visit to Berlin in September. It was the King who urged on Grey an invitation to the Kaiser at the end of 1907 and in the numerous clashes which preceded this visit it was always the King who took the conciliatory line.[3] Fitzmaurice summed up the situation in a letter to Lascelles: 'The Germans are wild about the King's so-called intrigues but I was on the contrary told the other day on a fairly good authority that the King was now frightened and said Grey was too anti-German for his tastes, etc.'[4] Despite a last-minute crisis, the Kaiser's visit went well. The King was carefully instructed by the Foreign Office 'on subjects which the German Emperor may possibly raise during the visit' but seems to have left political discussions to others. The new cordial mood did not fundamentally alter relations between the two monarchs. A series of royal trips in 1908, including ones to Paris and Reval, increased German suspicions, while a new German Naval Act and the Tweedmouth letter incident deepened the King's distrust of his German relative. Nevertheless, Grey urged the King to raise the question of naval disarmament at his meeting with the Kaiser at Cronberg in August 1908. Edward wisely let Hardinge take the initiative and it was the Permanent Under-Secretary who bore the brunt of the imperial displeasure. The only problem settled by the sovereigns was the question of Lascelles' successor at Berlin. The royal visit to Berlin in 1909 was of little political importance. The King was already unwell and spoke little and the meeting had few practical consequences.

By the end of 1909 the King was as fully committed to the policy of the ententes as was the Foreign Office. He shared Grey's views that the

---

[1] FO 277, Lansdowne to Lascelles, 17 January 1902; Salisbury to King, 22 January 1902.
[2] Newton, *Lord Lansdowne*, p. 330.
[3] Monger, *The End of Isolation*, pp. 326–7.
[4] Lascelles MSS, vol. III, Fitzmaurice to Lascelles, 8 May 1907, quoted in Monger, *The End of Isolation*, p. 326.

German fleet menaced the safety of Britain and his belief that Berlin would not compromise on this issue.[1] Though Edward had retained some doubts about the wisdom of the central Asian agreements with Russia, the annexation crisis swung him completely to the Russian side. The King felt that he had been deliberately misled by Franz Joseph; Aehrenthal became the object of much negative royal comment.[2] The Austrian press mounted a campaign against the British monarch and the King, in turn, had to be convinced to receive the Austrian ambassador and take his annual cure at Marienbad.[3]

The King's tours and visits contributed to the myth of 'einkreisung' but there was really little substance to these German fears. The royal difficulties with the Kaiser embittered already strained relations; the visits to Paris and Reval smoothed the way or strengthened already existing links with these countries. Even when the King did make an effort to check the anti-German mood of his Foreign Office, his attempts had little effect. He could not alter the course of foreign policy though he could make the Foreign Secretary's task either easier or more difficult. Basically, the King was in agreement with Grey and did not question the basic assumptions upon which Grey's policy rested. Edward VII neither led nor checked the Foreign Office. 'He not only accepted the constitutional practice that policy must be that of his ministers', Grey wrote in *Twenty-Five Years*, 'but he preferred that it should be so.'[4]

Although George V had travelled extensively while still heir to the throne, he did not reverse the trend towards non-intervention. He shared neither his grandmother's deep interest in foreign affairs nor his father's diplomatic flair and wanderlust. It was thought that his entourage was more pro-German and Austrian than that of his father's. According to Bertie, Lord Stamfordham, the King's private secretary, 'is for an understanding with Germany which is favoured by a section of the cabinet, and he is anti-Knollys, and anti-French, and pro all prerogatives'.[5] The Austrian ambassador, Count Mensdorff, was a frequent visitor and the King had decided early in his reign to make his first state visit to Vienna. During 1912 George tended to deprecate the French entente and supported the pro-German faction in the cabinet. In making plans for his tour of the European capitals, he suggested Vienna, Berlin, St Petersburgh and Paris in that order of

[1] BD vi, nos. 114, 207, Royal minutes.  [2] BD v, nos. 490, 508, Royal minutes.
[3] Sir Sidney Lee, *King Edward VII, a biography*, vol. ii, pp. 645, 649.
[4] Grey, *Twenty-Five Years*, vol. i, p. 197.
[5] Bertie MSS, FO 800/176, memorandum by Bertie, 2 October 1913. See other references to the King's private secretary in Hardinge MSS, vol. 69, Eric Drummond to Hardinge, 13 July 1913 and FO 800/351, Nicolson to Hardinge, 14 September 1911.

precedence.[1] Bertie immediately sounded the alarm and a minor Cabinet crisis ensued. The state visits were postponed; the Cabinet proposed an itinerary and insisted that Grey accompany the sovereign. In fact, the King's brief private meetings with the Kaiser were of little significance and his first official European visit was to Paris in the spring of 1914.[2] It is doubtful whether the royal sympathies (or Lord Stamfordham's) did more than worry the over-anxious Nicolson and Bertie. Even before the war brought an end to dynastic diplomacy, the British sovereign was playing little more than a ceremonial and symbolic role in the realm of foreign affairs.

[1] FO 800/186, memorandum by Bertie, 17 February 1912; FO 800/171, memorandum by Bertie, 19 February 1912.

[2] The German Emperor visited London in May 1911 for the unveiling of a memorial to Queen Victoria and despite Foreign Office fears to the contrary did not use the opportunity to discuss foreign affairs with Grey. The King and Queen made a private visit to Berlin in May 1913. To reassure the French, an invitation was sent to the President for a state visit the following month. Sir Harold Nicolson, *King George the Fifth* (London, 1952), pp. 182, 185–6, 216–17.

# CHAPTER 5

# The end of the old order

It was in the pre-war period that the Foreign Office reached the peak of its power. The foreign secretary was backed by an experienced, highly-educated and vocal staff which provided him with a steady stream of advice. The volume and complexity of business necessitated a far greater division of responsibility than Lord Salisbury would have imagined possible not to say desirable. The permanent civil servants in Sir Edward Grey's period thought it was their paramount duty to advise their chief in a way which Thomas Sanderson would have never contemplated. Part of this change was due to an administrative reform of the office. More important, a group of powerful men reached the highest positions in the Foreign Office and found in Grey a sympathetic chief. Yet the burden on the foreign secretary remained overwhelming and until the very end of the long peace the ultimate decisions were made by him. Institutions and civil servants can only aid or complicate the foreign secretary's task. Even when the Foreign Office was geared to an active role in the policy-making process, effective power rested with the foreign secretary. Thus, though after 1903 the Foreign Office became increasingly anti-German in tone, its judgements and advice remained only one factor in the foreign secretary's deliberations. Hardinge was powerful because his views concurred with those of his chief; Nicolson's influence was more limited because he was neither personally nor politically close to Grey and found himself in sharp disagreement with the Liberal Government. Similarly, Eyre Crowe's importance has been exaggerated. The power and consistency of his arguments have somewhat obscured the fact that his advice was not always accepted. In all cases, on major points of policy, Grey remained the key and pivotal figure. Yet to say all this is not to deny that the Foreign Office did play a new role in the formulation of policy and enjoyed a prestige and a position of power which it was never to recapture.

The balance between the Foreign Office and the Diplomatic Service swung in the direction of London. The senior officials had a broader view of the world picture than any single diplomat and the despatches of the latter were annotated before they reached the foreign secretary's desk. There were still a few outstanding figures, particularly Francis Bertie in Paris, but the group in Whitehall were a more impressive group than their overseas counterparts. Lord Salisbury relied on his diplomatists both for information and for the execution of his policy. Lord Lansdowne and, to an even greater extent, Sir Edward Grey, had an additional source of assistance within the walls of the Foreign Office.

The foreign secretaries of this period were well served by their officials. In Salisbury's day, it had been sufficient for clerks to be loyal, knowledgeable and industrious but with the changed position of the Foreign Office hierarchy came new responsibilities which required additional skills. Familiarity with the Foreign Office records increases one's respect for the pre-war department. The speed of response, the clarity of analysis and the attention to detail was indeed impressive. These officials had the courage of their convictions; even junior clerks were willing to state their views however unwelcome to their seniors. Grey's subordinates, particularly his under-secretaries, sought responsibility and considered decision-making a part of their daily work. Even when personal differences created difficulties at the senior level of the office, the departments acted with precision and a high degree of competence. The members of the Foreign Office shared a common language; they understood each other quickly and at a subtle level. Information could be collected with economy and despatch; advice given quickly and with a minimum of elaboration.

But if the pre-war Foreign Office enjoyed the advantages of a social and professional elite, it also suffered from the limitations imposed by its exclusiveness and isolation. The diplomats of this period were best at interpreting the world into which they had been born. With a few notable exceptions, they spoke to each other or to those similarly placed 'in society'. They operated in a closed circuit and tended mainly to hear each other's voices. Even Eyre Crowe, an exception to many of these generalizations, did not escape the consequences of his professional isolation. The Foreign Office saw the world in static terms and applied traditional solutions to new problems. It was assumed that all questions could be solved through rational discussion and officials repeatedly underestimated the erratic and emotional factors in foreign relations. Even Grey, in moments of crisis, was sometimes overwhelmed by waves of panic or despair which he did not explore or fully understand. Moreover, the whole structure of the Foreign Office discouraged any long-term analysis. Decisions were taken under pressure and the senior men often failed to consider the full implications of their proposals. It was Grey rather than Nicolson or Crowe who more accurately judged the full measure of defeat in July 1914.

Few bureaucracies respond quickly to changing circumstances. It is to the credit of the Lansdowne Foreign Office that the dangers implicit in the restless mood of Imperial Germany were recognized. The permanent officials accurately assessed the nature of the German malaise and the threat which it posed to the peace of Europe. It may well be true, as Thomas Sanderson argued in 1907, that these same men were unduly suspicious and insufficiently flexible in their response to this new mid-European giant. But it remains open to debate whether a more imaginative approach would have allayed German apprehensions or curbed her political ambitions. At the least, it was most unfortunate that a group of men who prided themselves on their intelligence and rationality should have had to deal with a country whose leaders were erratic and whose policies were often inexplicable. It is clear that all the diplomats exaggerated the power of Russia; her huge land mass and army obscured the signs of inner decay and social unrest. The British, too, erred in this direction though there was some disagreement on the proper respose to the Russian resurgence. The Foreign Office was conservative, socially, politically and diplomatically. It barely understood the disruptive tensions in its own society; it could only take a defensive stand against the challenges coming from abroad.

In London, the foreign secretary was the final arbiter in the field of foreign affairs and he was, even in the immediate pre-war period, relatively isolated from public demands and pressures. But the tendency to tolerate, bully or cajole other departments and to ignore the public had its negative side. The remoteness and aloofness of the Foreign Office created suspicion at home and discomfort abroad. It appeared to contemporaries that a few men sitting behind closed doors were determining the future of an unwary public. The complexity of diplomatic business had increased the power of the civil servants; the aura of secrecy dangerously increased the distance between Whitehall and the citizen. More publicity (for often the diplomats had little to hide) and public debate might have soothed the nerves of anxious powers and would certainly have better prepared the public for the final catastrophe. Ultimately, Grey's greatest failure was his unwillingness to explain the nature of the German menace and the steps he was prepared to take to meet it. It is not at all surprising that those who felt most betrayed by Grey in 1914 became the leading appeasers of the next decades. Grey and his officials believed that decisions could only be made by those trained in the complicated art of diplomacy; they did not believe it was necessary to either explain or educate. But if the Foreign Office prided itself on its skills, it was to pay a costly price for its detachment.

There were no 'grey eminences' at the Foreign Office. The men mentioned in this book made contributions to the policy-making process but no one man stands out as all-important or all-powerful. Since the days of Lord Hammond, those close to the foreign secretary had a voice in his deliberations. By the time of Sir Edward Grey, the Foreign Office as a department enjoyed a position of responsibility which was neither conceivable in the past nor possible in the time to come. But the fundamental distinction between a responsible minister and a civil servant remained. The civil servants were capable and even distinguished but they worked within the context of their department and a parliamentary Government.

Many myths have grown up about the 'old diplomacy'. Its virtues were never as obvious as its nostalgic supporters have suggested nor were its vices as great as the proponents of 'open diplomacy' proclaimed. The techniques used by the pre-war diplomats were most successful when employed in resolving the daily incidents and disputes arising between the major powers. The world in which this conception of negotiations flourished disappeared with the First World War. Baffled, Proust's M. de Norpois, that quintessence of the old diplomatic school, wondered how it was possible for families as distinguished socially as the Hohenzollerns to condone the grossness of Armageddon. Before 1914 the differences between the great and small powers were known and respected. Foreign affairs implied political decisions; economic matters, though the background to many disputes, rarely determined the course of policy. Though strategic considerations and military-naval strength came to play an increasingly important role in the thinking of foreign ministers, they were not all-powerful considerations. Moreover, when war was considered, it was not thought of in modern terms. Except to a few sensitive observers, military action in the old style was a possible extension of diplomacy. After the casualty lists of the Somme, this was never again to be the case. The public of the time, even in the most democratic of countries, was not only ill-informed but apathetic. Mass opinion presented only an ultimate check to the independence of the policy-makers. The 'third estate' could be a more formidable critic but no foreign secretary changed his stand as a result of a leader-writer. The distinction between professional and amateur was clearly drawn and the professionals considered themselves a separate and privileged class entitled to conduct their own affairs without outside interference.

To the contemporary diplomat the world described in this volume must seem like a distant remembrance. Those who look back with longing do so only in memory or in imagination. It is only within the walls of the Foreign Office that there are still echoes of this pre-war world. There are still those who claim that the Foreign Office has failed to catch up with the twentieth century. Its personnel continues to be recruited from a narrow social stratum; its preoccupations tend to be political rather than economic; it is isolated from the major currents of opinions which affect its domestic counterparts. A recent foreign secretary has complained of the 'mandarin atmosphere' in which he had to operate and the 'old-boys network' which controlled promotions and transfers. Like W. T. Stead, almost sixty years ago, George Brown called for an infusion of fresh air in the dusty corridors.

In my study I have tried to show some of the steps which led to the Foreign Office's rise and fall, its gain and loss of prestige and power. The Foreign Office had come to terms with a world Palmerston would never have dreamed of. But it did so only imperfectly—retaining modes of social sensibility and forms of organization that were already something of a handicap in July 1914. Paradoxically, it might have been better had the changes been more dramatic and drastic. Like many other English institutions, the Foreign Office tended to respond to an uncomely present by taking refuge in the forms of a splendid past.

## APPENDIX 1

# The departmental structure of the Foreign Office

The political departments included the following countries:

*African Department*

South-East, West and South-West Africa.

*African Protectorates Department* (separated from the African Department in 1900)

East Africa, Uganda, Central Africa, Somaliland and the Sultanate of Zanzibar. All but Zanzibar were transferred to the Colonial Office by 1906.

*American Department* (separated from American and Asiatic Department during 1899)

North, Central and South America, Pacific Islands.

*Eastern Department*

Greece, Montenegro, Roumania, Serbia, Russia, Turkey, Persia and Egypt, Abyssinia and Somaliland, Central Asia.

*Far Eastern Department*

China, Japan, Siam and Korea.

*Western European Department*

Austria, Bavaria, France, Germany, Italy, Portugal, Spain, Switzerland, Tunis, Wurtemberg, Belgium, Denmark, Netherlands, Sweden and Norway. Morocco, Newfoundland, Fisheries, Borneo and Eastern Archipelago. African colonies of European powers (1914).

The administrative departments included:

*Commercial and Sanitary*

Correspondence with H.M.'s ministers and consuls abroad, with the representatives of foreign powers in England, the Board of Trade and other departments of H.M.'s government as well as with commercial associations, etc., on matters strictly commercial. Sanitary questions, copyright, protection of industrial property.

# APPENDIX I

*Consular*

Correspondence with H.M.'s ministers and consuls.
Management of all matters related to the consular service.

*Financial* (Chief Clerk's Office)

Estimates, examination and control of accounts, diplomatic appointments, messengers, Cabinet keys, issue of salaries, diplomatic pensions, establishment questions.

*Librarian and Keeper of the Papers*

Custody, arrangement and registry of MSS, correspondence, confidential papers, treaties and printed library, preparation of memoranda on historical events, international cases, treaty questions. Correspondence on matters relating to the Public Record Office.

*Treaties and Superintendents*

Treaties, Orders in Council, commissions, credentials, exequators, royal letters, British and foreign orders, medals, and rewards, diplomatic privileges, questions of ceremonial and precedence, nationality and naturalization, protection, extradition, enforcement of Foreign Enlistment Acts, consular conventions, passports.

*Parliamentary Department* (created in 1903, expanded in 1911)

Preparation of Parliamentary Papers.
Ciphering and deciphering telegrams (1911).

*Registry* (created in 1906).

# The Diplomatic Establishment—1914

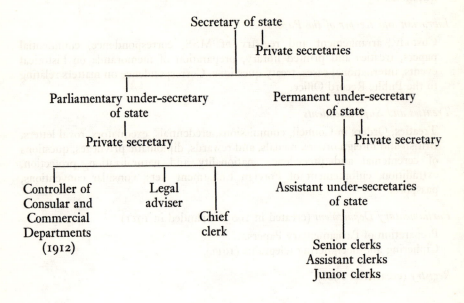

# Educational and family backgrounds, Foreign Office and Diplomatic Service candidates 1898-1913

1 Summary of educational backgrounds of successful Foreign Office candidates (clerks), 1898–1907

| | |
|---|---|
| Total number of clerks | 28 |
| Number traced | 22 |
| | |
| *Schools* | |
| Number of schools traced | 18 |
| Eton | 11 |
| Harrow | 2 |
| Marlborough | 1 |
| Repton | 1 |
| Radley | 1 |
| Wellington | 1 |
| St Augustine's College, Ramsgate | 1 |
| | |
| *Universities* | |
| Oxford | 7 (1 uncertain) |
| Cambridge | 4 |

2 Summary of educational backgrounds of successful Foreign Office candidates (clerks), 1908–13

| | |
|---|---|
| Total number of clerks | 16 |
| | |
| *Schools* | |
| Eton | 9 |
| Malvern | 1 |
| Radley | 1 |
| Wellington | 1 |
| Winchester | 1 |
| Rugby | 2 |
| Bedales School | 1 |

*Universities*
Oxford                   10
Cambridge       5
Edinburgh       1 (four months)

3 Summary of educational backgrounds of successful Foreign Office candidates (Diplomatic Service attachés), 1908–13

Total number of attachés      21

*Schools*
Eton                   16
Wellington       1
Harrow            2
Haileybury       1
Downside        1

*Universities*
Oxford               15
Cambridge       2
No university     4

4 Foreign Office clerks and attachés in the Diplomatic Service, 1908–13: age, school and university, and parentage*

| From limited competition of | | School | University | Father's profession | Age at date of examination |
|---|---|---|---|---|---|
| Aug. 1908 | Clerk 1 | Eton | Oxford | Clergyman | 22 |
| | 2 | Eton | Cambridge | Member of Stock Exchange | 23 |
| | Attaché 1 | Eton | Oxford | Peer | 23 |
| | 2 | Eton | Oxford | Banker | 24 |
| | 3 | Eton | | Peer; colonel | 22 |
| | 4 | Haileybury | | Comm. of Inland Revenue | 23 |
| | 5 | Eton | | Army officer | 23 |
| | 6 | Eton | Oxford | Chairman of bank | 23 |
| Aug. 1909 | Clerk 1 | Eton | Cambridge | Landowner | 24 |
| | Attaché 1 | Eton | Oxford | Peer | 22 |
| | 2 | Wellington | Oxford | Baronet; Diplomatic Service | 22 |

| Date | | | School | University | Career | Age |
|---|---|---|---|---|---|---|
| Aug. 1910 | Clerk | 1 | Eton | Oxford | Barrister | 24 |
| | | 2 | Malvern | Edinburgh (3 months) | Colonial Army officer | 23 |
| | | 3 | Private School Rugby (3 months) | Oxford; London (3 months) | Diplomatic Service | 23 |
| | Attaché | 1 | Eton | Oxford; Göttingen | Peer | 22 |
| | | 2 | Eton | Cambridge | Barrister | 24 |
| | | 3 | Eton | Oxford | Army officer | 22 |
| | | 4 | Harrow | Oxford | Peer | 24 |
| Aug. 1911 | Clerk | 1 | Radley | Oxford | Late judge of supreme consular court | 24 |
| | | 2 | Eton | Oxford | Naval officer | 24 |
| | | 3 | Eton | Cambridge | Banker | 24 |
| | | 4 | Wellington | Cambridge | Independent | 22 |
| | Attaché | 1 | Eton | Oxford | Independent | 24 |
| Aug. 1912 | Clerk | 1 | Winchester | Oxford | County Court judge | 24 |
| | Attaché | 1 | Eton | Oxford | *Merchant* | 24 |
| | | 2 | Harrow | | Baronet; colonel | 23 |
| | | 3 | Eton | Oxford; Munich (3 months) | *Merchant* | 23 |
| Aug. 1913 | Clerk | 1 | Eton | Cambridge | Knight; *merchant* | 24 |
| | | 2 | Bedales School, Petersfield, Hants. | Oxford; Marburg (1 month) | Artist | 23 |
| | | 3 | Eton | Oxford | Knight; surgeon | 23 |
| | | 4 | Eton | Oxford | Army officer | 24 |
| | | 5 | Rugby | Oxford | Principal and vice-chancellor of Montreal University | 24 |
| | Attaché | 1 | Downside School (near Bath) | Oxford | Civil engineer; former civil lord of the Admiralty | 24 |
| | | 2 | Eton | Oxford | Army officer | 22 |
| | | 3 | Eton | Oxford | Peer | |
| | | 4 | Eton | Cambridge | Foreign Office | 23 |
| | | 5 | Eton | Oxford | Peer's son; army officer | 23 |

* Cmd. 7749, 1914 Appendix LXXXIV, 306.

5 Foreign Office and Diplomatic Service clerks and attachés: unsuccessful competitors, 1908–13*

| School | University | Father's profession | Age |
|---|---|---|---|
| Charterhouse | Oxford | Indian Army officer | 24 |
| Eton | Oxford | Naval officer | 23 & 24 |
| Rugby | Oxford | Clergyman | 24 |
| Harrow | Oxford | Peer; Army officer | 23 |
| Haileybury | Cambridge | Prebendary and hon. chief sec. to Church Army | 24 |
| Not stated | Oxford | Civil servant | 24 |
| Harrow | Oxford | K.C.M.G., Diplomatic Service | 23 & 24 |
| Eton | — | Consular service | 23 & 24 |
| Eton | Cambridge | Barrister | 23 & 24 |
| Eton | Cambridge | Gentleman, D.L. | 23 & 24 |
| Wellington | — | Army officer | 22 |
| Eton | Oxford | Deputy judge advocate | 23 |
| School in Austria | Oxford | Peer | 22 |
| Charterhouse | Cambridge | Gentleman | 23 & 24 |
| Wimbledon College | — | Independent | 22 & 23 |
| None | Oxford | Independent | 24 |
| Eton | — | Knight; chairman, steamship company | 23 |
| Harrow | Cambridge | Schoolmaster | 24 |
| Eton | Oxford | Peer | 23 & 24 |
| Marlborough | Oxford; Grenoble (1 term) | Clergyman | 23 |
| Charterhouse; Private Tutor | Cambridge | Independent | 23 & 24 |
| Marlborough | Oxford | Naval officer | 23 & 24 |
| Rugby; Private Tutor | Cambridge; Göttingen (6 months) | Barrister | 22 |
| Eton | Oxford | Independent | 22, 23, 24 |
| Harrow | Cambridge | Solicitor and Barrister | 22 |
| St Christopher's School, Eastbourne | — | Knight, M.P. (deceased) | 23 |
| Winchester | Oxford | Peer | 22 & 23 |
| Eton | Cambridge (2 terms) | Banker | 23 |
| Harrow | Cambridge | Baronet, D.L., J.P. | 23 |
| Eton | Oxford | G.C.B. Ambassador, Privy Councillor | 23 |

| Cheltenham | Cambridge | Knight; Chief Justice of Hong Kong | 23 & 24 |
|---|---|---|---|
| Westminster | Oxford, Berlin and London (5 months each) | Civil servant | 24 |
| Eton | Oxford | Clergyman | 22 & 23 |
| Eton | Oxford | Baronet, ambassador | 22 & 24 |
| Eton | Cambridge | Clergyman | 23 & 24 |
| Winchester | Oxford | Consul (retired), University professor | 24 |
| Marlborough | Oxford | King's Counsel | 22 & 23 |
| Eton | Cambridge, Graz (3 months) | Banker | 22 |
| St Paul's | Oxford | Barrister | 24 |
| Eton | Cambridge | J.P. | 22 & 23 |
| Eton | Cambridge | Gentleman, J.P. | 23 |
| Winchester | Oxford | Bank director | 23 |
| Eton; Royal Military College, Sandhurst | — | Knight, late Lieut-gov. of Burma, member of India Council | 22 |
| Winchester | Oxford | Barrister and civil servant | 22 |
| Clifton College | Cambridge | Stockbroker | 23 |
| Eton | Oxford | Baronet, Army officer | 23 |
| Harrow | — | Army officer, J.P. | 22 |
| Eton | Cambridge | Independent | 22 |
| Winchester | Oxford | Not stated | 24 |

\* Cmd. 7749, Appendix LXXXIV, pp. 306–7.

# Arthur Ponsonby, the Diplomatic Service and the Foreign Office, 1900-1902[1]

Arthur Ponsonby, a second secretary in the Diplomatic Service, had been so repelled and bored by the life of a junior diplomat abroad that he had arranged an exchange which brought him back to the Foreign Office. On 17 October 1900 he presented a twenty-seven page memorandum to Thomas Sanderson with a covering note:

I have at last ventured to send the enclosed paper on reform in the D.S. and I trust you will not think it impertinent of me. I cannot help feeling very strongly on the subject for I can regard the prospect that lies before the junior members of the Service in no other way than despairing . . . My excuse for appealing to you in this matter is that I know that the initiative in any real reform lies more in your hands than in any other quarter and also that I am conscious of the gravity and pressing nature of the cause I plead. A time when reform is in the air has seemed to me an appropriate moment to speak out however inadequately on behalf of a service which may very well be left neglected for want of a proper champion.[2]

### Suggestions for reform in the Diplomatic Service

The growing importance of a speedy and extensive reform in the organization of the Diplomatic Service is strongly felt in many quarters and not least among the members of the Service itself. That as it now stands the system is greatly in need of being remodelled is obvious to those who seriously regard its present state of efficiency. For not only is it found necessary very frequently to look outside the Service for men to fill the more important posts in it but at the same time the percentage of men who are found unqualified to hold high positions of responsibility is curiously large when compared with the total number of members. And this latter circumstance which appears lately to have become more or less an accepted fact cannot be explained by the individual incapacity of the men but is undoubtedly due to the absence of all training or more correctly the demoralizing life of leisure and unprofitable exile to which the younger diplomatists are at present condemned.

Without organized work and training of some kind it is impossible to expect

1 I am indebted to Lord Ponsonby of Shulebrede who kindly gave me permission to see, copy and quote from his father's correspondence.
2 Ponsonby MSS, memorandum by A. Ponsonby, 17 October 1900.

a young man to develop statesman-like or even business-like qualities. And although it is of course true that either by resources in himself or by persistent energy and zeal in devoting himself to the study of questions of interest around him a diplomat can keep himself occupied and trained up to a certain point it is equally true that the majority, who are not endowed with these gifts find that an easy going career of prolonged leisure is surely rewarded by the eventual emoluments which fall to the lot of those who merely have to live long enough to enjoy them. The result being that as it stands at present the Diplomatic Service can more accurately be described as a position than as a profession.

In taking a general and broad view of the case to begin with; it would seem that the most obvious mistakes to be rectified are: firstly, the unnecessarily early age at which the attache is obliged to enter upon a more or less idle career; secondly, the numerous subordinate positions where little or no work is required the filling of which necessitates the employment of a far larger staff of secretaries than is either necessary or desirable; and thirdly, the rareness of the opportunity afforded to younger diplomats of obtaining work which might either serve as a training to themselves or be of use in the general conduct of Foreign Affairs.

As a means of possibly ameliorating these defects, I have drawn up the following suggestions after very careful consideration and discussion of the subject both with English diplomats, Foreign Office Officials and also with Foreign diplomats and after comparing our system with those of other countries the details of which have been supplied to me.

## I. *The examination*

There is little to be found fault with in the examination itself, but the fact that there is a limit of age for candidates is a regulation which has absolutely nothing to recommend it. Without doubt it is a serious mistake to admit boys who have scarcely had time to take their university degree if soon after passing the examinations they are to be sent abroad to fill posts where they are entirely exempted from either discipline or study. In all the principal foreign systems without exception far from there being an age limit there is a fixed time (in some cases 25 years of age, in others 27) before which candidates are not allowed to present themselves but after which they are at liberty to go up for the examination whenever they please within reasonable limits. By this means older and more experienced men who in many cases have had useful training in other professions receive nominations and are admitted into the service after an examination.

This idea should certainly be adopted. Candidates would be eligible after having completed their 25th year and, if there must be a limit, before their 36th birthday any period of service as attaché previous to the examination being permitted, if they so desire it, on passing a preliminary examination chiefly in French. A University degree or the passing of any public examination (army, Civil Service, etc.) would excuse candidates from that part of the examination which does not deal with foreign languages. An adequate knowledge of International Law is very necessary nowadays and the examination in this subject which is at present optional should certainly be made obligatory in fact promotion to the rank of Third Secretary should be dependent on passing it.

There is a point in the regulations for examination into the German and Russian Services that is worthy of imitation which is that part of the oral examination (possibly consisting only of an interview) would be conducted before an official of the Foreign Office who is naturally the best judge of whether the candidate is the sort of person required. For the passing of the examination is not a conclusive proof by itself of the candidate's fitness. But in order to avoid the contingency of a candidate who has passed satisfactorily being rejected because he is not considered a suitable person for the Service, it would be as well that he should be interviewed officially before receiving a nomination. This would secure a very careful selection of the few candidates required during the year.

## 11. *Chanceliers*

Having admitted an older man the next point is to prevent his spending the first fifteen or twenty years of his career (as at present) solely occupied with the mechanical work of the chanceries. This can be effected by the introduction of chanceliers and the consequent reduction in the number of Secretaries. The advantage of employing chanceliers can hardly be overestimated. I have heard from members of the German, Austrian and French services where this system is in force that by managing the routine work, and taking charge of the archives they ensure the work of the chanceries being conducted on the most efficient and business-like lines. While by their knowledge of the language and customs of the country in which they reside (if not permanently anyhow for long periods) they make themselves absolutely indispensable. The Secretaries are left free for the confidential and more responsible work and when in the smaller posts the whole staff is changed more or less simultaneously as sometimes occurs, continuity is secured by the chancelier who with his knowledge of precedent is a very considerable assistance to the newcomers. The Germans who favour the employment of chanceliers to a greater extent than any of the other countries have in their service thirty Secretaries and attachés less than we have.

To bring this scheme into force a circular on the subject could be addressed to our Representatives abroad and it would be found that in most places a man of the type required might be available in the capital itself, in fact in some posts they already exist with the title of translator or Vice Consul.

The eligibility of chancelier and his subsequent employment would be regulated by the following conditions.

(i) He must be a British subject.

(ii) He must have completed his 22nd year and should, if possible, have had some training in clerk's work.

(iii) He should have a thorough knowledge of the language of the country in which he is to reside and of English, French and arithmetic.

(iv) On passing an examination in the above subjects and in orthography and calligraphy he would receive pay ranging from £70–300 a year.

(v) He would have no access to the cyphers nor would any confidential documents pass through his hands.

He would in fact be the equivalent to the Foreign Office 2nd Division clerk. And the difficulty of finding men of this class who would be prepared to live abroad on so small a salary is met by the fact already alluded to, that in many if not the majority of cases the choice might be made out of the English Colony of the foreign capital in question . . .

By this means in a few years a Secretary will find himself Second or Head of the Chancery at an Embassy or second acting as chargé d'affaires at a Legation and the utterly useless not to say ignominious state of affairs of a Secretary of 35 to 40 after 15 to 20 years of service still copying out despatches in a subordinate position would be finally abolished. The numbers of the whole profession would be reduced to 100 or under and thereby a considerable decrease made in the expenditure. Attachés (who have not passed the final examination) and honorary attachés would be employed in the same way as now without any salary.

There appears however to be a certain prejudice against the introduction of chanceliers into the British Service but it is hard to say on what this can be founded, as the greater efficiency of the 2nd division clerk in the performance of the mechanical work is undoubted and the desire to entrust the younger members of the service with a higher class of work is keenly felt. If the danger of information leaking out is the objection this can surely be guarded against by the rule respecting cyphers and confidential documents being strictly enforced.

## III

By these first two reforms we get an older man and it is so arranged that he is soon released from being solely occupied with more mechanical work. The difficulty we are confronted with now is that in the majority of posts even with a reduced staff it is not easy to find sufficient work for a secretary although his presence at his post on the chance of any question of importance turning up or of his chief's absence on leave, is necessary.

The want of employment which is the gravest of all the disadvantages being the chief factor in leading to the present unsatisfactory results can only be adequately dealt with in one way—and that is by a freer amalgamation of the two services, the Diplomatic Service and the Foreign Office. In France this system is attended with the very best results. On the one hand it prevents the necessity of the prolonged exile which is neither beneficial nor pleasant and on the other hand it gives an opportunity of rest and change to Foreign Office officials whose interest and zeal for their work would be benefited rather than disturbed by a temporary relaxation from the continuous routine or work in the same atmosphere. Combinations and exchanges could be arranged which might be especially advantageous to Foreign Office clerks. While a year or two's work in the Office from time to time would be an immeasurable benefit to the diplomats. For by being compelled to live in one small capital after another they are naturally apt to attach too much importance to questions of local interest by regarding incidents of national politics apart from the general context of European or universal politics, a proper view of which can only be obtained from the centre of affairs at home.

In the report of the Royal Commission of 1890, amalgamation was referred to thus: 'Such a system would supply the office at home and the Embassies abroad with men of more varied training; it would enable times of pressure at any point to be met by more ready transfer; it would fill the ranks with men for whom from the first more steady work might be required; it might be expected to reduce the number of junior diplomatists and to secure more constant promotion.' This certainly suggests that times of pressure at the Foreign Office might be met by calling home diplomats from posts where they could be spared which was decidedly preferable to the present method of admitting a large quantity of young attachés.

The objection brought forward against amalgamation is that the advent of diplomats who want to spend a year or two in England is a disturbing element and an inconvenience to the work of the Office. And this is true if, as at present is the case, a diplomat only exchanges once while he is a junior. But this objection would be removed if constant interchange were encouraged and the advent of a diplomat who had probably served already in the Office would not be more disturbing to the work than the introduction of a clerk from one department into another. The interchange of course would not be obligatory. Those who preferred a leisurely career abroad (and many would be found who did) might easily be satisfied and those who were disinclined or could not afford to go out abroad might remain at the office, for the two examinations would still be kept distinct (the clerk being admitted at an earlier age but not being eligible for exchange into the Diplomatic Service before the age of 26, the attaché serving one year at least at the Office before being sent out abroad).

By allowing the services to be amalgamated to this extent it would ultimately be found that as far as diplomats were concerned those who took advantage of a period of service at the Foreign Office from time to time would be the ones who would prove themselves capable of filling positions of trust and responsibility in the long run. For by being at the centre of affairs they not only have the opportunity they desire of gaining some knowledge of various questions of foreign politics but they subject their own fitness for any particular post to the scrutiny of the higher authorities so that the men and their capacity would be *known* instead of their incapacity being guessed at as is now the case.

A minister in the French service who spoke very highly of the advantage of amalgamation assured me that ignorance of the central view of current politics and of questions of general interest, knowledge of which can be gained in London perhaps better than anywhere else, is a noticeable characteristic of the British diplomat of today. And indeed diplomats of the higher grades in our own service have confessed to me that the absence of opportunity and the life of prolonged leisure tends to deaden all effort and eventually produces an inactivity and indolency of disposition which is augmented by the certainty that promotion up to the high rank of Minister will come to all irrespective of their ever having been charged with duties of the smallest importance or having displayed the necessary tact and judgement without which no diplomat can be of any real service.

This leads me to the fourth point.

IV. *Superannuation*

There is no apparent reason why if a certain rank is not reached at a certain age, a diplomatic officer should not be obliged to retire on a pension just as much as an officer in the Army or Navy. For it is manifestly inconvenient that the promotions of the whole profession should be blocked by members whom the authorities have no intention of promoting further, being retained in the service solely because there is no way of dismissing them. It is true that there are posts which are of so little importance that no actual harm is done by converting them into shelves nevertheless it would surely be fairer and more beneficial to the service if these posts were treated as training grounds for the younger secretaries or anyhow as posts for active officials who desired a period of rest.

The regulation therefore as to ambassadors retiring at 70 might be further extended to Ministers Plenipotentiary and Ministers Resident who would be obliged to retire at 67 and 62 respectively.

We have now created a small and efficient working staff of officials for both home and foreign service the composition of which will be far better adapted to modern requirements than the present organization which in its main respects is entirely out of date. For by the introduction of the reforms specified members of the service while having every opportunity of studying special questions on the spot and of becoming familiar with foreign life and character will be thoroughly conversant with the views and dealings of the government at home.

It would be unreasonable to expect that any scheme could make quite sure of producing first rate men or could be in every way entirely satisfactory especially in diplomacy where so much depends on the particular character and special aptitude of the man himself. But in drawing up the above suggestions, one of the chief points which have been kept in view is an endeavour to allow a greater degree of responsibility to the younger members of the service. For although nowadays it has become customary to discourage Representatives from having too free a hand, it must be remembered that unless responsibility is taught and that at an early age it is probable that when the time comes for a diplomat to act of his own accord, possibly at a moment's notice, he will hesitate and be unable to take advantage of the opportunity before him in the same way as he would have had both confidence and sureness which alone can be acquired by his being accustomed to act alone and by his having learnt through mistakes in small matters the way to avoid mistakes when dealing with matters of great moment. In fact if responsibility is withheld from him from the first he will never prove himself worthy of being entrusted with it. Teach him the value of responsibility when he is young and his use of it while showing you what the man is made of will fit him in his day for the high posts which may fall to his lot.

There is one very significant consideration to be regarded with respect to the whole question of the reform of the Diplomatic Service and it can be appropriately mentioned in concluding this memorandum.

Diplomacy, it is true, has been shorn of much of the importance which gave it in former years so prominent a position in the state service. The surprising progress made in the means of communication has deprived diplomats of many of the grave responsibilities with which they were formerly charged. On the other hand in later years the prevailing and increasing desire to exhaust every possible means of negotiation and have recourse to arbitration before finally resorting to war, has done much and will do more still to rehabilitate the diplomatist and will perhaps in time elevate him to a higher position of importance than he has ever yet occupied. Reform therefore does not mean the patching up of an obsolete service but an endeavour to prepare and train the members of a rising profession with a view to the future where there is undoubtedly much work in store for them. If they do not equip themselves suitably for the competition, international jurists, military administrators and others will step into their places. But it is essential that they should be helped first, before they can effectively help themselves.

A marginal note on the memorandum suggests its subsequent history:

1900 presented to Sir Thomas Sanderson. He was very much annoyed. I followed it by a second memo: giving extracts from previous Royal Commissions. He showed it to one ambassador who disapproved. Nothing was done. When Hardinge succeeded Sanderson, some of the reforms were carried out and the position of the F.O. clerk very much improved—Royal Commission 1914 before which I gave evidence.

But there was a second part to the story. Two and a half years later, Ponsonby found the Foreign Office 'absolutely unbearable; the monotonous purely mechanical routine is quite intolerable'.[1] The reformer did not leave quietly; in his letter of resignation to Sanderson, he wrote, 'I have however also realized how very naif and foolish it was of me to draw up and send you such a paper as I ought to have known that reforms are not introduced in that way.'[2] Sanderson was outraged by Ponsonby's action and tone:

As to the decision itself I can only express my hope, as an old friend of your father, that you will, before leaving the profession for which you trained yourself with his approval, take all possible means to satisfy yourself that the new career you are choosing will really suit you better and offer you better prospects. I do not myself think that office work is what you are best fitted for . . . But in the Diplomatic Service abroad (whatever you may have thought on that subject, after six years experience divided between two posts) brilliant careers have been and are made by those who have the necessary qualities—I have not time at present to discuss the memorandum which you gave me two years ago containing your views on what the service ought to be and how it should be organized. I do not suppose you could have been so unreasonable as to expect that drastic changes such as some of those you advocated, were likely to be introduced on the recommendation of a junior 2nd Secretary—that would have been something more than 'naif'. I have from time to time consulted men of greater experience who have given portions of it a qualified assent and read others with expressions of considerable impatience. But the main point which I wish to impress upon you is that there is *no* profession or career, which after a certain experience, and again from time to time, does not seem disheartening and repulsive. It is the men who are not deterred by these considerations, who hold tight and do not wobble, who think mainly of their work and little of their prospects, who make steady or rapid or great careers as the case may be . . .

[1] Ponsonby MSS, undated copy of letter by Ponsonby.
[2] *Ibid.* Ponsonby to Sanderson, 5 August 1902. He also wrote to Eric Barrington and William Tyrrell (Sanderson's private secretary).

But I hope that you will consider carefully whether you are prepared to abide by your new selection as a permanency—for to return to the Service after once leaving it is becoming increasingly difficult, and a succession of changes generally goes, to put it mildly, in a descending scale.[1]

Ponsonby could not accept Sanderson's 'homily' and answered his rebuke. He was not unfitted to office work but 'the way all individuality is sacrificed and all personal responsibility suppressed for the sake of securing a smoothly working machine produced mechanical routine of a kind that appeared to me intolerable if it was to constitute the sole work of my life'.[2] The resigning diplomat claimed that the only notice Sanderson had taken of his memorandum was in a conversation of two of three minutes when the latter had made 'a reducto ad absurdum of my proposition [amalgamation] by instancing the exchange of Tilley and J. Ford and that was all—except one other occasion when you declared me to be an example of the failure of the system of exchanges'. Ponsonby assured his ex-chief that he would never return to the Foreign Office. He did return—as Ramsey Macdonald's parliamentary under-secretary in 1924.

Sanderson's final word on the subject throws a great deal of light on the tone and ethos of the old Foreign Office:

... As regards your Memorandum I cannot at this interval of time distinguish in my memory how much I discussed it with you directly and how much I asked Tyrrell to say to you at a time when I had very little opportunity for anything but pressing work. But I certainly have a very distinct recollection of having gone through it point by point, of having said that I myself had advocated an earlier age for retirement but found strong objections, that the use of Chanceliers had been deliberately rejected after trial though I also thought there were some cases in which they might tentatively be re-introduced and that I altogether objected to having the French Foreign Office (of which you have no knowledge or experience) being held up as a model, when its own Chief complained that it was enormously overmanned and yet inefficient, and it was notorious that our Embassy at Paris and others found it difficult to get any ordinary business through it. As regards the question of amalgamation, you altogether mistake or misrepresent my argument, which is simply that when two kinds of service are essentially different in their conditions and requirements you cannot justly or advantageously make them compulsorily interchangeable, though I advocate the largest amount of voluntary interchange subject to a right of veto when the exchange is manifestly undesirable, as in the individual case which you say I suggested. It is quite true that after a series of very annoying acts of carelessness in the room of which you were considered to have control, I said that it was not a remarkable illustration of the advantages of exchange—I think it was rather a mild remonstrance after what had occurred—and that it is a matter of fact true that constant practice is necessary to ensure

[1] *Ibid.* Sanderson to Ponsonby, 24 August 1902.
[2] *Ibid.* undated copy, letter from Ponsonby to Sanderson.

methodical attention to matters of details, which are yet of great importance. I have never argued that simply because you are a junior of small experience your suggestions are unworthy of being considered—But I certainly think experience is a great test of soundness of views—and that objection which others have made to your suggestions is that they are crude and not sufficiently considered—You will remember or I rather think you must have forgotten that at my request you extracted the evidence from the Royal Commission Reports bearing on the suggestions you made. I have got the collection in my box—I still study it on occasions, and I should be sorry that you should think you had taken the trouble for no purpose.[1]

Sanderson's concern and pique is obvious. What is typical of his period is that he should have taken the time to write two lengthy letters to a junior, albeit from a distinguished family, resigning from his office. Ponsonby had thought of a career on the stage; instead he turned to the Liberal party, became Campbell-Bannerman's private secretary and then radical-Liberal member for Stirling Burghs (Campbell-Bannerman's seat before his death). He soon became the leading radical critic of Grey's anti-German policy and kept up a steady attack on the exclusive character of the Diplomatic Service and the secrecy which shrouded its proceedings. In 1914, in his own right and as one of the leaders of the Foreign Affairs Group, Ponsonby gave evidence before the Royal Commission on the Foreign Office and Diplomatic Service.

[1] Sanderson to Ponsonby, 30 August 1902.

# APPENDIX 5

---

# Parliamentary work at the Foreign Office—suggestions for reform, 1901[1]

I am informed that formerly the Assistant in a Department was sometimes especially charged with Parliamentary work, but apparently the practice has fallen into desuetude with the result that the whole burden of this work is thrown upon the Head of the Department—a very severe addition, especially during the Session, for the Head of any Department dealing with questions of acute public interest.

Parliamentary business may be divided under three heads—the preparation of answers to questions, the collection of information required for Parliamentary debate, the preparation of Blue Books. As regards the first two I think it would be of great assistance to the Parliamentary Under Secretary if the system of having the Second in each Department especially charged with Parliamentary work could be revived. As regards the Blue Books by this allocation the business of the F.O. would benefit generally. But it is of course understood throughout this memorandum that while relieving them of the great mass of the Parliamentary work the Assistants should act under the supervision and direction of the Heads of these Departments. They should, however, have access at all times to the Parliamentary Under Secretary.

## 1. Parliamentary questions

It should be their duty to prepare the answers to questions and they should lay themselves out to learn from the Parliamentary Under Secretary the sort of answers which are required, both as to that which it is necessary to deal with and as to that which it is better to ignore.

## 2. Information

With the object of saving trouble when the critical moment arrives the Assistants should have special regard to any minute of the Parliamentary Under Secretary in which he calls attention to any papers or part of a paper which may become useful in Parliamentary controversy and should put it aside and in a short time they will be able themselves to supplement these selected papers by others which they may remark but which may have escaped the notice of the Under Secretary. With this object they should of course keep themselves in touch with the organs of public opinion. When the Parliamentary Under Secretary requires a special effort to be made it should be the duty of the Assistant to lay aside all other work until this effort is finished.

[1] FO 366/391, memorandum by Lord Cranborne, 18 November 1901.

## 3. *Blue Books*

It would save a great deal of time in the preparation of Blue Books if before the papers are selected in the rough the Assistant in each Department were to receive direction as to the general scope which is contemplated. For that purpose it would be well if the Parliamentary Under Secretary stated what should be inserted and omitted (especially the latter) from a Parliamentary point of view. The Under Secretary under whose supervision the particular Department happens to be should similarly suggest what should be inserted and omitted from a diplomatic point of view and, the thing being very important, their minutes on the prospective Blue Book should be submitted to the Secretary of State before they are acted upon. In carrying out these minutes in respect of Blue Books it is of course especially necessary that the Assistants should act under the immediate direction of the Heads of Departments, but in any case of doubt which may arise he should at once appeal to the Under Secretary, Parliamentary or otherwise, to whom the subject matter of the difficulty belongs, in order that no time may be lost.

# The Viceroy and the Consul-General:
# Lord Curzon and Lord Cromer

There were two men who stood outside the normal diplomatic channels and yet had more influence than any single diplomat. Lord Curzon was already an acknowledged expert on Middle Eastern affairs before his appointment as viceroy of India. In his book, *Persia and the Persian Question*, published in 1892, he argued that the Persian Gulf and southern Persia were of special concern to England and that all other powers were to be kept out of these areas by force if necessary.[1] The brilliant, if arrogant, Curzon had little patience with Lord Salisbury's 'buffer policy' and even when at the Foreign Office had criticized his chief's failure to take a more active stand against the Russian advance at Teheran.[2] The British position in Persia deteriorated sharply but Lord Salisbury, always a realist in diplomacy, found few means at his disposal to check this trend. Even before the Boer War, Salisbury knew that the military imbalance in central Asia gave the Russians an unassailable advantage and his pessimistic appraisal was fully endorsed by the military experts. Moreover, though the Prime Minister would have liked to compete with the Russians as the financial saviours of the bankrupt Shah, his efforts in this direction were defeated by Hicks Beach and by an unwilling House of Commons. 'Other Nations can lend money and we cannot', Salisbury complained in 1900 and all his efforts to forestall a Russian loan failed.[3] There was a third possibility, an arrangement with the Russians, but Salisbury's approach to St Petersburgh in 1898 bore no fruits.[4]

Once in India, Lord Curzon was determined to reverse the balance in central Asia. The Viceroy became the consistent advocate of a forward policy not only in Persia but in Tibet and Afghanistan. He had little faith in an

---

[1] The Persian question has been exhaustively studied. B. Busch, *Britain and the Persian Gulf, 1894–1914*; J. Plass, *England zwischen Deutschland und Russland, 1899–1907, Der Persische Gulf in der Britische Vorkriegspolitik*, and R. Greaves, 'British Policy in Persia, 1892–1903', *Bulletin of School of Oriental and African Studies*, 1965, particularly 284–307. Other material is found in FO 60/608, 630, 645, the Lansdowne Papers and Curzon Papers. Grenville, *Lord Salisbury and Foreign Policy*, and Ronaldshay, *Life of Lord Curzon*, vol. II (London, 1928) are indispensable.

[2] FO 60/601, minute by Lord Curzon, 18 May 1898.

[3] Grenville, *Lord Salisbury and Foreign Policy*, p. 301. Quotation from Salisbury papers, Salisbury to Currie, 8 June 1900.

[4] Greaves, 'British Policy in Persia, 1892–1903', 48–9.

agreement with the Russians and no confidence in the ability of these decaying Asian states to maintain their independence. In a critical memorandum sent to the India Office on 21 September 1899, Lord Curzon outlined his own suggestions for a policy in Persia.[1] This famous despatch contained a strong protest against Salisbury's policy of drift. It was essential that the British take a clear stand. Either the Russians should agree to a partition of Persia or the Persians and Russians be warned that any Russian move into Seistan or into the Gulf would be resisted by force. It was imperative for the safety of the Indian Empire that British influence in central and southern Persia be maintained and it was the duty of the Cabinet to make the position clear.

Curzon's demands for an active programme in Persia, like those of the British minister at Teheran, Sir Mortimer Durand, met with a lukewarm response in London.[2] Though supported by his friend and successor at the Foreign Office, St John Brodrick, nothing was officially done about Curzon's despatch until July 1900. The Cabinet decided it was unable to make a clear statement in favour of Persian independence given Russia's special position and could find no effective way of preventing other powers from establishing their influence on the Gulf. As Lord George Hamilton at the India Office explained to the Viceroy, Britain did not have the military power to take the diplomatic offensive in central Asia and there was no popular support for such a policy.[3] During the critical Boer War years, when the military and naval chiefs were particularly apprehensive of a Russian move, Lord Curzon's attempts to strengthen the British position on the Gulf, even when partially successful, were generally received with a certain degree of apprehension at home.[4]

Lord Curzon's opportunity came when Lord Lansdowne took over the Foreign Office.[5] Curzon rightly believed that Lansdowne, who had been viceroy of India, would prove more sympathetic to his demands. In an exchange of letters in the spring of 1901, Lord Curzon not only bitterly criticized Salisbury's 'hand-to-mouth' diplomacy but outlined a basic programme for Persia.[6] Lansdowne was already underwriting the efforts of Hardinge (the British minister at Teheran) to restore the British position at Teheran. He promised to find funds (from Secret Service money if not from

[1] FO 615, India Office to Foreign Office, 21 September 1899.
[2] For Durand's memorandum see FO 60/608, 12 February 1899. Despite his lack of success at Teheran, Durand was an acute observer and his despatch states the situation clearly. Yet when it was decided that a more active policy was essential, Durand, who was disliked by the Persians, was removed and replaced by Sir Arthur Hardinge. Hardinge, too, had his personal troubles but he proved far more successful in winning the confidence of the Persians than his predecessor.
[3] Grenville, *Lord Salisbury and Foreign Office Policy*, p. 299; Ronaldshay, *Life of Lord Curzon*, vol. II, p. 100. BD IV, pp. 363–5.
[4] See the evidence in FO 27/3492; Ronaldshay, *Life of Lord Curzon*, vol. II, pp. 45–50.
[5] The relevant letters are all found in the Lansdowne papers.
[6] Newton, *Lord Lansdowne*, p. 231; FO 277, Lansdowne to Curzon, 5 May 1901.

the Treasury) for a small loan and agreed to arrange for a visit from the Shah to London. Curzon wanted far more; he hoped that Lansdowne would designate the line in Persia beyond which the Russians would not be permitted to move without encountering British resistance. The Foreign Secretary refused, for like Lord Salisbury he knew he was unable to back the British position in Persia by force. Yet he fully considered Curzon's further detailed suggestions. The Viceroy's letter of June 1901 was an elaboration of his 1899 despatch but this time he was assured of a more friendly reception. Curzon demanded that a direct warning be given to the Persians with regard to southern Persia, Seistan and the Gulf. If the warning were observed, the British would do their best to see that the independence of Persia would be preserved. If, however, the Persians rejected British advice and encouraged the Russians in these areas we 'should protect and compensate ourselves in whatever way appeared best'. Curzon ended his long letter by recommending a protectorate over Baheria and Koweit to prevent either Russia or Germany (a new rival in the area) from advancing into the Gulf.[1]

Only a new crisis at Teheran delayed action on Curzon's recommendations.[2] The Shah, again on the point of total bankruptcy, appealed to the British for a loan but once more the Foreign Office was checked by the parsimony of the British Treasury. When these negotiations failed, Lansdowne became convinced that it was time to state the British position clearly in a comprehensive despatch for Hardinge which could be communicated to the Persian Government. After studying Curzon's suggestions during his summer holiday, Lansdowne had this despatch prepared and printed at the Foreign Office in September 1901.[3] It was not sent until January 1902, as in the autumn of 1901 Lansdowne made one final effort to come to an agreement with the Russians.[4]

Lansdowne's despatch followed Curzon's suggestions almost to the letter. In the Viceroy's exact words, the Persians were warned against granting military, naval or coaling stations to the Russians in the Gulf or any political concessions in southern Persia or in Seistan. Russia's special position in the north was recognized but the Persians were clearly warned that the British would not allow the Russians a similar ascendancy in the south. Though Lansdowne claimed that much in this despatch could be found in various earlier communications from London to Teheran, he had, in fact, acceded to Lord Curzon's demand for a clear definition of British policy in Persia. Both the Persians and Russians were now warned and all the other powers

[1] FO 277, Curzon to Lansdowne, 7 June 1901.
[2] For details, see material in FO 60/645.
[3] FO 277, Lansdowne to Curzon, 15 August 1901; BD IV, pp. 269–71.
[4] This approach was connected with the Anglo-Japanese negotiations. Steiner, 'Great Britain and the Creation of the Anglo-Japanese Alliance', *The Journal of Modern History* XXXI (1959), 27–36.

with ambitions in the Gulf were now alerted to Britain's special interests in that sea. The despatch to Teheran was backed by a strong statement in the Commons by Lord Cranborne. There was a full-dress debate, and the opposition spokesman, Sir Edward Grey, stated the case for an agreement with Russia, the policy which he was successfully to bring to fruition in 1907.[1] For the moment, however, it was Curzon's views which had triumphed. 'There is no greater fallacy in contemporaneous politics than the idea that England can come to an agreement with Russia over Asia', he wrote to Lord Lansdowne when the latter complained that he could not reveal that his approaches to Russia had been turned down by the Russians.[2]

The despatch of January 1902 marked a turning point in British policy in Persia. Despite setbacks, some rather ludicrous, Hardinge, Curzon and Lansdowne did manage to improve the British position at Teheran.[3] The Russian ascendancy was not checked but at least it was challenged. It was clear, however, that the Persian situation was highly unstable and that revolution was imminent. Hardinge warned the home government that plans would have to be made should the Persian Government collapse.[4] The professional army men were pessimistic; they did not believe they could successfully check Russian aggression in Persia.[5] Yet an inter-departmental committee (India Office, Foreign Office, War Office and Admiralty) did agree to a policy which, if it did not meet all of Curzon's wishes, went further than might have been expected. The committee's decisions checked the possibility of Russia turning Persia into a protectorate without a strong counter-move by the English.[6] It was not strategically possible to do any more.

In April 1903 the Government of India lent the Persians £200,000 through the Imperial Bank and supplemented this with another small loan. In the summer of 1903 when the Russians threatened to suppress the revolutionary movement in Tabriz, Hardinge warned the Persians that if Russia intervened, the British would move in the south and east.[7] As hoped, the news was quickly transmitted to St Petersburgh with gratifying results. In the autumn of 1903, Lord Curzon made a stately tour through the Gulf accompanied by an impressive naval escort. This was to be the high point of the Viceroy's power.

[1] Hansard, Parliamentary Debates, 4th series CI, pp. 574–87.
[2] FO 277, Lansdowne to Curzon, 16 February 1902; Curzon to Lansdowne, 16 March 1902.
[3] The British bought a road concession which, if it had gone to the Russians, might have led to Russian control of entry into the south. Subsidies were given to Lynch, to the Tigris and Euphrates Company to keep the concession in operation. By a judicious use of Secret Service money, Hardinge increased his influence with the clerical party at the Shah's court. The Shah arrived in England on 18 August but the visit was far from successful. The speed of the train made him ill and there was trouble with the King over the Garter.
[4] FO 277, Hardinge to Lansdowne, 15 September 1902. Balfour to Lansdowne, 6 September 1902; Lansdowne to Hardinge, 18 November 1902.
[5] FO 60/657, memorandum by W. R. Robertson, Lt.-Gen. Sir W. Nicolson, 4 October 1902, 16 October 1902.        [6] Ibid. memorandum of meeting at Foreign Office, 19 November 1902.
[7] BD IV, no. 322.

In the autumn of 1903 Count Benckendorff, the Russian ambassador in London, presented unofficial proposals for a settlement in Persia, China and Afghanistan. What had proved unattainable in 1898 and 1901 became a possibility in 1903. Lord Curzon's demands for a forceful policy in Afghanistan and Tibet were nervously considered in London where the Cabinet wished to avoid a military demonstration in central Asia.[1] The first open quarrel between the Viceroy and Cabinet occurred late in 1903 when Curzon's boyhood friend, St John Brodrick, replaced Hamilton at the India Office. Thereafter, a series of personal differences aggravated an already apparent split between Delhi and London.[2] Even before the clash with Lord Kitchener brought Curzon's viceroyalty to its unfortunate end, the Viceroy found his policies in Tibet and Afghanistan disavowed. In November 1905 Curzon left India for good, a disappointed and embittered man.

Lord Cromer enjoyed the same position in Egypt as Lord Curzon did at Delhi. Lansdowne wrote to the 'Lord' (as Tyrrell later dubbed him) at least twice a month and the Consul-General's authority extended far beyond Cairo. His policy in Egypt and in the Sudan was rarely challenged in the Cabinet and it was only the Treasury which sometimes blocked his schemes for irrigation and railway projects.[3] His advice was sought on a wide range of problems—the delimitations of the Abyssinian border with the Italians, the dispute over the Congo leases with King Leopold, the question of Tripoli, the organization of the consular services for Cairo and Constantinople.[4] Through his relations with the European representatives on the Caisse de la Dette, Cromer was able to provide the Foreign Office with a valuable evaluation of the attitudes of the different foreign powers. In a brilliant letter written on 11 December 1901 Cromer emphasized the pacific nature of French diplomacy in this traditional battleground of the two nations.[5]

It was during the Anglo-French negotiations of 1903–4 when Cromer most decisively affected the course of Lansdowne's diplomacy. On 2 February 1903, reading a specially placed press despatch printed in *The Times*, Cromer first picked up the possibility of an arrangement with the French. The Consul-General was preparing to complete the financial rehabilitation of Egypt and was anxious to bring about the abolition of the cumbersome

[1] FO 60/659, BD IV, nos. 289, 290, 291, 294, 465, 466. Ronaldshay, *Life of Lord Curzon*, vol. II, pp. 261–80.
[2] Ronaldshay, *Life of Lord Curzon*, vol. II, pp. 286–9.
[3] FO 277, Lansdowne to Cromer, 8 February, 31 March 1901.
[4] Re Abyssinia, see FO 277, Lansdowne to Cromer, 2 May, 17 June 1901. Congo Leases, Lansdowne to Cromer, 15 November, 25 November 1901; Sanderson to Phipps, December 1902. On the Consular Service, minutes by Villiers and Sanderson, 21 July and 22 August 1901.
[5] FO 277, Cromer to Lansdowne, 11 December 1901.

Caisse. During the spring, he urged Lansdowne to arrive at an under-standing with the French over Morocco and Egypt, and in August 1903 prepared the Egyptian clauses of the arrangement which Lansdowne sub-sequently presented to the French.[1] Lord Cromer sent Eldon Gorst, one of his subordinates (an adviser to the ministry of interior in Egypt), to London in November to explain Cromer's demands and to expedite the proceedings.[2] When the negotiations deadlocked on the vexed problem of Newfoundland, Cromer intervened: 'To allow negotiations to break down now,' he wrote to the Foreign Secretary, 'would in my opinion be little short of a calamity, whether from the general or the local Egyptian point of view.'[3] It was only on the question of Britain's freedom of action in Egypt that the Consul-General proved adamant; elsewhere he urged compromise or even sacrifice. It was, moreover, Cromer and Gorst rather than the Foreign Office who were most concerned about the future reaction of Germany.[4] Both men understood, as neither Balfour nor Lansdowne did, the full European implications of the new arrangement.[5]

Even before Cromer left Egypt because of ill-health, it was clear that a strong nationalist movement was developing. Eldon Gorst, who was his successor, had neither Cromer's prestige nor authority. He did, however, pressed by the home government, try to stem the tide through a series of reforms. The Foreign Office, or at least Hardinge and Grey, were apparently divided on the issue, but until 1909 the radicals, who were anxious to intro-duce measures of self-government into Egypt as well as into India, prevailed. 'I have urged Sir Edward two or three times during the last eighteen months to pull up a bit, as I saw that the Egyptians were getting out of hand. He, however, thought otherwise, as you gave no indication that your opinion in any way coincided with mine.'[6] Gorst had come to similar conclusions and had begun to follow a more repressive policy towards the nationalists even before his untimely death in 1911. His last report from Egypt in 1910 recorded the comparative failure of representative institutions in Egypt and counselled caution for the future.

[1] BD II, nos. 359 and 365.
[2] Lord Zetland (Lord Ronaldshay), *Lord Cromer* (London, 1932), pp. 278, 280–1.
[3] BD II, no. 367.
[4] Zetland, *Lord Cromer*, pp. 283–4.
[5] FO 277, Cromer to Lansdowne, 12 December 1903; BD II, no. 400. Lansdowne did see that the French entente opened the way to a settlement with the Russians which he had always wanted (see Lansdowne to Cromer, 10 September 1905) but did not realize that the Germans might react most negatively to this new departure in British policy.
[6] Hardinge MSS 1910. Hardinge to Gorst, 13 May 1910. See also *ibid.* 22 April 1910.

# Bibliography

PRIMARY SOURCES

Foreign Office papers:
For period until 1906

| FO | 5 | America |
|----|---|---------|
| | 27 | France |
| | 17 | China |
| | 46 | Japan |
| | 54 | Muscat |
| | 60 | Persia |
| | 99 | Morocco |
| | 64 | Germany |
| | 65 | Russia |
| | 63 | Portugal |

For period after 1906
FO 371 series
Other series:
FO 83 (general) 1623, 1647, 1791, 1813, 1879
FO 95/565, Foreign Office diplomatic specimens, indexes, etc.
FO 366/716–18, 731, 738, 740, Correspondence with Treasury
FO Confidential, general 4, 1844–1932
FO 5
FO General vol. 55/3, /5, /8
Librarian's Department 1890–1918, vol. 5

PRIVATE PAPERS

Ardagh, Sir John. Public Record Office, 30/40, vol. IX.
Balfour, first Earl of. British Museum Add. MSS 49683/962.
Bertie. Public Record Office, FO 800/160–91. (First viewed in Foreign Office Library under different citation; both citations used.)
Campbell-Bannerman. British Museum Add. MSS 43589.
Carnock. Public Record Office, FO 800/22, 336–81. Diplomatic Narrative—4 vols. Property of the late Sir Harold Nicolson.
Crowe, Eyre. Public Record Office, FO 800/243, 794/2 (later at Ashridge).
Devonshire. Chatsworth, 340/2679–2802.
Grey of Fallodon. Public Record Office, FO 800/35–113.
Hardinge of Penshurst. Public Record Office, FO 800/24, 192, 197, 198. Cambridge University Library, 15 bound volumes.

Langley, Sir Walter. FO 800/29–31.

Lansdowne. Seen in Foreign Office under FO 277; now in Public Record Office, FO 800/115–146.

Lascelles. Seen in Foreign Office Library, now reclassified FO 800/6–20. Public Record Office. (Both citations used.)

Ponsonby. Private permission of Lord Ponsonby of Shulbrede.

Ripon. British Museum Add. MSS 43510–43548.

Salisbury, third Marquis of. Christ Church Library, Oxford.

Sanderson. Seen in Foreign Office Library under Lansdowne MSS. Now FO 800/1–2, 115, 116. Also, some papers in private possession of the late Dame Lilian Penson.

Satow, Sir Ernest. Public Record Office, 30/33.

Spender. British Museum Add MSS 46386–46391.

Spring-Rice. Public Record Office, FO 800/241–242.

Tenterden. FO 363, vols. I–V, vol. II missing.

Villiers. FO 800/22–24.

*Printed Documents*

Command Paper 1634. Report of Committee appointed to inquire into the Constitution of the Civil Service. Misc. no. 3, 1903.

Command Paper 3610. Report by Sir Eldon Gorst and Mr Llewelyn Smith on the System of British Commercial Attachés and Commercial Agents. PP 1907.

Command Paper 7748, 7749. Fifth Report of the Royal Commission on the Civil Service, London, 1914. PP 1914–16.

Command Paper 8715. Memorandum by the Board of Trade and the Foreign Office with respect to the Future Organization of Commercial Intelligence, PP 1917–18.

Documents Diplomatiques Français, 1871–1914. Ministère des Affaires Étrangères. Commission de Publication des Documents Relatifs aux Origine de la Guerre de 1914, series II and III (Paris, 1930–53).

Expenditure, Civil Government Charges, Accounts and Papers 1901, vol. XXXVII; 1913–14, I.

The Foreign Office List and Diplomatic and Consular Year Book, London, 1895–1914.

Geiss, I. Julikrise und Kriegsausbruch 1914, 2 vols. (Hannover, 1963–4).

Gooch, G. P. and Temperly, H. (ed.). British Documents on the Origins of the War, 1898–1914. 11 vols. in 13. (London, 1926–38).

Hansard, Parliamentary Debates, 4th and 5th series, 1897–1914.

House of Commons 466, Select Committee on Public Offices (Downing Street) 29 July 1839.

Lepsius, J., Mendelssohn-Bartholdy, A., Thimme, F. (eds.). *Die Grosse Politik der Europäischen Kabinette, 1871–1914*, 39 vols. (Berlin, 1922–27).

Siebert, B. de and Schreiner, G. A. (eds.). *Entente Diplomacy and the War* (New York, 1921).

*Memoirs and Autobiographies*

Amery, L. S. *My Political Life*, 3 vols. (London, 1953–5).

Antrobus, G. P. *King's Messenger, 1918–1940: Memoirs of Silver Greyhound* (London, 1941).

Asquith, Herbert Henry. *The Genesis of the War* (London, 1923). *Memoirs and Reflections, 1852–1927*, 2 vols. (London, 1928).

Barclay, Sir Thomas. *Thirty Years Anglo-French Reminiscences* (London, 1914).

Bertie, Lord. *The Diary of Lord Bertie of Thame, 1914–18*, edited by Lady Algernon Gordon Lennox, 2 vols. (London, 1931).

Bethmann-Hollweg, T. von. *Reflections on the World War*, translated by George Young (London, 1920).

Blunt, W. *My Diaries, being a Personal Narrative of Events, 1888–1914*, 2 vols. (London, 1919–20).

Bruce, R. J. *Silken Dalliance* (London, 1946).

Buchanan, Sir George. *My Mission to Russia and other Diplomatic Memories*, 2 vols. (London, 1923).

Buckle, G. E. (ed.). *The Letters of Queen Victoria*, 3rd series, 3 vols., 1898–1901 (London, 1930).

Bullard, Sir Reader. *The Camels Must Go* (London, 1961).

Bülow, Prince von. *Memoirs*, 4 vols. (London, 1931–2). *Denkwürdigkeiten*, 3 vols. (Berlin, 1931–2).

Butler, Sir Harold. *Confident Morning* (London, 1950).

Cambon, P. *Correspondence, 1870–1924*, ed. Cambon, H. 3 vols. (Paris, 1940–6).

Campbell, G. *Of True Experience* (London, 1949).

Chamberlain, Sir Austen. *Politics from Inside; an Epistolary Chronicle, 1906–1914* (New Haven, 1937).

Chirol, Sir Valentine. *Fifty Years in a changing world* (London, 1927).

Churchill, Winston. *The World Crisis, 1911–14*, vol. 1 (London, 1923).

Cooper, Alfred Duff, Viscount Norwich. *Old Men Forget* (London, 1954).

Corbett, Sir Vincent. *Reminiscences: Autobiographical and Diplomatic* (London, 1927).

Conwell-Evans, T. P. *Foreign Policy from a Back Bench, 1904–1918* (London, 1932).

Crowe, Sir Joseph Archer. *Reminiscences of Thirty-Five Years of my Life*, 2nd edn (London, 1895).

Eckardstein, Baron von. *Lebenserinnerungen und politische Denkwürdigkeiten*, 3 vols. (Leipzig, 1919–21).

Esher, Viscount. *Journals and letters of Reginald, Viscount Esher*, ed. M. V. Brett and Oliver, Viscount Esher, 4 vols. (London, 1934–8).

Gregory, John D. *On the Edge of Diplomacy; Rambles and Reflections, 1902–1928* (London, 1928).

Grey of Fallodon, Viscount. *Twenty-Five Years, 1892–1916*, 2 vols. (London, 1925).

Gwynn, S. (ed.), *The Letters and Friendships of Sir Cecil Spring-Rice*, 2 vols. (London, 1929).

Haldane, Richard B. *Before the War* (London, 1920).
—— *An autobiography* (London, 1929).
Hambloch, Ernest. *British Consul: Memories of Thirty Years Service in Europe and Brazil* (London, 1938).
Hamilton, Lord Frederick. *The Pomps of Yesterday* (London, 1919).
Hamilton, Lord George. *Parliamentary Reminiscences and Reflections, 1886-1906* (London, 1922).
Hankey, Lord Maurice. *The Supreme Command, 1914-1918*, 2 vols. (London, 1961).
Hardinge, Sir Arthur. *A Diplomatist in Europe* (London, 1927).
—— *A Diplomatist in the East* (London, 1928).
Hardinge of Penshurst, Lord. *Old Diplomacy* (London, 1947).
Hayashi, Viscount. *Secret Memoirs*, ed. A. M. Pooley (London, 1915).
Hearn, Walter R. *Some Recollections; Memories of Thirty-Five Years in the Consular Service* (London, 1928).
Hertslet, Sir Edward. *Recollections of the Old Foreign Office* (London, 1901).
Hewlett, Sir Meyrick. *Forty Years in China* (London, 1943).
Hohler, Sir Thomas. *Diplomatic Petrel* (London, 1942).
Hornby, Sir Edmund. *An Autobiography* (London, 1929).
House, E. M. *The Intimate Papers of Colonel House*, arranged as a narrative by C. Seymour, 4 vols. (Boston, 1926-8).
Jones, L. E. *Georgian Afternoon* (London, 1958).
Kelly, Sir David. *The Ruling Few: or the Human Background to Diplomacy* (London, 1952).
Kennedy, A. L. *Old Diplomacy and New, 1876-1922* (London, 1923).
Kirkpatrick, Sir Ivone. *The Inner Circle: Memoirs of Ivone Kirkpatrick* (London, 1959).
Knatchbull-Hugessen, Sir Hughe. *Diplomat in Peace and War* (London, 1949).
Kühlmann, Richard von. *Erinnerungen* (Heidelberg, 1948).
Lawford, Valentine. *Bound for Diplomacy* (London, 1963).
Lichnowsky, Prince Karl Max von. *Heading for the Abyss*, translated by Sefton Delmer (New York, 1928).
Lloyd George, David. *War Memoirs of David Lloyd George*, 6 vols. (London, 1933-6).
Lockhart, Sir Robert H. Bruce. *Memoirs of a British Agent* (London, 1932).
—— *Friends, Foes and Foreigners* (London, 1957).
Loreburn, Earl. *How the War Came* (London, 1919).
Lucy, Sir Henry. *Memories of Eight Parliaments* (London, 1908).
Luke, Sir Harry. *Cities and Men*, 3 vols. (London, 1953-6).
Meinertzhagen, C. R. *Army Diary, 1899-1926* (London, 1960).
Meister, Leila von. *Gathered Yesterdays* (London, 1963).
Middleton, Earl of. *Records and Reactions, 1856-1939* (London, 1939).
Milner, Lord. *The Milner Papers, South Africa, 1897-99*, ed. Cecil Henderson (London, 1931).
Morley, Viscount. *Recollections*, 2 vols. (London, 1917).
—— *Memorandum on Resignation, August 1914* (London, 1928).

Müller, George von. *Der Kaiser: Aus den Tagebüchern des Chef des Marinekabinetts Admiral George Alexander von Müller*, ed. W. Görlitz (Göttingen, 1915).
Nicolson, Sir Harold. *Peacemaking, 1919* (London, 1933).
Oliphant, Sir Lancelot. *An Ambassador in Bonds* (London, 1954).
O'Malley, Sir Owen. *The Phantom Caravan* (London, 1954).
Oppenheimer, Sir Francis. *Stranger Within: Autobiographical Pages* (London, 1960).
Percy, Lord Eustace. *Some Memories* (London, 1950).
Peterson, Sir Maurice. *Both Sides of the Curtain* (London, 1950).
Ponsonby, Sir George Frederick. *Recollections of Three Reigns* (New York, 1952).
Rendell, Sir George. *The Sword and the Olive; Recollections of Diplomacy and the Foreign Service, 1913–1954* (London, 1957).
Repington, Charles. *The First World War, 1914–18*, 2 vols. (Boston, 1920).
Robertson, Sir W. R. *Soldiers and Statesmen, 1914–18*, 2 vols. (London, 1926).
Rodd, Sir James Rennell. *Social and Diplomatic Memories, 1902–19*, 3 vols. (London, 1925).
Rumbold, Sir Horace. *The War Crisis in Berlin, July–August 1914* (London, 1940).
Ryan, Sir Andrew. *The Last of the Dragomans* (London, 1951).
Steed, H. W. *Through Thirty Years, 1892–1922*, 2 vols. (London, 1925).
Strang, Lord (Sir William). *Home and Abroad* (London, 1956).
Thompson, Sir Geoffrey. *Front-line Diplomat* (London, 1959).
Tilley, Sir John. *London to Tokyo* (London, 1942).
Tirpitz, Alfred von. *Erinnerungen* (Leipzig, 1920).
Vansittart, Sir Robert. *Lessons of my Life* (London, n.d.).
—— *The Mist Procession* (London, 1958).
Wellesley, Sir Victor. *Diplomacy in Fetters* (London, 1944).
Widenmann, Wilhelm. *Marine-Attaché an der kaiserlichen deutschen Botschaft in London. 1907–12* (Göttingen, 1952).
Wilkinson, Spenser H. *Thirty-Five Years, 1874–1909* (London, 1933).
Wilson, Sir Arnold. *S.W. Persia, Letters and Diary of a Young Political Officer 1907–1914* (London, 1942).
Windham, Sir Walter. *Waves, Wheels, Wings* (London, 1943).
Winterton, Earl. *Pre-war London* (London, 1932).
—— *Orders of the Day* (London, 1953).

## SECONDARY WORKS

Albertini, Luigi. *The Origins of the War of 1914*, translated and edited by I. M. Massey, 3 vols. (London, 1952–7).
Allen, B. M. *The Rt. Hon. Sir Ernest Satow: A Memoir* (London, 1933).
Amery, J. *The Life of Joseph Chamberlain*, vol. IV (London, 1951).
Anderson, E. N. *The First Moroccan Crisis, 1904–6* (Chicago, 1930).
Anderson, P. R. *The Background of Anti-English Feeling in Germany, 1890–1902* (Washington, D.C., 1939).
Andrew, Christopher. *Théophile Delcassé and the making of the Entente Cordiale; a reappraisal, French foreign policy, 1898–1905* (London 1968).
Ashton-Gwatkin, F. T. *The British Foreign Service* (Syracuse, N.Y., 1951).

Askwith, Lord. *Lord James of Hereford* (London, 1930).

Barlow, Ima C. *The Agadir Crisis* (Chapel Hill, North Carolina, 1940).

Beloff, Max. *Lucien Wolf and the Anglo-Russian Entente, 1907–1914* (London, 1951).

Bishop, Donald G. *The Administration of British Foreign Relations* (Syracuse, N.Y., 1961).

Bloch, Camille. *The Causes of the World War*, translated by J. Soames (London, 1935).

Boveri, Margret. *Sir Edward Grey und das Foreign Office* (Berlin, 1933).

Brailsford, H. N. *The War of Steel and Gold* (London, 1914).

Busch, B. *Britain and the Persian Gulf, 1894–1914* (Berkeley, 1967).

Calvert, P. *The Mexican Revolution, 1910–1914* (Cambridge, 1968).

Campbell, A. E. *Great Britain and the United States, 1895–1903* (London, 1960).

Campbell, Charles S. *Anglo-American Understanding, 1898–1903* (Baltimore, 1957).

Cecil, Lady Gwendolen. *Life of Robert, Marquis of Salisbury*, 4 vols. (London, 1921–32).

Chapman, Maybelle Kennedy. *Great Britain and the Bagdad Railway, 1888–1914* (Northampton, Mass., 1948).

Churchill, Rogers P. *The Anglo-Russian Convention of 1907* (Cedar Rapids, Iowa, 1939).

Collier, B. *Brasshat: A Biography of Field Marshal Sir Henry Wilson* (London, 1961).

Collins, Doreen. *Aspects of British Politics, 1904–1919* (London, 1965).

Colvin, Ian. *Vansittart in Office: The Origins of World War II* (London, 1965).

Craig, Gordon A. and Felix Gilbert. *The Diplomats, 1919–1939* (Princeton, 1953).

Crewe, the Marquess of. *Lord Rosebery*, 2 vols. (London, 1931).

Dehio, Ludwig. *Germany and World Politics in the Twentieth Century* (New York, 1959).

Dugdale, Blanche E. C. *Arthur James Balfour, First Earl of Balfour*, 2 vols. (London, 1936).

Dugdale, Edgar T. S. *Maurice de Bunsen: Diplomat and Friend* (London, 1934).

Earle, Edward Mead. *Turkey, the Great Powers and the Baghdad Railway* (New York, 1923).

Ehrman, John. *Cabinet Government and War, 1890–1940* (Cambridge, 1958).

Elliott, A. R. D. *Life of Lord Goschen, 1831–1907* (London, 1911).

Escott, T. H. *The Story of British Diplomacy: its Makers and Movements* (London, 1908).

Eubank, Keith. *Paul Cambon, Master Diplomatist* (Norman, Oklahoma, 1960).

Evans, F. M. G. *The Principal Secretary of State, 1558–1680* (Manchester, 1923).

Feis, Herbert. *Europe, the World's Banker, 1870–1914* (New Haven, 1930).

Fischer, Fritz. *Griff nach der Weltmacht: Die Kriegszielpolitik des Kaiserlichen Deutschland, 1914–18* (Düsseldorf, 1961).

Flournoy, Francis. *Parliament and War* (London, 1927).

Foreign Office, Diplomatic and Consular Sketches, *Vanity Fair* (London, 1883).

Gall, Wilheim. *Sir Charles Hardinge und die englische Vorkriegspolitik, 1903–1910* (Berlin, 1939).

Garvin, J. L. *The Life of Joseph Chamberlain*, 3 vols. (London, 1931–3).

Gaselee, S. *The Language of Diplomacy* (Cambridge, 1939).

Gatzke, Hans. *Germany's Drive to the West* (Baltimore, 1950).

Gollin, Alfred M. *The Observer and J. L. Garvin, 1908–1914: A Study in a Great Editorship* (London, 1960).

Gooch, G. P. *Studies in Modern History* (London, 1932).

—— *Before the War: Studies in Diplomacy and Statecraft*, 2 vols. (London, 1936–8).

—— *Recent Revelations of European Diplomacy*, 4th edn (London, 1940).

Gosses, F. *The Management of British Foreign Policy before the First World War, especially during the period 1880–1914*, translated by E. C. Van der Gaaf (Leiden, 1948).

Gouswaard, J. M. *Some Aspects of the end of Britain's Splendid Isolation, 1898–1904* (Rotterdam, 1952).

Greaves, Harold. *Parliamentary Control of Foreign Affairs* (London, 1934).

Grenville, J. A. S. *Lord Salisbury and Foreign Policy: the Close of the Nineteenth Century* (London, 1964).

Guinn, P. *British Strategy and Politics, 1914 to 1918* (Oxford, 1965).

Gwynne, S. and Tuckwell, G. *The Life of the Rt. Hon. Sir Charles Dilke*, 2 vols. (London, 1917).

Hale, O. J. *Germany and the Diplomatic Revolution* (Philadelphia, 1931).

—— *Publicity and Diplomacy; with Special Reference to England and Germany, 1890–1914* (New York, 1940).

Halévy, E. *Imperialism and the Rise of Labour*, 2nd edn, revised (London, 1934).

Hallgarten, George. *Imperialismus vor 1914*, 2nd edn (Munich, 1963).

Hammond, J. L. *C. P. Scott of the Manchester Guardian* (London, 1934).

Hantsch, Hugo. *Leopold Graf Berchtold. Grandseigneur und Staatsmann*, 2 vols. (Cologne, Graz, Vienna, 1963).

Hauser, O. *Deutschland und der Englisch-Russische Gegensatz, 1900–1914* (Göttingen, 1958).

Headlam-Morley, James. *Studies in Diplomatic History* (London, 1930).

Helmreich, E. C. *The Diplomacy of the Balkan Wars* (Cambridge, Mass., 1938).

Hicks Beach, Lady Victoria. *Life of Sir Michael Hicks Beach*, 2 vols. (London, 1932).

Hinsley, F. H. *Power and the Pursuit of Peace* (Cambridge, 1963).

Hoffman, Ross. *Great Britain and the German Trade Rivalry, 1875–1914*, reissue (New York, 1964).

Hollingsworth, L. W. *Zanzibar under the Foreign Office, 1890–1913* (London, 1953).

Horne, D. B. *The British Diplomatic Service, 1689–1789* (Oxford, 1961).

Howard, C. D. H. *Splendid Isolation* (London, 1967).

Hubatsch, W. *Die Ära Tirpitz. Studien zur deutschen Marinepolitik, 1890–1918* (Göttingen, 1955).

—— *Der Admiralstab und die obersten Marinebehörden in Deutschland, 1849–1945* (Frankfurt am Main, 1958).

James, Robert. *Rosebery* (London, 1964).

Jenkins, Roy. *Mr Balfour's Poodle* (London, 1954).

Jenkins, Roy. *Asquith: Portrait of a Man and an Era* (London, 1964).

Johnson, F. A. *Defence by Committee: The British Committee of Imperial Defence, 1885–1959* (London, 1960).

Jones, Kennedy. *Fleet Street and Downing Street* (London, 1920).

Jones, T. *Lloyd George* (Cambridge, Mass., 1951).

Kennedy, A. L. *Salisbury, 1830–1903: Portrait of a Statesman* (London, 1953).

Krieger, H. and Stern, F. (eds.). *The Responsibility of Power, Historical Essays in Honour of Hajo Holborn* (New York, 1967).

Lamb, Alastair. *Britain and Chinese Central Asia: The Road to Lhasa, 1767 to 1905* (London, 1960).

Langer, W. L. *The Diplomacy of Imperialism, 1890–1902*, 2nd edn (New York, 1951).

Langford, R. Victor. *British Foreign Policy: Its Formulation in Recent Years* (Washington, D.C., 1942).

Lee, Sir Sidney. *King Edward VII, a biography*, 2 vols. (London, 1925).

Lindberg, Folke. *Scandinavia in Great Power Politics, 1905–1908* (Stockholm, 1958).

Louis, Wm. Roger and Stengers, Jean. *E. D. Morel's History of The Congo Reform Movement* (Oxford, 1968).

Lowe, C. J. *Salisbury and the Mediterranean, 1884–1896* (London, 1965).

Lutz, Hermann. *Lord Grey and the World War* (London, 1928).

—— *Die europäische Politik in der Julikrise 1914* (Berlin, 1930).

—— *Eyre Crowe, der Böse Geist des Foreign Office* (Stuttgart, 1931).

—— *Deutschfeindliche Kräfte im Foreign Office der Vorkriegszeit* (Berlin, 1932).

Luvans, Jay. *The Education of an Army: British Military Thought, 1815–1940* (Chicago, 1964).

Macdiarmid, W. D. *The Life of Lieut.-General Sir James Moncrieff-Grierson* (London, 1923).

Magnus, Philip. *King Edward the Seventh* (New York, 1964).

Mansergh, Nicholas. *The Coming of the First World War* (London, 1949).

Marcus, Geoffrey. *Before the Lamps went out* (London, 1965).

Marder, Arthur J. *The Anatomy of British Sea Power: A History of British Naval Policy in the pre-Dreadnought Era, 1880–1905* (New York, 1940).

—— *From the Dreadnought to Scapa Flow: The Royal Navy in the Fisher Era, 1904–1919*, 3 vols. (Oxford, 1961–7).

Maurice, Sir Frederick. *Haldane, 1856–1915. The Life of Viscount Haldane of Cloan, K.T., O.M.* 2 vols. (London, 1937–9).

Mayer, Arno J. *Wilson vs. Lenin: Political Origins of the New Diplomacy, 1917–1918* (New York, 1964).

Monger, George, W. *The End of Isolation: British Foreign Policy, 1900–1907* (London, 1963).

Montgelas, Count Max. *British Foreign Policy under Sir Edward Grey*, translated by William C. Dreher (New York, 1928).

Morel, E. D. *Morocco in Diplomacy* (London, 1912).

—— *The Secret History of a Great Betrayal* (London, 1923).

Mowat, R. B. *The Life of Lord Pauncefote* (London, 1929).

Murray, Gilbert. *The Foreign Policy of Sir Edward Grey, 1906–1915* (Oxford, 1915).

Namier, Sir Lewis, *Avenues of History* (London, 1952).

—— *Vanished Supremacies: Essays on European History, 1812–1918* (London, 1958).

Newton, Lord. *Lord Lansdowne: a Biography* (London, 1929).

Nicolson, Sir Harold. *Sir Arthur Nicolson, Bart: First Lord Carnock: A Study in the old diplomacy* (London, 1930).

—— *Curzon: the Last Phase, 1919–1925* (London, 1939).

—— *Diplomacy* (London, 1939).

—— *King George V* (London, 1952).

Nish, Ian. *The Anglo-Japanese Alliance: The Diplomacy of Two Island Empires, 1894–1907* (London, 1966).

Pelcovits, Nathan A. *Old China Hands and the Foreign Office* (New York, 1948).

Penson, Lilian. *Foreign Affairs under the Third Marquis of Salisbury* (London, 1962).

Piggott, F. S. G. *Broken Threads* (Aldershot, 1950).

Plass, J. B. *England zwischen Deutschland und Russland, 1899–1907. Der Persische Golf in der Britischen Vorkriegspolitik* (Hamburg, 1966).

Platt, D. C. M. *Finance, Trade and Politics in British Foreign Policy, 1815–1914* (Oxford, 1968).

Ponsonby, A. *Democracy and Diplomacy—a plea for popular control of Foreign Policy* (London, 1915).

Pope Henessey, James. *Lord Crewe, 1858–1945: the Likeness of a Liberal* (London, 1955).

Pribram, Alfred. *Austrian Foreign Policy, 1908–18* (London, 1923).

—— *England and the International Policy of the European Great Powers, 1871–1914* (Oxford, 1931).

—— *Austria, Hungary and Great Britain, 1908–1914*, translated by I. F. D. Morrow (London, 1951).

Renouvin, Pierre. *Les origines immédiates de la guerre* (Paris, 1925).

Rich, Norman. *Friedrich von Holstein: Politics and Diplomacy in the Era of Bismarck and Wilhelm II*, 2 vols. (Cambridge, 1965).

Ritter, Gerhardt. *The Schlieffen Plan: Critique of a Myth*, translated by Andrew and Eva Wilson (New York, 1958).

Robertson, John Henry. *The Office* (New York, 1958).

Robinson, Ronald and Gallagher, John with Denny, Alice. *Africa and the Victorians: The Official Mind of Imperialism* (London, 1961).

Ronaldshay, Earl of. *The Life of Lord Curzon*, 3 vols. (London, 1928).

—— *Lord Cromer* (London, 1932).

Saint-René Taillandier, G. *Les origines du Maroc français* (Paris, 1930).

Salet, R. *Der diplomatische Dienst* (Stuttgart, 1953).

Sanderson, T. *Observations on the Use and Abuse of Red Tape for the Juniors in the Eastern, Western and American Departments, 1891*.

—— *The Story of Forty Wise Men* (London, 1906).

—— *Four Stories for Children* (London, 1911).

—— *Evelyn, Earl of Cromer, Proceedings of the British Academy*, vol. VII (London, 1917).

Schmitt, Bernadotte E. *The Coming of the War*, *1914*, 2 vols. (New York, 1930).
—— *Triple Alliance and Triple Entente* (New York, 1934).
—— *The Annexation of Bosnia* (Cambridge, 1937).
Semmel, Bernard. *Imperialism and Social Reform: English Social-Imperial thought 1895–1914* (Cambridge, Mass., 1960).
Sommer, Dudley. *Haldane of Cloan: His Life and Times, 1856–1928* (London, 1960).
Sontag, R. J. *Germany and England: Background of Conflict, 1848–1894* (New York, 1938).
Spender, J. A. *The Life of the Right Honourable Sir Henry Campbell-Bannerman*, 2 vols. (London, 1925).
—— *Life, Journalism and Politics*, 2 vols. (London, 1927).
Spender, J. A. and Asquith, C. *Life of Herbert Henry Asquith Lord Oxford and Asquith*, 2 vols. (London, 1932).
Steinberg, Jonathan. *Yesterday's Deterrent. Tirpitz and the Birth of the German Battle Fleet* (London, 1965).
Strang, Sir William. *The Foreign Office* (London, 1955).
—— *The Diplomatic Career* (London, 1962).
Sun, E-Tu-Zen. *Chinese Railways and British Interest, 1898–1911* (New York, 1954).
Taylor, A. J. P. *Rumours of War* (London, 1952).
—— *The Struggle for Mastery in Europe, 1848–1918* (Oxford, 1954).
—— *The Trouble Makers: Dissent over Foreign Policy, 1792–1939* (Bloomington, Indiana, 1958).
—— *Politics in Wartime and other essays* (London, 1964).
Temperley, H. and Penson, L. A. *A Century of Diplomatic Blue Books, 1814–1914* (Cambridge, 1938).
Thompson, Mark. *The Secretaries of State, 1681–1782* (Oxford, 1932).
Tilley, Sir John and Gaselee, Stephen. *The Foreign Office*, 2nd edn (London, 1933).
*The Times, History of, The Twentieth Century Test, 1884–1912*, vol. III (London, 1947); *The 150th Anniversary and Beyond, 1912–1948*, vol. IV, pt I (London, 1952).
Trevelyan, George M. *Grey of Fallodon* (London, 1937).
Tuchman, B. *The Guns of August* (New York, 1962).
Tyler, John E. *The British Army and the Continent, 1904–1914* (London, 1938).
Ward, A. and Gooch, G. P. *The Cambridge History of British Foreign Policy*, vol. III (Cambridge, 1923). Ch. VIII, 'The Foreign Office' by Algernon Cecil.
Watt, Donald C. *Personalties and Policies: Studies in the Formulation of British Foreign Policy in the Twentieth Century* (South Bend, Indiana, 1965).
Webster, Sir Charles. *The Foreign Policy of Palmerston, 1830–1841*, 2 vols. (London, 1951).
—— *The Art and Practice of Diplomacy* (London, 1961).
Willis, Edward F. *Prince Lichnowsky Ambassador of Peace: A Study of Pre-War Diplomacy, 1912–1914* (Los Angeles, 1942).
Wilson, Trevor. *The Downfall of the Liberal Party* (London, 1966).
Wolf, Lucien. *Life of the First Marquess of Ripon*, 2 vols. (London, 1921).

Woodward, E. L. *Great Britain and the German Navy* (Oxford, 1935).
Wright, S. F. *Hart and the Chinese Customs* (Belfast, 1958).
Young, George. *Diplomacy Old and New* (London, 1921).
Young, Kenneth. *Arthur James Balfour* (London, 1963).
Zetland—*see* Lord Ronaldshay.

## ARTICLES

Ashton-Gwatkin, Frank T. 'Foreign Service Reorganization in the United Kingdom', *International Affairs* XXII (January 1946), 57–74.
Bindoff, S. T. 'The Unreformed Diplomatic Service, 1812–60', *Transactions of the Royal Historical Society*, 4th series, XVIII (1935), 143–72.
Butler, Rohan. 'Beside the Point', *World Review*, new series, no. 50 (April–May, 1953), pp. 8–13.
Butterfield, Herbert. 'Sir Edward Grey in July 1914', *Historical Studies* V (1965), 1–25.
Cooper, H. B. 'British Policy in the Balkans, 1908–1909', *The Historical Journal* VII (1964–5), 258–79.
Cromwell, V. 'An Incident in the Development of the Permanent Under-Secretaryship at the Foreign Office', *Bulletin of the Institute of Historical Relations* (May 1960), 99–113.
Edwards, E. W. 'The Far Eastern Agreements of 1907', *The Journal of Modern History* XXVI (December 1954), 340–55.
—— 'The Franco-German Agreement on Morocco, 1909', *The English Historical Review* LXXVIII (July 1963), 483–513.
—— 'The Japanese Alliance and the Anglo-French Agreement of 1904', *History* XLII, no. 144 (February 1957), 19–27.
—— 'Great Britain and the Manchurian Railways Question, 1909–1910', *The English Historical Review* LXXXI (1966), 740–89.
Greaves, R. 'British Policy in Persia, 1892–1903', *Bulletin of School of Oriental and African Studies* (1965), pp. 34–60.
Grenville, J. A. S. 'Lansdowne's Abortive Project of 12 March 1901 for a Secret Agreement with Germany', *Bulletin of the Institute of Historical Research* XXVII (November 1954), 201–13.
—— 'Great Britain and the Isthmian Canal, 1898–1901', *The American Historical Review* LXI (October 1953), 48–69.
Hargreaves, J. D. 'Lord Salisbury, British Isolation and the Yangtsze Valley, June–September, 1900', *Bulletin of the Institute of Historical Research* XXX (May 1957), 62–75.
—— 'The Origin of the Anglo-French Military Conversations in 1905', *History* XXXVI, no. 128 (October 1951), 244–8.
Helmreich, Jonathan E. 'Belgian Concern over Neutrality and British Intentions, 1906–1914', *The Journal of Modern History* XXXVI (December 1964), 416–27.
Howard, Christopher. 'Splendid Isolation', *History* XLVII, no. 159 (February 1962), 32–41.
Jones, R. B. 'Anglo-French Negotiations, 1907: A Memorandum by Sir Arthur Milner', *Bulletin of the Institute of Historical Research* XXXI (November 1958), 224–7.

Jones-Parry, E. 'Under-Secretaries of State for Foreign Affairs, 1782–1855', *The English Historical Review* XLIX (1934), 308–20.

Koss, S. E. 'The Destruction of Britain's last Liberal Government', *The Journal of Modern History*, 40 (June 1968), 257–77.

Louis, W. Roger. 'Sir Percy Anderson's Grand African Strategy, 1883–1896', *The English Historical Review* LXXXI (1966), 292–314.

Mackintosh, John P. 'The Role of the Committee of Imperial Defence before 1914', *The English Historical Review* LXXVII (July 1962), 490–503.

Monger, George W. 'The End of Isolation; Britain, Germany and Japan, 1900–1902', *Transactions of the Royal Historical Society*, 5th series, XIII (1963), 103–21.

Murray, John A. 'Foreign Policy Debated: Sir Edward Grey and his Critics, 1911–1912', in L. P. Wallace and W. C. Askew (eds.), *Power, Public Opinion and Diplomacy: Essays in Honor of Eber Malcolm Carroll by His Former Students* (Durham, North Carolina, 1959), 140–71.

Nightingale, Robert T. 'The Personnel of the British Foreign Office and Diplomatic Service, 1851–1929', *American Political Science Survey* XXIV (May 1930), 310–31 or Fabian Tract 232 (London, 1929).

Norton, Henry K. 'Foreign Office Organization', Supplement to *The Annals of the American Academy of Political and Social Sciences* CXLIII (1929), 1–81.

Papadopoulos, G. S. 'Lord Salisbury and the Projected Anglo-German Alliance of 1898', *Bulletin of the Institute of Historical Research* XXVI (November 1953), 214–18.

Penson, Lilian M. 'The New Course in British Foreign Policy, 1892–1902', *Transactions of the Royal Historical Society*, 4th series, XXV (1943), 121–38.

—— 'Obligations by Treaty: Their Place in British Foreign Policy, 1898–1914', in A. O. Sarkissian (ed.). *Studies in Diplomatic History and Historiography in Honour of G. P. Gooch* (London, 1961), 76–89.

—— 'The Principles and Methods of Lord Salisbury's Foreign Policy', *Cambridge Historical Journal* II, no. 5 (1935), 87–106.

Renouvin, Pierre. 'The Part played in International Relations by the Conversations between the General Staffs on the Eve of the War', in Alfred Coville and Harold W. V. Temperley (eds.), *Studies in Anglo-French History* (Cambridge, 1935), 159–73.

Selby, Sir Walford. 'The Foreign Office', *Nineteenth Century and After*, CXXXVII, no. 821 (July 1945), 3–13.

Sontag, Raymond J. 'British Foreign Policy, 1898–1912', *The Journal of Modern History* II (September 1930), 472–80.

—— 'British Policy in 1913–1914', *The Journal of Modern History* X (December 1938), 542–53.

Steinberg, Jonathan. 'The Copenhagen Complex', *Journal of Contemporary History* I, no. 3 (July 1966), 23–46.

Steiner, Zara. 'Great Britain and the Creation of the Anglo-Japanese Alliance', *The Journal of Modern History* XXXI (March 1959), 27–36.

—— 'The Last Years of the Old Foreign Office, 1898–1905', *The Historical Journal* VI (1963), 59–90.

—— 'Grey, Hardinge and the Foreign Office, 1906–1910', *The Historical Journal* XV (1965), 415–39.

Taylor, A. J. P. 'British Policy in Morocco, 1886–1908', *The English Historical Review* LXVI (July 1951), 342–74.

Temperley, Harold W. V. 'British Secret Diplomacy from Canning to Grey', *Cambridge Historical Journal* VI (1938), 1–32.

Trumpener, Ulrich. 'Liman von Sanders and the German–Ottoman Alliance', *Journal of Contemporary History* I, no. 4 (October 1966), 179–92.

Viner, Jacob. 'International Finance and Balance of Power Diplomacy, 1880–1914', *Southwestern Political and Social Science Quarterly* IX (March 1929), 407–51.

Williams, Beryl J. 'The Strategic Background to the Anglo-Russian Entente of August 1907', *The Historical Journal* IX (1966), 360–73.

Wolf, John B. 'The Diplomatic History of the Baghdad Railway', *The University of Missouri Studies* XI, no. 2 (April 1936), 1–107.

Zechlin, E. 'Deutschland zwischen Kabinettskrieg und Wirtschaftskrieg', *Historische Zeitschrift*, 199 (1964), 347–458.

DOCTOR OF PHILOSOPHY THESES

Anderson, Mary A. 'Edmund Hammond, Permanent Under-Secretary of State for Foreign Affairs, 1854–1873', London University, November 1953.

Bridge, F. R. 'The Diplomatic Relations between Great Britain and Austria-Hungary, 1906–12', London University, 1966.

Cosgrove, R. 'Sir Eyre Crowe and the English Foreign Office, 1905–1914', University of California, 1967.

Hilbert, L. 'The Role of Military and Naval Attachés in the British and German Service with particular reference to those in Berlin and London, and their effect on Anglo-German Relations, 1871–1914', Cambridge University, 1954.

# Index

Abyssinia, 237

Acland, Francis Dyke, parliamentary under-secretary (1911–15), 108

Addington, H. U., permanent under-secretary (1847–54), 6n

administrative divisions of FO, 3, 6n

Admiralty, in Landsowne period, 54, 65; naval estimates of, (1902) 52, (1908) 88, 89, (1909) 98, 99, (1914) 152n

Aegean islands, 145

Afghanistan, Curzon's policy in, 51, 233, 237; Russia in, 67, 133; settlement on (1907), 95; relations with (1909), 105

African Department of FO, 11, 12, 38

African and African Protectorates Department of FO (to 1900), 11; African Protectorates Department (from 1900), 44

Agadir crisis (1911), 91, 125, 141–2, 148, 180

Alaska boundary dispute (1903), 27

Albania, boundaries of, 135, 145, 146, 155

Algeciras Conference on Morocco (1906), 88, 117; Anglo-French entente during, 94, 96, 115

Alston, Beilby, of Far Eastern department, senior clerk (1907–18), 121

Ambassadors, query to (1905), 78; reports from, 81; London Conference of, 149, 152; *see also* Diplomatic Service, diplomats

American and Asiatic Department of FO (to 1899), 8, 11, 41; American Department (from 1899), 11, 41, 151n, 165n

Anderson, Percy, senior clerk of African Department (1883–93), assistant under-secretary (1893–6), 44

Angell, Norman, *The Great Illusion* by, 167

Anglo-French agreements on Africa (1898), 34

Anglo-French conversations, on West Africa and Niger (1896–8), 38; on Morocco (1902), 57; military, (1906) 67, 87, 108, 130, 193, (1911), 126n, 128n; naval, (1906) 67, (1912) 129–30, 152, 181, 193; on Newfoundland (1898–9), 35–6, 42

Anglo-French entente (1904), 196, 238; Edward VII and, 204; initiated as a colonial bargain, 47; Germany and, 48, 51, 54; prospects of conversion to alliance, 66, 124, 128, 129n, 181; attitudes towards of Brodrick, 51n, Cranborne, 59, Bertie, 66, 180–1, Lansdowne, 47, 238n, Grey, 66, 87, 94, Hardinge, 94, 98, Crowe, 112, 142–3,

Nicolson, 128; Gorst in negotiations for, 74n; Cabinet cabal against, 128n; German attempts to destroy (1911), 148; text published (1911), 126, 193; Anglo-German talks and (1912), 128

Anglo-German agreements, on Portuguese colonies (1898), 26n, 34, 39, 69n; on Portuguese colonies, proposed (1914), 128, 143–4; on China, (1900) 28, 34, 35, 36, 40, 56, 61, 69n; on Samoa (1902), 41; on Baghdad railway (1914), 144

Anglo-German conversations, (1898), 27, 196; (1901), 58, 60–1, 62, 64, 66, 69n, 196; (1908), 89; (1909–11), 87, 90, 100, 104, 116, 140–1; (1912–13), 91, 128, 181; Cabinet committee to deal with (1911), 90, 123, 124, 141n

Anglo-German Friendship Society, 124

Anglo-German relations, over Samoa, 41, 68n; in Persian Gulf, 57, 95; in Far East, 62–5, 69n; in Persia, 101, 116, 127; in Balkans, 96, 135, 137, 139, 145, 147; German naval expansion and, 68, 76, 88–90, 94, 98–9, 100, 108, 114, 119, 140, 146; détentes in, (1908) 98, (1912) 143, 144, 167, (1914) 152–3

Anglo-Japanese alliance (1902), 47, 48, 50, 54, 58, 63, 64, 196; attitudes towards of Bertie, 40, 63, Salisbury, 49, Chamberlain, 51, Hicks Beach, 52, Cranborne, 59, Percy, 59–60, Lansdowne 65; (1905), 45

Anglo-Portuguese negotiations on Delagoa Bay (1897–8), 27, 38–9; treaty, 144

Anglo-Russian convention on Persia (1907), 95, 132–3, 182, 193n

Anglo-Russian conversations, (1898), 196, 233; (1901, 1902), 47; (1903, 1904), 48; (1907), 86, 88, 99; (naval, 1914), 138, 139, 152

Anglo-Russian entente (1907), European implications of, 86, 87; attitudes towards of Hardinge, 94–5, 97, Nicolson, 97, 124, 131, 182, Mallet, 104, 105, Tyrrell, 120, Crowe, 143; discussions on (1914), 152; prospects of conversion to alliance, 124; Parliament and, 193n

Anglo-Russian relations, in central Asia, 51, 53, 87, 131, 138, 233, 234; in Persia, 59, 67, 88, 90, 97, 131–3, 138, 150, 233, 234, 236; over Dogger Bank incident, 74–5, 182; in Balkans, 96, 105, 132, 133, 134, 136, 150,

INDEX